Chinese Workers

Independent Chinese workers' organizations took a leading role in the 1989
Democracy Movement. They also suffered heavily for their political dissent in
the crackdown that followed, but attempts to form independent trade unions
have continued into the 1990s.

Jackie Sheehan traces the background and development of workers' clashes with
the Chinese Communist Party through mass campaigns such as the 1956–7
Hundred Flowers movement, the Cultural Revolution, the April Fifth movement
of 1976, Democracy Wall and the 1989 Democracy Movement. The author
provides the most detailed and complete picture of workers' protest in China to
date and locates their position within the context of Chinese political history.

Chinese Workers demonstrates that the image of Chinese workers as politically
conformist and reliable supporters of the Communist Party does not match the
realities of industrial life in China. Recent outbreaks of protest by workers are
less of a departure from the past than is generally realized.

Jackie Sheehan is a lecturer in international history at the University of Keele.

Routledge Studies in the Modern History of Asia

Chinese Workers

A new history

Jackie Sheehan

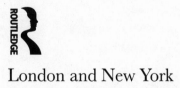

London and New York

First published 1998 by Routledge
11 New Fetter Lane, London EC4P 4EE

Simultaneously published in the USA and Canada
by Routledge
29 West 35th Street, New York, NY 10001

Typeset in Baskerville by Routledge
Printed and bound in Great Britain by Biddles Ltd,
Guildford and King's Lynn

British Library Cataloguing in Publication Data
A catalogue record for this book is available from the British Library

Library of Congress Cataloging in Publication Data
Sheehan, Jackie, 1966–
Chinese workers: a new history/ Jackie Sheehan.
p.   cm. – (Routledge studies in modern history of Asia: 2)
Includes bibliographical references and index.
1. Working class–China–History. 2. Labor movement–China–History.
I. Title. II. Series.
HD8736.5.S465   1999
305.5`62"0951–dc21   98–20170

ISBN 0–415–17206–3

Contents

Preface

This book has its origins in my doctoral thesis, which I began in October 1991. I had graduated in Chinese Studies in June 1989, and like anyone with an interest in China, I had spent the preceding two months watching events unfolding day by day in Beijing as the Democracy Movement moved towards its final, brutal suppression. I went off to Japan for a year after graduation with the images of the movement still fresh in my mind, and with a vague idea of beginning research on the subject at some point in the future.

A Chinese friend in Japan advised me not to expect any inspiration for my research in that country – 'Use it as a laboratory, but don't expect any ideas' – but fortunately my status back in Britain as a card-carrying anarcho-syndicalist enabled me to make contact with a group of Japanese anarchist labour activists, most of whom worked in low-status jobs such as that of school nightwatchman (hence their slogan 'Abunai keibin', 'Beware of the Nightwatchman') to make ends meet while devoting most of their energies to radical politics and union organization. In the spring of 1990 this group invited me to a talk and slide-show on the 1989 movement, and it was here that I first met Mok Chiu-yu and Teresa Hui, Hong Kong-based supporters of the Democracy Movement, and heard first-hand from them of the role of autonomous workers' organizations in 1989, which they convincingly portrayed as the really significant feature of the movement.

We met up again in Hong Kong in the summer of 1990, by which time Mok had co-edited a collection of documents from the movement (Mok and Harrison 1990). The workers' statements in this book further increased my interest in conducting research on the workers' movement, and once back in Britain at the end of 1990 I began looking at the secondary literature to investigate possible PhD topics. It struck me immediately that Chinese workers prior to 1989 were always portrayed as a politically passive and reliable group which took little part in mass protests. Knowing that the Chinese working class of the pre-1949 period had been anything but passive, and that the post-1949 official unions in China were famous for their ineffectiveness in representing their members' interests, I was troubled by the insistence that workers' protests of 1989 were unprecedented. Either this was true, in which case something very interesting had been going on in China which enabled or compelled workers there to accept a position against which their counterparts in Eastern Europe had rebelled; or it was not completely true, in which case there must be evidence of previous confrontations between workers and the regime. The evidence I found to support this latter possibility forms the basis of this book.

Acknowledgements

Given this book's origins in my doctoral research, thanks are first of all due to my supervisor at the School of Oriental and African Studies, London University, Gary Tiedemann, for his unfailing support, interest, efficiency, and generosity with his time. My examiners, Stephan Feuchtwang and Kaoru Sugihara, were both kind enough to show an interest in the project in its early stages as well as offering much useful advice and criticism during and after the examination itself. Anita Chan and Elizabeth Perry also offered their encouragement when I contacted them in the course of the PhD, and Gregor Benton offered very valuable advice on rewriting the thesis for publication. Needless to say, any remaining flaws in the study are my responsibility alone.

A travel grant from London University enabled me to visit the Universities Service Centre at the Chinese University of Hong Kong in 1993, and I owe thanks to the Centre's Jean Chen and her staff for their assistance during that trip. I arrived with maximum inconvenience as they were moving into new premises on campus, but they went out of their way to enable me to use the collections even as they were still being unpacked so that I could make the most of my limited time there, for which I am very grateful. Thanks are also due to others in Hong Kong: Mok Chiu-yu, Teresa Hui, Haymann Lau, Yuen Che Hung, Trini Leung, and all the staff of the Independent Trade Union Federation for the use of the library and archives at their offices in Portland Street.

I completed my thesis and began work on transforming it into a book while lecturing here at the History Department of Keele University, and I thank my present and former colleagues first for agreeing to the appointment in a mainstream History Department of a China specialist, and more particularly for their award to me of a semester of research leave in 1997 to enable me to concentrate on writing. The university also granted me a semester's sabbatical in 1997–8 in which to finish the book, for which I express my thanks; and a grant from the Economic and Social Research Council under its Pacific Asia Initiative funded short field-trips to Chinese factories in 1995, 1996, and 1997 which, although devoted to a separate project, also contributed to the last two chapters of this book. I thank my companions on these trips, John Hassard and Xiao Yuxin of Keele and Jon Morris of Cardiff University, for their excellent company, friendship, and support over the past few years.

My family and friends have found out more about Chinese workers over the past seven years than they can ever have wished to know, and tolerated with patience and good grace the typical obsessiveness of the doctoral student. Finally, in a slight twist to the usual pattern of these dedications, I wish to thank my ex-husband, Colin Clifford, who had to listen to more, and more prolonged, perorations on the general topic of the Chinese workers' movement than all the rest of my friends and relatives put together, and without whose support I would have faced serious financial obstacles to beginning full-time doctoral study back in 1991.

Jackie Sheehan
Keele, Staffordshire
February 1998

Introduction

Over the six years since the suppression of the Chinese pro-democracy movement, the initial view of most observers – that the involvement of autonomous
workers' groups in that movement was merely an epiphenomenon – has shifted
somewhat. The publication of the accounts of actual participants (Lu Ping 1990)
and the possibility of interviewing them has helped to reveal the true significance
of workers' activities and organizations in the spring and early summer of 1989.
But the seriousness with which the Chinese leadership, right from the beginning,
regarded the threat posed by the workers should perhaps have alerted more
observers to the significance of workers' activities. Leaders had good reason for
their concern, as Anita Chan observed:

> Whereas most Chinese, above all the younger generation, generally assumed
> that 1989 was the first time that Chinese workers had turned upon the Party
> in protest, the Party elite was painfully aware that this in fact was the fifth
> time that a portion of the Chinese working class (at times led by the official
> trade unions) had asserted itself politically.
>
> (A Chan 1993: 32)

In view of this statement that politically-charged confrontations between workers
and the party had in fact occurred before, the question arises as to whether
workers' activities in 1989 were really unprecedented, as is often claimed.

In the light of the recent re-assessment of the significance of workers'
Democracy Movement activities, it now seems appropriate to look afresh at
previous instances of workers' protest to find out whether or not they offer any
sort of precedent for the events of 1989. In particular, this study looks for pre-
1989 precedents for the formation of independent workers' organizations. It is of
course possible that the circumstances of workers' political activities in 1989
were unique, since the progress of the economic reforms had by then created a
China quite different in some respects to the one which existed before 1978. But
given that the political significance of the Workers' Autonomous Federations has
now been recognized, even though the party line is still that workers on the
whole remained aloof in 1989 and more often defended the party than attacked
it, there is also the possibility that in the past, outside observers were too easily

convinced by the Chinese authorities' line that the vast majority of workers were loyal and politically reliable, that only a small minority had anything to do with anti-party protests, and that where workers had become involved in protests, their motives and grievances were selfish and narrowly economic, and represented opportunistic demands rather than any deep-seated disagreement with the policies or line of the regime.

Part of the problem in weighing the arguments regarding workers' relationship with the party is that the divisions between different groups of workers have not always been recognized (with the partial exception of the Cultural Revolution, where research has revealed the importance of socio-economic background and status in determining factional allegiance). However, the common picture of Chinese workers as basically supporting the party, and even intervening on its behalf against other groups involved in anti-party protest, is not at all convincing when applied to the whole range of workers in all types of enterprise across the country. It only holds true to any extent, and even then not entirely, when applied to the relatively privileged group of permanent workers employed in the largest state enterprises, a minority of the industrial workforce as a whole. The work of Elizabeth Perry and François Gipouloux on the Hundred Flowers has been very welcome in this respect, since it shifts attention to disadvantaged groups within the workforce who have been prepared to confront the party and to take their protests onto the streets.

It is not the claim of this study that *all* workers, or even a majority of them, have regularly been involved in confrontations with party-state authorities which had a political aspect to them. But it is my contention that conflict, often originating from economic grievances, but quickly developing into a political dispute as a result of the dominance of the party within enterprises, has been a far more common feature of industrial life in China than is generally recognized. This background of conflict and discontent within enterprises provides the context in which workers' involvement in movements such as the Hundred Flowers, the Cultural Revolution, April Fifth and Democracy Wall can be understood properly. If workers' activities at these times had merely represented economically-motivated opportunism, it is hard to see why the regime should have been greatly concerned about them. But in fact, protesting workers have consistently been treated more harshly than any other social group in the repression of such protest movements, and there is considerable evidence to suggest that the party regards workers' involvement as its cue to bring protests to an end by whatever means necessary. This has been the case in particular since the emergence of Solidarity in 1980, but even before this spectre of the working-class overthrow of a ruling communist party began to haunt the socialist world, the Chinese Communist party (CCP) on several occasions demonstrated that workers' protests were more disturbing to it and constituted a more serious problem than did student or intellectual activities.

This study, then, will look back at a series of crises in the always strained relationship between the Chinese working class and its self-proclaimed vanguard, the CCP. These occurred in the early post-liberation period (1949–52); during the

Hundred Flowers movement (1956–7); during the Cultural Revolution (1966–76); and in the late 1970s and early 1980s, beginning with the April Fifth movement (the Tiananmen incident) of 1976 and continuing through the subsequent Democracy Wall movement (1978–81). We will examine the attitudes and activities of workers in each of these confrontations with the authorities, and use this as the basis for a re-examination of the history of the working class in China under CCP rule.

Secondary sources relevant to this study can be divided into three broad groups: those which relate to the movements mentioned above; those which focus on the Chinese working class since 1949; and those which deal with the position of workers under socialist rule in countries other than China. Starting with the first group, we find that most accounts of the Hundred Flowers movement, the Cultural Revolution and the Democracy Wall movement portray these as being primarily intellectual and/or student movements, with any involvement on the part of workers being of secondary importance. This is, of course, the attitude taken by many in the immediate aftermath of the 1989 Democracy Movement, hence the need for a critical re-examination of this assessment now.

Not only has workers' involvement in these movements been given little attention but, in many cases, workers only appear in large numbers in these accounts after the backlash has already begun, when they are mobilized by the party or the official unions to criticize and attack the original protestors; this is particularly true when the Hundred Flowers movement and the early stages of the Cultural Revolution are discussed. A notable exception to this tendency, as mentioned above, is François Gipouloux's study of the confrontation between workers and the party which developed towards the end of the First Five-Year Plan, *Les Cent Fleurs A L'Usine* (1986). The conclusions of this study are in keeping with my own findings that far from industrial unrest and protests by workers being an episode in the Hundred Flowers movement, the reverse may be closer to the truth.

But generally speaking, the significance of workers' involvement in these movements has been unduly neglected. Workers' initial reluctance to become active in such movements may be taken as a sign of satisfaction with the status quo rather than caution in the face of the serious risks involved, while the Chinese leadership's attribution of selfish and narrowly economic motives to protesting workers is too often accepted at face value. Why the Chinese leadership should be intent on 'down-playing and even obliterating any collective memory' (A Chan 1993: 32) of its confrontations with workers is not difficult to understand: desirable though the support of intellectuals and students might be, it is on its claim to be the vanguard of the most advanced class, the working class, that the legitimacy of the CCP regime rests. It is less obvious why outside observers should thus far have devoted relatively little attention to workers in this context, since sources dealing with workers are for the most part no less accessible than those relating to other groups. However, it is hoped that this study will go some way towards redressing the balance and, in focusing exclusively on the role of workers, will shed some new light on the movements concerned.

The second group of sources includes studies of various aspects of the official trade unions in China (Lee Lai To, Paul Harper), as well as work on industrial organization, enterprise management, and industrial democracy (Andrew Walder, Steven Andors, Bill Brugger, Charles Bettelheim, Martin Lockett). The latter topic is particularly important for our purposes, as the absence of democracy and of opportunities to participate in management has been a perennial cause of complaint amongst Chinese workers, as well as being one of the more obviously political causes of disputes at the enterprise level. The legitimacy of workers' complaints has been acknowledged by the party, which has made its most strenuous efforts to establish satisfactory representative institutions for workers at precisely those moments when worker discontent has reached a peak (1950, 1956–7, 1967, 1980). Deborah Kaple has identified the contradiction between the centralized, Stalinist system of industrial organization and management which the Chinese adopted after 1949, and the Chinese Communists' own earlier experiences of more democratic management, pointing out that the democratic institutions the CCP set up within factories were never going to be able to play their proper role in the rigidly hierarchical system of one-man management, adopted from the Soviet Union, which will be discussed in more detail in Chapter 1 (Kaple 1994). Nevertheless, the party continued to pay lip-service to the importance of democracy in factories, and it is possible that this very insistence on its desirability helped to inflame workers' resentment when reality failed to match rhetoric.

Although the works of Andors, Brugger, Bettelheim and Lockett deal with the development of various structures for workers' participation in management at some length, they give very little indication of the role which workers' own demands and pressures from below have played in pushing the authorities towards these more democratic forms of management. Similarly, in describing the limitations and ultimate failure of all such structures or institutions, little attention is given to the possible reactions of disappointed workers, leaving the impression that when their aspirations have been thwarted, workers tend simply to accept the situation, whereas in fact, as leaders of the official trade unions in China have been aware since at least 1957, in certain circumstances workers with a grievance and no legitimate official channel for resolving it will resort to illegitimate methods, such as organizing themselves independently or taking unofficial industrial action. So the overall picture is one of workers as the passive recipients of top-down reforms, not as active proponents of changes in the direction of greater democracy.

There are similar problems with the picture of relations in a Chinese industrial enterprise which emerges from Andrew Walder's *Communist Neotraditionalism*. In emphasizing the successful working of the networks of patron–client relationships and organized dependency which the party, 'under normal circumstances' (Walder 1986: 11), can use to control workers in the enterprise, and in particular to prevent them from taking any sort of organized collective action outside official auspices, this study tends to go along with the official line that cases of this sort of action are extremely rare among Chinese workers, which, as we will see in the following chapters, is not the case. In contrasting these party methods with more overt forms of repression, Walder observes that:

> A state or elite which must use a large amount of force to repress emerging or ongoing collective action exercises less effective control than a state or elite which is able regularly to prevent organized group action in the first place. The most brutal and violent regimes are not necessarily the most effective at imposing political control; their brutality and violence is often a mark of a poorly organized and ineffective effort to stem collective action.
>
> (Walder 1986: 18–19)

It is generally agreed that in the aftermath of the 1989 pro-democracy protests it was workers who suffered the harshest and most violent repression, and in fact this is true of the party's reaction to workers' involvement in earlier protest movements as well. As well as testifying to the party's perception that independent action by workers poses the most serious threat to its rule, this would also seem to indicate that the party has been much less successful at controlling workers, and conversely that workers have been a great deal more active on their own behalf, than Walder supposes.

As has been pointed out elsewhere, Walder's work to a great extent focuses on the relatively privileged group of permanent workers in large-scale state enterprises, and this means that his conclusions may not hold good for other groups. Some of the apparent disagreement about workers' political awareness and attitudes can be traced to the fact that different observers are talking about different groups within the working class, so clearly it is important to identify where possible which workers are under discussion. However, Walder's focus on the penetration of party control right down to the workshop level within the enterprise is relevant to this study, since it illustrates the point that, with the official unions and enterprise management also ultimately deferring to party authority, disputes even at this low level tend quickly to develop into a confrontation between workers and the party.

As for the official trade unions, since membership among Chinese workers is the norm, although it is not actually compulsory, it might be assumed that an account of conflicts between the official unions and the party would subsume any discussion of conflicts between workers and the party. But it becomes clear on the most cursory reading of, for example, letters from workers in the Chinese press during the 1956–7 period, that in most cases the official unions were definitely part of the problem as far as workers were concerned. It was in fact not at all unusual, as Chapters 1 and 2 will show, for enterprise unions to side with management against the workers when disputes arose, and even when unions were inclined to support their members, they usually lacked the power to do so in any effective way. More will be said about the precise role of the unions later; for now it will suffice to note that it is important, wherever possible, to distinguish between the attitudes and interests of workers themselves and those of their official representatives, since they by no means always coincide. Consequently, while accounts of confrontations between the official unions and the party may be of interest to us, particularly at those moments where the unions sided with the workers, e.g. 1951, all too often these accounts relegate workers themselves to a minor role. As with discussions of management reforms and changes in industrial organizations, the active role of workers in pushing for preferred options is largely left out of many of these accounts.

By drawing on the above two groups of sources it is possible to piece together a general account of how the position of workers in the enterprise and in wider society has developed in China since 1949. However, this tends to be a distorted account in which workers' independent activities – industrial action or unrest not backed by the official unions, or the formation of independent organizations of varying degrees of formality, up to and including independent unions – are consistently down-played or even ignored. There is an over-emphasis on higher-level, institutional conflicts between the official trade union organization and the party, concentrating on the unions' periodic attempts to gain greater autonomy from the party, with relatively little attention given to union members' own aspirations and demands and the ways in which these might influence the actions of higher-level union leadership.

In addition, the political content of workers' protests is given less prominence than economic causes of disputes, and workers' actions under official mobilization (such as organized criticism of intellectuals during the anti-rightist campaign in 1957, or the entry of worker-picket teams into universities and schools to restore order during the Cultural Revolution) tend to be regarded as more reliable indicators of working-class opinion (and support for the party) than actions undertaken independently by workers on their own initiative, often at considerable personal risk. Thus workers emerge as a rather passive section of society which basically supports the party, and which is only occasionally moved to protest in defence of its economic privileges when a relatively safe opportunity to do so appears; this might take the form of an intellectual- or student-led protest movement, or a shift in the attitude towards workers on the part of either the party or the official unions.

What is missing from such an account, above all, is any sense of workers as active political players in their own right, responding to developments in their enterprises and in wider society not merely in accordance with their own narrow economic interests, but in the light of their political beliefs and aspirations; workers who, having undergone many hours of education as to their leading role in the state as well as in the factory, in which their status as management's political equals has been stressed, are prepared to defend their rights and protest against management authoritarianism and cadre privilege, in the first instance through officially sanctioned channels, such as the trade union or the workers' congress, but later, when these prove inadequate, by methods such as independent organization and strike action which, if not actually illegal, certainly lack official approval.

Since little evidence for this sort of portrayal of Chinese workers is offered in most existing accounts, is it safe to assume that their role in the major political movements in contemporary China has indeed been a minor one, and that those workers whose protests have become visible are an unrepresentative minority? Here it is useful to refer to the third group of relevant secondary sources, studies of workers in the former socialist countries of Eastern Europe and the Soviet Union. There are of course important differences between the People's Republic of China (PRC) and these countries, but it would be unreasonable to exclude these sources from consideration altogether for that reason. We are, after all, considering workers' experiences under socialist rule and socialist management, and the fact of the various regimes' coming to power under different circumstances and developing in different directions should not be allowed to obscure the basic similarity in workers' situations. The Chinese leadership itself has always been keenly aware of possible parallels between events in Eastern Europe and in China, as will be shown in Chapter 2 when we see how knowledge of the uprisings in Poland and Hungary in 1956 influenced the policies of the Hundred Flowers period in China, and in particular attitudes towards workers. In more recent years it is the example of Solidarity in Poland which seems to have preoccupied the Chinese authorities and informed their responses to workers' independent activities, especially attempts to form independent unions (Wilson 1990b: 3–4), as we shall see in Chapter 6.

From studies of workers in Eastern Europe and the former Soviet Union dealing with the issues which concern us in China (the functioning of official trade unions; participation, democracy and workers' councils; workers' involvement in popular protest movements; the causes and development of disputes; the question of independent unions), a consensus seems to emerge that there are certain basic problems inherent in the position of workers in a socialist state which are bound to emerge sooner or later (Triska and Gati 1981; Ruble 1981; Sturmthal 1964; Zinner 1956). In general terms, the dilemma faced by workers in an avowedly socialist system is as follows. A ruling communist party usually defines itself as the vanguard of the working class, an elite organization of the most advanced elements of that class. But this does not mean that the party represents the interests of the working class as opposed to those of other groups in society; as the highest national authority, it must act in the best interests of the country as a whole. It is an article of faith that the long-term interests of the working class are identical with those of the party-state, but it is accepted that in the short term there may be discrepancies, and that in any case, workers need their own organization to protect their specific rights and interests against any violations of policy or law which enterprise management might commit. So official trade unions are organized, under the leadership of the party.

All such trade unions are organized in accordance with the 'dual function' Soviet model, i.e. they have responsibilities towards management and the party with regard to mobilizing workers for production as well as being responsible for protecting the rights and interests of their members, rather than being solely the representatives of workers and (usually) the adversaries of management, as has been more common outside the socialist world. They are commonly described as a 'transmission belt', passing on the party's policies and instructions to the workers and also communicating the opinions and problems of the workers to the party. Unions are also to act as 'schools of communism', responsible for ideological as well as technical and cultural education of workers. An additional feature intended to distinguish socialist enterprises from capitalist ones is their system of democratic management, involving workers' participation in management through either representation on managing bodies or the election of a workers' council or congress with specific rights and powers in the enterprise. Although the division of labour demanded by modern, large-scale industry means that workers mainly engage in physical labour while management mainly occupies itself with mental labour, this does not imply any inequality of social or political status; the position of workers in a socialist enterprise is fundamentally different from that of capitalist wage-labourers, as the means of production are owned not by a private individual but by the state, which is led by the working class.

That, then, is the theory. But in practice, conflicts quickly begin to emerge. A study of Eastern European and Soviet sources does not reveal any case where the official unions were able to perform their dual functions satisfactorily for any length of time; many union activists in China in the mid-1950s complained that their task was simply impossible, and they may well have been correct. What generally happens is that the unions have to side either with the party and management or with the workers. If they support the workers, they lay themselves open to party accusations of economism or syndicalism; if they side with management and the party, they risk losing the trust and allegiance of workers who come to regard them as little better than a tool of management or an arm of the state. They are in any case much less powerful than either the enterprise party organization or its management, and therefore unable to offer much effective support to workers. Workers' councils (the workers' representative conference or workers' congress in China) fare little better, as they tend to require the goodwill and active cooperation of senior management, especially the factory director, to be able to function as intended. In fact, far from welcoming and supporting it, managers generally regard workers' participation in management as a time-consuming and unnecessary burden, and rank-and-file workers seem to have particular difficulty in using this sort of organ to bring their influence to bear on workplace decision-making (Pateman 1970). Given that these problems with official unions and workers' representative bodies seem to be universal in socialist states, it becomes apparent that workers can actually find themselves in a weaker position vis-à-vis managerial and political authorities in socialist enterprises than they would in capitalist ones. They are urged, or compelled, to give up such traditional methods of defending their interests as strikes, and indeed are assured that any such action would be pointless since they, as the leading class in society, would only be striking against themselves.

Yet the democratic socialist management systems which are supposed to render this type of action unnecessary, and which are an essential foundation for workers' new status as the masters of the state and of the enterprise, seem to be fatally flawed. And, as we shall see when we examine events in China in more detail, whereas workers' relationships with capitalist employers before 1949 had at least been unambiguously antagonistic, the shift to state ownership could leave workers in a very difficult position, where legitimate disagreements with enterprise management could be presented by the latter as an attack on the authority of the state organization which they represented, tantamount to an attempt to 'overthrow the leadership'.

The central contradiction faced by workers in socialist enterprises is thus that while the authorities insist that workers are the masters of the enterprise and stress the ownership of the means of production as the decisive factor, in reality workers often find that they are virtually powerless to exercise any control over their working lives or any influence over the officials who are supposed to be their political equals. One writer has described the likely result of this contradiction between rhetoric and reality thus:

> No matter what political apathy or cynicism may prevail, the official values of the regime are a standing incitement to trouble. A regime basing its legitimacy on the power, if not the dictatorship, of the working class, and a regime which spreads the classics of Marxism-Leninism through its educational and propaganda work, is bound to face sharp, persistent and spontaneous tests of the reality *versus* the stated norms ... the official ideology makes claims on behalf of the industrial workers which the day to day reality contradicts.
>
> (Denitch 1981: 254)

From the above sources it is clear that conflict between workers and the authorities in a socialist enterprise tends to become a regular feature of industrial life, since the mechanisms which are meant to avert open confrontation between workers and the enterprise leadership do not function as intended. One point which greatly exercises writers on industrial disputes and conflicts under socialism is the extent to which such disputes have political content and significance. A view commonly expressed in writings on workers in Eastern Europe is that conflicts between the working class, 'the professed mainstay of the political order in communist polities' and its 'erstwhile vanguard' (Triska and Gati 1981: xi–xvi) are inherently political; as was indicated earlier, the opposition of even a section of the working class to a ruling communist party is uniquely damaging to that party's legitimacy.

At first glance, specific disputes often seem to be based on purely economic grievances: the Polish strikes of 1970, for example, were sparked by meat price increases, and Solidarity was later formed as a result of a similar outcry over price increases. But closer examination of a dispute as it develops usually reveals much more profound concerns on the part of workers which centre on problems of social and political inequality. To return to the Polish example, the first demand of workers in the Szczecin shipyards in 1970 was not for the rescinding of the meat price increase, but for the abolition of the official unions in favour of independent unions organized by the workers themselves, and for rectification of the situation in which management and the state industrial bureaucracy (the ones who took decisions regarding the price of meat, wage levels and other questions of great importance to workers) were inflated in numbers, paid far too much in relation to workers, and provided with disproportionate material benefits and other privileges (Montias 1981: 181).

In other words, the problems were that social inequalities existed between workers on the one hand and managers and officials on the other, while workers lacked the political power to remedy these inequalities as their official unions and structures for participation in management were ineffective. This is why demands for the formation of independent unions to protect workers' interests are such a common feature of the latter stages of such disputes, and why some workers eventually develop the view that party and management officials constitute a new ruling class (Montias 1981: 182), a class which does not and cannot represent the interests of workers since it is mainly concerned with perpetuating its own powerful and privileged position. Thus we see how a dispute triggered by a specific economic grievance can escalate rapidly into a serious political conflict; examples of this progression in China can be found in reports of industrial unrest during the Hundred Flowers period.

We now have two rather different portrayals of how workers fare under socialist government and management: one, drawn from studies of China, which depicts Chinese workers as basically loyal supporters of the party who are politically passive and whose participation in popular protest movements is marginal; and the other, based on research on Eastern Europe and the former Soviet Union, which strongly suggests that sharp, persistent and escalating conflict between the working class on one side and management and the party on the other is an inevitable product of the state socialist industrial system, and that workers will repeatedly be driven to take independent collective action including the formation of their own organizations. That the former portrayal is now beginning to be revised in favour of the latter is shown by the remarks of Anita Chan quoted above, and by other reassessments of the significance of the Workers' Autonomous Federations formed in 1989, and of workers' involvement in the Hundred Flowers movement.

But in my view there is still a need for a reappraisal of the experience of workers in China's cities since 1949, and that is what this study is intended to provide, focusing on workers themselves, as opposed to the official unions, and, bearing in mind the findings of studies of workers in other socialist countries, examining workers' responses to party policies, their degree of satisfaction with the functioning of the official unions and the various bodies set up to represent them in the enterprise, the development of their relationship with political and managerial authorities, and the underlying causes, nature and possible political significance of any conflicts or disputes which might arise. Tracing the development of the major crises in workers' relationship with the CCP regime up to 1989 can also aid a reassessment of the significance of workers' involvement in the wider movements, such as the Hundred Flowers movement or the Cultural Revolution, with which these crises coincided. It is hoped that a more detailed picture of workers' attitudes and concerns, particularly in the very early stages of each of the periods of confrontation, will provide insights into the underlying causes of these confrontations and a fuller and more intelligible account of their development.

This account will provide the context, which has hitherto been missing, in which the series of major confrontations between workers and the CCP can be understood not as aberrations, but as the most serious manifestations of fundamental contradictions which have always been present in their relationship. Looked at in isolation, and without detailed knowledge of the background in terms of workers' attitudes, living and working conditions, and their position within the socialist enterprise, it is possible to see why the view has gained ground that workers' activities in each case have been of only marginal importance. Yet if we consider these 'aberrations' together, equipped both with knowledge of Chinese workers' lives and with some understanding of workers' experiences in other socialist states, then a more accurate depiction of Chinese workers' experience of, and responses to, CCP rule will emerge. It is only by taking into account all of the crises identified in workers' relations with the CCP that we can see both the similarities between them and the ways in which they have become progressively more acute and harder to resolve with each recurrence. We can also see how workers have progressed, gaining in organizational and political confidence through their experiences in these periodic confrontations.

For example, over the years the official trade unions were first criticized then rejected in favour of independent, though informal and small-scale organizations, and then ceased to exist altogether for much of the Cultural Revolution and the years up to 1976, as workers organized themselves into Red Guard and other groups. This experience of larger-scale collective political activity meant that after the Cultural Revolution, workers were quick to organize independent trade unions during the unrest surrounding the Democracy Wall movement, with some making explicit reference to similar movements in Eastern Europe by appropriating the 'Solidarity' title. We will also see how criticism of cadres' bureaucratist and undemocratic attitudes after liberation gave rise during the Hundred Flowers period and after to the idea that the political power of the bureaucracy over workers might lead it to develop into a new class. This serious political division between the workers and their leaders meant that in the aftermath of the Cultural Revolution, with workers' attitudes towards authority radically altered by their experiences, the confrontation between workers and the party was expressed in terms of class conflict, i.e. a conflict between the workers and the new ruling class.

This study will show that conflict between Chinese workers and the leadership of their enterprises has been a much more common feature of industrial life in China than is generally realized, and, in investigating the underlying problems of social and political inequality in the workplace (which seem to be of far greater significance in motivating workers to protest, and eventually to organize themselves, than the purely economic grievances usually stressed in official accounts), will demonstrate the wider political implications of apparently limited industrial disputes. It will pay particular attention to Chinese workers' attempts to organize themselves outside party control, a subject given renewed importance by the widespread formation (and suppression) of Workers' Autonomous Federations in many Chinese cities in 1989. This most recent confrontation with workers, regarded by many at the time and since as of slight importance, a sideshow to the main student demonstrations, will thus be seen in its proper context, not as an unprecedented action on the part of Chinese workers, but as the latest, and most serious, in a series of crises in workers' troubled relationship with the CCP regime.

1 Chinese labour under 'New Democracy', 1949–55

The first major confrontation between the CCP and Chinese workers began to develop immediately after the communist victory in 1949. The newly-organized official trade unions played an important part in it, so much so that accounts of the period often focus exclusively on the unions' struggle for greater autonomy from the party at this time, a struggle which culminated in the removal of the veteran CCP leader Li Lisan as Chair of the All-China Federation of Trade Unions (ACFTU) in early 1952. This concentration on the higher levels of the union hierarchy has tended to obscure the activities of workers themselves at the grassroots level, and may perhaps explain why 'the incident went down in popular memory as simply a power struggle among the Party's top leaders' (Chan 1993: 33). In fact, the confrontation had its roots in the conflict between workers' expectations of their new role and status after liberation and the party's more moderate policies towards the takeover of industry, particularly in later-liberated areas such as southern China.

Many elements of the ongoing conflict between workers and party authorities in the early 1950s will become familiar as we examine later crises in this problematic relationship. They include the difficulties faced by basic-level trade unions in carrying out their dual functions, presented with the dilemma of either alienating their own members with their obedience to party and managerial authorities in the enterprise, or supporting the workers and risking accusations of economism, syndicalism, and attempting to usurp party leadership over the working class. We will see how, beginning in late 1949, the new official unions shifted between these two positions in response to conflicting pressures from the workers below them and the party above, apparently unable to find any viable middle way, and ultimately succumbed to absolute dominance by the party at the Seventh ACFTU Congress in May 1953, thus incurring the disappointment, even disgust, of many workers, who complained that the unions had 'lost their guts' after the Congress (*Workers' Daily* 21 May 1957).

Another familiar feature making its first appearance in this period is the promotion of management democratization in response to workers' demands for a greater say in the running of their enterprises, both state and private. There is a marked similarity between the problems encountered in the establishment and operation of various workers' representative bodies at this early stage, and again in 1956–7 and the early 1980s, which supports the view that there are fundamental flaws in such organizations which eventually undermine them all. Deborah Kaple's work has suggested that the Chinese attempted in the early post-liberation period to implement an idealized, and correspondingly harsh, version of the Stalinist industrial organization and management practices then prevalent in the Soviet Union, and that the attempt to graft onto this provisions for democratic management was always doomed (Kaple 1994: 58–69). This is a persuasive view, since one so often has the impression that workers and grassroots cadres alike in this period are struggling with systems which are fundamentally unworkable.

Workers' criticisms of cadres, whether union, management or party, and indeed the self-criticisms of these same officials, also return repeatedly to what seem to be the perennial problems in the attitudes and workstyle of leadership cadres: bureaucratism, isolation from the rank and file, a preference for coercive or commandist methods, failure to trust in the workers, arrogance and high-handedness, formalism, and a lack of democracy within enterprises and in the trade unions. In the early post-liberation period many such problems might be attributed to the difficult economic situation, the inexperience of large numbers of cadres, or workers' 'unduly high' (Harper 1969: 91) expectations of the new regime, were it not for the fact of their repeated recurrence during later confrontations between party and workers. It is this which gives them added significance in the years under consideration in this chapter.

In order to understand why many workers, especially in later-liberated areas, found the party's moderate policies on the takeover of industry difficult to accept, we must first look at workers' earlier experiences of both economic and political struggle and how these shaped their attitudes and expectations of communist rule. Immediately after liberation, CCP propaganda made much of the working class's contribution to the party's victory, even though this often meant going back to the 1920s heyday of the Chinese labour movement (Wales 1945; Chesneaux 1968) to find events to celebrate. For example, reporting the liberation of the southern city of Guangzhou (Canton) two days after the event, the *Workers' Daily* reminded readers of the 'glorious tradition' of the labour movement in that city during the Republican period, describing Guangzhou as 'a hotbed of the 1925–27 revolution', and recalling workers' role in the Guangzhou uprising and the establishment of the short-lived Guangzhou Commune, 'the first worker-peasant-soldier revolutionary regime in China', in December 1927 (*Workers' Daily* 16 October 1949; Dirlik 1997).

The CCP itself had been driven into rural exile after 1927, with only a relatively small number of organizers remaining behind in the cities under Guomindang (GMD), and later Japanese, control, so this presentation of workers' revolutionary role could be taken simply as the wishful thinking of a communist party anxious to prove its proletarian credentials after more than twenty years of rural peasant organizing and guerrilla warfare. But this would ignore the extent to which 'in the rank and file of labour itself . . . the tradition remained much more than a matter of words' (Epstein 1949: vi). Even during the Cultural Revolution, some workers' organizations still harked back to the struggles of the warlord era in the nomenclature of their groups (Perry and Li 1997: 73). Workers' own sense of the traditions of Chinese labour does genuinely seem to have encompassed the early years, particularly 1919–27, when the labour movement was above all highly politicized, with the gaining of improved material conditions by workers a secondary goal.

Economic struggles did dominate the 1930s, but the spirit of the more politicized unions reappeared periodically in upsurges of activity in which they 'repeatedly incorporated the entire rank and file of purely economic and even government-controlled "yellow" unions' (Epstein 1949: v). Throughout the 1930s and during the Anti-Japanese War, 'an "unorganized" labor movement . . . seethed constantly below the surface and burst out in sporadic and spontaneous strikes and disputes, in which Chinese labor [showed] remarkable resourcefulness, tenacity and courage' (Wales 1945: 67). With or without the leadership of underground communist activists, the labour movement continued in the cities and rose to new heights after the Japanese surrender, with more than 3 million workers taking part in strikes during 1947 alone (Zhu Xuefan 1948: 57). Workers' linking of economic and political struggles in areas under GMD control drew praise and encouragement from the CCP at labour movement congresses during the civil war years and after. A speaker at the Sixth All-China Labour Congress in 1948 noted with approval a rise in workers' political consciousness and an understanding that 'livelihood and starvation are not just economic questions, but also political ones' (Zhu Xuefan 1948: 50). In similar vein, the Seventh ACFTU Congress in 1953 recalled that in GMD-ruled areas,

> it was necessary for the trade unions to lead the workers to wage both legal and illegal economic struggles under every possible and favourable condition, and to link these struggles closely with the political struggle . . . [before liberation] all economic struggles waged by the trade unions had political significance.
>
> (Xu Zhizhen 1953: 86)

Thus the political aspects of the labour movement before liberation were regarded as not only acceptable, but absolutely necessary. This is in sharp contrast to the role mapped out for unions under the new communist government and, as we shall see, the transition for unions and workers alike was not an easy one.

Given the militant and politicized history of the labour movement in cities under GMD control, it is easy to see why workers' expectations of their new position after the anticipated communist victory were high. The emphasis in GMD labour policy and legislation was always on controlling workers (Epstein 1949: viii), and needless to say the restrictions on labour did not ease under Japanese occupation of the cities of the eastern seaboard. What is perhaps more surprising is the extent to which the GMD, on their return to southern and eastern urban areas after the Japanese surrender, maintained this level of control over workers and even intensified it (Epstein 1949: 75–6). In these circumstances workers would clearly expect a marked contrast between their treatment under GMD and Japanese or 'puppet' rule, and life under an avowed party of the working class. It was noted in the second half of 1948 that workers were 'greatly encouraged' (Zhu Xuefan 1948: 51) by what they heard about rural land reform in areas already liberated, and they looked forward to a similar process taking place after the liberation of their cities.

But from about the middle of 1948 it began to become apparent that workers' expectations were not going to be met, or at least not immediately, as CCP policy on the takeover of industry shifted, and the idea that 'the ultra-egalitarianism of the "peasant socialist" period of land reform should be applied to the industrial sphere' (Brugger 1976: 64) was supplanted by the more moderate policy of 'bene-fitting both labour and capital'. Under this new policy, as many capitalists and private enterprise managers as possible in cities like Shanghai and Guangzhou were to be encouraged to stay on under the new regime and to keep in operation any enterprise which was of benefit to the national economy and to the people as a whole. Expanding employment and alleviating shortages were the priorities, and the overriding need to restore and develop industrial production was the main motivation for pursuing a policy towards private industry which top party leaders admitted was essentially 'reformist' (Li Lisan 1949: 84) rather than revolutionary.

Given their preference for a radical, land reform-type takeover of industry and commerce, it comes as no surprise that many workers were highly suspicious of the party's policy of 'benefitting both labour and capital' in private enterprises, which they viewed, not without reason as we shall see, as a cover for their continued exploitation by capitalists. The problem of the clash between workers' expectations and actual party policy was addressed by Li Lisan in May 1949, when he discussed the differences between the situation in the countryside and in the cities as follows:

> Some people say that the Communist Party's method of liberating the peas-ants was good and very simple: they took the landlords' property and distributed it equally to the peasants, so why can't they distribute the capital-ists' property to the workers, instead of carrying out the development of production and only then being able to improve workers' lives?
>
> (Li Lisan 1949: 73)

In the countryside, he explained, the peasants worked harder and produced more once freed from the exploitation of landlords, 'so the result of the equal distribution of land was that we were able to increase agricultural production', with consequent benefits for peasants' purchasing power, which in turn expanded markets and gave impetus to industrial production. But applying the rural policy to industry would mean that 'society would move backwards and livelihoods would decline', as a literal dividing up of capitalists' property – facto-ries and machinery – would make it impossible for factories to go on producing. Workers, he insisted, 'certainly cannot divide up the capitalists' factories; on the contrary, they must do their utmost to protect the factories and increase produc-tion, for only that will be of benefit to the workers' (Li Lisan 1949: 73–4).

In Li's analysis, the three main causes of workers' hardship in the past had been imperialist, bureaucratic capitalist and feudal oppression and exploitation; oppression and exploitation in enterprises owned by the national bourgeoisie; and the under-development of Chinese industry. The first of these had already been erad-icated and the second considerably restricted by the new people's government and the leading position of the working class, leaving just the third to be tackled by workers' own efforts in a 'production alliance' with capitalist employers. Their capital was vital to the transformation of China's backward economy; increases in production brought about by workers' hard work would unavoidably benefit capi-talists, and their increased profits from the surplus value produced by workers would be exploitative in nature, but this situation was historically necessary, and 'excessive exploitation' (Li Lisan 1949: 74) could and would be prevented. The sole criterion on which private enterprises were judged was whether or not they were beneficial to the national economy (*Xinhua News Agency* 21 September 1948).

Li's point about the need to persuade the national bourgeoisie to stay on and keep investing in enterprises was a reasonable one, but his overly literal interpre-tation of what workers were demanding when they called for capitalists' property to be distributed to them failed, perhaps deliberately, to address workers' real political aspirations. He was careful to concentrate on the impracticality of phys-ically taking factories apart and 'distributing' them to workers, but never mentioned the possibility of workers' taking control of the (intact) enterprises in which they worked. That this possibility existed was shown by the experience of the north and northeast, the earliest industrialized areas to be liberated, where many private enterprises were in fact run by workers after being abandoned by their former owners and all or most of their management personnel.

This more radical, as well as often more violent, takeover of industry in the north and northeast illustrates the general principle that 'the earlier a particular city was liberated the more radical was the takeover of its industries likely to be' (Brugger 1976: 67). The policies towards private industry implemented in the later-liberated cities where large numbers of private enterprises remained in private hands for up to seven years after liberation, were very moderate when compared with those of earlier-liberated areas; and workers in these cities, with their history of labour movement militancy and high expectations for the new era under communist rule, found these policies correspondingly difficult to accept. That the new CCP city government never entertained the idea of allowing workers to take over and run their own enterprises did little to deter workers from pushing in this direction; nor did it prevent some 'overzealous union organizers who had interpreted Marxism-Leninism far too literally' from 'forcibly concentrating power in the hands of the workers' (Vogel 1969: 76) in the early spring of 1950. Thus the scene was set for conflict between the CCP and workers as soon as the party took power.

After liberation: management democratization and the new unions in the 'last difficult year'

There is no doubt about the seriousness of the economic problems facing both workers and the new CCP government at the beginning of 1950, the 'last difficult year' (*People's Daily* 6 February 1950). The main industrialized areas had all suffered considerable damage during twelve years of civil and international warfare, from Japanese bombing to sabotage by the retreating GMD in 1949. In Guangzhou, for example, it was reported in December 1949 that less than a quarter of the city's enterprises were operating at full capacity, while nearly a third of the entire workforce was unemployed (*Guangzhou Labour Movement* 1950: 85). In these circumstances, the CCP stressed the responsibilities of workers as the leading class in the new society and warned them of compromises which would have to be made. In order to consolidate the leading position of the working class, Ye Jianying informed Guangzhou workers,

> we must be good at uniting our own class, raising our political conscious-ness, and distinguishing between immediate and long-term interests and between partial and overall interests, and must subordinate immediate and partial interests to long-term and overall interests . . . and so, under certain circumstances, it will sometimes be necessary to make some concessions to other classes.
>
> (*Guangzhou Labour Movement* 1950: 79)

But the moderate policy towards industry, with its emphasis on compromise for the sake of production, economic recovery and keeping enterprises in business, did not mean that workers' interests and aspirations were to be ignored alto-gether. They could not be, for it was recognized that the mood among workers was such that management democratization in state enterprises and an improve-ment in labour–capital relations in private enterprises were urgently required if this policy were to succeed, as was the rapid organization of workers into new, official trade unions. The demand for democratization and participation by workers in enterprise management was also clearly present in the earliest weeks and months of CCP rule, although, as would be the case with later campaigns for democratization, its importance for the restoration and development of production was the point most strongly emphasized: the *People's Daily* insisted that the participation of workers in democratic enterprise management was 'the reason why labour productivity in New Democratic or socialist societies tends to be higher than in capitalist countries' (*People's Daily* 6 February 1950).

But in addition to its role in promoting production, democratization of enter-prise management was also the main symbol of the changed status of workers after liberation. While the right to use the traditional weapons of labour, such as strikes, was not withdrawn from workers under the new regime, workers were told that they '[did not] need to and should not use [these] methods of struggle which harm production' (Peng Qingzhao 1951: 29–30). Whether disputes arose with state enterprise administrators or with capitalists in private enterprises, they could all be resolved by consultation and negotiation through workers' 'own trade unions and own government'; these methods were adequate because 'there could certainly be no circumstances where the government, led by the working class itself, would fail to protect the interests of the working class' (*Questions on the*

Labour Movement 1950: 56). The fact that workers were being asked to exchange their cherished weapons of struggle from the pre-liberation labour movement for the new structures of democratic management, which would make them the partners, rather than the opponents, of management, demonstrates how important it was for these structures to live up to expectations and give workers some genuine role in enterprise management. We turn now to a detailed examination of the nature of the management reforms undertaken in both private and state enterprises, and of the extent to which they provided workers with real influence in the enterprise, before looking at the new official unions and their changing relationship with both workers and management, and the influence this had on the progress of the reforms.

The labour–capital consultative conference (LCCC)

In all the CCP's efforts to improve labour–capital relations after liberation the emphasis was on compromise, with workers' wages and conditions being improved only to the extent that struggling enterprises could afford, and capitalists being allowed a reasonable level of profit. The labour–capital consultative conference (*laozi xieshang huiyi*) was intended to be an institution where representatives of both labour and capital could discuss all matters relating to pay, conditions, profit, and production in an enterprise (or sometimes in a trade or industry), on the basis of equality, in a way which took into account the fundamental interests of both sides.

Opinions differ as to the effectiveness of the LCCC as an institution for workers' participation in the management of private enterprises in this period. As we shall see in the next chapter, when management democratization and workers' participation returned to the top of the agenda in the second half of 1956, state and joint state-private enterprises were criticized for having 'neglected the democratic tradition allowing workers in private enterprises to participate in management' (Lai Ruoyu 1956a). This would seem to imply that management reforms in this direction had been fairly successful in the private sector, at least in comparison with state enterprises.

On the face of it, LCCCs seemed to be weighted in favour of the labour side: disputes which could not be resolved were to be referred to the local Labour Bureau, which in all probability would be staffed by officials with a union background who could be expected to come down on the side of labour in most cases. 'A capitalist was still a capitalist and the machinery worked against him' (Harper 1971a: 121). Added to this, the two sides took turns in chairing the conference's meetings, and the secretary of the enterprise party committee was a labour representative, both of which militated against the institution being dominated by the factory director or manager (this was a major problem with the factory management committee in state enterprises, about which more will be said later).

But it should be remembered that the LCCC was primarily 'a potent instrument for use by the Party or union against the capitalists' (Harper 1971a: 119). Whether or not workers themselves could actually exercise any influence

depended on the attitude of their union representatives, who would not necessarily share or support workers' views. Nor were capitalists always as constrained
by their somewhat ambiguous status under the new regime as might be
supposed: one writer finds that the LCCCs 'did not function well, if at all'
because managements' fears of 'unreasonable demands' from workers and
'infringements on their administrative authority' (Lee Lai To 1986: 90) led them
to impede the operation of the conferences by their non-cooperation. In cases
where the trade union was ineffective in defence of workers' rights, it was even
possible for capitalists 'to achieve the goal of "benefitting only the capital side"'
(*Guangzhou Labour Movement* 1950: 56) by means of the LCCC.

During negotiations with private employers, the lack of experience of cadres
representing workers' interests often showed. The capital side generally appears
to have been much better prepared and more effective than were the cadres and
workers' representatives on the labour side, who, for example, found themselves
unable to dispute capitalists' assertions about their finances and what constituted
a reasonable level of profit at an enterprise as they had not worked out their own
figures beforehand. This led to 'a lot of difficulties which could have been
avoided' (*Guangzhou Labour Movement* 1950: 66). From this experience we can see
how it might have been possible for capitalists, who on occasion turned up for
negotiations accompanied by their lawyers, to turn institutions such as the
LCCC and collective agreements to their own advantage.

Democratization in state enterprises: the factory management committee and workers' representative congress

Progress in management democratization in state enterprises also encountered
difficulties in the first few months after the establishment of CCP rule.
Government regulations provided for the establishment of a factory management committee (FMC) and a workers' representative conference (WRC) in
every state enterprise (North China People's Government 1949).[1] Workers in
private enterprises were also encouraged to persuade management to adopt
these forms, although in keeping with the policy of cooperation and equality
between labour and capital, this could not be done by the workers alone without
the agreement of the capital side.

The FMC (*gongchang guanli weiyuanhui*) consisted of the factory director
(as Chair), the deputy director, the chief engineer, and the Chair of the trade
union as *ex officio* members, plus other 'responsible production personnel, and a
corresponding number of representatives of workers and staff'. This made a
total of between five and seventeen members, with the participation of responsible personnel being decided by the factory director, and workers'
representatives elected 'by a general meeting of all workers and staff, or by a
representative conference, called by the trade union'. The FMC was to be 'an
administrative organization for unified leadership of the factory or enterprise',
with the following duties: 'on the basis of production plans and various directives

laid down by higher-level enterprise management organs, and in accordance with actual circumstances in the enterprise, to discuss and decide upon all important questions to do with production and management'. These included production plans, management systems, the organization of production, appointment and dismissal of personnel, wages, welfare, etc.

All the committee's decisions were implemented by order of the factory director and as Chair, the director had the power to take emergency decisions alone, subject only to seeking the committee's retrospective approval, and to veto majority decisions which were judged to be 'in conflict with the interests of the enterprise, or not in keeping with higher-level directives', provided immediate guidance on the matter was sought from higher-level organs. In cases like this, the majority on the committee could also report its divergent views to higher-level organs, but had to implement the factory director's decision pending further guidance. In large enterprises a standing committee consisting of the director, the trade union Chair and one elected representative could be formed to take charge of day-to-day business and oversee implementation of the committee's decisions. In newly-liberated cities, military representatives stationed in factories were also automatically members of the FMC and the standing committee.

The WRC (*zhigong daibiao huiyi*) was the forerunner of the Workers' Congress (*zhigong daibiao dahui*) which was promoted from 1956 as an antidote to the excesses of Soviet-style 'one-man management' and a solution to workers' alienation from both management and the official trade unions. It was to consist of representatives directly elected by workers and staff from their own production small group or shift. These representatives were 'directly responsible to the workers and staff electing them', and if found to be unsatisfactory, they could be recalled and dismissed by their electors at any time. Barring such recalls, representatives were to be re-elected annually. Meetings of the WRC were to be held once or twice a month, generally outside working hours, and were to last not more than half a day. In enterprises with less than 200 workers, monthly or bimonthly meetings of the entire workforce would serve as the WRC. In large enterprises which consisted of more than one factory or production site, each constituent part was to elect its own, basic-level WRC which could then delegate representatives to a general WRC covering the whole enterprise, but the principle of direct election by all workers and staff of the basic-level WRC was strongly emphasized.

The WRC was essentially intended to be a forum for consultation and communication between management, in the guise of the FMC, and workers and staff. Its powers were limited to hearing and discussing FMC reports, checking on the committee's administrative management and leadership work-style, and making proposals or offering criticism. The WRC's decisions would not come into force until ratified by the FMC and implemented by order of the factory director. The WRC also served as a representative conference of the factory's trade union organization, and the trade union committee was obliged to implement all its decisions on trade union business.

It is clear from the above description of the structure and workings of the

FMC that early concerns about the 'potentially undemocratic nature of the [factory director's] veto' (Brugger 1976: 220), and about the dominant position of the director or manager in general, were not without foundation. Given the active cooperation of the director and other 'responsible personnel', it is possible that workers' own views, expressed by their union representatives on the committee, could carry some weight. Harper considers that since union cadres could be drawn from among political activists and outstanding producers in the workforce, the union presence on the committee 'did provide for some actual worker representation', particularly in the few months immediately after liberation when '[a]s enterprises were taken over by the state, the initial surge would be for some significant workers' role' (Harper 1971a: 117), but concedes that both the FMC and WRC could equally easily be ignored, especially when the enterprise leadership was preoccupied with economic difficulties. In most circumstances, 'it is very likely that the manager, together with the chief engineer, could always play down the opinions of unions and workers' representatives' (Lee Lai To 1986: 98).

The WRC tended to act as 'a rubber-stamp body' (Harper 1971a: 115) for decisions of the factory director and the FMC; since its own decisions were not binding on the FMC, it could have little real influence. Reports on the workings of the WRC in the first few months after liberation are scarce, especially in comparison with the LCCC. However, there are signs that workers initially attempted to turn the WRC into a rather more influential body than had been intended in the regulations. For some reason meetings of the WRC, rather than taking up only half a day as specified in the regulations, were going on for at least three or four days, and quite often for ten days or more, taking up production time (*Workers' Daily* 9 March 1950). Inadequate preparatory work and a failure to focus discussion on key issues were blamed for the excessive length of meetings, but it is likely that workers' eagerness to participate in discussions on all aspects of the enterprise's work in this, the only official forum for workers' views, was the cause of these prolonged discussions. The excessive length of the meetings could also be taken as evidence of possible conflict between workers and unions on the one hand and the administration and party on the other.

Slow progress in the democratization of state enterprise management seems to have been a national phenomenon in early 1950. A *People's Daily* editorial in February 1950 mentioned progress in the northeast of China, but qualified this with the statement that 'we must frankly admit that we are still not managing all enterprises well, and indeed are managing some very badly' (*People's Daily* 6 February 1950). The absence of FMCs in some state enterprises was also noted in the *Workers' Daily* the following month (*Workers' Daily* 5 March 1950), and even where structures for democratic management were set up, workers' problems in actually using them to exert influence over the running of the enterprise were still considerable. In order to understand what was happening in both state and private enterprises in this period, and to find the root causes of workers' problems with management democratization, it is necessary to examine the development of the official unions. Workers' ability to make use of the formal participatory structures available to them, with union cadres representing workers on the LCCC and FMC and being in overall charge of the WRC, depended on the unions' degree of support for workers' views and demands. This was the decisive factor in determining whether or not workers could actually participate in the management of their own enterprises. The official unions had a duty to protect workers' democratic rights, and as we will see in the next section, whenever they were unable or unwilling to discharge this duty, workers lost any chance of exerting influence through the formal channels of democratic management.

The trade unions after liberation

The dual-function model of trade union established by the Soviet Union and adopted by the PRC requires the official unions to represent the interests of their members on the one hand, and of enterprise management and the state on the other. Since these interests are often in conflict, in practice the Chinese unions have shifted between siding with workers and allying themselves with enterprise and party authorities, with these shifts depending on the broader political climate in China and the amount of pressure being brought to bear on the unions from above and below. In the first two years of the new CCP regime the newly-established official unions were still finding their way, and so it is not surprising that their shifts in emphasis, from worker-oriented relative autonomy to complete subjugation to the party and back again, took place more rapidly than was ever the case in later years. From an early period of sometimes backing worker militancy (although some union organizers also displayed a deep distrust of workers who had belonged to the compulsory GMD-run 'yellow' unions or to secret societies, about which more will be said later) and pushing for meaningful democratization of management, the unions shifted from about March 1950 to siding with management and acting to curb workers' demands, concentrating solely on production. This attitude was not at all what many workers had expected of the CCP victory, and the powerful backlash of worker criticism forced the unions to reconsider and, from about late 1950, stress their role as the defenders of workers' interests first and foremost. This in turn provoked a party reaction against excessive autonomy and syndicalism at the higher levels of the union hierarchy which culminated in the purge of the ACFTU's top leader, Li Lisan, and the taming of the unions as effective workers' advocates until the mid-1950s.

There is an obvious contrast between the proper role of the trade unions under a socialist government and the way in which unions and workers were operating in Chinese cities immediately before liberation, in the militant labour movement with strong political overtones which existed then. Such was workers' belief in the importance of unions that, in spite of the overwhelmingly negative picture of the GMD's 'fake' trade unions painted by CCP propaganda (which, it must be remembered, had considerable basis in fact), when it came to the dismantling of these organizations, there was a feeling among workers that 'they knew that the fake trade unions were bad, but in the end they were better than no trade unions at all, and if a labour–capital dispute arose, what then?' (*Guangzhou Labour Movement* 1950: 30; Friedman 1949: 128). This strong support for the traditional, adversarial type of union created difficulties in the transition to a cooperative rather than a confrontational role for unions, one in which they would have responsibilities to management and the state as well as to their own members. It proved to be a transition which union organizers were not always immediately able, or willing, to make.

The first few months after October 1949 have been characterized as a period 'when workers struck at will and frightened capitalists closed their factories' (Harper 1969: 91), and given the mood among many workers before liberation and their expectations of the new era, this is a credible description. The annual report of the All-China Federation of Labour (forerunner of the ACFTU) published in May 1950 confirms this impression, acknowledging as 'unavoidable' the fact that 'workers who have long been under capitalist exploitation and oppression become rather retaliative and show an extreme leftist tendency' (*Chinese Worker* 15 May 1950). What seems to have caused particular concern was the inclination of some unions to support these 'leftist' workers, and to attempt to use institutions like the LCCC, set up in support of the policy of 'benefitting both labour and capital', to make gains for workers at the expense of private management (*Chinese Worker* 15 July 1950). Management cadres and the factory director in some state enterprises also came up against union-led opposition from workers.

Union cadres were criticized in the press for continuing to regard the enterprise administration as an enemy after liberation, and it was reported from Tianjin that union officials there were reluctant even to hold discussions and consultations with the enterprise administration in the latter's offices, for fear of workers' branding them 'the running dogs of the administration' (*Workers' Daily* 13 October 1949). This sort of pressure and criticism from workers was not union cadres' only motive for their stand, although it must have been a powerful one, given that the new unions were anxious to differentiate themselves from the GMD's 'fake' trade unions, which they dismissed as having done nothing at all for the workers who were forced to join, except control them on behalf of management and the state (*Guangzhou Labour Movement* 1950: 86). But in addition to this, some union cadres also seem to have thought that the proclaimed policy of democratization in enterprises justified their attitude.

A series of articles by the paper's editor, Chen Yongwen, published in *Workers' Daily* in early March 1950 dealt with various questions concerning enterprise democratization, and in particular attempted to clear up any confusion among union cadres as to the difference between democratization aimed ultimately at improving workers' work performance and increasing production, and what was termed 'extreme democratization', which was how workers' demands to take control of their own enterprises were characterized (*Workers' Daily* 3 and 8 March 1950). Chen observed that some union officials had forgotten about the production goals of democratization and were instead concentrating on mass mobilization and the launching of a 'democratic movement':

The result is that they intentionally or unintentionally 'mobilize the masses' and stir up opposition to and disputes with the administrative leadership;

and they intentionally or unintentionally lead the masses in raising a lot of demands relating to purely economic interests which cannot all easily be resolved straight away. Problems thus cannot be solved, but on the contrary become a barrier between the leadership and the masses.

(Workers' Daily 3 March 1950)

This sort of 'extreme democratization' was described as 'very harmful to production' and as 'even worse than no democracy at all' *(Workers' Daily* 3 March 1950). A later article in the same series revealed that some union officials saw the factory director's right to veto FMC majority decisions as incompatible with management democratization and therefore opposed it, but this view too was condemned as likely to undermine state leadership over enterprises and lead to 'anarchist, syndicalist extreme democratization' *(Workers' Daily* 8 March 1950).

But union support for workers' apparent preference for 'extreme democratization' was short-lived. As industry and commerce in China's cities slipped into a period of crisis between March and June 1950, the party intervened to curb the number of industrial disputes and enforce its policy of giving priority to economic recovery and stability. Pressure was brought to bear on the unions to concentrate on production and support the leadership of their enterprises, whether state or private, with the result that:

> during the spring months of 1950 the unions stressed compromise and ignored class struggle, often siding with the plant administration. In private enterprises, unions approved capitalists' suggestions for reducing wages and welfare benefits. In state-run enterprises, the same conservative tendency appeared, with the unions and the management 'speaking the same phrases' and the unions behaving as no more than an arm of the administration.
>
> (Harper 1969: 92)

Party pressure was not the only reason, however, why unions across China took this line during the spring and early summer of 1950. Alongside those 'overzealous union organizers who . . . were forcibly concentrating power in the hands of the workers' (Vogel 1969: 76), many cadres in the official unions as well as in enterprise management and party organizations had a much less positive attitude towards urban workers. Not all union organizers, it must be remembered, had any background in the labour movement or in urban areas at all; many had only rural or military experience prior to the CCP victory in 1949, and those from the earlier-liberated areas who had long been party members or fought in the Red Army tended to distrust the workers who 'had made rifles for the enemy' (Brugger 1976: 71).

Two main factors affected union cadres' attitudes towards workers. The first of these was a tendency to over-emphasize what a union journal euphemistically referred to as the 'complex nature of the working class' in China, 'the dark side created and left behind by the old society' *(Chinese Worker* 20 December 1950). Instead of the clean-cut proletarian heroes pictured in party propaganda, union cadres saw dominating workers' ranks such features of pre-1949 industrial labour as gang-bosses and secret-society members (Brugger 1976: 42–7; Chesneaux 1968: 54–64). They were so concerned about not letting any of these undesirables into the new unions that in Guangzhou, for example, where gang-boss and secret-society influence over labour had been very strong, union recruitment proceeded at a snail's pace, with some new unions not having recruited a single member by March 1950 (*Guangzhou Labour Movement* 1950: 11). In the case of the Guomindang's 'yellow' unions, some effort had to be made to distinguish active participants and leaders from unwilling or indifferent conscripts into these compulsory organizations, but again, in the early months of union recruitment organizers were ultra-cautious in evaluating workers for union membership. Eventually instructions came from the party to organize first and worry about weeding out the 'dark side' later, and to have faith in the majority of workers' ability to spot real counter-revolutionaries (*Guangzhou Labour Movement* 1950: 40). Former gang-bosses who did slip through the net and continued to wield influence in the workplace were then targeted in later campaigns such as the Democratic Reform Movement, discussed below.

As well as these suspicions of socially degenerate elements among the workers, we can detect in many union cadres a more general lack of confidence in workers' ability to understand and contribute to the running of their unions and workplaces. This lack of faith was even more common among enterprise managers, and it was of course the job of union officials to combat such conde-scension and insist that workers be able to exercise their right to participate in management, hence the difficulty for rank-and-file workers if union leaders themselves did not believe their own rhetoric about the talents and wisdom of the shopfloor workforce. Given the existence of 'retained personnel' in later-liberated areas, some of the evident disregard for workers' intellectual capabilities can perhaps be traced back to typical employer–worker relations in the Republican era, when, as described by Julian Friedman,

> [t]he situation could profitably have done with far less contempt for manual laborers on the part of the non-manual managers and employees. . . . Employers, even after the war, lorded it over the workers in an autocratic manner. They viewed manual labor with disdain and frequently paid wages consistent more with their feelings than with the value of output. Some employers imperi-ously imposed penalties and humiliations which the workers, lacking the usual peasant reticence and forbearance, reciprocated with non-Confucian abuse.
> (Friedman 1949: 111–12)

Better could surely be expected of party personnel, including those in the union hierarchy, but here as well workers did not in practice enjoy particularly exalted status. Rather, the revolutionary victory of 1949 was seen as very much the achievement of the party and the army, with liberation bestowed by them on a grateful but relatively passive proletariat and peasantry (Rosen 1982: 78). This view of the Chinese revolution did not put workers in a strong position to assert their right, as members of the leading class in society, to a role in workplace deci-sion-making, and even in 1957, management and unions in some places were still treating recalcitrant workers more like naughty schoolchildren than as the 'masters of the enterprise' (Sheehan 1995: 191).

Workers' criticisms of unions and cadres in 1950

In spite of all the talk of the importance, not least the political importance, of democratization in enterprises, the reality in the first part of 1950 was that the remaining private employers retained considerable freedom of action in their businesses, including the freedom to reduce wages and fire surplus workers, and factory directors in state enterprises similarly ran things with little regard to workers' opinions or preferences. Moreover, both sets of managers were aided in this by the official unions, who themselves exhibited a lack of faith in workers by failing to involve them in the organization and running of 'their own' organiza-tions. It was a far cry from what some workers had expected of the CCP's takeover of industry, and the backlash of criticism was not long in coming.

Particularly in the second half of 1950, the extent of workers' discontent with 'their' unions, and the consequences for enterprise democratization which the unions' attitude entailed, became apparent. Reminders to union cadres of the importance of internal democracy and of trusting in and relying on the workers abound in labour movement and other press articles from this time, but their very frequency (and their continual reappearance over the years) attests to the difficulties encountered in making the official trade unions truly democratic and representative organizations which workers would treat as their own. Some early problems can probably be excused as teething troubles, although we should beware of making too great an allowance for cadres' heavy workload, since this was often caused by their own reluctance to delegate work to activists or ordi-nary union members. Year-end reports on the progress of trade union work during 1950 confirm that throughout the year, workers in all parts of the country were voicing the same sort of complaints about the unions.

In Shanghai, union cadres' emphasis on production tasks, at the expense of welfare, safety and hygiene work, and the protection of workers' interests, meant that workers were entirely at the mercy of administrative cadres in their enter-prises. These cadres were described as:

> lacking in the concept of relying on the working class . . . the workers' management committee is treated as a cipher, very little attention is paid to workers' positive proposals, [and] workers' safety and problems which must and could be solved are often brushed aside. When the administration has no regard for workers' safety and hygiene and doesn't respect workers' opin-ions, and the trade union doesn't care either, this makes the workers see the trade union as merely the administration's union and not their own.
>
> (*Chinese Worker* 20 January 1951)

It is clear from this comment that workers had identified the role played by the new unions in this period, correctly, as that of an arm of the administration. The unions' adoption of this role demonstrates the difficulties inherent in their mandate to act in the interests of both workers and management, particularly at this early stage where they were under strong party pressure to enforce stability and order in enterprises, while at the same time lacking the necessary integration with workers which could have balanced the emphasis on industrial peace at all costs with a deeper understanding of workers' views and essential interests.

The lack of democracy within unions is a common theme in 1950 criticisms. Cases occurred where candidates to chair enterprise trade unions 'only had to put their names forward, and didn't allow workers to cast ballots to elect them' (*Guangzhou Labour Movement* 1950: 58). Problems also arose in union elections when cadres did not trust the workers to vote for the activists who had been on training courses and were thus the best qualified for the posts, and were tempted to apply 'official safeguards of correctness' (Liu Zijiu 1951) to ensure the election of the 'right' candidates. This sort of conduct was definitely not in keeping with the injunction that democracy should be 'the soul of the trade union' (*Workers' Daily* 1 January 1951).

Union cadres were also said to 'attach little importance to suggestions put forward by workers, or brush them aside' (*Chinese Worker* 20 January 1951). When cadres did take action, for example on welfare, it was reported that 'they don't consult the workers beforehand and give no explanation after the event. What is more serious, however, is that they . . . don't have the slightest scrap of fraternal class feeling or affection for the workers and staff' (*Chinese Worker* 20 January 1951). Decisions were made by higher-level trade union organs without regard to the actual situation on the factory floor, leading workers to accuse union cadres trying to implement these decisions of being 'the higher-level trade union's trade union, not a union for us workers' (*Chinese Worker* 20 January 1951).

Union officials were also criticized for their treatment of the many trade union activists who had emerged during various movements, who felt that cadres 'only emphasize[d] making use of them and not training them; only require[d] them to be active and [gave] no consideration to their actual level and difficulties; criticize[d] a lot and [gave] little encouragement' (*Chinese Worker* 20 January 1951), causing widespread demoralization. The basic problem with the official unions was that of responsibility without power, and this problem was most acute for union activists, the lowest level of the hierarchy and at the sharp end of workers' discontent while having the least ability to do anything to meet their demands. We will find these comments from demoralized union activists repeated almost verbatim during 1956, showing the persistence of the problem.

A *Workers' Daily* article published around the same time as the report quoted above included some reference to the achievements of the new trade unions during 1950, but also featured a similar litany of complaints and criticisms. Union organization, particularly at the basic level, was described as 'not very sound', and the persistence among union cadres and in many unions of 'the serious phenomenon of separation from the masses' was noted:

some trade union cadres are still not good at showing consideration for the interests of the broad working masses. For example, in state-owned enterprises, the common task of the trade union and the administration is of course to guarantee the completion of state production plans, but because of this, some trade union cadres forget to give consideration to the interests of the working masses in their daily life, and turn a blind eye to their most urgent requirements.

(Workers' Daily 1 January 1951)

The article repeated the charge that problems which could and should be solved were being neglected, and that unions were failing to exercise their legal right to represent workers' interests and to seek solutions to problems from the administration. Nor did it find the performance of trade unions in private enterprises to be without defects:

> In private enterprises, there are a few trade union cadres who not only are not good at giving consideration to the interests of the working masses, but who even take the place of the capitalists in carrying out 'firing workers and lowering wages', and who openly speak on the capitalists' behalf. Because of this, in some trade unions the phenomenon of the masses' not trusting the trade union and the trade union being divorced from the masses has appeared.

(Workers' Daily 1 January 1951)

These observations confirm the unions' tendency to act exclusively in the interests of management, whether state or private, and of production and stability, thereby neglecting the interests of workers.

Problems with democracy within the unions were also noted in this article, with reports that some union cadres both at the higher and basic levels were still being appointed rather than elected, and showed some reluctance to promote worker activists to cadre status, rejecting these 'mass leaders who really are supported by the broad masses' because of their lack of qualifications or seniority. This attitude was said to be 'fundamentally wrong. . . . All trade union organizations must come from the bottom up, democratically elected by the masses'. Some unions were 'still lacking various systems of democratic life', such as regular meetings, consultation with members and reporting back on decisions and progress, and opportunities for criticism and self-criticism. The article reported that 'work-styles of coercion, commandism, and monopolizing all work oneself' still existed, and gave another example of a factory where union cadres interfered in the running of a union election, insisting that workers voted for candidates who had returned from union training classes, 'incurring the masses' universal dissatisfaction' (Workers' Daily 1 January 1951). Finally, there seems to have been a particular problem with union finances, with some union organizations collecting dues but failing to do anything for their members and not publishing accounts, and even cases of waste and corruption. In view of the main criticisms of the GMD's 'fake' trade unions, i.e. that their leaders were corrupt and simply pocketed members' dues with no intention of using the funds for the benefit of workers, the effect of this sort of conduct on workers' attitudes towards the new unions can be imagined.

These criticisms of unions show how, after a brief initial period in which some union personnel had sided with workers and sought to continue their traditional role as the representative of workers' interests first and foremost, all union officials were soon pressed towards the other extreme of their remit, almost invariably siding with management and the party against workers. This change was not only the result of the change in party policy, which now leaned heavily towards subordinating workers' demands to economic recovery and stability. It also stemmed from the separation of union cadres from their worker members: union cadres had slipped into the undemocratic workstyle of the old-style bureaucrat, and since they were not consulting with workers and seldom sought their opinions, they were unlikely to come under effective pressure from workers to support their preference for 'extreme' democratization of enterprise management.

The implications of the unions' shift from siding with workers to siding with management can be seen if we examine the way in which the policy of 'benefitting both labour and capital' developed in private enterprises during the first half of 1950, and in particular the way that union cadres' attitudes affected the functioning of the LCCC. The early post-liberation surge of union-supported leftism among workers must have confirmed many capitalists' fears about their likely fate under the new regime. In some places they were reported to be understandably nervous about how their workers, now officially the masters, would treat their former oppressors: in Zhengzhou 'panic' amongst capitalists was reported, some of whom 'did not even dare to show their faces and run their businesses' (*Guangzhou Labour Movement* 1950: 70). But we have already seen that there was scope within the LCCC system for the capital side to further its own interests at the expense of labour, and this became even easier once party pressure on the unions to curb workers' 'retaliative' tendencies in private enterprises began to take effect in March 1950.

Reviews of labour–capital relations after the Three- and Five-Anti movements (discussed below) maintain that before these movements, it was commonplace for capitalists to use the LCCC to assert their managerial authority, insisting on the right to sack workers or reduce wages without consultation (*Workers' Daily* 7 April 1952). A report on unions in north China's private enterprises admitted that:

> Before the Five-Anti movement, because of deficiencies in trade union work the masses were not mobilized, and so in very many factories and shops the policy of benefitting both labour and capital was not genuinely implemented, and in a good number [the policy] was to 'benefit only the capital side'.

> (*Workers' Daily* 20 September 1952)

Since capitalists had come under sustained attack during the Five-Anti movement, with great efforts in the labour movement press in particular to whip up
feeling against them, reports such as these are likely to take an especially negative, and quite possibly exaggerated, view of the extent to which LCCCs and the
'two benefits' policy in general were used against workers. Yet there is earlier
evidence from several parts of China which confirms this tendency (Sheehan
1995: 46–7). So it seems probable that during 1950, the pressure on workers to
moderate their demands and even accept pay cuts or dismissals to help enterprises stay afloat was indeed exploited by some capitalists, who

> lack[ed] sincerity and [were] always trying to 'use' the trade union and
> control the workers, or use overcoming difficulties and tiding [the enter-
> prise] over a difficult time as a pretext to force workers to reduce their wages
> and standard of living, to achieve the goal of 'benefitting only the capital
> side'.
>
> *(Chinese Worker* 15 July 1950)

From the middle of 1950, capitalists were widely criticized for having sought
advantage for themselves at workers' expense during the spring economic crisis,
'totally violating unity and the spirit of "all being in the same boat"' (*Shanghai
Labour News* 24 May 1950). Warnings had been given to cadres in the earlier-
liberated areas about the tendency to 'one-sidedly stress the interests of the
capital side, connive at the capitalists' law-breaking and violation of discipline,
and fail to intervene on encroachments on workers' legally established rights, so
that we sacrifice the fundamental interests of the workers' (*Xinhua News Agency* 21
September 1948). But despite this early awareness of the likely problems, this
tendency soon came to the fore in later-liberated areas as well, and was given
additional impetus by CCP policy, as unions in private enterprises were exhorted
to concentrate on productivity and discipline, using the same methods as in state
enterprises, e.g. labour emulation competitions, in an effort to persuade capitalists to stay in business (*Workers' Daily* 23 June 1950).

Enterprise democratization and workers' participation fared little better in
1950 in state enterprises. It was reported that administrative cadres commonly
regarded institutions like the FMC 'not . . . as effective instruments, but as an
extra burden, with the result that meetings are held purely for formalism' (*Chinese
Worker* 15 July 1950). In some cases, administrative cadres agreed to the setting
up of the FMC 'merely in order to "complete" the "task" of setting up the FMC
decided upon at the higher level, and not because they genuinely want[ed] to
implement democratic management'. This sort of committee might either have
a majority of cadre members, or might simply take no notice of worker
members' views and not bother to assist them by explaining things or educating
them for real participation, 'so when the time comes for an FMC meeting the
worker members don't feel that it has any meaning. . . . Some worker members
say: "We've come to listen to the meeting"' (*People's Daily* 3 May 1950).

Typical cadres' comments on the faults of FMCs reported in the press included the following: 'Holding a meeting of cadres will solve the problem just the same, so why do we have to hold FMC meetings? . . . Workers only know what happens in one workshop, so how can they participate in democratic management of a whole factory?' (*People's Daily* 3 May 1950). 'The FMC has a lot of members, it's a bother to convene it, it drags on for ages and can't decide any issue'. 'The workers don't understand the overall situation and can't make speeches'. The factory director's right of veto seems to have undermined administrative cadres' respect for the FMC, as they tended to 'set the factory director's right of final decision against the FMC', describing their respective functions thus: 'You discuss, then at the end I make the decision' (*Northeast Daily* 9 June 1950). In this context, puns on the Chinese word for democracy, *minzhu*, abounded, as in 'workers are the *min* (people), and the factory director is the *zhu* (ruler)' (*Chinese Worker* 15 July 1950). Frequent exhortations to cadres to implement resolutions passed by the WRC in this period also seem to indicate that the workings of that body were being largely ignored.

Strong criticisms of these attitudes, and of cadres' bureaucratist and commandist workstyles in general, reminded cadres that management democratization was 'not merely a question of methods, but in fact a question of ideology' (*Chinese Worker* 15 July 1950). Proper operation of FMCs and WRCs was the 'key link' in transforming old, bureaucratic capitalist enterprises into New Democratic enterprises, and it was emphasized that cadres must grasp 'the basic idea of relying on the assistance of the working masses in managing enterprises well' (*People's Daily* 6 February 1950) if workers were to feel that they genuinely were masters of the enterprise and work accordingly. While it was conceded that worker delegates on FMCs, many of them with minimal education, were not always well equipped to play a prominent role in participatory structures, unions were reminded that it was their task, as 'schools of communism', to educate and assist workers so that they could participate effectively; it would be most unjust to keep workers in a subordinate position because of their lack of education, when this was a result of their low status in the old society.

The stream of negative reports on cadre attitudes and the failure of democratization prompted an early rethink on how both private and state enterprises had been dealt with in the immediate post-liberation period. It had earlier been maintained that the policy of 'benefitting both labour and capital' itself was not at fault, but that 'some private industrialists and commercial proprietors . . . twist[ed] the meaning of government policy, wilfully behaving illegally in violating the proper rights of workers' (*Xinhua News Agency* 21 September 1948). Later, however, there was some recognition that the policy had erred too far in the direction of benefitting the capital side. Most of the blame was attributed to the unions for failing to protect workers from exploitation, which was rather unfair as their line had been 'a correct interpretation by union leaders of CCP directives in those days of economic crisis' (Harper 1969: 92). But whether the fault lay with the policy itself, as framed by the party, or with its implementation by the trade unions, there was a clear acknowledgement that workers' dissatisfaction with it was to some extent justified.

The reassessment of party policy on private enterprises was paralleled by a reconsideration of whether moderate policies on the takeover of state enterprises had been entirely appropriate. From quite early in 1950 it began to be suggested that although slogans such as 'don't smash the old structure to pieces' and 'preserve original positions, salaries and systems' had been correct at the time of liberation, the policy of maintaining the status quo had had the disadvantage that 'we could not help inheriting temporarily the many disruptive phenomena of disunity, irrationality, anarchism and disorganization, and some corrupt systems' (*People's Daily* 6 February 1950; Brugger 1976: 231). A union report in May of the same year went further, conceding that the decision to 'maintain the status quo at various national enterprises so as to keep them intact . . . was suitable for the taking-over stage, but not for stages when enterprises had been brought under control', and that 'some of the cadres in managements and trade unions misapplied the policy of the taking-over stage to the control stage' (All-China Federation of Labour 1950: 4). The reluctance in many state enterprises to make the radical changes favoured by workers, it was now admitted, had hindered progress in management democratization. Once again, the trade unions were at fault for their failure adequately to represent and protect the interests of workers: union cadres could hardly defend workers' right to participate in management against the indifference or hostility of administrative cadres, who regarded workers as incapable of participating effectively, when they themselves were only paying lip-service to the idea that trusting and relying on the workers should be the heart of all work, including enterprise management.

The unions' subordination to state enterprise management during much of the first half of 1950 left workers with no means of enforcing their right to participate in enterprise management, because, as we noted earlier, the mere existence of democratic structures such as the FMC and WRC was not enough to guarantee that workers' participation would become a reality. Despite the official insistence that democratization was essential for the development of production, many cadres still regarded it as an optional extra on which, given their other pressing tasks, they should not waste too much time, and unless union officials were effective in insisting on workers' democratic rights in the enterprise, the dominant position of the factory director in the state enterprise management structure would allow management to brush workers' views aside.

Pressure for a change in policy grew as the results of the shift of unions' allegiance away from workers and towards enterprise management became apparent, and as serious and damaging criticism of the unions by workers mounted. Given its prominence both in official union reports and the main newspapers, there seems to be little doubt that it was mainly the volume and seriousness of workers' criticism and discontent which prompted the change. A union rectification campaign began in August 1950 in which union cadres undertook self-criticism of the commandist and bureaucratist attitudes they had earlier displayed. There was no sudden switch to all-out support for workers' opinions and demands; in order to do this, union cadres would first have needed to know what precisely those opinions and demands were, and as we have seen, it was their alienation from the workers and ignorance of their views which brought about the crisis in the first place.

But all levels of the union hierarchy seem to have agreed that their previous neglect of workers' welfare and interests had allowed both capitalists in private, and administrative cadres in state enterprises, to ride roughshod over those interests, and that if workers' new status as 'masters of the enterprise' was to mean anything, this state of affairs had to be remedied forthwith. So while there was no immediate reversion to supporting workers' demands for 'extreme democratization', from the beginning of 1951 unions did place greater emphasis on their role as workers' representatives and advocates of workers' specific interests. This was soon to bring party accusations of economism down upon basic-level unions, while at the higher, national level it was paralleled by moves towards increased union autonomy from the party which were similarly unacceptable. In both cases, unions were much more inclined to position themselves on the side of the workers in their ongoing confrontation with the CCP, something which the party could not be expected to tolerate.

The union 'crisis' of 1951 and democratic reform

When commentators discuss the early post-liberation crisis in relations between the official unions and the CCP, it is usually just the events of 1951 to which they refer, although as we have seen, unions' support for workers' leftist inclinations immediately after the CCP victory in 1949 was a source of friction as well. Although the party took action to curb the related trends of economism and syndicalism within the unions and the ACFTU hierarchy at the end of 1951, replacing Li Lisan as head of the ACFTU with Lai Ruoyu, it was not until early 1953 that any reports or analyses of these problems were made public. Belated attacks on both economism and syndicalism featured prominently in reports to the Seventh All-China Congress of Trade Unions in May of that year, but these criticisms were for the most part directed specifically at the top leadership of the ACFTU. The question thus arises as to how far this high-level conflict was reflected in events at the enterprise level, and how the confrontation which had unfolded after liberation between workers and the party, centred on the latter's policies on industrial management, developed under these circumstances.

Following the outpouring of workers' criticism which they had faced in the second half of 1950, and much of which they accepted, the trade unions in 1951 gave far more attention to their role as the advocates of workers' specific interests in the enterprise. It was this attitude, and in particular their attention to the immediate material interests of workers, which was condemned as economism in 1953: enterprise-level unions were criticized for seeing a contradiction between improvements in workers' welfare and the development of production and for failing to understand that the former was in fact dependent on the latter, and were accused of irresponsibility in failing to persuade workers not to raise excessively high demands which could not be met under present circumstances (Lai Ruoyu 1953: 52, 66). Party concern about these tendencies was increased by the fact that they coincided with an attempt by Li Lisan to win greater independence from the party for the ACFTU and its affiliated unions; syndicalism thus appeared to the CCP leadership to have permeated the unions from the lowest level to the highest. If the unions' previous tendency to operate as an arm of management had been completely unacceptable to workers, its new emphasis on workers' interests proved equally objectionable to the party. The problems in private enterprises were not so serious, being mainly of a practical rather than an ideological nature. That is, despite their obligation to mobilize workers for the completion of production plans, there was no ideological obstacle to unions' taking an independent line in defence of workers' interests when these were threatened by the actions of private management. Opposing 'excessive' exploitation of workers by the remaining capitalists while continuing and developing production had long been the unions' proper role in private enterprises, and represented a much less drastic shift away from their pre-1949 function. The practical problems concerned the ability of basic-level union organizations to fulfil this role, an ability which was brought into question by the conducting of repeated rectification and reform campaigns, including the Democratic Reform Movement and the Three- and Five-Anti movements, to put union organizations on a sound footing. More will be said about these campaigns later.

But in the case of state enterprises the proper role of the unions was less obvious, and was the subject of a debate within the labour movement during 1951 (Harper 1969: 92–6). This debate centred on whether or not the standpoint of the trade union in a state enterprise should differ in any way from that of the administration. The official party view was that it should not: since the long-term, collective interests of the working class were identical with those of its vanguard, the CCP, and of the party's representatives in state enterprises, the administration, there was no possibility of antagonism between them. Under these circumstances, the unions were responsible for persuading the less advanced section of the working class of this identity of long-term, overall interests, while at the same time keeping the party informed on workers' own immediate interests; the unions were definitely not to become advocates of workers' short-term or purely material interests, since this would amount to a syndicalist challenge to party supremacy.

The opposing position, taken by some union officials, was that the division of labour between management and workers still existed in state as in private enterprises, necessitating a difference in standpoint if unions were genuinely to be the workers' own organization which defended their interests. Unions would thus on occasion be justified in opposing the administration where its actions infringed on workers' interests, even though this ultimately meant opposing the party, which appointed and controlled the administration. It was this view which was criticized in 1953 as 'a tendency in the trade unions of departing from the leadership of the Party' (Lai Ruoyu 1953: 52).

It was not coincidental that the attempts of the top-level ACFTU leadership under Li Lisan to win greater union independence from party control took place at the same time as basic-level unions were taking a more independent line, siding with workers in defence of their interests in the enterprise. However, while

Li Lisan's actions as ACFTU leader probably helped to create a climate in which basic-level unions were able to move towards a stronger and more consistent advocacy of workers' interests, this shift did not necessarily represent a response to instructions or even direct influence from above; in fact, the weakness of vertical control of basic-level unions by ACFTU organs at this point precluded that possibility (Harper 1969: 96).

What is more likely, given what we know about how the unions had operated during most of 1950 and about workers' reaction to their deficiencies, is that unions at various levels, including the highest, were responding to the same pressures, having realized that unless they made a real effort to represent workers in the enterprise and uphold their demands, their position would be untenable as they would be rejected by the workers. This same realization of the threat of irrelevance and redundancy was behind unions' efforts to win back workers' trust and allegiance in the Hundred Flowers era of 1956–7 and again in the early 1980s, as will be seen in later chapters. The union 'crisis' which is usually referred to as having occurred in 1951 thus becomes, in this version of events, a third phase of the ongoing confrontation between workers and the party, with the official unions now once again inclined to side with workers. Looking at the 'standpoint' debate in this context, it is evident that those union cadres who were insisting on a more independent stance for unions in state enterprises were responding to workers' earlier accusations that they were 'the administration's union and not [workers'] own' (*Chinese Worker* 20 January 1951). In opposition to this, the party's formulation of the correct standpoint and role of the unions in state enterprises as described above would mean that unions were to continue to act as an arm of enterprise administration (albeit the 'workers' own' administration).

It is difficult to gauge from contemporary press reports the actual extent of the economist and syndicalist leanings of basic-level unions during 1951, as all criticism of them seems to have been postponed until early 1953 (*Southern Daily* 19 May 1953). It is possible that the unions might only have seemed to overemphasize workers' interests during 1951 in contrast with their usual stance of backing and enforcing the decisions of enterprise authorities whatever the impact on their members. But it is safe to assume that the accusations made against union cadres at the Seventh ACFTU Congress had some basis in fact, since we know that the union rectification campaign of late 1950 was intended precisely to move the unions away from unconditional support for the enterprise administration and towards stronger support for workers' views and interests. After their experiences of 'the administration's' unions, too, workers were likely to try to push the unions as far as possible in the opposite direction, so that they would at times cross the boundary between acceptable reflection of workers' views to the party and syndicalist advocacy of those views. However, flaws in the organization of the unions still remained, calling into question the degree to which unions even now were actually capable of pressing workers' demands and making 'economist' gains on their behalf.

Assuming that workers now had, in some cases at least, the support of their unions in upholding their interests and democratic rights in the enterprise, it might be expected that rapid progress would be made in the democratization of enterprise management, with a corresponding rise in workers' level of satisfaction with their new position under CCP rule and an easing of the conflict between them and the party. But in fact continuing problems within union organizations seem to have undermined their inclination to support workers' demands for democratization. In the summer of 1951 we find that enterprise democratization in the central-south region of China was judged still to have made very little progress, leading workers to complain that 'they [were] masters but [did] not have a say' (Liu Zijiu 1951). It was admitted that most enterprises had 'not been able to solve their problems. Some of them did not go through any fundamental changes; only a limited number have undergone comparatively thorough reform'. This meant that 'the neglected lesson in democratic reform [had to] be made up' in the south (*Southern Daily* 10 July 1951). The problems which the Democratic Reform Movement (DRM), as well as the subsequent Three- and Five-Anti movements, was intended to tackle were present not only in state organs and the management of both state and private enterprises, but also within the trade unions, where they continued to provoke dissatisfaction and discontent among workers. The period during which these three movements were carried out in the south (mid-1951 to early 1953) constitutes the final phase of this first confrontation between workers and the party, as the party sought to promote enterprise democratization and the purification and strengthening of the official unions without, however, unleashing the pent-up demand among workers for what it termed 'extreme democratization'. These campaigns were prompted by workers' protests and demands over the previous two years as well as by the tenets of the CCP's guiding ideology, but even as the party implicitly acknowledged that many of these protests and criticisms had been justified, it still displayed a lingering mistrust of workers and a reluctance fully to mobilize them to achieve democratization, and was quick to intervene whenever it feared that workers might be taking these movements to extremes.

The Democratic Reform Movement

The DRM was launched in the area under the jurisdiction of the Central-South Bureau of the CCP Central Committee in May 1951. It had already taken place immediately after liberation in the northeast of China and was subsequently implemented throughout the country, but it was the central-south area which 'bore the brunt of the 1951 movement' (Brugger 1976: 105). The reform, described as an historical phase 'which the workers must pass through in the process of emerging from the position of the ruled to that of the masters' (*Xinhua News Agency* 20 August 1951), was intended to complete the transformation of enterprises, changing bureaucratic capitalist enterprises into socialist (state) enterprises, and changing old democratic (private) enterprises into new democratic ones. As such, it seemed to promise the sort of radical reform of the old order in industrial enterprises which many workers had demanded immediately after liberation.

The movement was mainly directed against remaining so-called feudal or reactionary influences, and more specifically against the gang-boss system and secret societies:

> The aim and purpose of democratic reform is to introduce a thorough reform of the gang labour system which imperialism, feudalism and bureaucratic capitalism purposely established and cultivated in factories and mines to rule the masses of workers.
>
> (Liu Zijiu 1951)

But as with earlier measures for workplace democratization, emphasis was also placed on the beneficial effect the campaign would have on production. The official directive on the launching of the DRM in the south explained that

> the idea is to rely upon the working class to rid the enterprises of all feudal, reactionary elements, reactionary systems and bad styles of work, to thoroughly wipe out obstacles to production, and to establish an overall system of democratic management to lead the workers' enthusiasm into production efforts, so that a new labour attitude and discipline can be established and the workers be made into a strongly organized class.
>
> (*Xinhua News Agency* 20 August 1951)

The movement was to be carried out in three stages. The first, democratic struggle, would include mass meetings at which workers could identify and accuse gang-bosses and other 'feudal remnants'. It was emphasized that the struggle was 'anti-feudal, not anti-capital' (*Southern Daily* 9 October 1951), at least in private enterprises. The aim of the second stage, democratic unity, was 'to solve . . . problems concerning the relations between workers and [white-collar] employees, between the leadership and the masses, between old and new workers, between skilled and unskilled workers, and between different groups of workers' (*Xinhua News Agency* 20 August 1951). The main methods used would be criticism and self-criticism. It is interesting that problems are identified not only between workers and cadres, but also between different segments of the workforce within an enterprise. The divisions between old and young, skilled and unskilled, etc. will also be visible when we come to look at industrial unrest and workers' protests in the Hundred Flowers era, when the 'have-nots' of the industrial workforce, including the young, the less-skilled, apprentices and so on were particularly prominent among the party's critics (Perry 1994).

The third and final stage of the DRM was democratic construction, which involved raising political awareness in enterprises, establishing a new labour attitude, reforming and strengthening mass organizations, including enterprise trade unions, and establishing a democratic management system (*Xinhua News Agency* 20 August 1951). This stage was to include 'provision for the regular reelection of labour union committees' (Brugger 1976: 111), a vital measure if unions were to be democratically controlled by their members. The inclusion of this measure can be taken as a sign that criticism of those basic-level organizations which failed to hold regular elections the previous year had not resulted in any marked improvement in the situation. The official unions were to have a major role in carrying out the DRM except in those enterprises where the union itself was considered 'impure' (Brugger 1976: 250), i.e. contaminated by undesirable 'feudal' elements. This provision is further evidence that serious problems remained in many recently-established unions, particularly in areas where gang-boss influence had been strongest. Re-election of FMCs was to take place during the DRM as well (*Workers' Daily* 22 October 1951), indicating that the demo-cratic operation of these institutions was not proceeding as planned either. In practice, progress through the three stages of the movement was often slow, with the first stage not being completed in some cases until December 1951. The second stage did not take place in many enterprises until early 1953, while the third stage, the one intended finally to establish democratic management in all types of enterprise, was postponed in its entirety until after the Three- and Five-Anti movements had been completed (*Workers' Daily* 22 October 1951).

Back in March 1950, the *Workers' Daily* had insisted that, contrary to the belief of many workers and union cadres, there was no need for any mass movement for democratization in enterprises (*Workers' Daily* 3 March 1950). However, as the DRM was launched it was acknowledged that in fact a mass movement was necessary to accomplish a real transformation of the many enterprises where little had changed since 1949: 'Mere dependence on government orders to abolish these [feudal remnants and] systems is ineffective; the labouring masses must be mobilized to stamp out the evils of such systems and remnants' (*Southern Daily* 20 August 1951). But a mass movement in enterprises where reform since liberation had had such limited success could in itself create problems, and concerns about the possible dangers are evident in many of the early documents on the conduct of the movement.

The fear among many cadres directly in charge of the movement was that it might finally offer workers a chance to settle old scores, not just with the desig-nated 'feudal' targets, but with managers, white-collar staff, even engineers and technicians, all of the old enterprise elite which in many cases had remained intact since 1949. Not only the survival of gang-boss influence, but also the general policy of leaving systems intact and retained personnel in place wherever possible, had in effect kept enterprise management back in its pre-liberation state in places. Workers' attitudes towards this situation is revealed in statements justi-fying the need for the movement. It was claimed, for example, that workers in private factories in Guangzhou who were still 'ideologically and organizationally controlled' by gang-boss and secret-society influences felt that they 'had not yet achieved genuine liberation, as is reflected in their comments that "we are in a place that the sun doesn't reach", "the streets have been liberated, but not our factory"' (*Southern Daily* 1 December 1951). Clearly those workers still working for the same private boss two years after the revolution might also feel that 'liber-ation' had made little difference to the power structure in their workplaces.

Thus there were fears among those about to launch the DRM that this long-postponed movement to establish workers as 'the masters', finally meeting their 1949 expectations of the CCP takeover, might prove too popular among workers and would quickly get out of control. These fears were not in fact realized during the DRM itself as mass mobilization was generally unsuccessful, but something very similar did occur at the height of the anti-capitalist Five-Anti movement. Cadres proceeded very cautiously with the DRM and tried to pre-empt worker extremism. While admitting that workers' feelings with regard to enterprise elites, technical and managerial, were not entirely unreasonable, the authorities stressed that technical personnel were 'an important force, indispensable to factories' (*Xinhua News Agency* 20 August 1951), and that all those not found to be political counter-revolutionaries must be won over and reformed, 'despite the dissatisfaction of the working masses' (*Southern Daily* 10 July 1951). Workers' disputes with staff and technical personnel were classed as 'internal' (*Southern Daily* 10 July 1951) matters which 'should be openly discussed and settled', but which had nothing to do with the movement to eradicate the minority of feudal elements 'who politically oppress and economically exploit and defraud' (*Xinhua News Agency* 20 August 1951) the workers.

The united front against these elements was to include not only staff and technicians who, 'under the old regime, might have offended the workers and aroused their dissatisfaction' (we recall Friedman's comments on the contempt for manual workers shown by even the lowliest office clerk in the Republican era (Friedman 1949: 111)), but also capitalists in private enterprises who 'had employed the feudal reactionary influences to maintain "order"', incurring similar hostility among workers. Capitalists were deemed to have suffered the ill effects of these influences as well, and therefore their support for the movement '[could] and [had to] be secured' (*Southern Daily* 10 July 1951).

The reservations which are apparent in these documents about the advisability of mobilizing workers for an all-out mass movement give the impression that enterprise cadres were unlikely to give the movement their wholehearted support, and in fact cadres' lack of commitment to reform was soon to be identified as a factor hindering the development of the DRM in the south. To get the campaign back on course, a directive was issued calling for administrative, party, youth league and union cadres to be 'ideologically aroused into attaching importance to the democratic reform movement' (*Southern Daily* 20 September 1951). Cadres were warned against the 'highly erroneous attitude' of 'overcautiousness under the pretext of avoiding confusion, hesitation to mobilize the masses, and withholding of support for the workers' righteous demands [which would] result in detachment from the masses' (*Southern Daily* 10 July 1951). 'Avoiding confusion' usually meant restricting the scope and duration of the struggle to prevent the workers from going too far, and also to ensure the maintenance of production. It was repeatedly stressed to unconvinced enterprise leaders that the DRM would not damage production:

> On the contrary, it will render a service to production. Even if it yields temporary ill effects on production, yet in the long run it will be all to the

good. It [would] be an error to resist or give up democratic reform under the pretext of maintaining production.

(Southern Daily 10 July 1951)

All available evidence on the conduct of the DRM in the south during 1951 indicates that in most enterprises, cadres held back from complete ideological and practical commitment to the movement, mainly because of fears that workers, if they were allowed free rein, would quickly expand the movement to include almost all those in positions of power in the enterprise, and also because of related worries about its likely effect on production. Given the prevalence of this attitude, workers' own enthusiasm for the movement tended to evaporate (*Southern Daily* 9 October 1951). The DRM's lack of success is shown very starkly by reports on what amounted to a re-launch of the movement in large sections of Guangzhou's industry at the end of 1952. Only the docks and state enterprises were said to have successfully completed the reform, while workers in private enterprises were still either openly or covertly controlled by 'feudal remnants and reactionary forces' (*Southern Daily* 1 December 1951), and the gang-boss system of labour contracting was still in operation in the construction industry. Implicitly admitting the failure of the DRM, in late 1951 and early 1952 the CCP launched the Three- and Five-Anti movements to remedy some of the very deficiencies in state organs, state and private enterprise management, and in the unions, which had hitherto impeded democratic reform.

The Three- and Five-Anti movements

The Three-Anti movement was launched towards the end of 1951 to combat the problems of waste, corruption and bureaucratism in the state bureaucracy, including the administration of state-run enterprises and the official trade unions. The campaign was later extended to the private sector in the form of the Five-Anti movement, which was directed against the so-called 'five poisons' practised by some capitalists: bribery, tax evasion, theft of state property, cheating on government contracts, and theft of secret state economic data. The movements are of interest to us in that they were intended, among other things, to solve the problems of bureaucratism and separation from the masses in both enterprise management and the unions, the extent of these problems having been revealed by the failure of the DRM to achieve its aims of management democratization in enterprises of all types and the establishment of workers as the 'masters of the enterprise'. Both movements were hailed as great successes on their completion, but later official analyses revealed serious shortcomings which cast doubt on the efficacy of the whole series of reform campaigns in industry. However, by the time doubt was being cast on the success of the various reform campaigns in early 1953, the party's emphasis had shifted away from democratization and management–worker relationships; instead production output and labour discipline were the dominant concerns, and thus no further campaigns were embarked upon.

The Three-Anti movement exposed worrying cases of bureaucratism and corruption among basic-level trade union cadres, leading to warnings from the party that the unions would have to reform their own organizations, satisfying the workers as to their probity and financial rectitude, if they were to be able credibly to lead workers against 'lawless capitalists' in the Five-Anti movement (*Workers' Daily* 16 December 1951, 20 February and 9 April 1952). Unions were supposed to lead the Five-Anti movement 'at the action level' (Harper 1969: 99) in enterprises, and the movement is generally regarded as the high point of the influence of both workers and unions in private industry, establishing their rights over private management in what were subsequently known as 'state capitalist' enterprises. However, there was another side to the Five-Anti campaign: attacks on capitalists who had committed the 'five poisons' also revealed numerous cases nationwide of corruption of union cadres by these same capitalists (*Workers' Daily* 29 February, 5 and 16 April 1952, and 11 March 1955). So while the movement is, rightly, regarded as an overall victory for unions and workers over the remaining capitalist employers, it also served to reveal the depth of the problems in some union organizations up until 1952–3.

Uncertainty about the conduct and the results of the Five-Anti movement is evident even in articles published in June 1952 to applaud its achievements and anticipate its final victory. While not all commentators would go so far as to say the movement had had a 'devastating effect' (Ong Shao-erh 1953: 37) on production and employment, there is general agreement that at its height (Brugger 1976: 116) it did cause a number of enterprises to cease operations, and interfered with production in many others as workers' and union cadres' time was taken up with the movement, despite the slogan of 'struggling and carrying on production at the same time' (*Southern Daily* 15 June 1952). In the aftermath of the Five-Anti the terms used were strongly reminiscent of the time immediately after liberation, as industrial and commercial workers were urged to unite with the 'educated and reformed' (*Southern Daily* 15 June 1952) capitalists in restoring and developing production and enlivening the economy, while capitalists were offered loans and tax concessions to assist those in difficulties (*Xinhua News Agency* 18 June 1952). Capitalists were also reassured that 'the object of the "Five-Anti" was not to exterminate the capitalist class, but to purge the "five poisons" among law-breaking capitalist elements' (*Southern Daily* 15 June 1952). Clearly the movement had had a big impact in remaining privately-owned enterprises.

A reminder to workers of the need to respect capitalists' property rights, right to manage, and right to hire and fire within the limits of the law (*Southern Daily* 15 June 1952) strengthens the impression that the authorities were anxious to curb a movement which had got out of hand. If we bear in mind how little successful reform there had been in enterprises to give workers a real say in their running, especially in areas where a significant private sector continued to exist, it is possible to understand the strength of feeling among workers which was unleashed by this first genuinely successful mass mobilization against private employers. It was precisely the sort of reaction from workers which had been feared at the launch of the DRM, but which had not materialized as the move-ment stagnated with little active involvement on the part of rank-and-file workers. Anti-capitalist feelings among workers during the Five-Anti movement seem to have created an atmosphere in which virtually no-one in an enterprise was prepared to act as an agent of private management 'for fear of being considered to be serving the interests of the capitalists'. Workers had to be reminded that as long as capitalists ran their enterprises lawfully and in a way which benefitted the state and the people, 'serving such capitalists would not conflict with [their] desire to serve the people' (*Southern Daily* 15 June 1952).

By early 1953 the Three- and Five-Antis and the DRM in industry were being quite harshly re-evaluated and judged to have had only limited effects. Cases of corruption of union cadres by private employers continued to surface in the press from time to time, showing that even the Five-Anti movement, the most effective of the three carried out since 1951, had not ended all such prac-tices. A survey of union cadres on a training course in Guangzhou in 1955 found that almost 90 per cent of them admitted having assisted capitalist employers in cheating the state in various ways, or turning a blind eye to such conduct (*Workers' Daily* 11 March 1955).

The original verdict on the success of the Three-Anti movement was also revised considerably. Some cadres themselves referred to the Three-Anti as 'only the "Two-and-a-half-Anti" or the "Two-Anti", or even the "One-Anti" – only opposing corruption' (*Southern Daily* 13 February 1953). But despite the doubts now cast on the success of the Three- and Five-Anti movements, the time for reform campaigns dedicated to improving workers' position in the enterprise had passed. The remaining problems with institutions and mechanisms for workers' participation in management were left unresolved, soon to resurface in the next bout of workers' discontent during the Hundred Flowers era, as will be seen in the next chapter. The first half of 1953 saw an anti-bureaucratism campaign which was in effect an extension of the Three-Anti movement, yet the emphasis during this period was not on management democratization and the promotion of workers' participation in management, the original aims of both of these movements; the anti-bureaucratism campaign was aimed at the party and state bureaucracy rather than basic-level cadres in enterprises (*Southern Daily* 11 February 1953). Within enterprises, a strong emphasis on discipline and a shift in workers' activism from politics to production became evident. Workers were constantly reminded of their responsibilities in production, and were warned that violations of discipline were incompatible with their status as 'masters of the enterprise' (*Southern Daily* 28 August 1953).

This tendency was reinforced by the effects of the Seventh ACFTU Congress held in May 1953, at which unions were criticized for having paid far too much attention to welfare and to supporting workers' 'excessive' demands in the past, at the expense of their duties in production. All unions were now reminded that production was their central task, even in private enterprises, where it was not for the sole benefit of capitalists and their profits, but was vital to the national economy and to workers' own long-term interests (*Southern Daily* 31 May 1953).

Although only a few months earlier the persistence of bureaucratism in the unions had still appeared to be a cause for concern, with the absence of democratic life within them and the failure to hold elections and to report back to the WRC specifically mentioned, workers' continued dissatisfaction with their unions seems subsequently to have been put to one side as all attention was directed towards production.

The criticism of unions at the Seventh Congress was of course aimed at the economist and syndicalist tendencies which some of them had displayed during 1951. But time had not stood still for the unions since then, and we must also consider what impact the criticism was intended to have in the light of other events, such as unions' activities during the Five-Anti campaign. It seems likely that the down-playing of unions' political activities in favour of their central task of production was also a measure designed to bring to a decisive end the struggle of workers and unions against capitalists in private enterprises, a struggle which had at times threatened to escalate out of control and which in some cases adversely affected production. It was now firmly denied that workers in private enterprises were 'only half masters' (*Southern Daily* 28 August 1953), and they were discouraged from further attempts to enlarge their power within the enterprise.

Although it is true that the Five-Anti movement 'was designed to increase the power and participation of workers in management' (Andors 1977a: 52), this increase in participation was not promoted purely for its own sake. Had this been the case, one would have expected to see a further expansion of participation once enterprises were taken into state ownership in 1955–6, whereas in fact the role of workers and unions in management was curtailed once private ownership was ended. More will be said about this in the next chapter. The involvement of workers and the leadership of the Five-Anti campaign by unions in enterprises should be seen in the context of general party policy towards industry. While the influence exercised by workers and unions definitely increased as a result of the campaign, 'the primary purpose of the mobilization of workers into management in private enterprises by unions was for the ultimate nationalization of the economy' (Lee Lai To 1986: 99). After nationalization, production would be their central task and great emphasis would be placed on discipline and obedience to party and administrative leadership, as was already the case in state enterprises.

Management, unions and workers in the mid-1950s

In 1954 a *People's Daily* article on labour discipline set out the new line, advocating enforceable rules and regulations as a guarantee of order and discipline in the enterprise (rather than relying on education and group pressure), something which had hitherto been regarded as the 'working style of warlords'. It was now claimed that 'what threatens the normal progress of production and affects the labour activism of the masses is not that discipline is too strict but that it is too slack' (quoted in Brugger 1976: 117–18). Along with this renewed emphasis on obedience rather than activism, 'the growth of a planning system restricted [workers'] participation to matters of detail', while there was a growing tendency for management 'to take increased production as the sole success indicator' (Brugger 1976: 137–8), subordinating issues of democracy and participation to the goal of fulfilling state production plans.

From 1953, the first year of the PRC's First Five-Year Plan, until about the middle of 1956, there was a strong emphasis on centralized national planning in industry and on the Soviet system of one-man management, a strictly hierarchical system of management with the enterprise director at its apex. Although this system was never introduced in all sectors or in all areas of the country (P N Lee 1987: 29–32), and was officially repudiated and replaced in 1956 with the factory director responsibility system under the leadership of the enterprise party committee, its appearance in China at this time was in keeping with the changed emphasis in enterprise management. This was a period when '[t]he management–worker split grew wider from the control system and the realities of decision-making' (Andors 1977a: 57).

The new atmosphere also affected the work of the official trade unions: Brugger notes 'an increasing tendency to relate everything to matters of production' (Brugger 1976: 247) in union work as well as in management. The unions' role was reduced to that of a one-way transmission belt, passing on production plans and the instructions of management to the workers but not carrying any feedback in the opposite direction. Structures for workers' participation such as the FMC and WRC, which as we have seen were of limited effectiveness even when initially introduced, also declined further under the new system, with the tendency to use the WRC 'to instruct workers' (Lee Lai To 1984: 30) reinforced by one-man management, and the role of the FMC much reduced. Brugger finds few mentions of the existence of FMCs after the end of the Three- and Five-Anti movements, and concludes that 'their very existence could not be reconciled with one-man management forms of organization' (Brugger 1976: 249–50). This new emphasis on labour discipline and production seems to have been successful in bringing about a temporary suspension of the conflict between workers and the party which had been unfolding since liberation.

Workers' response to the thwarting of their aspirations to run their own enterprises in this early period does not seem to have extended to organizing themselves in opposition to management or the party, but judging from press accounts and official reports, it did include often harsh criticism of leading cadres which could not safely be ignored. Workers' alienation from enterprise leadership is frequently mentioned, and there are references to strikes, although these are blamed on agitation by 'feudal remnants'. However, this first confrontation between workers and the party left a legacy of dissatisfaction among workers and unresolved problems regarding the implementation of democratic management which would also form the basis of the second major confrontation in 1956–7.

It might be argued that some degree of conflict in the years immediately following liberation was inevitable, as workers, unions, enterprise management and the party explored the limits of their respective roles under the new regime and reached some sort of *modus vivendi* in the enterprise. The ambiguities of the official trade unions' role, in particular, would mean that they could not be expected to make a smooth, swift transition to a means of operation which would be equally acceptable to them, to their members, and to their party superiors. But once the various movements for democratization launched by the party had been carried out, even if they did not go as far as some workers would have wished, conflict could be minimized and the attention of all parties turned towards the tasks of modernization and industrialization.

But conflict between workers and the party not only broke out again a few years later, as the First Five-Year Plan neared its end, but did so in a way which bore striking similarities to this early period of confrontation. On this occasion workers did not stop at criticizing union, administrative and party cadres for their attitudes, but bypassed the official unions and organized themselves to force concessions from enterprise authorities; there was even talk of organizing fully independent trade unions. It is to this more serious crisis in workers' relationship with the party that we now turn.

2 Contradictions among the people, 1956–7

The Hundred Flowers movement of 1956–7 is generally viewed as a confrontation between intellectuals and the party, provoked by the call for criticism by non-party people to help the organization to rectify itself and avoid the type of Stalinist errors for which the Polish and Hungarian ruling parties were punished by popular rebellions during 1956. But less attention has been given to the confrontation between industrial workers and the party which developed in these years, and which came to pose at least as serious a challenge to party authority by the spring of 1957 as anything said or written by discontented intellectuals and students. The lack of contact, indeed the hostility, between worker and student protesters in 1956–7 (Perry 1994: 23, n. 106) might account for the relative absence of scholarly attention to workers' activities at this time. Yet in a sense workers were ahead of intellectuals and students in challenging the status quo. Although the movement to 'let a hundred flowers bloom, and a hundred schools of thought contend' had little effect when first launched by Mao in May 1956, as few responded to his invitation to speak out freely, and intellectual and professional criticism was only really unleashed the following spring after his 27 February speech, 'On the correct handling of contradictions among the people', criticism and industrial unrest among workers did not wait for this second stimulus, becoming prominent by the end of 1956 and continuing through the spring of 1957.

In the Hundred Flowers campaign, contradictions within the ranks of the people, rather than between the people and its enemies, were identified as the main source of conflict in Chinese society now that acute mass class struggle had basically come to an end, and these non-antagonistic contradictions were to be resolved by peaceful methods such as debate and criticism and self-criticism. After the launching of an open party rectification movement in March 1957, particular importance was attached to criticism of the higher levels by the grassroots. Cadre–mass relations were now on the agenda, and given the nature of worker grievances in the early 1950s, this clearly provided an opportunity for workers to air once again their resentment at how they, nominally 'the masters', were treated in their workplaces. It is not usually emphasized that Mao's report on contradictions within the people was prompted at least as much by the industrial unrest of 1956 and early 1957 as by intellectual agitation and discontent among the peasantry. François Gipouloux has pointed out, however, that Mao's report contains frequent references to 'various trade union reports' and quotes workers' angry criticism of administrative cadres as contained in an internal ACFTU report. One particular remark noted in the ACFTU report and quoted by Mao must have set alarm bells ringing among the Chinese leadership: some workers had reportedly expressed the opinion that in their disputes with the enterprise administration, 'if you don't learn from Hungary, you won't get anything' (Gipouloux 1986: 191). Protesting workers in Shanghai also used the slogan 'Let's create another Hungarian Incident!' (Perry 1994: 11).

The possibility that the sort of popular protest and revolt which had occurred in Poland and Hungary during 1956 might be repeated in China was something which the Chinese leadership took extremely seriously, particularly in view of the wave of industrial unrest which developed at the enterprise level during 1956. Knowledge of the events in Eastern Europe was undoubtedly a further motive for the policy of (limited) liberalization and democratization and increased scope for criticism of the party which took shape during 1956 and the first half of 1957, particularly as it related to workers. Articles in the Chinese press on the Hungarian Incident, in particular, show Chinese awareness of the similarities between the conditions which had given rise to the rebellion in Hungary and those created during the course of the First Five-Year Plan in China. It was noted that in Hungary:

> some party leaders in their work failed conscientiously to rely on the masses and mobilize the masses, and did not have sufficient concern for the masses . . . with regard to improving the people's livelihood, they did not adopt effective measures; workers' real wages increased very little. . . . [These mistakes] greatly damaged links between the party and the masses, restricted the people's democratic rights and hindered improvements in their standard of living.
>
> (Yi Han 1956)

This is very similar to Chinese accounts of how the institutions of democratic management in enterprises had over the years degenerated into formalism, as the leadership became complacent and 'did not care about the masses, did not respect the masses' opinions, did not solve difficulties which could have been solved', leading workers to become 'sceptical, negative, disappointed, and even dissatisfied' (Li Chun 1957). Thus it reflects the same problems in the relationship between workers and their leaders which gave rise to the first confrontation in China after liberation.

The mid-1950s outbreak of unrest occurred at a point where workers were least well provided with effective mechanisms or organizations through which they could defend their interests in the workplace, while at the same time they were subject to acute economic and social pressures resulting from the First Five-Year Plan's emphasis on accumulation and heavy industrial development. Some sections of the workforce, such as employees of former private enterprises, apprentices, and younger workers, were much more prominent in the unrest than others (Perry 1994), but many of the grievances giving rise to protests were common to all enterprises by 1956–7, and many of the protests had an unmistakably political nature, as the absence of effective intermediary structures pitted disgruntled workers directly against party authorities. Just as workers have often been written out of the Hundred Flowers story as protesters, being present only as defenders of the party during the anti-rightist campaign (*People's Daily* 10 June 1957; *China Youth Daily* 17 June 1957), so the party took pains not to acknowledge this political challenge from the working class as it reimposed control, denying workers the political status of 'rightists' and punishing them as criminals instead (Chan 1993: 33).

Background to the 1956–7 industrial conflict

Democratic management

From about the middle of 1956, something of a backlash against authoritarian or undemocratic management in general, and against the system of one-man management in particular, began to emerge in the trade union press in China. It has already been noted that this system of management was never introduced in all areas or all industrial sectors in China, and indeed there were early signs of less than wholehearted support for it at the highest level (Andors 1977a: 59). But even where this specific system was not in operation, the tendency mentioned in the last chapter to emphasize strict labour discipline and to regard production as the sole criterion on which to judge an enterprise's performance was by 1956 very pronounced, and seems to have resulted in a very authoritarian style of management in most if not all industrial enterprises.

In one analysis in 1957 of what had gone wrong in the system of democratic management set up in enterprises after liberation, the problem was traced back beyond the spread of Soviet management practices in China to defects in the organization of FMCs, specifically the excessive powers of the factory director as *ex officio* chair of the committee with the right of veto over its decisions. The author of this report observed that

> From certain articles of the regulations, it would appear that the FMC possessed very great power, but in reality, when it came to implementation, power was completely concentrated in the hands of the factory director. Moreover, at its meetings it mostly discussed the problems raised by the higher level and the administration and very few questions raised by the masses. Because of this, the masses' interest in the FMC declined, while the leading administrative cadres found its existence no longer justified, and it could not but decline into formalism.
>
> (Su Ke 1957)

This description of the weaknesses of democratic management in Chinese enterprises accords with our findings in the previous chapter. The WRC seems to have suffered the same fate as the FMC, with workers in Guangzhou in 1957, for example, reporting that their housing problems had been repeatedly raised in this forum without any response from enterprise leaders (*Guangzhou Daily* 19 May 1957).

This lack of democracy and absence of genuine participation in state enterprises spread to private enterprises on the latter's transformation to joint state-private status. How much scope there had been for democratic participation in private enterprises between the end of the Five-Anti movement in mid-1952 and nationalization in early 1956 is difficult to gauge. Much is made in articles advocating the expansion of enterprise democracy in 1956–7 of the powerful role of the trade unions in the old private enterprises, and of the supervisory powers over private management enjoyed by the production-increase-and-economy committees (formed during the campaign of the same name) made up of workers and staff (*People's Daily* 30 November 1956). Chen Yun, discussing the transformation of industry at the Eighth Party Congress in 1956, said that unions had had 'a high degree of authority over the enterprise management' (*Xinhua News Agency* 21 September 1956) after the Five-Anti campaign.

But according to one 1956 account from Wuhan, the union participation in the democratic management of private enterprises mandated by workers after the Five-Anti movement virtually ceased during 1953 under the influence of one-man management, causing great dissatisfaction among workers who did not feel that they were the masters of the enterprise in any real sense (*Workers' Daily* 4 December 1956). So it seems that democratic management in private enterprises may have reached a peak in the year or so immediately after the Five-Anti movement before going into decline. Whatever the actual extent of management democratization in private enterprises during these years, it is clear that there was a feeling among workers themselves that powers and influence in the enterprise which they once enjoyed had been lost when their enterprises were nationalized: at the Eighth Party Congress, workers were said to be asking 'Why it is that workers' and staff members' powers have actually declined since joint management? Why do former capitalists still have power and position in the enterprise today?' (*Xinhua News Agency* 21 September 1956).

Regardless of the actual limits of their influence over pre-1956 private employers, workers and trade unions alike had at least been in a much less ambiguous position in the event of a confrontation with private management than they were in any disputes after 1956, when ultimate power in the enterprise had passed into the hands of state representatives:

> The administrative cadres headed by representatives of the state . . . placed under their control the entire administrative work of the enterprises. Trade union cadres and the masses, finding it impossible to enquire into the management of enterprises, had quite some cause for complaint.
>
> (Su Ke 1957)

It does seem to have been difficult in this period for workers to make any criticism of administrative cadres. Such was the attitude of factory directors and other high-ranking cadres to their own authority that they tended to react to any criticism, justified or not, as if it were an act of rebellion and a serious attack not on their personal actions or style of work, but on the state organization which they represented. Thus workers raising perfectly reasonable criticisms found themselves accused of, and often punished for, 'undisciplined and unorganized behaviour' (*Chinese Worker* August 1956, 16: 4), or 'opposing the management' (*Chinese Worker* October 1956, 19: 11). It was reported that 'some enterprises even draw up a lot of 'prohibitions' to restrict workers and staff', for example banning criticism of the higher level by the lower, i.e. production workers, in production conferences and other meetings (*Chinese Worker* August 1956, 16: 5).

The phenomenon of retaliation by factory directors against their low-ranking critics was by all accounts widespread, with the imposition of arbitrary and 'unlawful punishments' common in many enterprises and 'very serious' in some (*Workers' Daily* 18 May and 14 July 1956; *Chinese Worker* August 1956, 16: 5). In extreme cases, reassignment to unsuitable workposts, perhaps forcing a worker to travel much longer distances to work, could be arranged by a director (*Chinese Worker* October 1956, 19: 11), but the favoured method of warning off critics appears to have been 'one-to-one chats' with the director, or 'one-to-one threats' (*Chinese Worker* August 1956, 16: 4) as they were perhaps more accurately termed. Such an attitude on the part of the factory director could easily spread commandist and coercive methods to all levels of the enterprise, as reflected in the workers' saying that 'each level orders the next about, and the workers order the machines about'. With this style of management rapidly becoming the norm, it was not long before the question was posed: 'This quite simply is feudal order; the "managers" in these enterprises have become the feudal kings of petty king-doms. How can this phenomenon be allowed to continue to exist in socialist enterprises?' (*Chinese Worker* August 1956, 16: 5).

So we find that in state enterprises, early fears about the tendency for the factory director to override institutions for workers' participation in management had been realized, as Soviet-influenced styles of highly centralized management spread through Chinese industry and cadres appointed by the state came to behave as if their every action had the personal sanction of Chairman Mao himself. This, then, is the style of management and enterprise atmosphere which the remaining private enterprises inherited when they were taken into joint state-private ownership early in 1956, as the 'transition to socialism' in the Chinese economy was completed. But it was in sharp contrast to the expectations of many workers in those private enterprises who seem genuinely to have looked forward to attaining the status of a state employee, and who were gravely disappointed by the reality of their working lives as 1956 progressed.

The nationalization of private enterprises

The nationalization, or socialist transformation, of industry and commerce in China took place earlier than originally expected, at the beginning of 1956.

As of September 1955, the transformation of the many remaining private enterprises into joint state-private enterprises was projected to take five years to complete. In November, after Mao's speech of 29 October calling for a speed-up in the transformation process, this was revised to two years, and in fact all industrial and commercial enterprises were transformed, on paper at least, early in 1956 (Vogel 1969: 156–73). The term 'joint state-private enterprise' is slightly misleading, for although former capitalists were to continue to receive fixed interest for a specified period (originally seven years) after the takeover of their enterprises, and would in many cases become ordinary employees of the enterprise in a managerial capacity, the enterprise would actually be run by representatives appointed by the state. These new joint enterprises were particularly strike-prone in 1956 and the spring of 1957, which made for a very high level of industrial unrest in the cities which had retained the largest private industrial sectors after 1949. For example, in Guangzhou the nationalization of remaining private firms involved 4,727 industrial units employing 60,000 workers; these were reorganized into 700 joint enterprises (*Wen Hui Daily* (Hong Kong) 4 February 1957). Similarly, 75 per cent of Shanghai's industrial workforce was still privately employed in the autumn of 1950, and this translated into 72 per cent employed in new joint state-private enterprises at the end of 1957 (Perry 1994: 7–8).

Workers do seem to have had high expectations of their enterprises after nationalization, especially in terms of improved welfare benefits and living conditions of the sort enjoyed by workers in some older state enterprises; this was precisely the impression they were given in official propaganda about the change (*Guangzhou Daily* 19 April 1957). Besides the expected material benefits, though, the shift to state ownership might also have been welcomed as an end to the politically second-class status which some workers in private enterprises felt they had. Some of the worker extremism evident in the Five-Anti movement, for example, seems to have been motivated by workers' desire to prove themselves untainted by working for a 'capitalist' and to show that they were every bit as progressive and patriotic as state workers were portrayed as being in the press. They did not anticipate, however, that the transformation of private enterprises would lead to a sharp decrease in their opportunities for participation in management and would reduce almost to nothing the influence of the remaining democratic institutions such as the WRC. This should not have come as a complete surprise, since, it will be recalled from the last chapter, the scope of action allowed to workers and their union representatives in private enterprises at the height of the Five-Anti movement was granted not for its own sake, but for the specific purpose of extending state control over private firms in preparation for nationalization (Lee Lai To 1986: 99). Once nationalization was complete there could be no question of any antagonism between workers and state representatives in industry, since it was an article of faith that the long-term interests of the workers were identical to those of the state and were best served by diligence and obedience to state instructions. The implication was that there was no longer any pressing need for workers themselves to participate directly in management since state representatives were already running the enterprise on their behalf.

The decline in democracy and participation in private enterprises after nationalization clearly came as a great disappointment to many workers, doubts about the real extent of their power under private management notwith-standing; the unavoidable impression is that however limited workers' and unions' influence had been once the peak of the Five-Anti passed, after the tran-sition to state ownership the situation worsened. Towards the end of 1956 workers' disappointment was officially acknowledged to be entirely reasonable, since the new joint state-private enterprises had 'neglected the democratic tradi-tion allowing workers in private enterprises to participate in management' (Lai Ruoyu 1956a). A *People's Daily* editorial in November of that year deplored the fact that

> the greater part of the enterprises brought under state-private ownership failed to carry on as a good tradition the experience of the masses in management. . . . The machinery of democratic management was done away with . . . some state representatives would not consult with the masses . . . [and] many workers were doubtful of their position as 'master of the enterprise'.
>
> (*People's Daily* 30 November 1956)

The article asserted that the democratic tradition 'should not only be carried on but also enlarged upon. The power of the trade unions to exercise supervision [over the administration] should be restored'. This was the thinking behind proposals for management democratization, and specifically for the establishment of the workers' congress with the enterprise trade union committee as its standing organ, which gained widespread acceptance during the second half of 1956.

Workers' expectations that they would benefit materially from the transforma-tion to joint state-private ownership were also disappointed during the course of 1956 as many found that in terms of housing, welfare provisions, and sometimes real wages, any improvement in their situation was minimal in spite of the rapid progress made in production. 'Economic activity had seen an unprecedented expansion, but this was not always translated in tangible fashion to the daily life of the worker' (Gipouloux 1986: 165). In these circumstances it is not surprising that so much of the industrial unrest of 1956–7 occurred in joint state-private enterprises (Perry 1994: 8), since it was here that workers felt most cheated of the material benefits they had been led to expect, and here that they now had even fewer resources at their disposal with which they might make their grievances known and exercise some influence in the enterprise in defence of their interests. It would have been bad enough to have new state managers appointed, over whom workers accustomed to some influence in the workplace had no control, but the fact that retained personnel, former capitalists and private managers, in some cases moved seamlessly into a factory director's job in the same enterprise (*Southern Daily* 9 January 1957), and at the stroke of a pen became state appointees with unimpeachable political authority over the rank and file, intensified workers' resentment. With retained personnel able to keep their old positions of authority while in effect evading the supervision which workers had been able to exercise over them in private enterprises since the Five-Anti movement, some workers argued that

> before joint management, capitalists had to accept the workers' supervision; after joint management, some capitalists were assigned by the state to take up the duties of factory director or manager and the workers instead had to heed the capitalists instructions . . . since joint management, the capitalists have been riding roughshod over the workers even more, and the workers' power is actually less than it was before joint management.
>
> (*Chinese Worker* March 1958, 5: 21)

The official explanation offered to workers was that such personnel were 'serving socialism under the leadership of the working class and of the state' and '[could] not in the slightest belittle the leading position of the working class in jointly-managed enterprises', and that workers had no need of their old powers of supervision as they had now 'moved from supervising production to managing it directly together with the state representatives'. This argument could hardly persuade workers, given that institutions for direct participation such as the workers' congress were subject to important restrictions on their powers and were easy for cadres to ignore or evade if they so wished. In practice, state representatives could run joint enterprises as they saw fit, without consulting workers or allowing them to participate in management. So workers were left with the thought that 'since joint management, the capitalists have a professional position, and also have fixed interest [payments] and high salaries; they live an easy life in the same old way while workers still have their noses to the grindstone'. It was not surprising that 'some workers even [thought] that the party's policy [was] rightist' (*Chinese Worker* March 1958, 5: 22). The large increase in management numbers under joint ownership (typically increasing to more than a third of total employees in Shanghai's joint enterprises, for example) stoked further resentment against those who did not actually produce anything on the part of hard-pressed production workers (Perry 1994: 15).

Workers' discontent: welfare, wages and privilege

The high incidence of strikes in China at the height of the Hundred Flowers movement in the first half of 1957 is now quite well documented (Perry 1994; Gipouloux 1986), but the relatively high level of discontent and unrest already evident during 1956 is not so widely appreciated. An internal ACFTU report for the year 1956 noted twenty-nine strikes and fifty-six petitions during the year, not including incidents registered by the trade union statistical service. Oral accounts mentioned in this report give much higher figures for individual cities: for example, there were said to have been more than forty incidences of strikes and petitions in Xi'an alone, while Shanghai saw a total of eighty-six incidents, increasing throughout the year from six in the first quarter to forty-one in the final quarter (Gipouloux 1986: 189). This apparent escalation tallies with accounts of wage reform disputes which resulted in industrial action, which seem to have peaked in November 1956 in cities such as Tianjin, Wuhan, and Guangzhou (*Workers' Daily* 25 and 30 April 1957; *Southern Daily* 25 April 1957; *Guangzhou Daily* 10 May 1957). A number of new features of enterprise life during 1956, in addition to the reduction in democracy and participation in newly nationalized enterprises, were behind this early outbreak of discontent, and we need to look at these in more detail before going on to examine why the official unions failed to help workers resolve their differences with management and higher authorities.

Looking at disputes in 1957, we find that '[w]ages, authoritarian assignments, working and living conditions were at the centre of all demands' (Gipouloux 1986: 189), with inequality between workers' and cadres' households a particular cause of friction, and the picture is similar in 1956. We have already noted the pressures on workers during 1956 as the deadline for meeting the production targets of the First Five-Year Plan approached, and one of the results of this pressure was an increase in industrial accidents and injuries which followed. After the nationalization of the remaining private enterprises in January 1956, calls for a 'high tide' of production were made, with workers encouraged to focus their efforts on increasing production during a six-month period of 'business as usual' in enterprises (*Southern Daily* 3 February 1956; *People's Daily* 12 February 1956). It was denied that the retention of old management systems during this period would dampen workers' enthusiasm for socialist transformation (*People's Daily* 12 February 1956), and cadres were instead warned of the dangers of lagging behind workers who, it was claimed, were themselves supporting this policy and pressing for increased norms and production targets (*Southern Daily* 23 March 1956). Our natural scepticism about such claims should perhaps be tempered by the undoubted enthusiasm for the new era of joint management initially expressed by some workers, but it is likely that any such enthusiasm swiftly dissipated under the pressure for results in production at the expense of basic safety during this period. One worker, recalling the mood in his factory when joint management was first introduced, expressed workers' subsequent disappointment:

> I remember when joint management first came in, when we celebrated our enterprise starting out on the socialist road with a great fanfare, we were all really happy thinking that now we had joint management, we would become the masters of the enterprise, just like in state enterprises today, and we would go to and from work by bus and have state housing to live in . . . but now that we have joint management, the factory's production has increased, but our lives have not only not improved, but are actually worse than before.
>
> (*Guangzhou Daily* 13 April 1957)

The CCP had whipped up enthusiasm for nationalization with a strong emphasis on the material benefits it would bring for workers in terms of wages and welfare provision, raising expectations which were subsequently ignored in the drive for increased production. The forced pace of industrialization in 1956, the penultimate year of the First Five-Year Plan, to some Soviet sinologists 'stands out . . . for policies inimical to the interests of workers' (Rozman 1985: 113), as 'the call for efficiency and productivity tended to intensify industrial work . . . placing additional strains on industrial workers' (P N Lee 1987: 40). Given these priorities, workers' welfare and even safety tended to be ignored. Coupled with the further weakening of enterprise democracy which occurred once private enterprises were taken over, this created a mood of bitterness and disillusionment among workers which fuelled increasingly frequent bouts of industrial unrest.

Complaints surfaced early in 1956 about the consequences for workers of the overriding emphasis on bringing down enterprise costs and increasing production (*People's Daily* 21 January 1956), and following an ACFTU conference on labour protection, welfare and housing in May 1956, a renewed emphasis on workers' safety, livelihood and welfare is evident in articles in the labour movement and local press. From 12–18 June, the *Southern Daily* published a series of articles exposing bureaucratist indifference to workers' substandard working and living conditions among enterprise administrative and union cadres and the staff of various industrial bureaux in Guangzhou. In the wake of revelations about the failure of the DRM and Three- and Five-Anti campaigns in the city in 1953 local journalists had been castigated for their lack of courage in exposing cadre misdeeds (*Southern Daily* 13 February 1953), but no-one could charge the paper's reporters with cowardice this time. In the time-honoured style of investigative reporting they first detailed blatant violations of workers' basic rights, and then presented their evidence to the relevant authorities, recording in detail for their readers the unconcerned, evasive, or downright hostile responses this provoked. These articles, accompanied by editorials reinforcing their message on welfare, safety, excessive overtime, etc. were followed by admissions from one of the top leaders of the ACFTU, Liu Ningyi (Liu Ningyi 1956), and the CCP's Minister of Labour, Ma Wenrui (*Southern Daily* 2 July 1956), that progress in these areas had lagged far behind improvements in labour productivity, not just in the six months since nationalization, but going right back to the beginning of the First Five-Year Plan in 1953.

Workers' grievances uncovered by this journalistic campaign ranged from serious matters of health and safety to the apparently trivial, although in the latter cases, it was often the very pettiness of enterprise management's actions which enraged workers most. In one factory, for example, workers were forbidden to use the enterprise's tap water for washing when they came off shift from high-temperature glass workshops, thus reducing the plant's water bill by about 10 *yuan* per month, but creating shopfloor resentment out of all proportion to this paltry saving (*Southern Daily* 18 June 1956). At one of the enterprises visited by a *Southern Daily* reporter, a construction site on the outskirts of Guangzhou, the deputy chair of the union recounted how the cost of the tea-leaves provided to workers had been transferred from the welfare to the construction budget and then the provision had been withdrawn, to achieve a 'saving' on construction expenses. This and other problems on the construction site had been repeatedly raised by the union, but, as the union cadre put it, 'the higher-ups always pretend not to know anything about it' (*Southern Daily* 12 June 1956).

These sorts of 'little problems' also existed on other sites, but were not going unsolved because of a lack of funds. On the contrary, tens of thousands of *yuan* in medical subsidies and enterprise reward funds were piling up unused, and the labour insurance fund of the No. 3 Construction Company, for example, was running a monthly surplus of 2,000 *yuan*, with 22,000 *yuan* left unspent from 1955. Various 'responsible personnel' at the company and at the Municipal Construction Engineering Bureau denied any responsibility for deciding how the money should be spent and were apparently unconcerned at the amounts accumulated; one official in the company's finance department, 'in response to repeated questioning', finally retorted: 'Surely you don't think we should spend the whole day encouraging the use of this money?' (*Southern Daily* 12 June 1956). The finance departments did not publish details of the money they had accumulated, 'so the workers and union organizations on the building sites don't know how much money the company or Bureau has which could be used to improve workers' livelihood and welfare'. Senior union cadres in any case claimed to have been too busy with other campaigns to concentrate on these problems, leaving the reporter to conclude that with these 'bureaucrats' and 'leading cadres who don't know anything about anything' in charge, the prevalence of bureaucratism and indifference to workers' welfare was hardly surprising (*Southern Daily* 12 June 1956).

Two of the remaining articles dealt with the problem of excessive overtime and extra shifts, which by all accounts was widespread at this time (*Workers' Daily* 5 July 1957). Not only were enterprise leaders using this as their main method of fulfilling and over-fulfilling production quotas, in some cases regularly exceeding the legal maximum of thirty-two hours overtime by any worker in one month, but they were also finding ways to avoid paying workers the proper rates for this overtime (*Southern Daily* 14 June 1956). In some cases the job was done for them, when higher-level organs approved the overtime or extra shifts requested but then refused to provide any extra money for wages, so that the enterprise had to cut bonuses and other payments to workers to make up the amount, leaving workers at best no better off than if they had not worked the extra hours, and at worst reducing their income.

Another plant had come up with a 'clever scheme' whereby overtime was 'borrowed' from workers during the enterprise's busy period, and workers could then request time off when production tasks were less pressing in lieu of the free time they had foregone (*Southern Daily* 15 June 1956). However, since workers needed the administration's permission to regain their 'borrowed' time off, there was often a considerable delay before they could actually take it, with 'arrears' in some cases of more than a year, after which many gave up hope of ever getting the time off to which they were entitled. The deputy manager claimed that overtime was not a problem at the plant and was all strictly voluntary, something which workers flatly told the reporter was 'not true'. When he took his findings to the manager himself, the reporter was told: 'Comrade, I have to point out to you, we have backward workers here!' (*Southern Daily* 15 June 1956). The union in this enterprise also helped to enforce the new system, and criticized as 'backward' workers who protested against it. As well as the obvious effect on workers' health and morale, excessive overtime was also said to have had 'undesirable political consequences' (*Southern Daily* 15 June 1956) in some enterprises.

The pressures on workers' incomes were also revealed by various sections of the press during the summer of 1956. Reference was made to the profiteering of public utilities which were levying high charges (Liu Ningyi 1956), and fares on public transport and rents were also singled out as too high for many workers to afford (*Workers' Daily* 31 May and 7 July 1956; *Southern Daily* 4 September 1956). The emphasis on economizing in enterprises led to a policy of 'commercializing' canteens and other facilities, i.e. raising the prices paid by workers so that these facilities made a profit (*People's Daily* 5 March 1956; *Workers' Daily* 11 March and 31 May 1956). Enterprises missed no opportunity to recoup money from workers for services; sick workers could even be charged for petrol and the depreciation of factory-owned vehicles when an accident in an out-of-town plant necessitated travel to a hospital within the city (*People's Daily* 5 March 1956). There was reportedly some misappropriation of welfare and medical funds in the new joint enterprises (*Southern Daily* 18 June 1956), and many enterprises let their medical and hygiene funds (constituting 5 to 7 per cent of the wage bill) pile up unused while workers and their dependents fell behind with hospital bills. In some cases patients who had recovered were 'detained' in hospital until money could be borrowed by their relatives to pay off their bills (*Southern Daily* 19 June 1956). Funds for workers' housing were also improperly diverted to other uses, and planned housing construction cancelled as an economy measure (*Workers' Daily* 6 and 24 June 1956; *Southern Daily* 25 June 1956).

Once the seriousness of the neglect of workers' welfare and the ignorance on the part of administrative and union cadres about workers' genuine difficulties became clear, a campaign against bureaucratist indifference to workers' problems and the separation of cadres from the masses was launched. Delegations of cadres, especially from the unions, visited workers' homes to find out the real circumstances of their lives and to offer emergency relief to those in difficulties, and newspapers ran articles detailing the large amounts of money now being spent on welfare and housing (*Southern Daily* 16 and 19 July, 8 August, and 2 September 1956). Indeed, a report from Shanghai on 'unprincipled accommodation' by cadres of all workers' welfare demands, regardless of merit, accused cadres of picking out isolated points from higher-level directives to support their own 'deviations', with the result that enterprise welfare funds for the whole year had been exhausted during the first half or even the first quarter of the year (*Southern Daily* 12 October 1956). It is significant that this intervention came from Shanghai, where First Party Secretary Ke Qingshi had always taken a hard line on workers' pay and conditions, 'insisting on an exceptionally harsh implementation of wage policy' in an attempt to gain favour with national party leaders

(Perry and Li 1997: 99). A *People's Daily* editorial criticized sections of the press for making too much of some workers' problems and raising expectations with regard to welfare and living standards (*People's Daily* 27 November 1956), and the working-class tradition of 'hard work and plain and frugal living' was promoted once again as an antidote to the one-sided emphasis on opposing bureaucratism and improving workers' lives (*Workers' Daily* 23 December 1956).

However, despite this mini-backlash against excessive concern for workers' welfare and living conditions, it is clear that the 'welfare wind' of the summer of 1956 had little effect. In fact, problems with housing and union cadres' refusal to grant emergency assistance to workers from welfare funds were still exercising workers in the spring and summer of the following year: they are the subject of many of the contributions from workers to the *Guangzhou Daily*, with one worker reporting that the findings of union cadres' home visits had been ignored by the administration, and that the union had subsequently failed to press workers' requests (*Guangzhou Daily* 29 May 1957). Workers also said that they had been criticized for demanding improvements in working conditions during this period and that their complaints had been suppressed (*Guangzhou Daily* 17 May 1957). It is evident from workers' comments at this time that many of them still considered welfare after nationalization to have been 'one step forward and two steps back' (*Guangzhou Daily* 17 April 1957), with the old, 'irrational' and 'egalitarian' benefits such as double pay at the end of the year and allowances for meals, haircuts, laundry, etc. abolished, but nothing of any substance put in their place.

One problem which clearly had not been successfully tackled, the withholding of welfare funds from workers, re-emerged as a source of conflict the following year. We saw earlier that the accumulation of unspent funds while welfare problems went unsolved continued largely because workers and even lower-level union cadres did not know that the money existed. However, when awareness that money was available but was not being used for workers' benefit did begin to percolate down to workers, this caused enormous resentment and generated suspicions of cadre corruption. It was reported in the *Guangxi Daily* in October 1957 that four months earlier, a worker of the Guilin Construction Engineering Company had 'collected fragmentary financial statements of the company, and distorted them by saying that the cadres "split the welfare funds among themselves" and that "the workers were denied any of them"'. Passing on this information to others, a group of workers was alleged to have violently disrupted a mass meeting called to discuss workers' grievances and assaulted a union cadre whom they believed to be primarily responsible for the corrupt dividing-up of welfare funds; they then called a strike which lasted for three days (*Guangxi Daily* 16 October 1957).

We have no way of knowing whether these accusations against cadres were true, but it is clear from earlier reports concerning the construction and other industries in Guangzhou that large sums were being accumulated in welfare funds for no apparent reason, and cases of corruption were not unknown. The Guilin incident shows how unresolved problems of this nature which first surfaced during the 'welfare wind' of 1956 could eventually result in serious disturbances, if nothing was done to allay suspicions that cadres were benefitting themselves at workers' expense. Even where corruption was not suspected, workers still resented the accumulation of welfare funds by unions which they considered to be worse than useless at protecting their members' interests, and the demand that union funds should be divided up amongst workers has been noted as a common feature of strikes and protests in Shanghai in 1956–7 (Perry 1994: 17).

It was often suggested during the second half of 1956 that the programme of wage reform carried out in all enterprises between April and October of that year would solve many of the difficulties workers were experiencing (*Southern Daily* 25 June 1956). But not only did wage reform not solve many of these prob- lems, it actually created some of its own and became a major source of discontent and protest among workers. The programme was intended to remove all remaining irrationalities and inconsistencies in the wage system left over from the pre-revolutionary era. The resulting integrated system would reflect the party's priorities for 'decisive' heavy industrial sectors during the First Five-Year Plan (*Chinese Worker* June 1956, 11: 6). It was a general principle in the reform that if workers were evaluated according to the new system and found to be in a lower grade or on a lower wage than before, they would keep their original grade and wage, so that the reform seemed to be in effect a general wage increase, with no workers seeing their pay reduced as a result of the new system of assessment (*Chinese Worker* May 1956, 10: 4; July 1956, 13: 6), and most seeing an increase. It was admitted, however, that wage reform would not solve all workers' liveli- hood difficulties, and workers were encouraged to help themselves by improving their technical skills, with those in serious difficulties to rely on trade union emer- gency allowances or mutual assistance funds (*Chinese Worker* May 1956, 10: 4). Given the evidence of workers' difficulties in getting assistance from these sources, this shows the limitations of the reform and the likelihood of continued hardship for some workers and their families.

Workers inclined towards more egalitarian forms of distribution and anxious about the widening of the gap between the highest and lowest wages both within and between grades were assured that

> In a socialist society, disparities in wage standards are entirely necessary, and this sort of disparity is rational, and is an important part of the guiding principle for the realization of socialism of 'more pay for more work, to each according to his work', and material incentives.
>
> (*Chinese Worker* June 1956, 11: 7)

A regular system of evaluation, testing and promotion was to be put in place in every enterprise, with criteria for evaluation including workers' technical skill, speed of work, cultural level, and attitude to labour. No consideration was supposed to be given to workers' age or length of service in itself, since it was assumed that this would be reflected in higher technical capabilities and profes- sional experience, both factors which could legitimately be taken into account when assessing workers' grades (*Chinese Worker* July 1956, 13: 4). In fact, many veteran workers who were poorly educated or even illiterate found their wages rapidly overtaken by those of the new intake of young workers in 1956–7, many of them at least middle-school graduates, in spite of the latter's lack of work experience, and this caused considerable resentment and friction in some enterprises (*Chinese Worker* June 1957, 11: 3–4; Perry 1994: 19).

If the new wage structure sounded reasonable enough in theory, its actual application could entail considerable arbitrariness and injustice. It had always been claimed that the reform would end the phenomenon of workers receiving different pay for the same work, but in fact this was still a frequent occurrence. It was one of the main grievances of Wang Cai, a turner in an unnamed Guangzhou factory, whose letter to the *Guangzhou Daily* on 10 April 1957 complaining of leadership bureaucratism and lack of concern for workers' welfare in his enterprise began a two-month debate in the paper's pages. Wang had been evaluated as a grade-four worker during wage reform, but considered this unfair as he was capable of grade-five work, and many workers with records similar to his had in fact been promoted to grade five. His own assessment of his abilities was apparently vindicated when, due to pressure of work in the factory, cadres asked him to do the work of a grade-five worker. Incensed, he refused, adopting the principle of 'work according to payment' (*an chou fu lao*, a pun on Marx's 'to each according to his work', or *an lao fu chou*, the main slogan of the 1956 wage reform) which gained widespread support among workers at this time.

Many of the workers who joined the debate supported Wang's decision not to do any work for which he was not paid: what else, they asked rhetorically, did 'payment according to work' mean (*Guangzhou Daily* 12 and 25 April 1957)? Workers protested that the new wage regulations had been inconsistently applied with no regard to the real situation on the factory floor, resulting in numerous mistakes. In some enterprises the problem of undemocratic management affected the reforms, with very little democratic discussion or consultation taking place before wage grades were decided on. In contravention of national guidelines, cadres instead resorted to 'closed-door' reform in these plants, just posting a list of names and grades for workers to read (*Southern Daily* 4 October 1956; 25 April and 5 May 1957; *Guangzhou Daily* 14 and 30 May 1957). There were also instances of partiality and corruption where reforms were implemented in this way: in one enterprise, the entire department in charge of wage reform was promoted in the process, in marked contrast to the proportion promoted in other departments, and there were cases of preferential treatment for party and youth league members who gained undeserved promotions without the requisite approval by workers (*Southern Daily* 4 May 1957; *Guangzhou Daily* 17 May 1957). All of the above criticisms of the wage reform process were admitted to be correct and justified in June 1957, in the article which brought to a close the 'Wang Cai' debate (*Guangzhou Daily* 8 June 1957).

Another aspect of wage reform which provoked discontent and protests was the promotion of piece-work. In 1956 the percentage of the Chinese workforce on piece-rates rose to a new high of 42 per cent (Richman 1969: 314). Workers on this form of pay found that the frequent upward revision of norms which became common practice following the completion of wage reform 'systematically eroded [their] income', with wage gains 'eaten away by increases in pace [of work] and productivity' (Gipouloux 1986: 169). Workers had been assured during the progress of the reform that the new piece-work system would include a basic wage as well as a piece-rate element, which would protect them from the old problem of severe or even complete loss of income in the event of work stoppages which were beyond their control, but in reality this measure does not seem to have had the intended effect. During the 'Wang Cai' debate, an official of the Guangzhou Municipal Textile Bureau conceded that the allowance paid to piece-rate workers in the new joint enterprises in the event of unavoidable stoppages in work was 'not enough to live on' (*Guangzhou Daily* 11 May 1957).

The reorganization and amalgamation of enterprises after nationalization also affected the income of piece-workers, with norms in some factories being aligned with those of all other enterprises in the same line of work, regardless of factors such as the varying degree of mechanization or other differences in conditions of work. Workers affected by this sort of realignment of norms could see their pre-wage reform pay reduced by as much as 40 per cent, or in extreme cases 70 per cent (*Guangzhou Daily* 8 May and 10 June 1957). Not only were workers' protests about this ignored, but the management 'reproached the recalcitrant workers for their passivity and poor spirit' (Gipouloux 1986: 169), treating the matter as an ideological problem on the part of the workers. In May 1957 some of the undesirable consequences of wage reform in Guangzhou were acknowledged when the Guangdong Party Committee cited dissatisfaction with wages as the prime cause behind thirteen instances of 'strikes and trouble-making activities' in the province since the beginning of the year. The 'giving of a bigger increase to factory [directors] and leading personnel and a smaller increase to workers' was specifically mentioned as a cause of discontent (the lack of democracy in enterprises was also cited as a major source of unrest) (*Xinhua News Agency* (Guangzhou) 14 May 1957), showing the importance of cadre–worker inequalities in generating unrest.

Finally, housing, which came very low on the list of investment priorities at this point, was a serious problem in many urban areas. This might have been a less divisive issue if the available housing had been fairly allocated, but instead the crisis 'was exacerbated by social inequality' (Gipouloux 1986: 183), as cadres, often with the connivance of the enterprise trade union, allocated a disproportionate share of any new housing to themselves (*Guangzhou Daily* 9 June 1957). Workers protested that they and their families were stuck in dangerous, leaking housing while cadres' dependents, and even siblings, had ample accommodation (*Guangzhou Daily* 29 May 1957). It is evident from workers' statements, and indeed it was officially acknowledged as the 'Wang Cai' debate was brought to a close, that it was not the housing shortage in itself which had provoked so much anger among workers, but rather the unfair allocation of the limited stock (*Guangzhou Daily* 8 June 1956). The crux of the problem was, as ever, the still subordinate position of workers, and cadres' isolation from them. One of the first workers to contribute to the debate made the point that all talk about workers having 'stood up' and being 'masters' was meaningless so long as they could still be treated unfairly and with disdain by those with power over their lives (*Guangzhou Daily* 11 April 1957).

The trade union crisis

The enterprise trade unions must bear some responsibility for the state of affairs described above, since they patently were failing in their duty to protect workers' interests. The accusation by one worker that the trade unions had 'lost . . . their guts since the Seventh National Congress' (*Workers' Daily* 21 May 1957) in 1953 has some basis in fact, since the charges of economism which were made at that time, and the accompanying purge of many of the top leadership of the ACFTU, had left the unions cowed and reluctant to be outspoken in defence of workers' rights when such statements could easily be construed by party authorities as further outbreaks of economism and syndicalism. It was acknowledged by Lai Ruoyu and others in the ACFTU leadership that although it had been necessary to attack these tendencies, the unions had subsequently gone too far in the opposite direction, committing the error of bureaucratism and showing no concern for their members' interests and failing to support their proper demands (*Workers' Daily* 24 September 1956; 12 and 22 May 1957).

Careerism among union cadres must also be mentioned in this context: the fact that being a union official was often the first rung on the ladder of promotion which might eventually lead to party membership and all its attendant privileges created its own pressures on cadres not to rock the boat by siding with workers against factory leadership. The same applied to union cadres who were already party members. In practice, as had happened in the spring of 1950, unions tended to side with the administration in any case where workers' views conflicted with those of the factory leadership. Union cadres were roundly criticized for making 'unprincipled concessions' (*Workers' Daily* 4 May 1957) and giving in to administrative cadres without an argument whenever they expressed divergent views. Many union officials were ruled by their fear of 'spoiling relations' (*Workers' Daily* 2 March 1956) with the administration and thereby losing its support for their work in future; they were afraid that a stand against the administration on whatever issue would be remembered when the time came to evaluate them for wage increases and promotion (*Workers' Daily* 4 May 1957). The safest course for the unions was to concentrate on the welfare matters which came under their jurisdiction, and on the organization of labour emulation competitions and other activities which promoted production and so were unlikely to lead to any conflict with the administration.

Union defence of workers' rights in private enterprises seems to have been greatly weakened after their transfer to joint state-private ownership, as the authoritarian tendencies of many state representatives affected their performance of their duties and undermined their supervisory role. It was reported in December 1956 that

Some state representatives think: when the enterprises were privately run, trade unions had to exercise supervision to prevent capitalists' illegal activities. Now that enterprises have implemented joint management, with state representatives heading the administration, they are managing it on behalf of the state, and if the trade union wants to exercise supervision, won't it just be stirring up opposition to the administration and seeking trouble for its own people?

(*Chinese Worker* December 1956, 23: 3)

Some state representatives, it was said, 'even demand that the trade union obey the administrative leadership'. And some union cadres were themselves unsure of their rights in the new situation, thinking 'the state representatives are cadres appointed by the state, of a higher level than us, so how can we possibly supervise them?' (*Chinese Worker* December 1956, 23: 3).

Enterprise union cadres were reminded in this article, which appeared in the ACFTU's official journal and therefore can be assumed to have the backing of the union leadership, that they had the full authority of the constitution (Article 17) and of the Trade Union Law (Article 7) to ensure mass criticism and supervision of the enterprise leadership and to protect workers' interests and supervise the administration's adherence to party policy and the law. Although the common task of the administration and the trade union was 'to promote the development of production and on that basis to improve the material and cultural lives of the working masses', and although the trade union was supposed in normal circumstances to exercise its authority in support of the administration, there was a possibility that administrative power might be used inappropriately, in which case

this [would] often tend to distort party and state policy and laws and harm the democratic rights and material interests of the working masses. So the trade union, as a mass organization and a body representing the interests of workers, must exercise supervision in respect of the administration, to prevent the misuse of administrative power.

(*Chinese Worker* December 1956, 23: 3)

Unions were urged to 'struggle against any abuse of administrative power, failure to act on the masses' proposals, attacks or reprisals against people making complaints, arbitrary punishment of workers, etc.' (*Chinese Worker* December 1956, 23: 3), reflecting their failure to do this during 1956. The Soviet sinologist A P Davydov noted that in the drive for production at this time, 'not only were the opinions of workers ignored, many unions at the enterprise level dealt harshly with those who complained. The unions' neglect of worker interests is evident in the greatly increased number of occupational injuries' (Rozman 1985: 112). In Guangzhou the root cause of the 1956 increase in industrial accidents involving injury or death was identified as leadership bureaucratism, i.e. a lack of concern for workers' health and safety and the view that safety precautions would hinder the completion of production quotas, and should therefore be dispensed with. Unions were frequently criticized not only for their failure to protect workers' interests, but even more for their role in actually enforcing dangerous practices such as excessive overtime (*Southern Daily* 14 and 15 June 1956).

Why was it that the unions were so ineffective in defence of workers' rights? In 1957 workers in Guangzhou were said to have 'dubbed their trade unions "workers' control department" . . . "tongue of bureaucracy" and "tail of administration"' (*People's Daily* 9 May 1957). Their bitterness towards the unions is understandable, but it must be remembered that there were genuine difficulties inherent in the role of the official unions. They were obliged both to support the administration and to protect workers' rights and interests. In theory there was no conflict between these two tasks, but in practice many union cadres did see their dual responsibilities as incompatible (*Workers' Daily* 4 and 7 May 1957), and when a conflict arose, as it all too often did, it was extremely difficult for unions to side with the workers without provoking charges of economism, syndicalism, or challenging party and state authority.

It might have been possible for unions to fulfil their obligations towards their members if they had had the necessary support from the administration, but often the actions of the administration would undermine the union's authority and prestige among workers. In some enterprises there were 'even instances where production plans and safety and welfare measures were kept "secret" from the trade unions' (*Xinhua News Agency* 23 November 1956) by administrative cadres. When workers made requests for welfare benefits to which they were entitled (such as emergency loans or allowances for visiting sick relatives, etc.) the request would be dealt with by the Chair of their union small group or section committee, in other words by a fairly low-level union cadre with little real authority in the enterprise and no control over budgets. Cases were reported in the second half of 1956 where such requests had been arbitrarily turned down several times, whereupon the worker or workers concerned would go over the head of the ineffectual group-level union cadre to an administrative cadre or to the enterprise trade union Chair, who was usually a party member and therefore did have real power in the enterprise. The request would then be granted without further ado, leaving workers to conclude that the union at the lower level would not bother to do even a simple thing for them, and that in future it would be better to rely on their own resources to get things done (*Chinese Worker* August 1956, 15: 4; and October 1956, 19: 12).

The outlines of the union crisis which came to a head in the spring of 1957 can be discerned in the above comments. The basic problem was the same as in 1950, that of obligation without authority: the union did not have the right to give orders to anyone in the enterprise, but had to rely on persuasion and education to see that the work it delegated to activists or ordinary trade union members was accomplished. Since it relied on this sort of mobilization, the vicious circle of ineffectiveness in helping its members, and lowered prestige among workers, was a particularly destructive one. Union cadres were forced to conclude that their organization 'really has no position and no power, when there's a problem, what the trade union says doesn't count, it can't take responsi-bility, and the factory director must ratify [anything] before it can take effect' (*Chinese Worker* October 1956, 19: 12).

A series of articles in the labour movement journal *Chinese Worker* between August and November 1956, consisting mainly of contributions from workers, described in considerable detail the nature of the crisis in union work as experi-enced by union activists and lower-level cadres, and in particular highlighted the effect of the reformed wage structure and the system of material incentives then in force in industry on these people's willingness and ability to do union work. The problem of responsibility without authority was, as ever, most acute for union activists who had no official position and whose union work was purely voluntary. Their complaints and the universal demoralization which is evident in these 1956 accounts show that activists' position had not improved since their original protests about the lack of support for their activities in 1950.

It emerges from these accounts that most activists and lower-level cadres felt that union work was a thankless task which frequently got them into trouble both with the administration and with their fellow workers. Many frankly admitted that they were waiting impatiently for the next round of union elections when they would have a chance to pass their responsibilities on to someone else (*Chinese Worker* August 1956, 15: 6). The reasons behind activists' plummeting morale are not hard to find. First, all their trade union work was supposed to be done in their spare time. One problem with this, which also applied to lower-level union cadres, was that after work workers who did not live in enterprise dormitories would disperse and go home, making it impossible to do any union work with them. Another was that however well organized and experienced in their jobs activists were, they simply did not have enough spare time for all the work they were supposed to do, mainly because many of them held more than one post concurrently. Judging from the evidence in these articles, it was not unusual for a union small-group head, for example, to hold five or six posts simultaneously, and an individual might in the past have held as many as nine.

When union work did encroach on working hours, it not merely 'incurred the displeasure of the administration' (*Chinese Worker* August 1956, 15: 5), but could also have a direct effect on the income of the activist or cadre concerned and that of their colleagues. Under the newly established eight-grade wage system, workers were appraised for promotion with reference to factors such as their performance in production, technical skill and attitude to labour. Any enforced absence from the shopfloor on union business would adversely affect an activist's rating on all these criteria. In enterprises which practised a system of group piece-work, an activist's poor performance might mean the group as a whole failed to reach its target and thus lost income, not something calculated to boost the prestige of the union. And if activists and cadres did spend all their spare time doing union work they still lost out, falling behind their colleagues in tech-nical skill as they had no time for study. One small-group head recounted how in the course of his union career, my apprentices all overtook me, and some had already been promoted from grade two to grade six; quite a few workers who were originally grade six workers like me have gone ahead of me, and all get paid more than me.

(Chinese Worker August 1956, 15: 6)

The common feeling among activists and lower-level cadres was that far from their union work doing any good, it was actually harmful, not only to themselves in terms of their performance in production, technical progress and pay, but also to their colleagues, since they could do nothing to assist them without the cooperation of the enterprise administration and might drag down their income and lose them bonuses through time spent away from production on union work. A common theme was the lack of support from the enterprise administration, and also, in the case of activists, from the enterprise union leadership, who were accused by one worker (in terms almost identical to those we saw in 1950) of 'treating us like "a brick picked up to knock on the door"; when they can use us, they press us into service, and when they can't they cast us aside, and nobody gives a damn'. According to this worker, the leadership's attitude 'not only turns dedicated and energetic trade union activists into demoralized ones, but also produces a bad impression of activists among the masses, so no-one is prepared to do trade union work'. He insisted that he was fully aware of the importance of union work and would be willing to undertake it at any time, but only on condition of 'understanding, concern and support' for activists from the union and administrative leadership. Otherwise, he felt that he could make more of a contribution to socialism by doing a good job in production and improving his skills, and some of his more sympathetic colleagues had urged him to do exactly that (*Chinese Worker* October 1956, 19: 13).

It was of course quite convenient for the higher levels to have the basic-level union in the enterprise bearing the brunt of workers' discontent at their lack of material progress and democratic influence after the socialist transformation of industry. When, for example, a union's inability to stand up to the administration and protect workers from excessive overtime resulted in damage to workers' health and posed the risk of a serious accident (*Chinese Worker* August 1956, 16: 5), workers' anger would, not unnaturally, be directed primarily at the union. But in spite of some harsh criticism from workers of union cadres' bureaucratism and general ineffectiveness during 1956 and the spring of 1957, workers seem to have been well aware of the difficulty of their position as 'fourth-class' cadres, ranking below party and youth league cadres and technical personnel in terms of influence and authority in the enterprise. They did not agree with the view that cadres' workstyle was the main problem, and pointed instead to their lack of authority in the enterprise and the almost total lack of cooperation they received from management and enterprise party committees.

Workers felt that unions were 'not in a position to support the proper demands of the masses' (*Workers' Daily* 21 May 1957), and could do nothing about the arbitrary rejection of such demands. They were aware that union cadres who did try to defend workers' rights and so came into conflict with the administrative or party leadership in the enterprise tended to be accused of trying to perpetuate class struggle even though enterprises were no longer privately owned, as in the comment that '[y]our trade union is not the labour side and the administration is not the capital side. No reason for staging the same play!' They also pointed out their own difficulties in selecting union cadres who would actually defend their interests: cadres who 'always backed up the masses' had problems with their careers and with getting or keeping party membership (Harper 1969: 88), and those who 'persisted in the proper demands of the masses, were accused of "conceit", "no respect for party leadership" or "fomenting discord and independence"' (*Workers' Daily* 21 May 1957).

In fact, the problem with the unions as far as workers were concerned, as in 1950, was a dual one: not only that CCP policies put pressure on them not to respond to workers' demands and to side with the administration, but also that they still were not democratic organizations elected and controlled by their members. New ACFTU regulations on the election of basic-level union committees were published in February 1956 (*Workers' Daily* 24 February 1956), and an article the following month revealed the sort of practices which these regulations were intended to curb. It was reported that many unions were failing to hold regular elections and meetings of members, that where meetings were held, most of the time was taken up with the Chair's report, leaving little time for discussion, and that workers were being prevented from discussing or approving candidates for election to the committee, being compelled instead to elect, by acclamation rather than balloting, whatever list of candidates was presented to them (*Workers' Daily* 17 March 1956; *Guangzhou Daily* 17 May 1957). This resulted in weak basic-level union organizations which were separated from workers, led by cadres who were the 'bosses', rather than members, of the rank and file (*Workers' Daily* 11 May 1957). As had happened in 1950, the weakness of 'the administration's union department' and its lack of contact with its members militated against its being able to defend their interests effectively even where union cadres were inclined to support workers against the administration, while undemocratic election practices reduced workers' chances of getting into office cadres who would support them.

Given workers' low regard for their unions and their awareness of the constraints on union cadres' activities, it is not surprising that they were quick to abandon the official union organization whenever they felt the need to confront the enterprise leadership on an issue. The enterprise union thus became an irrelevance in disputes, and workers who had become accustomed to taking individual problems and demands straight to the administrative leadership or to the party began to do the same thing collectively, organizing themselves to present their demands to those they knew had the power to meet them. Together with the absence of any effective means of influencing the administration through democratic representation or participation in management, this meant that there remained no intermediary structures between the discontented workers on the one hand and the party and administrative authorities on the other, which meant that '[t]he decisive confrontation took place between the party and the working class. . . . All disputes developed into a political confrontation' (Gipouloux 1986: 101).

By the late spring of 1957, the high point of both the Hundred Flowers campaign and the wave of industrial unrest which had built up through the previous year, party authorities were thus facing not just individual discontent, but organized collective resistance from some parts of the workforce. Autonomous unions were formed, often termed *pingnan hui* ('redress grievance societies'), and while many of these groups were confined to a single enterprise, there was also some liaison and coordination of action between enterprises and districts (Perry 1994: 11). These independent organizing efforts were short-lived, being brought to an end by the anti-rightist campaign from June 1957, but nevertheless highly significant, and of great concern to the party and to the official, and now apparently redundant, unions alike. Workers themselves knew that the difficulties they were experiencing were by and large a direct result of national decisions on industrial and management policy, now that everything from wage rates to lengths of apprenticeships had been standardized across all industries and regions, and accordingly 'much of their wrath was directed against cadres in factory, government, Party and union positions' (Perry 1994: 15). Even where less-privileged sections of the workforce (apprentices or young workers, for example) were moved to protest by resentment of the advantages employed by permanent workers in the larger state enterprises (or by permanent workers in their own workplace, in the case of temporary workers), their anger was mainly directed at those responsible for the inequality rather than at its beneficiaries.[1]

The whole direction of wage and other policies, with their emphasis on piece-work, frequent raising of norms, and material incentives as a spur to productivity, had by early 1957 contributed to a change in many workers' attitudes towards enterprise leadership and towards their own labour. The most striking thing which emerges from newspaper articles, and particularly from workers' letters to the press, at this time is the extent to which workers regarded the leadership of their enterprises as adversaries, and adopted the methods of the withdrawal or selective application of their labour to gain concessions and the reversal of unacceptable decisions (*Workers' Daily* 25 and 30 April 1957; *Southern Daily* 19 May 1957; *Guangzhou Daily* 10 and 24 May 1957). It was frequently argued by workers that unless they took this sort of action their views and demands would continue to be ignored by the leadership and problems would go unsolved, and many even recommended creating disturbances (*chaonao*) as the only effective means of influencing enterprise authorities, claiming that workers had to stand up for themselves in this way against leaders who 'bullied the good, but feared the bad' (*Guangzhou Daily* 19 and 21 May 1957). Many of the workers who advocated actions like working to rule under the sarcastic 'work according to payment' slogan admitted that such tactics really belonged to the capitalist era of wage relations (*Guangzhou Daily* 3 and 8 May 1957) and were not suited to workers' role as masters of the enterprise under socialism, but they nevertheless defended them as necessary given the bureaucratist and undemocratic nature of enterprise management as it actually existed. This came close to accusing enterprise leaders of behaving like the capitalist employers of the old society, showing the seriousness of the split which was developing between leaders and led in the industrial sphere.

In Gipouloux's view, the widespread adoption of this overt 'wage-labour mentality' by workers 'exposed what the mythology which held the political economy in place wished to cover up: the relations of exploitation which bound the working class to the party' (Gipouloux 1986: 173). The policies of the First Five-Year Plan, as we have seen, placed a heavy burden on workers, who by 1956 found that 'pay was meagre, the rhythm of work exhausting, and living conditions deplorable. To say nothing of the exclusion of workers from the whole process of decision-making' (Gipouloux 1986: 270). The last point is particularly important, as participation in management was supposed to be the feature which distinguished socialist enterprises from capitalist ones (Lai Ruoyu 1956a) and showed that workers really were the 'masters of the enterprise' in some meaningful sense.

Yet despite workers' pressure for far-reaching democratization and participation in management immediately after liberation, the CCP had held back from full mobilization of workers to achieve these goals, creating tensions in its relationship with workers which fuelled the first major confrontation between them. These same tensions also underlay the second confrontation with its accompanying industrial unrest, and were exacerbated by workers' disappointment and disillusionment at the results of the final nationalization of industry. If workers' democratic rights in state and joint-managed enterprises were ignored and they had no accepted legal means of protesting or of attempting to enforce those rights, then there really was a sense in which they were in a weaker position than had been the case under capitalism or in private enterprises, since in a state enterprise under a socialist government, any attempt at self-organization or strike action would be treated as a challenge to the regime, which based its legitimacy on its status as the vanguard of the proletariat.

If the description of relations between the party and workers as exploitative sounds extreme, we should remember that in 1956–7, workers were being required to work all-out for socialist construction without enjoying the benefits of socialist democracy or the protection of socialist unions in the enterprise; they were keeping their side of the bargain, but the promised benefits of their new status as the partners, not the adversaries, of management, had not materialized. It is in this context that some workers' comments that they were freer in the old society, when they could at least vote with their feet and seek work elsewhere if working conditions were intolerable, should be understood. This sort of freedom was officially condemned as 'nothing more than the freedom to sell labour power, the freedom of the wage-slave' (Wen Jin 1956), but it is clear that under the policies in force in 1956, some workers actually *felt* like wage-slaves, in the absence of any concrete manifestation of their theoretical status as 'masters of the enterprise'. The scale of the crisis in the CCP's relationship with the working class is evident from the prevalence of this view among workers.

The party's response

Just as signs of serious trouble within the industrial workforce were evident during mid-1956, long before the peak of the Hundred Flowers strike wave in April and May 1957, so the party's awareness of the need to respond was apparent by the autumn of 1956. Indications of a high-level shift in industrial policy emerged from the Eighth Party Congress in September 1956, where the Soviet model of strictly hierarchical one-man management was finally rejected in favour of the mass line in industry and the collective leadership of the enterprise party committee. The Congress called for the strengthening of mass supervision as part of the 'further broadening of democratic life in China' (*People's Daily* 22 March 1957), and decided on the establishment of experimental workers' congresses, consisting of directly elected representatives who could be recalled by workers at any time, as the best means of ensuring the 'expansion of democracy and introduction of the mass-line method of work in state enterprises' (*People's Daily* 29 May 1957). Two months later, at a conference of enterprise-level union cadres from joint enterprises, the ACFTU Chairman Lai Ruoyu identified democratization of management as the feature which distinguished socialist enterprises from capitalist ones and called on unions to 'preserve and improve the system of workers' congresses' (Lai Ruoyu 1956a) in order to make workers feel that they really were 'masters of the enterprise'.

This change of policy was clearly designed to avert the danger of serious open confrontation between restive, alienated workers and party and administrative authorities in the workplace and beyond; it was a recognition that policy had gone too far in the direction of only emphasizing production and neglecting democracy, welfare and workers' rights. The decision must also have been influenced by events in Eastern Europe during 1956, which the CCP took as an indication that it could not safely ignore the pressures that were building up in China. The parallels between Hungary and China are particularly striking when one looks at unrest among workers. Hungary's official unions, for example, had been suffering from the same problems of a lack of authority and respect in the enterprise, and from workers' lack of confidence in their own mass organizations, as had their Chinese counterparts, with the 'belittling of the trade unions and trade union work . . . quite frequently observable' (Zinner 1956: 366) there as in China. Chinese workers themselves had advertised their intention to emulate their Hungarian counterparts in their slogans and banners, and they showed a clear awareness of the wider socialist world of which China was a part: 'Another slogan in 1957 was "We'll take this all the way from district to city to Party central to Communist International"' (Perry 1994: 11).

The high-level support for increased democratization, participation in management, and concern for workers' material well-being displayed after the Eighth Party Congress might have been expected to improve the situation in China's enterprises, but the action taken to meet workers' complaints seems to have been a case of too little, too late, with some workers having so little faith in the system of workers' congresses, for example, that they refused to elect representatives to them (*Southern*

Daily 3 June 1957). It is equally possible that the new policy's very prominence, rhetorically if not in fact, actually exacerbated workers' anger and bitterness against the official unions, enterprise administration, and ultimately the party, thus precipitating even more acute conflict in the spring of 1957. This can be taken as a Chinese example of the situation noted in Eastern Europe before 1989, where 'the official ideology [made] claims on behalf of the industrial workers which the day to day reality contradict[ed]' (Denitch 1981: 254), resulting in sharp and persistent conflict between workers and the regime.

In promoting wider democratization as an antidote to workers' growing discontent, the CCP did in fact reach the heart of the matter, for it was not primarily the fact that China was a relatively poor and under-developed country which provoked so much unrest among the working class, but issues of democracy and equality. Herein lies the political content of workers' protests: these were not just that their living and working conditions were poor and sometimes downright dangerous, but that their requests for modest improvements could be disregarded with bureaucratist indifference by cadres who did not share these hardships, and who even criticized workers for venturing to complain; not just that wages were still low and that there were irrationalities in the system, but that reforms intended to remedy this had been carried out in a high-handed and sometimes corrupt way which violated all principles of democratic management and workers' participation, and were manipulated by cadres for their own advantage while many workers lost out; not just that there was a serious shortage of housing, but that the limited stock was not allocated according to need, instead being monopolized by a privileged group. In short, the state and party bureaucracy, right down to the level of enterprise management and including the official unions, had control over virtually all important aspects of workers' lives, including the organizations and institutions through which they were supposed to participate in decision-making and act as the 'masters'. This left workers with no option but to resort to illegal or semi-legal methods to have any influence on the most fundamental issues affecting their lives.

The workers' congress

The intention behind proposals for enterprise democratization was to restore and reinvigorate intermediary structures in the enterprise, including the official trade union and a revised version, with more extensive powers, of the sort of participatory structure which had existed in state enterprises after liberation (the workers' representative congress (WRC)) and in private enterprises before nationalization (the production-increase and economy committee). As we saw, the absence of these sorts of intermediary structures had come to mean that rebellious workers quickly came into direct conflict with the party itself. With the advantages and defects of earlier institutions as a guide, a debate unfolded from late 1956 on what the powers of the new democratic body should be, and various models were tried out on an experimental basis in enterprises. A description of the role and powers of the workers' congress as they emerged from the debate clearly shows its relationship to the earlier WRC, although given that it was accepted that the WRC had quickly declined into formalism, there was evidently a need to modify the institution in order to ensure that workers' participation would go beyond 'making a guarantee' (Li Chun 1957; *People's Daily* 29 May 1957) at meetings to carry out managers' instructions.

Over the seven months from November 1956 to May 1957, the ACFTU's Lai Ruoyu was a consistent advocate of wider and more clearly defined powers for the workers' congress, although these were always conditional on the 'non-violation of plans, decisions and orders of the higher levels' (Lai Ruoyu 1956a). It was emphasized that if workers and cadres alike were not to feel they were wasting their time at congress meetings, *all* congress resolutions which met this condition had to be implemented without fail (Zai Heng 1957), but of course similar statements had been made with regard to the WRC in previous years without these good intentions being translated into reality. Under Lai's proposals, the workers' congress would have the right to take decisions on matters concerning workers' interests and benefits, such as the use of factory bonuses and state appropriations for safety, and the right to 'recommend the appointment and removal of leading officials' and ask for revocation of 'inappropriate' decisions (Lai Ruoyu 1957a). The congress was also entitled to 'hear reports of the leadership, discuss . . . criticize and make proposals' (Lai Ruoyu 1957a), although this entitlement was backed by nothing stronger than moral pressure on cadres not to ignore workers' opinions and dismiss their suggestions as they had tended to do in the past. Congress representatives were to be 'nominated and elected by the masses', and in turn management cadres would be 'elected by the workers' congress or the general meeting of all workers' (*People's Daily* 30 November 1956).

The workers' congress as formulated by Lai had the additional advantage of providing a positive role for the enterprise union committee, which was to act as the standing organ of the congress, organizing the election of delegates, convening the congress regularly, and carrying out its resolutions and day-to-day business when it was not in session. In this way it was hoped that unions would regain the respect and trust of workers and authority in the enterprise: according to Lai, 'the trade union management committee should be a regular organization under the leadership of the workers' congress, and also an organization with authority' (Lai Ruoyu 1956a). In fact, the effect was the opposite of that intended: rather than the effectiveness of the workers' congress rescuing the prestige of the unions, the unions' dismal reputation among workers tended to tarnish the workers' congress in their eyes even before it was formally established in many enterprises (*Workers' Daily* 11 January and 25 February 1957).

Early proposals that workers should elect their factory director (*Xinhua News Agency* 27 December 1956) had already been rejected by the end of May 1957, when a *People's Daily* editorial stated that:

Inasmuch as the state enterprises are owned by all the people and not collectively owned by the workers . . . the leading administrative personnel of the enterprise should be appointed by the state administrative organs representing the interests of all the people and should not be elected by the workers' congresses.

(*People's Daily* 29 May 1957)

This was a rather ominous statement, since it was precisely this unchallengeable authority of the state representatives which had weakened enterprise democracy and workers' participation in management in state enterprises since 1949 and which had the same effect in joint enterprises after nationalization; the leading role of the factory director, the highest state representative in the plant, had been identified as the main reason for the FMC's decline into formalism. Similarly, proposals that the workers' congress should be the 'highest administrative organ' (*Xinhua News Agency* 27 December 1956) in the enterprise, or that it should be on 'an equal footing with the management' (*Xinhua News Agency* 9 January 1957) were discarded after trials in only a few enterprises.

However, the free election by workers of congress representatives was strongly emphasized: union cadres, who were to oversee the process of nomination and election of candidates, were reminded that although it was important for representatives to be competent, 'it is advisable to make no mention of the required qualifications so that the masses may have a wider latitude in choosing the persons to represent them' (*People's Daily* 29 May 1957). But elections, like all other congress activities, were subject to higher-level approval and could be strongly influenced by the enterprise party committee. Cadre interference in elections was evidently still common, although it might be disguised as concern for democracy:

> Some people, although they don't say anything to oppose democracy, still don't much trust the masses; they are afraid that the masses' 'consciousness is low, their cultural level is very low', 'they don't know how to apply democracy', 'they raise excessively high demands', and so, at election time, [they think] it is necessary to circulate a list of names and make the masses 'pledge' that they will elect these people ... the masses will not be the slightest bit interested in this sort of 'democracy', and will not be prepared to act as some sort of 'voting machine'.
>
> (Li Chun 1957)

This is exactly the attitude towards elections found among union cadres in the months immediately following liberation, one which aroused a great deal of discontent then among workers who were being deprived of their democratic rights. It should be remembered that these same union officials who were supposed to run democratic elections for workers' congress representatives had themselves been castigated for undemocratic practices and rigging union committee elections early in 1956, something which casts doubt on their ability or inclination to adhere to democratic principles in organizing workers' congresses.

Overall, in spite of the good intentions of at least some of those concerned, no institutional arrangements were put in place during late 1956 and the first half of 1957 which would have enabled the workers' congress to avoid the fate of its predecessors. What was actually on offer in any case fell far short of the claims made for it by the state-controlled media and the official unions, and even the limited version of the workers' congress which was implemented ran into considerable cadre resistance, with concerns soon voiced that it might encourage workers to demand 'extreme democratization' (*Workers' Daily* 17 April 1957). It is hard to see how any representative or participatory institution could have succeeded in giving workers a say unless party and management cadres were compelled to take notice of it. As it was, cadre attitudes towards workers had not changed, and once proposals for cadre elections were dropped, they were able to ignore congress resolutions whenever it suited them.

Workers vs cadres: the failure of democratic reform

The sheer contempt for workers displayed at this time by many who had power over them is quite startling, and this in an era which is looked back on as a time of 'special closeness between the Chinese people, particularly the working class, and their new socialist government' (Perry 1994: 2). Cases abound where industrial disputes arose because workers were simply lied to in order to get them to do something disadvantageous to them, and cadres' response to resistance was more likely to be punishment, repression and political labelling of protesters than a reconsideration of the issue (Gipouloux 1986: 193–8; Perry 1994: 15–16). Many cadres, faced with workers' grievances, traded shamelessly on the heroic pre-1949 reputation of party and army regardless of whether their own service extended back to that era. When workers in a Guangzhou machine works asked for improved ventilation in a workshop where temperatures regularly reached 110 degrees even in winter, they were told: 'When the Red Army was on the Long March, they managed to survive by eating tree bark, and you're saying when it's a bit warm in the workshop you can't work?' (*Guangzhou Daily* 17 May 1957). Coming from a cadre with an electric fan in his office, this remark provoked outrage rather than a shamefaced withdrawal of the demand. Such attitudes were hard to reconcile with the official insistence that workers and cadres were political equals, with their different roles in the enterprise merely reflecting the division of labour necessary in a modern industrial organization.

One of the better-known disputes of spring 1957, the undeclared strike on the Guangzhou docks – a mass stay-away from work by, at its height, more than half of the total workforce (*Workers' Daily* 9 May 1957; *Guangzhou Daily* 15 June 1957) – is a good example of typical cadre responses to genuine grievances.[2] In brief, the dispute arose because a new, physically demanding shift system (eight hours on and eight off for two days followed by a day off) was driving down the wages which could be earned on piece-rates to the point where workers were actually better off on sick-pay than at work. To force them to work nevertheless, the union was enlisted to help by barring the enterprise clinic's doctors from signing anyone off on sick-leave, and work discipline was tightened to the point where workers arriving a few minutes late would not be allowed to work for the rest of the day, instead being detained by the personnel department for a full eight-hour shift in which they had to write self-criticisms; this time was unpaid, with only a fifty *fen* meal allowance provided (*Southern Daily* 19 May 1957). Thus a shift system which threatened workers' health and safety and drove down wages was being enforced, with union assistance, by means of penalties plucked out of the air by managers determined to force compliance, and workers who did not cooperate were treated like naughty school-children being put in detention. This is one of the more egregious illustrations of the depths to which cadre–worker relations had sunk by 1957, but it is not untypical.

Constant exhortations to workers not to rely on the state for everything also risked a dusty answer, as workers were not slow to point out that if anyone relied on the state for everything, it was the cadres, with their special sanatoria and cadres-only canteens; they, not workers, were 'entering communism ahead of schedule', as the joke went, with everything provided for them according to need (*Workers' Daily* 21 May 1957). The re-launch of the Hundred Flowers as an open party rectification campaign in the spring of 1957 gave the boldest workers scope for outspoken criticism of cadres, as the top leadership had declared open season on bureaucratism, arrogance, separation from the masses, authoritarianism, dishonesty, and misapplication of policy at the lower levels. Mao himself had expressed the view that disturbances were not necessarily a bad thing if they helped to expose bureaucratism, and that the blame for them might more fairly be placed at the door of those cadres who had failed to deal with a grievance when it was first presented rather than with the protestors themselves; the knowledge that the Chairman himself took this line must have acted as an encouragement to discontented workers. Mao showed some awareness of this likely effect in a meeting with local leaders, joking that 'you're not all to go back to your cities and provincial capitals and say there was a meeting in Beijing and now the whole country can go on strike, the Chairman said so [laughter]' (*Mao Zedong Sixiang Wansui!* 1969: 94).

But even if Mao was characteristically sanguine about the prospect of the rank and file giving their bosses a hard time, those lower-level cadres on the receiving end of workers' anger (and occasionally physical violence) could not be expected to share this view (nor, in fact, did some among the national leadership who feared that popular criticism might get out of hand). Cadres at the enterprise level, particularly in joint enterprises, had been under pressure from discontented workers for almost a year by the time the 1957 peak of the strike wave arrived, and as they saw groups of workers abandoning the official unions and organizing themselves, the last thing they were inclined to do was to listen politely to the protests and resolve to mend their ways by enlarging workers' role in decision-making. Instead they became increasingly fearful of any measure which might allow workers to give vent to their feelings, holding back from the democratic discussion which was supposed to take place over, for example, wage-grades and promotions, and also displaying reluctance to implement the revised workers' congress in case this too was used as a forum for attacks on cadres and pressure for 'extreme democratization'.

So the higher levels were encouraging workers, like other citizens, to speak out and expose problems in the workplace, while closer to home cadres fearful of losing control were responding to workers' protests with repression and secrecy rather than a renewed commitment to democracy and participation for the rank and file. A vicious circle thus developed, as the reluctance of enterprise leaders to broaden democracy as a means of defusing workers' discontent led them into repressive measures which actually exacerbated that discontent. When the officially approved, democratic channels for dealing with their grievances were thus denied to workers, they resorted to other methods, including strikes, which in turn confirmed leaders' fears of workers' militancy and extremist tendencies and reinforced their inclination to respond with authoritarian measures, provoking a further escalation in the unrest. The new era in which workers would be able to exercise their rights as 'masters of the enterprise' for the first time was still trumpeted in the press, but it never really began, thanks to the nervousness of cadres already very concerned at the level of resistance and hostility they were facing on the shopfloor. This is the key to the crisis which had developed by May 1957: workers' discontent was being met with quite limited concessions for which exaggerated claims were made in the press and national leaders' statements, while in fact even such improvements in their situation as were on offer were resisted and hampered by cadres at the enterprise level.

The anti-rightist campaign: the end of 'blooming and contending'

The usual explanation offered for the launch of the anti-rightist campaign in June 1957 is that criticism of the party by intellectuals had exceeded Mao's expectations when he launched the movement, extending by May and June 1957 to calls for an end to the CCP's monopoly of political power (MacFarquhar 1960: 87–8, 106–9). The CCP itself tried to portray the Hundred Flowers as a trap set by Mao to tempt rightists into the open, but although this 'cunning plan' theory gained some credence within China, it seems more plausible that although always prepared to deal harshly with any enemies who were exposed during the campaign, Mao did not anticipate the scale and seriousness of the criticism which actually emerged. Moreover, this criticism did not just come from intellectuals. By the time the backlash began, workers too were striking, surrounding enterprise offices, attacking cadres verbally and occasionally physically, and calling them worse than the capitalists of the pre-revolutionary era; the party itself was cast by some as rightist, corrupt, exploitative and privileged (*Guangzhou Daily* 10 June 1957). It is certainly hard to believe that the CCP leadership was fully aware of the depth of the division between workers and their leaders before spring 1957, since it attempted to paper over the cracks with a revised version of democratic institutions which had failed in the past, together with token participation in physical labour on the part of cadres (*Workers' Daily* 1, 3 and 4 May 1957).

The targets of the anti-rightist campaign were all intellectuals of one sort or

another. The fact that only a relatively small number of union leaders were officially branded as rightists and punished for their activities during the Hundred
Flowers period has given the impression that workers did not suffer any reprisals
once the brief interval of liberalization and democracy had come to an end,
being involved in the anti-rightist campaign only to the extent that they 'spoke
out' at meetings organized to condemn the main rightists. One of the first articles to report veteran workers' criticism of rightist intellectuals was somewhat
disingenuously titled 'Workers start to speak up' (*People's Daily* 10 June 1957);
workers had of course been doing precisely this for months, but not in support of
the party. No explicit reference was made during the campaign to the industrial
unrest of the preceding eighteen months which had exposed the crisis in the
party's relationship with the working class, although some of the points made as
veteran workers compared their lives before and after liberation touched on the
issues involved. For example, claims by intellectuals that the CCP was exploitative and lived in luxury at the expense of ordinary people were denied, but with
no hint that broadly the same conclusions had been reached by many workers
(*Guangzhou Daily* 10 June 1957).

But even if it was not publicly acknowledged, given the extent and nature of
workers' protests, it is not credible to suppose that they would escape punishment. As early as January 1957, long before the anti-rightist campaign began,
Mao had warned provincial and municipal party secretaries that nothing short of
a counter-revolutionary revolt should be met with armed force, but the very fact
that such a warning against 'the methods of the Guomindang' (*Mao Zedong
Sixiang Wansui!* 1969: 88) was necessary shows how disturbances were likely to be
dealt with. Once the anti-rightist campaign began, it was much easier to brand
anyone involved in disturbances as a counter-revolutionary (particularly if they
had violated the conditions for legitimate criticism laid down in the revised
version of Mao's speech on contradictions among the people, which was only
now published), and thus to resort to harsher repressive measures. Workers, and
some union officials, were in fact imprisoned and sent to labour camps in the
aftermath of the Hundred Flowers movement, and some were executed, but
only a few were 'labelled as "rightists opposed to the Party and socialism"'
(Bennett and Montaperto 1971: 56). Most were distinguished from the intellectuals by being labelled 'bad elements' (A Chan 1993: 33) rather than rightists, a
term which has criminal rather than political connotations. The state-controlled
press took pains to portray arrested workers as a small minority hoodwinking
others into rebellion, and stressed their allegedly non-proletarian family backgrounds and historical problems (*Chinese Youth* 16 August 1957; *Chongqing Daily*
22 September 1957; *Guangxi Daily* 16 October 1957) in order to give the impression that 'real' workers had remained loyal to the party.

In fact, the workers involved in strikes and disturbances in 1956–7 were
usually a minority of those employed in the enterprise concerned (Perry 1994:
12), and were disproportionately drawn from among the younger sections of the
workforce. It should not surprise us that even with an invitation from Mao
himself to speak out and criticize cadres, many people were reluctant to risk the

'settling of accounts after the autumn harvest', knowing very well that everything they said or did during the course of the campaign could be noted in their file and used against them in future. Anita Chan recently observed that:

> Throughout the Maoist period, much as in Stalinist Russia, it required extraordinary courage – to the point of foolhardiness – to exhibit any truly dissident sentiments. Horrific prison conditions or execution awaited any such effort – and there were very few takers.
>
> (A Chan 1996: 178)

This applied just as much to workers as it did to intellectuals; perhaps even more so, as the latter group had always been regarded as ideologically suspect, while the working class was always referred to as the leading and most progressive force in society and the social base of the ruling party. Working-class criticism of actually existing socialism in China was thus extremely threatening to party legit-imacy. One of the reasons for the greater boldness of apprentices and younger workers might have been that they were less encumbered with family responsibil-ities (as well as having some particularly clear-cut grievances against the authorities), and had less to lose and more to gain by taking the very risky step of overt protest. The extent to which workers felt the effects of repression in the second half of 1957 is shown by the marked reluctance, even nine years after the event, of many workers to get involved in the next major national mass move-ment, the early stages of the Cultural Revolution (Bennett and Montaperto 1971: 56) in spring and summer 1966.

The official unions had played a role in encouraging workers' protests in spring 1957 by their sympathetic attitude towards disturbances. Following Mao's lead, they suggested that the responsibility for strikes and protests should be laid at the door of cadres who had let serious problems develop, not that of the workers involved (*Chinese Worker* June 1957, 11: 4; *Workers' Daily* 11 November 1957). With workers across the country casting aside the official unions and orga-nizing themselves in disputes (*People's Daily* 9 May 1957; *Workers' Daily* 9 May 1957), the ACFTU faced the prospect of complete irrelevance if it could not regain workers' allegiance. In this climate, ACFTU head Lai Ruoyu and other leading officials such as Li Xiuren and Gao Yuan began to formulate a role for the unions in which they would concern themselves mainly or exclusively with the interests and demands of the workers, without the usual riders about the identity of their long-term interests with those of the state; in other words, the unions would now side with the workers rather than the party or management (*Workers' Daily* 22 October, 11, 12 and 19 November 1957).

Gao Yuan was particularly vilified during the anti-rightist campaign for having pointed out that it was legal for groups of workers to organize their own unions outside ACFTU auspices if they so wished (*Workers' Daily* 22 October, 12 and 19 November 1957). All talk of independent unions was blamed on rightist conspira-cies to overthrow the CCP (*Chinese Worker* August 1957, 16: 3), ignoring the fact of spontaneous self-organization and inter-factory liaison by workers in some mid-

1950s disputes. Again, the intention was to give the impression that a few enemies of socialism had stirred up the trouble, rather than admitting the actual extent of resistance and protest among workers themselves. Throughout the second half of 1957 and into 1958, the official unions were subjected to a purge, similar to that of 1951–2, which again left them under the thumb of the party and profoundly unwilling to risk any action or statement which could be construed as a syndicalist attempt to usurp party leadership over the working class, and left workers virtually bereft of any protection of their interests in the workplace.

'Repression, persuasion, or concession'

Despite the severity of the crackdown from June 1957, there was no immediate cessation of the rumblings of discontent from workers; these continued sporadically until the end of the year, and were accompanied by further promotion of democratization and the establishment of workers' congresses, and by a rectification campaign in enterprises in the autumn of 1957 which consisted chiefly of criticism of enterprise leaders by workers as a means of correcting the former's bureaucratist errors. In this way, the CCP attempted to deal harshly with those it considered most culpable, whose words and actions had gone far beyond what was permissible, and to make some limited concessions to the rest who had not gone so far and whose grievances were recognized as legitimate. No less a person than Zhou Enlai admitted that many workers' complaints, particularly those related to wage reform and apprenticeships, were justified and should be dealt with (MacFarquhar 1960: 281–2).

But to keep this continued campaign under control, it was coupled with a 'systematic socialist propaganda and education movement' (*Southern Daily* 12 September 1957) which was intended to strengthen political and ideological education of workers. The same newspaper which announced this campaign in Guangzhou had a few months earlier ridiculed the leadership on the docks for resorting to the 'talisman' of political and ideological education to suppress fully justified protests by workers (*Southern Daily* 19 May 1957), showing the abrupt change in atmosphere which had taken place. The appearance of democratization given by the methods to be used in the campaign, such as 'great debates' and 'free airing of views' (*Southern Daily* 12 September 1957), is belied by the subject matter prescribed for it, namely the correct relationships between democracy and centralism, freedom and discipline, individual and collective interests, and so on. Organized discussion of these issues had long been the standard method of peacefully suppressing unrest among workers.

Reports on the progress of the campaign throughout the second half of 1957 show how the sharp conflict between workers and cadres which had dominated the preceding six months refused to die down. While workers' 'candid and incisive' (*Southern Daily* 5 October 1957) criticisms of their leaders in big-character posters were praised by visiting higher-level officials, such as Guangdong Party Secretary Zhao Ziyang (*Southern Daily* 11 October 1957), they were evidently a little too candid for some of the cadres to whom they referred, who had reportedly restricted the development of the movement by failing to dispel workers' suspicions that the invitation to speak out was some sort of trap (*Southern Daily* 25 October 1957; Gipouloux 1986: 247). Some had also prevented certain posters from being put up, covered them up or even destroyed them, and had taken reprisals against their critics (*Southern Daily* 25 October 1957). But despite the persistence of some workers in asking difficult questions about who really was the master of the enterprise, workers or the party, by the time of the Eighth ACFTU Congress in December 1957, the CCP's application of 'repression, persuasion or concession' (Gipouloux 1986: 256) had been largely successful in bringing to a close this second period of confrontation.

Conclusions

Stemming from the same basic contradiction in workers' relationship with the party as the first confrontation between the two, but taking it a stage further in terms of both political ideas and methods of action, this second confrontation can be seen in some respects as transitional, linking the first outbreak of conflict between workers and the CCP with the third, the Cultural Revolution. Where workers in the early 1950s had criticized their official unions, in 1956–7 they ignored them altogether, preferring to organize themselves in the event of a dispute and confront party authorities directly; and during the Cultural Revolution, such was the degree of animosity felt by workers with regard to the unions that they actually ceased to operate for some years. Similarly, forms of enterprise democratization offered to protesting workers with limited success immediately after liberation were summarily rejected in the second confrontation, as workers began to pose more probing questions about who the masters of the enterprise really were, and by 1966–7 the debate had moved on altogether, from participation in management by workers to 'mass management' with workers in the dominant position. Thus these periodic confrontations, all rooted in the same basic conflict, escalated with each reoccurrence and became progressively harder for the CCP to control.

One important change which took place in this second confrontation was a shift of attention from questions of attitude and workstyle to actual inequalities of power and their consequences. Workers were not simply protesting that cadres *behaved* as if they were old-style bureaucrats or capitalists, bossing workers about and treating them with disdain, but that they actually possessed power over workers' lives which allowed them to take decisions in an autocratic and arbitrary way, and that workers had no legitimate power available to them to counteract this. This is why the workers' congress was rejected as soon as it became apparent that it would not be allowed to become an institution with real power in the enterprise, with workers instead going back to the illegitimate methods of industrial unrest and causing disturbances which seemed to them to be the only ones which had any effect.

This imbalance of power between workers and cadres was of course not a new development, but the more time passed after liberation, and the more the party's reputation became tarnished by cadre privilege and corruption and the failure of improvements in workers' conditions to keep pace with improvements in production, the more starkly it appeared. All the different points of contention in this second confrontation, from corrupt and undemocratic practices during wage reform, unfair housing allocation, and the failure of promised welfare benefits to materialize, to the criticism, labelling, and punishment of workers expressing legitimate grievances, came down to this inequality of power. The party never admitted it, and even at the height of the conflict workers too spoke mainly of attitudes and workstyles (keeping to established practice in officially-sanctioned criticism campaigns), but their ready resort to withdrawing their labour and organizing themselves shows their awareness of their own lack of power if they kept to the structures of participation and representation which had been set up for them. They quickly realized that the new system of workers' congresses would not give them any real authority in the enterprise, and so rejected it, with some refusing even to elect representatives (*Southern Daily* 3 June 1957).

This focus on the question of power brings us to an idea which would become increasingly important in discussions of the conflict between workers and their leaders, playing a vital role in particular in the third confrontation which began with the launch of the Cultural Revolution. This is the idea that the bureaucracy, including its lowest level, the enterprise bureaucracy, can constitute a new 'class' or stratum wielding political power over the workers. The idea that cadres could become detached from workers and begin to act as a privileged class or stratum as the process of bureaucratic routinization set in was behind one of the most important policies in industry during the Great Leap Forward, that of the 'two participations', i.e. the participation of workers in management and of cadres in manual labour (the latter, the beginnings of which we have already seen as part of the party's response to rebellious workers in 1957, was particularly strongly emphasized). A rather defensive theoretical article published in December 1957, before this policy really began to be promoted, provided tacit acknowledgement of the dangers inherent in the division of labour, claiming that:

> It is true that, comparatively speaking, the personnel of state organs do not take a direct part in productive labour but directly exercise the administrative power, while the people take a direct part in productive labour and do not directly exercise administrative power. But it does not follow from this that the personnel of the state organs form a privileged class standing above the people and that the contradictions between the Government and the people are the contradictions between this so-called 'privileged class' and the people who do not enjoy such privilege.
>
> (Fu Rong 1957: 20)

But in spite of protestations that the socialist ownership of the means of production would prevent such an occurrence, during the Socialist Education Movement in the early 1960s the danger of the emergence of a new bureaucratic class was frequently mentioned by Mao. He warned that:

If the management staff do not go down to the [production] teams in work-shops, practice 'three togethernesses' [with workers], and treat workers as teachers and learn [from them], they will end up in a fierce, life-long class struggle with the working class. Eventually they as the bourgeois class will be defeated by the working class.

(P N Lee 1987: 100)

As Maurice Meisner has described it,

In a society that has abolished private property and private ownership of the means of production, Mao early recognized that the principal social contra-diction is no longer primarily economic but rather political, the elemental distinction between those who hold political power and those who do not . . . between (as Mao put it in 1957) the leadership and the led. From there he was inexorably driven to the conclusion that China's bureaucrats were becoming a new exploiting class . . . 'bourgeois elements sucking the blood of the workers' – in effect, a functional (albeit propertyless) bour-geoisie able to exploit society and appropriate much of the fruits of social labour by virtue of the political power they wielded.

(Meisner 1983: 123)

Much more will be said about the debate on exploitation and class in the context of relations between workers and enterprise authorities in later chapters, and in particular with reference to the Cultural Revolution. For now it is sufficient to note that the protests of restive workers in 1956–7 were already starting to touch upon these ideas, indicating the seriousness of the crisis in their relationship with the party only seven years after liberation.

The 1956–7 industrial unrest cannot be dismissed as merely another outbreak of economism among workers (Harper 1969: 100). Studies of workers in other socialist countries point out that the 'latent political content and overt political significance' (Pravda 1981: 56) of such activities as absenteeism and go-slows should not be disregarded even if they are prompted by mainly economic demands. In Eastern Europe it appears that when protests broke out among workers, 'dissatisfaction with economic progress promote[d] political and social dissatisfaction that tend[ed] to spill over quickly into more radical worker demands for political and workplace liberalization, especially in the form of workers' councils' (Tyson 1981: 130). We can see the beginnings of a similar process in China in 1956–7, as the final years of the First Five-Year Plan saw the 'usual progression from economic to sociopolitical demands' (Montias 1981: 173) beginning to develop among workers. Although workers' self-organization at this time was limited (Gipouloux 1986: 211), being mostly confined to a single enter-prise and of relatively short duration, given a few more weeks or months before the reimposition of repressive controls, workers' activities in China might well have developed in this direction.

Certainly the experience of autonomous, collective political action which many workers gained through their involvement in independent mass organizations in the Cultural Revolution between 1966 and 1969, as well as the effect of this activity on their attitudes to authority, made the formation of independent unions more of a possibility in the event of conflict with enterprise or higher authorities in the late 1970s and 1980s, as we shall see in subsequent chapters of this study. Although the unrest of 1956–7 cannot really be classed as national in scope, since it involved no nationwide organization or coordination of action by workers, it did occur in virtually every Chinese industrial centre, bringing it close to the sort of nationwide disturbance identified by Mao as a sign of errors in the party's overall line, rather than merely its methods or policies. It is clear from his comments in 1957 that, had those involved in the disturbances attempted to organize themselves in the same way as activists in the Workers' Autonomous Federations did in 1989, they would have met with a similar response from the regime: even if errors of line resulted in protests reaching all the way to West Chang'an Avenue in Beijing,[3] he asserted, 'as long as we build up the army, we will not lose the country' (*Mao Zedong Sixiang Wansui!* 1969: 87). The severity of the repressive measures to which the Chinese leadership was prepared to resort testifies to the seriousness of this second confrontation; during the Cultural Revolution, the third confrontation, it did in fact become necessary to send the army in to restore order in factories, marking a further escalation in the conflict.

3 'Hard work and plain living', 1958–65

Through the autumn and winter of 1957 the policy of combining suppression, persuasion and limited concessions restored order in enterprises, stifled workers' protests, and stopped in its tracks the trend towards the formation by workers of their own, small-scale independent organizations. Yet in the autumn and winter of 1966, workers began forming unprecedentedly large organizations of their own, first illegally and then with the blessing of some top-level leaders, and a wave of protest involving millions swept through urban China, the force of which threatened to push the Cultural Revolution in entirely unintended directions. To describe what happened in these months as a crisis in workers' relationship with party-state authorities is something of an understatement, since the actions of some for a short period constituted an all-out attack on those authorities in an attempt to overthrow them completely. In this chapter we will look at what happened in enterprises over the nine years after the end of the Hundred Flowers, examining how old issues developed and new ones emerged to create groups of workers who by 1966 were only too ready to answer Mao's call for rebellion.

The Great Leap Forward

Even while it denied the very existence of working-class protest during the Hundred Flowers, let alone the political content of such protest, the party showed by its actions that it had in fact understood the seriousness of the hostility between leaders and led in factories. Following on from the December 1957 article quoted in the last chapter, the national and labour movement press returned time and again to issues of the political consequences of the division of labour in enterprises and workers' status and role under socialism, protesting perhaps too much that workers really were 'the masters' (despite the fact that others could determine where they worked, what they earned, where they lived, and even when and to whom they got married). At the same time as the improvements in pay and conditions for which workers had fought in the strikes of 1956–7 were being condemned and withdrawn, other policies of the Great Leap Forward (GLF) in industry were specifically designed to try to tackle the growing divisions between workers and cadres, and in particular to remind the latter that their exercise of management powers over production workers was merely the job to which they were assigned and not a form of political power or superiority.

Worker–cadre relations and the 'two participations'

An example of this is the Leap policy of 'two participations' (of workers in management and cadres in physical labour), 'one reform' (of irrational rules, regulations and systems in enterprises), and 'three-in-one technical groups' (of workers, technicians and cadres working together on technical reforms and innovations), commonly known as the 'two-one-three' policy. A *People's Daily* editorial on an early pioneer of the policy, the Qinghua Machine Tool Plant in Heilongjiang, stressed its political benefits above all else, admitting that relations between cadres and workers were sometimes not so different from those of the pre-revolutionary era:

> Politically [workers and cadres] are absolutely equal and their relations at work are comradely relations which are fundamentally different from the relations of exploitation and oppression between the managers and workers of the old society. But . . . certain survivals of the old relations of production are still constantly found between them.
>
> (*People's Daily* 7 May 1958)

Thus the 'two-one-three' policy was necessary 'radically to change the thinking and working style of cadres' who did not treat workers as equals and issued orders from the safety of their offices, seldom being seen on the factory floor and never getting their hands dirty with physical labour. The 'two participations' were singled out as especially important as 'a strong proof that in a socialist enterprise there is only a difference in division of labour and duties and no difference in social status between the leader and the led' (*People's Daily* 7 May 1958).

The 'two participations' policy is most strongly associated with the Great Leap Forward of 1958–60, but it continued to be emphasized to a greater or lesser extent into the mid-1960s. Initially introduced in response to workers' criticisms, cadre participation in labour had been stressed since the spring of 1957 as a valuable method for tackling bureaucratism, bringing cadres closer to the rank and file workforce and preventing their political degeneration. However, its success in reforming the arrogant and high-handed attitudes which did so much to fuel workers' protests in 1956–7 is questionable to say the least. The profoundly anti-cadre and anti-authority character of the Cultural Revolution among many workers (Liu Guokai 1987: 46) suggests that it had very little success in mitigating the 'them-and-us' antagonism in enterprises so evident during the Hundred Flowers period; the attacks on cadres' bureaucratism and lack of concern for workers during the nationwide wave of 'counter-revolutionary economism' among workers in December 1966 and January 1967 were strongly reminiscent of those made in 1956–7. It thus seems unlikely that participation in labour brought about any major or lasting change in cadres' attitudes. Andors has noted that '[b]y itself, participation did not lead to better and more egalitarian relationships between workers and managers. Cadres had to change subtle aspects of their behaviour' (Andors 1977a: 72).

Where cadres did go down to the shopfloor, this did not always have the desired effect of dispelling workers' hostility towards their leaders. Many cadres lacked the necessary skills to participate in productive labour, and so tended to end up hanging around on the factory floor leaning on a broom for much of the time (*Southern Daily* 22 September 1964), in which situation, far from appreciating cadres' presence among them, workers generally suspected them of using 'participation' as an opportunity to supervise workers more closely (Andors 1977a: 73), or even to spy on them. There were also reports indicating widespread reluctance among cadres to participate in labour, with one early article finding that they had to be 'driven' to participate (*People's Daily* 27 November 1958); 'nominal' participation, avoiding any dirty or strenuous work, was also noted (*Southern Daily* 22 September 1964). It should be said in their defence, however, that cadres' reluctance stemmed in part from a genuine and quite well-founded conviction that regular participation in manual labour was not compatible with the efficient performance of their other duties (*People's Daily* 7 August 1963).

The other half of the 'two participations', workers' participation in management, initially seemed to offer 'a further expansion of democracy in the management of enterprises ... a new form of direct participation of the workers in management' (*People's Daily* 26 April 1958), by allowing workers at the production-team level to take over certain tasks, such as attendance and production record-keeping, planning, management of tools, quality inspection, and maintenance of equipment (Chung 1980: 147). This new form of direct participation was not intended to replace the representative system of workers' congresses, which was to continue alongside it, but was seen as putting management 'on an even broader mass basis' (*People's Daily* 26 April 1958), further strengthening mass supervision and participation. Clearly, a policy of more direct participation in management should have been a major step forward in meeting workers' demands for more influence in the workplace, yet there were a number of reasons why it proved a disappointment in practice.

One limitation was inherent in the system: participation was limited to the level of the production team. This aspect of the policy drew particularly harsh criticism from Soviet observers of China (as ever, far more vitriolic about their fraternal socialist ally than any anti-communist could have been) who, noting that 'participation was very modest and occurred only at the lowest level with little possibility of influencing the enterprise plan', condemned the party's rhetoric on the subject as ' "social demagoguery that was directed at the creation of illusions in the working class" ' (Rozman 1985: 120). But even at the team level, not all workers had an opportunity to participate: figures for 1960, according to Wang Haofeng of the Heilongjiang Provincial CCP Committee, the main promoter of the policy, showed that 30 to 50 per cent of workers were involved (Wang Haofeng 1960: 9) and this percentage 'seemed to have been even less in 1958 and 1959' (Chung 1980: 147, n. 53). It seems likely that this figure represented relatively high levels of participation in a small number of 'model' enterprises where the policy was first tried out and experiments went furthest, but fairly low levels elsewhere.

Workers' participation in management does seem to have been the most problematic component of the 'two-one-three' policy, not least because of the 'active and passive resistance of cadres' (Andors 1977a: 73; *People's Daily* 7 August 1963) which Stephen Andors finds to have been the 'major obstacle' (Andors 1977a: 70) to its implementation. As we saw earlier with the WRC, even where structures for representation and participation exist which have the potential to give workers a significant role in decision-making, cadre attitudes can render them virtually useless to workers. This seems to have been the case with GLF participation in management, where some workers' own lack of enthusiasm for the policy could be traced to the intimidatory effect of cadres' known opposition to it (Andors 1977a: 77). As the retreat from the GLF gathered pace from 1961, variations in the degree and importance of workers' participation continued to exist, but in general this aspect of the 'two-one-three' policy declined more than either cadre participation in labour (which gained renewed emphasis as the Cultural Revolution-era preoccupation with the political degeneration of those in power began to take hold (*Southern Daily* 22 September 1964; *People's Daily* 24 September 1965), or the three-in-one technical groups. Some regional and sectoral variation is evident, with a greater persistence with workers' participation in heavy industry (dominant in the northeast), while light industrial management (more prominent further south in cities like Shanghai and Guangzhou) remained 'closely related to pre-1949 methods' with cadres 'less likely to accept the GLF revolutionary concepts of human relationships' such as the equality of workers, technicians and cadres (Andors 1977a: 77).

Unions during the Leap

Another factor undermining workers' ability to take advantage of the 'two participations' policy, or to make use of the workers' congress, a form which continued to exist throughout these years, was the lack of powerful union support. Again, this is something we noted as an obstacle to meaningful participation by workers in the early post-liberation period and in 1956–7. Union organizations had been purged in the anti-rightist campaign of 1957 and again in 1958, a year which saw a debate on whether there was any point in the unions' continuing to exist (*Workers' Daily* 3 February 1958). ACFTU head Lai Ruoyu had already become ill during 1957 as the anti-rightist campaign developed; he died during 1958, and was succeeded by Liu Ningyi, under whom 'the ACFTU became a docile tool of the Party' (Lee Lai To 1984: 65). Although the CCP did wish the unions to continue to exist, this was now only for the purpose of indoctrinating workers and mobilizing them more effectively for production, and was on condition of total obedience to the party (*Xinhua News Agency* 3 September 1957; *Workers' Daily* 11 July 1958).

Lai's illness and untimely death exempted him from the purge of all those who had been outspoken in their support of workers' protests, but there were other prominent victims. The editor of the *Workers' Daily*, Chen Yongwen, was branded a 'class dissident' who had refused to print party propaganda while making great efforts to gather the 'incorrect views' of a few 'backward workers' and using these to incite workers to oppose management and the party and government (in fact, 1956–7 was a rare period in which the voices of real workers could be heard in the *Workers' Daily*; they were seldom heard there again until the late 1970s). It was claimed that under Chen's leadership, the *Workers' Daily* had more or less invented the trade union 'crisis' of 1956–7 as well as dwelling on the 'dark side' of workers' lives; just for good measure, accusations of a bourgeois background and a corrupt private life were added to the charge-sheet (*Workers' Daily* 13 August 1958). The other main labour movement organ, the monthly *Chinese Worker*, which had been so frank during 1956–7 about the crisis within the unions, ceased publication altogether during 1958 and did not reappear until after the Cultural Revolution. All things considered, the official unions were left in their weakest position yet and were very unlikely to be able to support workers in exercising increased influence at any level in the enterprise.

Welfare and conditions during the Leap

As well as undermining the possibility of meaningful participation in manage-ment, the weakness of the unions must also have contributed to other problems for workers during the GLF, such as the rescinding of many of the concessions on welfare and livelihood which had been won in the strikes of 1957. Demands made during that period were invariably characterized as 'excessive' (*Workers' Daily* 3 February 1958), while the main problem in welfare work was now identi-fied as the fact that 'the enterprise takes too much care of the staff's welfare' (*People's Electricity Industry* 20 February 1958). The press strove to create the impression that workers themselves were in the forefront of the return to 'plain living' (*Workers' Daily* 7 July 1958), voluntarily giving up over-generous welfare benefits which they saw as an insult to their proletarian values of frugality and sacrifice.

In the case of piece-rate wages the argument that workers themselves pushed for abolition is more plausible, as this form of pay had always proved divisive and was at the root of some of the bitterest disputes over wage reform in 1956–7; it is evident that many workers supported the move away from piece-rates, even if they did not initiate it. However, the claim that large numbers of workers were also volunteering to give up overtime pay and bonuses for the sake of 'building socialism with more, better, faster and more economical results' (*Liberation Daily* 19 October 1958) should be treated with much greater scepti-cism, not least because excessive overtime was such a serious problem in many enterprises during the GLF. Given the angry reaction to the ingenious schemes devised to avoid giving workers the overtime pay to which they were legally enti-tled in 1956–7, it seems unlikely that workers' attitudes towards compulsory, excessive and unpaid overtime had undergone such a complete transformation in barely two years, however much ideological education they were subjected to.

One of the bleakest assessments of workers' experiences during the GLF is that of the Soviet sinologist A P Davydov, who finds that during these years, workers

> were made to labour almost without rest. Exhausted by that gruelling experience, they then experienced the years of hunger and, for many, relocation to villages. The Great Leap Forward was characterized by reduced worker participation in management, wages that provided little incentive to diligent work, unconcern about well-being of workers . . . the rate of accidents sharply increased.
>
> (Rozman 1985: 117)

Blunt as they are, these comments are not untypical and evidence can be found to support them with regard to the three main points: participation, safety, and overtime. We have already seen that both workers' direct participation in management and their supervision of cadres through the workers' congress were undermined by cadres' lack of commitment, or even hostility, to these institutions, as well as by the weakness of the unions, purged and now under very tight party control.

Fears that safety was being sacrificed in the pursuit of ever higher production quotas surfaced very early in the GLF (*Workers' Daily* 26 March 1958), and reappeared frequently thereafter. Furthermore, the increase in accidents observable during the GLF came on top of an already high rate identified as a cause of concern following nationalization in early 1956. The regular appeals to cadres to view safety measures as a help, not a hindrance, to increased production seem to have had little effect, apparently unable to compete with the enormous pressure on all enterprises to meet by whatever means necessary the impossibly high targets set in this period. The extent of the safety problem in these years is well illustrated by a *Workers' Daily* editorial *promoting* safety in production, which nonetheless also includes praise for the 'advanced experience' of a certain enterprise in carrying out cleaning and maintenance of machines without stopping them (*Workers' Daily* 9 June 1959). 'Innovations' of this sort initially drew great praise in the party-controlled press, despite the fact that there was nothing inherently proletarian, revolutionary or progressive about losing one's fingers in a machine while proving that it could be operated faster if the safety-guard was removed.

As for excessive overtime, the problem of overwork was quite frankly acknowledged in the press by 1960 (*Workers' Daily* 26 July 1960), although it was attributed, not very plausibly, to workers' own excessive enthusiasm for production (the era when flashes of honesty in the press became ever fewer and further between had already begun; it culminated in the Cultural Revolution, by the end of which many newspapers had degenerated into almost unreadable compilations of slogans and polemical abuse). As late as 1965, editorials on combining labour and rest in correct proportions were still appearing, indicating a very persistent problem (*People's Daily* 21 June 1965). This aspect of the situation in enterprises must be kept in mind when evaluating the extent and significance of workers' participation in management during the GLF. Since participation in certain production-team management tasks was to be done in workers' spare time, on top of the usual eight hours of production work, overwork and poor safety standards must have greatly undermined workers' enthusiasm and ability with regard to these extra tasks.

Finally, it should be noted that many of the problems of overwork and neglect of safety during this period are directly attributable to the 'one reform' component of the 'two-one-three' policy, i.e. the reform of irrational regulations and systems in enterprises. Intended to promote the revision of 'those regulations and systems that restrict the activism of the masses and the development of their productivity' (*People's Daily* 26 April 1958), this policy instead resulted in measures essential to safety at work being abolished as 'irrational', without any adequate replacement first being developed by 'the masses' (*Workers' Daily* 9 June and 19 July 1959). This is a clear example of a measure intended to benefit workers, not least by facilitating their participation in management and breaking down some of the unnecessarily rigid regulations by which cadres exercised control in the enterprise, actually having a very negative impact on vital aspects of their conditions of work.

It is now well known that the GLF resulted in a widespread famine in the countryside which claimed as many as 30 million lives in 1959–61 (Becker 1996). Although there is little evidence of actual starvation in the cities, the effects of food shortages were clearly felt, and the overall impact of the nationwide damage to living standards and economic output was significant for urban workers. As shortages of rural materials and markets worsened, more industrial workers found themselves laid off and often forced to return to the countryside. The pain was not shared equally throughout the urban workforce, however, as the fault lines evident during the Hundred Flowers period became even clearer, with permanent, unionized workers in the larger state factories at an advantage, while 'the contract workers were the first to be sent back to their villages' (L T White 1989: 159). As well as this direct 'support for agricultural production', workers were also strongly encouraged to grow their own food wherever possible, using vacant land around factories and even roadside verges as vegetable plots in an effort to achieve food self-sufficiency (*Workers' Daily* 20 July 1959, 2 April 1961).

As had happened during the anti-rightist campaign, politically-reliable veteran workers were again mobilized in organized sessions 'to show how much worse the pre-1949 situation had been' (L T White 1989: 162). But despite the down-playing of the catastrophic effects of the GLF as merely 'temporary and local difficulties' (*Workers' Daily* 2 April 1961), it is evident from many articles in the press purporting to explain how to improve workers' welfare and living standards that what is actually being discussed is a desperate response to an economic and social crisis, hence all the talk of self-sufficiency and praise for model workers who could make do and mend anything from their factory's equipment to co-workers' worn-out cooking-pans and socks (*Workers' Daily* September 1961 *passim*). Workers' families were brought into the campaign, with 'model dependent' titles awarded to those spouses who 'would not waste even one grain of rice, one drop of water, one lump of coal, or a single match' (*Workers' Daily* 14 September 1961). There were some reports of strikes during the GLF (Lee Lai To 1986: 104), but in general workers and their families were kept too busy with the drive to fulfil production quotas and to make ends meet at home for any widespread rebellion against the impositions on them to develop.

The end of the Great Leap Forward

With the GLF manifestly a failure, from 1961 onwards industrial policy and management were characterized in practice by a general retreat from the 'mass line' of the GLF. But this did not mean that the latter was completely discredited or repudiated. On the contrary, the GLF line still had its powerful partisans, notably Mao. The outlines of what came to be known as the 'two-line struggle' in industry can be discerned in the debates of the early 1960s, as the 'revisionist' and 'revolutionary' programmes for enterprise management began to coalesce around the Seventy Articles[1] and the Anshan Constitution[2] respectively. With Mao's endorsement of the Anshan Constitution in 1960, 'the issue of the mass line in industrial management continued to become politicized' (P N Lee 1987: 67). In broad terms, the Anshan Constitution (closely identified with Mao's line all through the Cultural Revolution and in the Gang of Four's disputes with Deng Xiaoping in the 1970s) stood for: politics in command in enterprises; stronger party leadership in management and politics; mass movements and the methods of mass mobilization in enterprises; the continuation of the GLF's 'two-one-three' policy; and technical revolution (*Guangming Daily* 21 March 1970).

If the Anshan Constitution could thus be seen as upholding the GLF emphasis on the mass line in industry and associated policies, then the Seventy Articles were 'essentially aimed at negating the GLF experiments and returning to one-man management' (Andors 1977a: 129), with the stress on the primacy of the economic role of enterprises and of production (economics in command, as the Cultural Revolution polemics had it); the authority of the factory director and the chief engineer; strict responsibility systems and regulations and tighter labour discipline; material incentives and some reintroduction of piece-rates; and less political study (P N Lee 1987: 87–93). Of course, the distinction between these two 'lines' was not as clear-cut in theory or in practice as it might appear from the outline above. Yet neither was the so-called 'two-line struggle' in industrial management a total fiction: there were real issues behind the debate which concerned not only top-level leaders but also workers themselves.

Although the results of the GLF were often inimical in the extreme to workers' interests, this was mainly due to the continual upward revision of production targets already at unrealistically high levels and the consequent pressure to increase production at all costs, and to the general sharp economic decline which the Leap engendered. The stated aims of GLF policies in industry, however, did not necessarily run contrary to workers' interests and aspirations: workers did want to participate more in management; they did want cadres to lose their arrogant disdain for workers and reform their workstyle by coming out of their offices and participating in productive labour; and they did want their suggestions for innovation and reform taken seriously and, if feasible, implemented promptly, rather than being shunted off into some labyrinthine process of upward referral and endless discussion. So support for GLF policies both at the highest and lowest level did exist, and to a certain extent continued in the 1961–6 period.

Needless to say, GLF-era austerity measures affecting pay, bonuses and welfare would have been much less welcome to workers, and they ended up in effect with the worst of both worlds, as the material incentives condemned as extravagant, bourgeois and divisive were abolished without, however, being replaced by the non-material or political incentive of a real change in workers' role and status in the enterprise. Thus as the GLF developed, '[r]evolutionary rhetoric not backed by worker participation in management and cadre participation in labour could lead to cynicism' (Andors 1977a: 150), which in turn would precipitate a shift away from these sorts of political incentives and back to material incentives. But this is an example of the tendency already observed whereby the discrepancy between official rhetoric about workers' position as the masters of the enterprise and their actual experience in the workplace creates disillusionment and discontent. It should not be mistaken for the out-and-out rejection by workers of political incentives such as increased participation in management and more control over their own work. Rather, the failure of these incentives to materialize (mainly because of cadre opposition) led to dissatisfaction which could only undermine performance, necessitating greater reliance on other forms of incentives which could actually be implemented.

Enterprises under the Seventy Articles (1961–5)

Although workers' interests, like those of virtually all ordinary citizens, generally suffered as a result of the GLF, this did not necessarily translate into great support for the policies, based on the Seventy Articles, which despite some high-level opposition began to replace the GLF line from 1961. It has already been noted that these policies in many ways represented a return to one-man management (Andors 1977a: 129), with a strengthening of the authority of the factory director, the chief engineer (P N Lee 1987: 89) and administrative and technical staff in general. One-man management and the cadre attitudes which tended to accompany it had been a major cause of the discontent and protests which built up during 1956–7, so a certain amount of resentment among workers at the resurrection of such policies could be expected once relief at the end of the Leap began to wear off. Additionally, if the GLF had disdained material incentives completely, under the Seventy Articles improved pay and benefits were only on offer to a limited group of unionized state workers, while many others lost out (L T White 1989: 184–5).

Policies based on the Seventy Articles were 'intensively implemented' (P N

Lee 1987: 91) between 1961 and 1966, and any adjustments made seem to have resulted from pressure from Mao:

> For instance, a fresh effort was made to institutionalize the cadres' participation in manual labour . . . an attempt was made to accommodate workers' participation in managerial functions through an institutionalized, rather than a mobilizational, channel (the congress of the representatives of workers and staff).
>
> (P N Lee 1987: 88)

But the revision of the Seventy Articles suggested by Mao in September 1962 at the 10th Plenum of the Eighth Party Congress was not carried out until 1965, and few changes were actually made even then (P N Lee 1987: 92). However, sensitivity to workers' likely opposition can be detected in early articles on the new direction in enterprise management, where it was often stressed that management systems were not intended to control workers, but merely reflected their own practical experience (*Liberation Daily* 5 June 1961). A distinction was made between the operation of, for example, responsibility systems in socialist enterprises, which were said to reflect 'the comradely and mutually cooperative relations between the workers', and systems such as Taylorism, which Lenin 'most appropriately called . . . the "blood and sweat system of science"' (*Economic Research* 3 August 1962: 30). The debate on what constituted rational and necessary regulations and what rules and systems designed for 'control, check and suppression'[3] of workers continued well into the 1970s, but these concerns were clearly already present in the aftermath of the GLF. As the retreat from the Leap gathered pace, it once again became difficult to explain how exactly the relationship between workers and managers in China's socialist enterprises differed from that in capitalist ones.

To help demonstrate the difference, the 'two participations' were continued into the mid-1960s, although since their impact had been so limited even at the height of the Leap, it is hard to see how they could have much effect as older patterns of authority in the enterprise reasserted themselves. Cadres' participation in labour received renewed emphasis as part of the Socialist Education Movement (SEM) from the end of 1962. With the ideological fervour of the GLF receding, the practical difficulty of finding suitable production tasks which cadres could usefully do was acknowledged as a real problem from about the middle of 1963. The search for improved practical methods of participation was, however, accompanied by a strong emphasis on the political importance and benefits of participation (*Red Flag* 10 July 1963; *People's Daily* 22 September 1964; *Southern Daily* 22 September 1964).

Yet articles on improved systems for participation from this time still identify cadre resistance as a significant problem, and their portrayal of the majority of enterprise cadres indicates that little progress had been made since 1957 in improving workstyles and overcoming bureaucratism, as can be seen from this description of cadres at the Guangzhou Chemical Works:

[S]ome leadership cadres were seriously affected by bourgeois individualism . . . for a long time they estranged themselves from the masses and from reality and . . . made rather grave errors of bureaucratism and commandism. . . . Among the leadership cadres, some indulged in an extravagant life and demanded privileges. Some individual cadres even succumbed to bribery and thievery and became degenerate.

(*Southern Daily* 22 September 1964)

Despite the renewed emphasis from mid-1963 on the necessity of cadre partici-pation in labour as 'an effective guarantee against corruption by bourgeois thinking' (*People's Daily* 22 September 1964), in 1965 we find that:

Massive and overlapping administration, detailed and anomalous scholasti-cist regulations, complicated administrative procedures, and the pompous airs of administrative personnel which separate them from production and alienate them from the masses continue to be the common defects of many industrial enterprises.

(*People's Daily* 24 September 1965)

Evidently the 'revolution in enterprise management', which this article identifies as having begun a year earlier, had yet to make much progress in breaking down the 'invisible barrier' (*Southern Daily* 22 September 1964) between workers and cadres which had caused so much resentment and hostility over the past ten years.

Renewed efforts to promote the workers' congress are also evident from the end of 1961, but the emphasis was now always on the role of the congress in solving production problems and increasing productivity (*Workers' Daily* 11 November 1961; *Red Flag* 16 January 1962). This showed, first, that the workers' congress was being revived after the GLF largely because more direct (although low-level) forms of participation were no longer in favour; second, that workers' role in the enterprise was now for the most part restricted to matters directly connected to production; and third, that cadre resistance to the implementation of the congress system necessitated a strong emphasis on its beneficial, not harmful, effect on production. But in spite of signs of revival of the workers' congress in 1961, this and other concessions to workers unhappy with the influ-ence of the Seventy Articles in industry made little headway until 1965.

In that year it was announced that in some enterprises the system of workers' congresses had been 'overhauled and improved' as part of the SEM. The inten-tion was to remedy defects such as the use of congress meetings simply to give instructions to workers and concomitant neglect of their opinions, and the prac-tice whereby 'the workers' representatives were nominated by the leadership. Most of them were cadres' (*Workers' Daily* 13 October 1965). Monthly 'demo-cratic life meetings' organized by the enterprise union committee also began to be promoted towards the end of 1965 as a forum where workers could speak out freely, report on conditions at the shopfloor level and participate in democratic problem-solving (*Workers' Daily* 9 October 1965). But there is nothing in any of the 1965 accounts of how the system was to be improved which would lead one to expect a significant increase in meaningful participation by workers in the running of their enterprises by means of the workers' congress. So it seems that neither of the 'two participations' was able to make significant progress while the Seventy Articles were in force in industry, in spite of renewed political pressure for their implementation as the SEM gathered momentum; nor did the workers' congress enable production workers to bring much influence to bear on enterprise decision-making.

Hierarchy and division: enterprises on the eve of the Cultural Revolution

As the SEM sought to re-politicize China's citizens through the early 1960s, the discrepancy between the radical leftist rhetoric of the state press and workers' actual experience of factory life under the Seventy Articles became ever greater. The accident rates during the GLF were held up by managers as a justification for the overwhelming emphasis on discipline and obedience in these years, even while political concern built up among those on the left that enterprise systems and regulations were being formulated by cadres to control or 'rule over' workers. The growing tendency was to see the relations between cadres and workers in an enterprise as those between a minority who had power and a majority who did not, or between 'rulers' and 'ruled'.

We have already seen how during the GLF the movement to reform irrational regulations and systems led to the removal of vital safety measures as well as genuinely superfluous rules, and thus contributed to the high rate of industrial accidents and poor working conditions in these years. But it must be remembered that, along with the 'two participations', this 'one reform' policy was in part intended to correct the impression, which had gained ground among many workers in 1956–7, that cadres in their enterprises and above constituted a separate, privileged group which had great power over workers' lives, including the power to make the rules in enterprises. Giving workers a stronger role in reforming regulations would be one concrete way in which their theoretical status as the masters of the enterprise could actually begin to become a reality. It is in this context that the criticism, from 1964 onwards, of excessive regulations in enterprises designed specifically to *control* workers should be understood:

> In some cases, leading cadres of a number of enterprises have even set up sections and sub-units as well as other administrative organs for the purpose of controlling workers. They have laid down regulations and instituted systems for the express purpose of bringing workers into line. . . . It is wrong for the leadership and administrative personnel of enterprises to stress 'control' and their authority, to make every decision, and to act in accordance with the dead letter of the regulations instead of trusting and relying on the working masses.
>
> (*People's Daily* 24 September 1965)

While some backtracking on GLF reforms for the sake of safety was obviously necessary, it is clear that the Seventy Articles, with their emphasis on the over-riding authority of administrative and technical cadres, gave free rein to those enterprise officials who preferred a very clear division of labour whereby they gave instructions and the workers followed them. Workers' position in the enter-prise was summed up in the saying: 'The leadership makes the laws, the managers enforce the laws, and the workers obey the laws' (Gong Xiaowen 1976: 67). It is important to bear in mind that this issue of excessive regulation and control of workers was not just a convenient stick with which leftists such as the Gang of Four could beat 'revisionists' like Deng Xiaoping, but that workers' resentment at petty regulations governing even the time they were allowed to spend in the toilet[4] (P N Lee 1977: 90–1) was real, and was building up in the years immediately preceding the Cultural Revolution while the Seventy Articles held sway in industry:

> The deep-rooted feeling was that the workers were excluded from mean-ingful participation in making decisions about production and industrial operations that constituted an intimate part of their lives ... the workers operated machinery, used equipment and manufactured products, yet they were not permitted to have any say about their work environment. Instead, 'experts' controlled every move of the workers and every step of the opera-tion or process. While excluding workers from participation in management, the experts did not necessarily do a better job.
>
> (P N Lee 1977: 91)

Resentment of strict discipline, and a combative attitude among workers towards those who tried to enforce it, crop up repeatedly in reports on conflict in indus-trial enterprises even at the end of the mass-movement phase of the Cultural Revolution in 1969 (*China News Analysis* 15 August 1969), and continued indisci-pline and 'anarchy' in enterprises, blamed on the influence of the Cultural Revolution, was a frequent complaint in the late 1970s and early 1980s. Even now, the potential of excessive regulation and discipline to arouse strong feelings among Chinese workers should not be underestimated (*Far Eastern Economic Review* 18 November 1993: 63–4).

Temporary and contract employment: the worker-peasant system

One final feature of the industrial landscape of the early 1960s which helped to fuel workers' protests during the Cultural Revolution was the so-called 'worker-peasant' system of temporary and contract employment.[5] By 1966 it was not only the workers actually employed on these terms who had cause for protest, but also many of those still benefitting from permanent employment status who nevertheless feared that they might soon be forced into contract working.

The disadvantages to the worker of contract or temporary employment had been clear since the late 1950s. During the strike wave of 1957, temporary workers had been among the protesters, expressing their resentment at having no security of employment or union rights while often doing exactly the same work as permanent employees and in some cases having been in their 'temporary' post for as long as four years (Perry 1994: 13). During the GLF it could be seen even more clearly that some groups of workers, namely new recruits to the rapidly expanding workforce and temporary or contract workers, were not enjoying the same rights and benefits in terms of job security, pay and conditions, and in some cases union membership, as were longer-established and more skilled and experienced workers. New recruits during the GLF, according to a Soviet commentator, 'were paid badly and had little chance of advancement as they acquired new work skills and experience. They received little in the way of social benefits. These workers were not only underpaid, they were without rights' (Rozman 1985: 117). And as the GLF ground to a halt in 1960 amid confusion, shortages, and even famine, getting rid of temporary and contract workers was the first resort of managers who needed to make reductions in their workforce (L T White 1989: 159).

From about 1962, and especially after 1964 (L T White 1989: 160), this system of reducing costs by restricting the number of workers in secure, higher-paid, unionized posts, and making up the shortfall with lower-paid contract or temporary workers with fewer or no rights in the enterprise, was consolidated and expanded, and became generally known as the worker-peasant system. Although there was a political rationale to the scheme, namely the gradual diminution of two of the 'three great differences' which had to be overcome during the transition to communism (those between urban and rural areas and between workers and peasants),[6] the system appealed to enterprise management mainly because of the savings on welfare spending which it offered. Contract workers did not have the right to bring their dependents to the city with them, reducing pressure on housing, nurseries, etc., and could be sent back to their homes or communes when not needed, where other units would be responsible for their welfare. There were also clear advantages to the system where cadres faced protests from workers, as any temporary or contract workers who showed signs of causing this sort of trouble could swiftly be got rid of (L T White 1989: 189).

In fact, welfare for the better-established, unionized workers was actually expanded during 1962–5 as material incentives and welfare in general came back into favour, 'but cost-conscious managers tried to limit the groups receiving such benefits' (L T White 1989: 184–5). As in 1957, many of the temporary and contract workers employed in large numbers as the workforce expanded during the GLF had over the years come to be doing the same work as permanent workers in the same enterprise, and therefore felt that it was unfair for them not to enjoy the same basic rights as permanent workers. In July 1963 the State Council appeared to recognize this claim of unfair treatment when it promulgated the 'Notice on the question of shifting temporary workers doing regular work to the permanent establishment'.[7] This notice allowed enterprises to employ these workers as permanent workers on the usual terms and wages, provided this did not violate the state's labour plans for enterprises in 1963.

But this clearly ran contrary to the desire to restrict the number of workers enjoying permanent status and the 'iron rice-bowl' benefits which went with it, and so from mid-1964, as the employment of fewer permanent workers and more on temporary contracts began to be promoted for all enterprises, the transfer of temporary or contract workers to permanent status was discouraged, until in March 1965 the 1963 'Notice' was declared null and void. Dissatisfaction with and resistance to the contract labour system seem largely to date from this point, as workers who believed they had a good case for transfer to permanent employment, and who thought, in 1963, that this case had been conceded by the authorities, were now refused permanent status. Some provincial Labour Department officials reportedly warned the Labour Ministry that this decision would be hard for workers to accept.

The Seventy Articles emphasis on material incentives had already begun to create divisions in the workplace, just as similar policies had in 1956–7: 'the rewards to workers who produced more encouraged an elitism that separated officials and technicians from the masses. This separation undermined the doctrine of "politics in command" and the enthusiasm of the ordinary worker' (Vogel 1969: 319). With the development of the worker-peasant system, the division became more pronounced between much of the rank-and-file workforce on one side, and on the other a group (sometimes a majority but sometimes not, especially in smaller enterprises) of well-established and relatively privileged, more skilled workers, together with cadres, technicians and activists. It was only this limited second group which really benefitted from post-GLF policies in industry, as the worker-peasant programme 'lowered costs for managers; and it raised the relative status of well-established union members. But it repressed most others' (L T White 1989: 182).

The roots of the division were already visible in the 1956–7 protests, where the most active protesters were often the 'have-nots' of the urban workforce: younger workers, especially apprentices, or workers from smaller joint enterprises who enjoyed fewer benefits and lower pay than workers in large state enterprises. But during the Cultural Revolution the split became impossible to overlook for even the most blinkered CCP ideologue convinced of working-class unity as an article of faith; the two categories of worker identified above largely coincide with the two mass factions, rebel and conservative, which emerged during the movement. The most significant impact of the worker-peasant system thus came in the Cultural Revolution, when not only those workers already affected, but also any who feared they might be about to lose permanent status, flocked to the rebel faction to demand that what they saw as an unjust and unacceptably discriminatory system be abolished.

Maoism, revisionism, and the 'two-line struggle' in industry, 1964–6

When policies related to the Seventy Articles and the worker-peasant system were criticized by the Maoists in the Cultural Revolution, they were invariably referred to as part of Liu Shaoqi's so-called 'bourgeois reactionary line' in industry, with Deng Xiaoping identified as the other major representative of this tendency. However, contradictions in this line of argument soon become apparent. As the Cultural Revolution developed, Liu Shaoqi stood accused simultaneously of promoting the authority of 'bourgeois experts' in the enterprise and supporting their strict control over workers, and of encouraging the tendency of some rank-and-file workers to overthrow all cadres without discrimination, rather than just targeting a handful of 'capitalist roaders in authority'. The point here is that loyalty to Mao and to the Chairman's 'revolutionary line' were the *sine qua non* of Cultural Revolution activity, and conversely any tendency which a participant in the movement opposed had to be identified with Liu Shaoqi, the 'number one person in authority taking the capitalist road'. (When some individuals did begin to have doubts about Mao himself as the Cultural Revolution wore on, they generally kept them to themselves; some activists, such as Yang Xiguang of Hunan province's *Shengwulian*, the author of 'Whither China?', tied themselves in ideological knots trying to make their own strongly-held views conform to Mao's writings (Unger 1991a)).

Since there is no need for us to follow the sort of convoluted reasoning necessary to blame Liu Shaoqi for absolutely everything with which workers were dissatisfied prior to the Cultural Revolution, we can instead look at why Mao's SEM and allied policies failed to benefit the majority of workers in the years 1964–6 despite endless rhetorical glorification of the proletariat, and at how aspects of Mao's 'line' also motivated workers to take action during the Cultural Revolution. One reason why the SEM brought few improvements in the position of most workers is of course that, as a political campaign, it had little impact on the economic structure of enterprises, which in fact was still largely determined by the Seventy Articles. Thus the SEM was 'an attempt . . . to sing the superiority of work and the worker when the social structure militated against it' (Vogel 1969: 319). The main beneficiaries of the SEM's renewed emphasis on 'proletarianism' (L T White 1989: 199) were actually those who could claim to be the vanguard of the working class: 'local leaders of party branches and activists in Socialist Education struggles. Many workers received no new benefits at all' (L T White 1989: 218). The promotion of 'politics in command', particularly Mao's thought, could also be used to give unpopular programmes such as the worker-peasant system unimpeachable ideological authority, and did in fact make the system difficult to criticize in 1966–7; high-level public support for protesting contract workers from members of the Central Cultural Revolution Group (CCRG), notably Jiang Qing, proved short-lived (Solomon 1968: 9–12; Perry and Li 1997: 101–2).

The other main development in enterprises in the mid-1960s which is closely identified with Mao's policy preferences is the establishment of political departments, usually staffed by ex- People's Liberation Army (PLA) personnel, to promote the idea of 'politics in command' in all areas of an enterprise's work, and also to control the confidential files compiled on all individuals for which more information had been gathered in urban areas during the SEM (L T White 1989: 197).

'Learning from the PLA' had been a common slogan since the campaign to emulate Lei Feng began in 1962, but intensive efforts to apply it to industrial enterprises can be observed from 1964. The official unions seem to have resisted it (Lee Lai To 1984: 70–1), bringing up many practical difficulties in mechanically applying the military style of work to enterprises (*Workers' Daily* 28 March, 7 April, and 19 September 1965), and it is striking in discussions of the campaign that all those insisting that the PLA's style is easily applicable, and must be applied, to enterprises and to union work are political departments and militia cadres, while all those raising objections are union cadres, generally basic-level. It is also very noticeable that exhortations to learn from the PLA are almost entirely absent from the pages of the *Workers' Daily* during 1965, in sharp contrast to most other newspapers. Mao, as in the rest of the press, is on virtually every page, so the objection seems to have been specifically to military influence in industry.

If union cadres were displeased with the growing influence of the political departments, so too were many workers, as was shown once the Cultural Revolution started, when in at least some places cadres staffing political departments became workers' preferred target of attack:

> The spearhead of the workers' rebellion had at first been directed against some of the Party authorities at their work units. . . . At the time of the Cultural Revolution, China's grassroots work units contained two kinds of cadre. One kind consisted of the people who had actually been managing the work units before 1964; the other . . . were those demobilized armymen in the political departments. When the Cultural Revolution broke out, the workteams sent by Liu Shaoqi often employed members of this second group to criticize members of the first, pre-1964 group as revisionist. But when the workers spontaneously rebelled they seldom directed their attacks against the management cadres, but rather against the much-hated cadres in the political departments.
>
> (Unger 1991a: 18–19)

An added incentive for attacking the political departments was that during the summer of 1966, when it was still not at all clear to the majority of people what sort of campaign the Cultural Revolution was going to be and many treated it as another anti-rightist campaign (Wang Shaoguang 1995: 68), still more 'black material' had been collected, in industrial enterprises as well as schools, on the usual suspects (those from 'bad' class backgrounds, those criticized in previous campaigns or who had made political errors or crossed powerful people in their unit, and anyone given to making cynical remarks and complaints), and political departments held this material also (Liu Guokai 1987: 22). The existence of and control over dossiers remained an explosive political issue, particularly for the rebel faction, throughout the first three years of the Cultural Revolution (Wang Shaoguang 1995: 91–2).

From the point of view of this study, the main development of the Cultural Revolution as far as workers are concerned is not that they followed either of the 'two lines' – Mao's revolutionary line, or the 'revisionist' line identified with Liu and Deng – because, as we have just seen, there were important elements of both programmes which were objectionable to at least some workers. Instead, the striking feature of the Cultural Revolution, as will be seen in the next chapter, is that workers acted with an unprecedented degree of autonomy and spontaneity. Whichever faction they joined, they to some extent shared in the experience of large-scale self-organization and independent political action and expression in 'independent mass organizations which leant real power to the voice of workers for a fleeting period' (Walder 1982: 229). It is this which makes the Cultural Revolution a turning point, if not in terms of workers' achievement of their desired position and influence in the enterprise and beyond, then at least in terms of the autonomous collective action which might ultimately be able to bring this about.

Both the Maoist and Liuist 'lines' in industry between 1958 and 1966 played a part in creating the grievances and discontents which found expression in the Cultural Revolution. Some of these dated back to the 1950s, being essentially unresolved issues from the 1956–7 round of protests and strikes, while others reflected new features of industrial life in the 1960s, such as the growing threat to employment security posed by expansion of the worker-peasant system. Liu and Deng's Seventy Articles, with their emphasis on discipline, hierarchy and obedience, had brought back many of the features of one-man management to which workers had objected during the 1950s, together with a new stress on austerity and limiting the numbers eligible for the so-called 'iron rice-bowl' of permanent employment and welfare benefits. Mao's line, on the other hand, while taking away material benefits, had promised much in the way of promoting workers' political status and voice in the enterprise, but had not delivered during the GLF, leaving workers with the worst of both worlds. It then influenced an intensification of political indoctrination and control of workers in the shape of enterprise political departments and the campaign to emulate the PLA. Ultimately, of course, it was Mao's line which had the greatest impact, not necessarily because it stoked up more anger among workers than did the revisionists' policies, but because, in the shape of the August 1966 'Sixteen Points' document (Schoenhals 1997b: 33–43), it then unleashed that anger by allowing workers to organize themselves outside party control for the first time since 1949. Once workers' mass organizations came into existence, these autonomous and representative bodies reflecting 'the genuine but divided concerns of the workers' (Rozman 1985: 128) proved extremely difficult for the authorities to bring back under control, in some cases defying the party and the army in pursuit of their goals.

4 'To rebel is justified'

Workers in the Cultural Revolution, 1966–9[1]

To judge from the rhetoric of the party centre and the state-controlled press, by 1969 workers' status and influence had reached a new high point as a result of the Cultural Revolution: to be designated 'proletarian' became the highest possible praise for anyone or anything. However, this much-trumpeted new era of the working class 'leading in everything' (Yao Wenyuan 1968) was a far cry from the reality for most workers, and this is even true of Shanghai, the only city in which leaders of workers' mass organizations actually took power.[2] Even there, as Elizabeth Perry and Li Xun have shown, the limited gains made by some worker-leaders of the rebel faction did not translate into any 'class crusade to improve the lot of their fellow laborers' (Perry and Li 1997: 187–8), leaving workers in the city's enterprises in much the same position in terms of workplace authority at the end of the Cultural Revolution decade as at its beginning.

What had changed, however, is that large numbers of workers were by then prepared and equipped to act autonomously and collectively in pursuit of their own interests and in opposition to party-state authorities in the enterprise and beyond. This is the truly significant legacy of the Cultural Revolution as far as workers are concerned: the experience of large-scale collective action outside normal party controls which left workers ready to resort to self-organization and strikes at times of unrest in the 1970s and 1980s. Ironically, this key aspect of workers' Cultural Revolution experience has been denied by subsequent party leaderships who have been unable to deal with such manifestations of overt opposition to the existing power structure in the PRC, preferring a version of the movement in which 'the masses', led by Deng Xiaoping after Liu Shaoqi's demise, do battle with the forces of evil represented by the Gang of Four and a minority of hooligans who followed them. A large part of the rebel faction disappears from this formulation altogether, and not by accident: the CCP could not find a convincing answer to the arguments of the rebel faction's radicals that the party was coming to constitute a new ruling class in China, so it simply avoided the issue as best it could by writing this key idea out of the history of the Cultural Revolution (A Chan 1992).

The Cultural Revolution in factories May–December 1966

What began in May as an effort to mobilize workers to criticize a small number of intellectuals singled out by the party centre in Beijing gave way, over the summer and early autumn of 1966, to more genuine protest activity in some enterprises by a minority of restive workers, with some involvement of student Red Guards. At first this activity seems to have been quite successfully suppressed by enterprise authorities, but as workers' organizations, especially rebel organizations, grew through November and December, mass action by workers became more and more common. When the existence of these organizations was legitimized by the CCRG in Beijing on 17 November 1966 (Lee Lai To 1986: 108–9), the last important obstacle to workers' organizations was removed, and December and early January 1967 saw the nationwide outbreak of what became known as 'counterrevolutionary economism'. This movement in fact bore a close resemblance to the outpouring of workers' criticisms in 1956–7, as the following description by Liu Guokai shows:

> In an upsurge of democracy unprecedented since the founding of the People's Republic, the long-pent-up thoughts and reasonable demands of the masses all burst out like a flood from an opened sluice gate. The prolonged wage freeze, the delay in turning contract labour into regular workers, insufficiency of labour insurance, fringe benefits, and subsidies or employment for high school graduates, the assignment of dormitories, and overdue overtime compensation – in a word, all tumbled out as pressing problems. . . . Once the masses in one unit took the first step to rise in rebellion, the news would spread to other units, and the masses there would immediately follow suit. In a rage, the rank and file took the cadres to task, reprimanding them and complaining about the unreasonable treatment they had been subject to over the years. They accused the leadership of being relentless and brutal towards the workers and showing no concern for them, and they set forth their demands . . . those who had been poorly paid and had suffered horrendously in their working conditions and everyday lives were many. Therefore, the protests were manifestations of a genuine mass movement, much more vigorous than the campaign to criticize the bourgeois reactionary line.
>
> (Liu Guokai 1987: 45–6)

The force of the 'economism' movement pushed the Cultural Revolution completely off course for a time and caused severe economic disruption in many areas as workers' demands were temporarily met. The mobilization of large numbers of ordinary workers into the movement also paved the way for another key feature of the Cultural Revolution, the January 1967 power seizures in which enterprise authorities were frequently overthrown in their entirety (Walder 1996: 187).

Just another campaign (May–July 1966)

Early developments in the spring and summer of 1966 showed few signs of leading to a movement markedly different from the ongoing leftist campaign for 'politics in command' and ideological revolutionization in enterprises. However, although in the course of the SEM cadres had already been prevailed upon 'to give up their privileges in housing, in children's education, and in life-style' (P N Lee 1987: 99), as the experiences of the model Daqing oilfield began to be promoted more strongly it did appear that a fairly radical critique of the existing power structure in factories might be the basis of more far-reaching changes: 'The revisionists turn an enterprise practically into the private property of the bourgeois privileged stratum; they manage an enterprise by commandism, the imposition of penalties and the enforcement of rigid systems' (*Economic Research* 20 April 1966). To counter this and implement the mass line in enterprises, workers were to have the right to elect basic-level cadres and to criticize cadres at any meeting. For their part, cadres were to agree to forego special privileges:

> They will not build office buildings, auditoriums, hostels, and reception houses; they will live in 'makeshift dwellings' or single-storey houses. They will hold no parties and present no gifts; they will neither dance nor put a sofa in their office. They will eat in collective dining rooms. And they will teach their children not to seek privileges for themselves. . . . They must persist in participating in physical labour and must never be bureaucrats sitting high above the people.
>
> (*Economic Research* 20 April 1966)

These ideas about the need for workers to elect their own leaders, who would be subject to recall and would not enjoy high pay or other special privileges, were at the heart of calls made later in the year, and especially during the 'January Storm' of 1967, for a new form of social and industrial organization based on the Paris Commune, by which the rebels who advocated this form meant four main things:

> the people govern themselves; they do this through elected leaders; these do not become a new and oppressive bureaucracy because they can be recalled at any time and do not get a higher wage than those who elected them; and the people are armed.
>
> (Mehnert 1969: 12)

Mao of course returned to the virtues of the Paris Commune form of mass organization, with leaders elected and subject to instant recall by the rank and file, in the seminal 'Sixteen Points' of August 1966 (Schoenhals 1997b: 39–40), the document in which he laid down the approved form which mass participation in the movement should take. But already early in 1966, the development of this trend was foreshadowed by an article in *Red Flag* in praise of the Paris

Commune, which, following Mao, emphasized the importance of this form of self-government in preventing a new regime from degenerating into the dictatorship of a privileged and exploitative elite after a successful workers' uprising (*Red Flag* 1 April 1966). As a contrast to this ideal, the article criticized the existence of privileges, high pay, corruption and widespread material incentives in Khrushchev's Soviet Union (*Red Flag* 1 April 1966: 14). Thus even before the Cultural Revolution officially got underway, there were signs that a fairly radical reform of enterprise management and worker–cadre relations might be on the horizon.

But no such radical solutions to the still-present problems of worker–cadre relations were visible in the first months of the Cultural Revolution, May–July 1966, as what unfolded was a very conventional campaign of criticism, easily mistaken for a re-run of the 1957–8 anti-rightist campaign. In enterprises some workers did try to rebel against their own leaders, but were swiftly suppressed, and the movement in factories as well as on school and university campuses generally targeted the 'usual suspects'. Where workers were mobilized to attend meetings and rallies for criticism of the intellectuals who were the very first targets of the Cultural Revolution (mainly the writers Deng Tuo and Wu Han), only politically-reliable activists and workers already co-opted into the power structure could take part; the right to participate in the Cultural Revolution was at this point still limited to people of 'high political quality' (Liu Guokai 1987: 43) who would later mostly be found in the conservative faction. These 'progressive' workers and staff are the ones credited in official reports with refuting the intellectuals' alleged claims (not made explicit in their satirical writings, but quite clear to those at whom they were aimed, notably Mao), that the GLF had been a costly and disastrous failure which had brought only suffering to the ordinary Chinese people, and that the CCP despised the masses and ignored their views. Workers were said to have countered these slanders with specific evidence of the progress made in their own industries and enterprises during the GLF.[3]

It should not surprise us that workers displayed more caution in their response to the earliest phase of the Cultural Revolution than did school and university students. While the focus of the movement remained primarily cultural, many workers in any case did not see the relevance to their lives of a debate over what a few writers in Beijing might or might not have implied about the Great Helmsman in a newspaper column three years before. But even where they detected in the new movement an opportunity to voice their many grievances and criticisms of workplace leadership, they were well aware of the serious risks involved, particularly those of them who had already been in the workforce during the anti-rightist campaign and had seen for themselves the penalties for plain speaking (Bennett and Montaperto 1971: 56). Most workers therefore stuck to activities 'permitted, encouraged, or even required by the authorities' (Wang Shaoguang 1995: 68) for the time being. The few who did speak out faced house arrest or detention at their work-unit, denunciation as 'ghosts and monsters' by factory authorities and outside work-teams, transfer to less desirable jobs and bonus cuts (Perry and Li 1997: 64–5), and in extreme cases 'struggle sessions and beatings that brought some close to death' (Walder

1996: 174). Torture was much less common at this stage in factories than in schools and universities, but cases did occur (Perry and Li 1997: 65). This was sufficient to deter all but a few from speaking out.

Factory authorities, as ever, had a formidable array of weapons which could be deployed against rebellious workers, but they remained concerned that radical students might be able to stir up protests if they were able to make contact with discontented workers. In Guangzhou, rumours of the 'brutal suppression' (Bennett and Montaperto 1971: 57) of workers who had criticized their leaders in May and June 1966 prompted middle-school students who had been involved in a work-study programme at the warehouse concerned to go and offer moral support to these oppressed proletarians, although they were unable to get into the plant until after the party work-team assigned to guide the Cultural Revolution there had been withdrawn late in August. Once they did gain access and persuaded workers to speak to them, they were given a sample of the type of grievances most commonly expressed by workers in the mid-1960s, and in many cases typical also of the mid-1950s: 'family difficulties to which the factory leadership paid no heed', many years of service in the same unit 'with little adjustment in wages', and the transfer of a worker's wife from the warehouse to the countryside (the worker-peasant system particularly affected transportation and storage enterprises such as this one (Solomon 1968: 3–4)).[4] The students found that 'other workers bore a grudge against the warehouse leadership for its bureaucratic style of work, staying always in their office and hardly ever descending into the shops to labour along with the workers' (Bennett and Montaperto 1971: 58–9). This last is a complaint which could justifiably have been made at any time in the previous ten years.

The students in this case only happened to hear how workers in Guangzhou who spoke out early in the movement had been treated because a teacher and some class-mates had relatives among the factory workforce (Bennett and Montaperto 1971: 56); enterprise authorities were quite successful at this stage in keeping conflicts within the unit. Some of the workers involved had vented their animosity towards the main beneficiaries of the Seventy Articles in industry – technicians and cadres – while taking care to phrase their criticism in the terms of the new campaign, casting them as 'bourgeois academic authorities' in the workplace who looked down on production workers and paid too much attention to 'bookish rules and foreign stereotypes'; they were also accused of failing to respect or make use of workers' own newly-gained technical expertise, despite the GLF's emphasis on the 'three-way combination' to involve workers in technical matters. But this impeccably Maoist line of attack had not spared the workers swift retaliation and denunciation by enterprise leaders who saw the attack on the leadership 'unmistakably implied' (Bennett and Montaperto 1971: 56) in it. Workers were aware that they would always be treated more harshly than students for the same offence of attacking the authorities, and up to the end of July 1966 most played safe by doing only the minimum required to be seen to be supporting the new campaign. Those who sought to form connections with like-minded workers did so secretly (Wang Shaoguang 1995: 88).

August 1966: 'Bombard the Headquarters'

Whether Mao intended the Cultural Revolution to be just an extensive purge of non-Maoists in the party or a real and far-reaching anti-bureaucratic revolution, it was clear by August 1966 that it was not having the desired effect, as the work-teams dispatched under Liu Shaoqi's instructions to guide the movement were in fact controlling it and suppressing any real criticism of local leaders. Mao's response was the publication of the 'CCP Central Committee Decision on the Great Proletarian Cultural Revolution', usually known as the 'Sixteen Points', on 8 August. This document defined the targets of the movement as 'capitalist roaders in authority in the party' and 'bourgeois reactionary "authorities"', thus indicating that this was not, after all, a campaign aimed at finding rightists among the ordinary people (Liu Guokai 1987: 23–4), but was aimed at those in power who had deviated from the correct line. This change of tack brought to an end the campaign against the obvious targets in enterprises (the 'usual suspects' identified in the last chapter, including rightists, people of bad class background, and anyone ever criticized, labelled or otherwise punished by enterprise authorities), but did not immediately lead to any radical new developments within enterprises.

Cultural Revolution committees and groups were set up in all units to direct the campaign, but since it was 'mostly mainstays from the previous period of the campaign, namely, persons with high "political qualities"' (Liu Guokai 1987: 24) who were elected to these bodies, few attacks against 'capitalist roaders in authority' in enterprises transpired. The 'Sixteen Points' itself had a strong emphasis on the importance of production, stipulating that the Cultural Revolution was 'a powerful motive force for the development of the social productive forces' (Schoenhals 1997b: 42), and should not be seen as any sort of obstacle to production; the masses were to be mobilized to 'grasp revolution and promote production' simultaneously. This gave enterprise leaders scope to limit workers' activity in the name of safeguarding production, and this they continued to do through August and September 1966, with both party cadres and managers interpreting the 'Sixteen Points' exclusively

> in terms of its emphasis on production and discipline. For instance, workers' spare time was filled with endless rounds of meetings to discuss the problems of production and daily life. Workers who wished to exchange 'revolutionary experiences' were transferred from day to night shift or from one workshop to another so as to make it difficult for them to organize political activities. When workers did go to other factories or to file petitions to the higher echelons of authority they were charged with 'wrecking production' and undermining the 'Sixteen-point Resolution'.
>
> (P N Lee 1987: 107)

These are the usual tactics of enterprise leaders faced with awkward criticism from workers, and bear a close resemblance to the methods of control employed under one-man management up to 1956. It was seen in the last chapter that protesting temporary and contract workers could be dealt with quite simply by being laid off, but it seems that even permanent workers could be kept under control at this stage of the movement using similar methods; enterprise authorities had control over so many vital aspects of workers' lives that there was endless scope for effective retaliation against trouble-makers. It was later revealed that many workers, permanent and temporary, had in fact been laid off or had their pay cut since the Cultural Revolution began (*People's Daily* 26 December 1966) as a direct result of their criticism of enterprise leaders.

Where success in the Cultural Revolution in factories was claimed, close inspection of the reports often reveals only token or formalistic changes taking place. In Guangzhou it was claimed that 'rules have been broken and difficulties resolved',[5] as workers, influenced by their study of Mao's thought, abolished irrational rules and regulations, including, in one plant, the system of attendance cards for clocking-in, something which was described as 'a big insult to workers' revolutionary spontaneity'. However, the report went on to make clear that clocking-in had not been abolished in this plant at all; the hated attendance cards had simply been re-named 'revolutionary cards', and the system continued as before under this new name. However, the way had now been opened in theory for ordinary workers to attack certain individuals in the leadership, and particularly once practical safeguards against reprisals were introduced from October 1966, workers did begin to feel able to participate in the Cultural Revolution in more than a token way. As activity among workers increased through the autumn of 1966, though, it became apparent that workers' groups, like those of other sections of society, were divided into two broad factions, conservatives (*baoshoupai*) and rebels (*zaofanpai*), which had quite different interests and were seeking to develop the movement in different directions. It is to the causes of this factional division that we now turn.

Factional division among workers

The conventional wisdom on workers during the Cultural Revolution for some time was the same as that for the Hundred Flowers period: that workers' relatively privileged position in society and political status led them to stand aloof from protests and defend the party from attacks by other social groups. As we saw, this view is a travesty of workers' actual activities in 1956–7 since it takes no account of the powerful wave of workers' protest and strikes which preceded as well as accompanied the well-known intellectual and student movement. The idea that *some* workers supported and defended party authorities during the Cultural Revolution is well-founded: this was why the conservative, or 'royalist' (*huangshoupai*), faction was so named by its more radical rivals. But care must be taken not to overlook the significance of rebel workers' militant opposition to these same authorities.

Generally speaking, factional allegiance was influenced by an individual's place in the hierarchy of status and benefits after seventeen years of socialism in

China, and sometimes by more specific personal experiences as well. Liu Guokai (memoirist and rebel-faction member in a Guangzhou factory) uses the terms 'had-it-good' and 'had-it-bad' faction to encapsulate this division between those benefitting from the 1966 status quo, who therefore defended the existing order (conservatives), and those who were at a disadvantage because of family (class) background, employment in a smaller or less prosperous work-unit, holding a lowly position in any enterprise (apprentices, young, temporary and contract workers, and anyone doing menial auxiliary jobs), or previous political or personal indiscretions (including those of family members, where guilt by association applied), who tended to become rebels and to attack everyone in a position of authority, not just a minority of 'capitalist roaders'. This formulation has been criticized, and one can instantly think of exceptions to the general rule, but the overall framework of beneficiaries of the existing order as conservatives and those who felt they were unfairly missing out as rebels remains useful, in my view, provided it is not regarded as absolute.

Andrew Walder has developed a model of patronage networks in enterprises by which activists and model workers were bound in loyalty to the leadership by personal, clientelist ties (Walder 1986, 1996), and could thus easily be mobilized in defence of enterprise and higher authorities, as they were when these authorities came under attack in the early stages of the Cultural Revolution. This model of division and conflict where the key split is between activists and non-activists has sometimes been set in opposition to models of division which rely on socioeconomic position and relative status as explanatory factors, but in fact these two are not necessarily contradictory. If as well as material conditions and benefits we include political power and influence in calculations of who were the 'haves' and who the 'have-nots' among workers, then the two are quite compatible; those included in political networks are beneficiaries of the status quo in all respects, and hence conservatives, while the 'have-nots' outside the networks are both materially and politically disadvantaged, and often display considerable hostility towards the activists.

The 'political networks' approach is valuable in explaining the development of conservative workers' organizations (Perry and Li 1997: 5), but Walder's assertion that the activist/non-activist split has been 'easily the most politically salient social-structural cleavage' (Walder 1986: 166) in industry in the PRC is contradicted by the evidence of this study. Workers involved in factory political networks are visible as loyal defenders of their cadre-patrons both during the Hundred Flowers period and in the Cultural Revolution, but only because the latter needed defending from many other workers, often disadvantaged in some specific way in the distribution of benefits and opportunities in socialist China. The insistence that it is the division between the two groups of workers, rather than between some workers and those in power, which is most politically significant is as unconvincing as Walder's other claim that the existence of patronage networks of loyalists in factories has been able to prevent the emergence of collective resistance among the workforce, when in fact this has been happening periodically since the 1950s, as this study shows (and as Walder has recently acknowledged, although still without recognizing the political content of many outbreaks of protest, classing them instead as the expression of 'occupational grievances' (Walder 1996: 168–9)). His claim of the efficacy of the networks is a qualified one, that is, that they have been able to keep control of workers 'under normal circumstances' (Walder 1986: 11), but if we exclude from consideration as 'abnormal' periods of campaigns, political extremism, war, famine, rebellion, etc., we are left with a system of control which functioned perfectly, but only during 1954–5.

Conservative workers' groups (who sometimes called themselves 'Scarlet Guards' (*zhiweidui*) to distinguish themselves from the student Red Guards, the name harking back to the communist base areas of the republican era (Perry and Li 1997: 72)) have been taken as representative of workers in general, mainly because they are judged to have constituted a numerical majority among industrial workers, particularly in the larger, more modern state enterprises.[6] Rebel workers almost always comprised less than half the workforce in large enterprises, which might lead us to assume that these groups were less important and less representative of workers' opinions in general than were their conservative counterparts. But it must be remembered that there were severe pressures on workers not to stick their necks out by forming or joining rebel groups, especially in large enterprises where the influence of the party and mass organizations and of the political and militia departments was strongest:

> In factories, particularly big factories, most of the 'conservative' organizations were stable and powerful. This was because in big factories the old order had held powerful control. From the factory party committee, political department, and public security section down to cadres and staff members of the trade union and of youth and women's associations and even workshop superintendents and shift foremen joined the 'conservative' workers' organizations almost as a bloc. What could a rank-and-file worker do but throw in with the tide? The political and security cadres were 'prestigious' persons . . . and the workers were used to obeying them. The consequences would be grave if anyone dared to disobey them by joining a 'rebel' organization. One would be up against a formidable opponent and duly penalized. For instance, one could easily be transferred to an undesirable job. It was true the workers made up the majority, and if they were courageous enough to rebel the situation could be different. . . . But . . . it was not easy for the majority of workers to rise to the occasion with spontaneous action. As a result, just a small number of backbone elements were able to coerce the rank-and-file workers to form organizations that really did not have genuine mass support.
>
> (Liu Guokai 1987: 75)

Thus the influence brought to bear through political networks could restrict the number of workers prepared to risk overt rebel allegiance, although it could not prevent such groups emerging altogether. This is the view of a former rebel, but it makes a great deal of sense and is supported by other findings that many workers who initially joined the conservative faction did so not out of any conviction that it was the right thing to do, but because, as the home of activists and model workers, lower-level cadres, and party and youth league members, it seemed to be the safest place to be judging by experience of past campaigns (Perry and Li 1997: 76–7, 85). Conversely, given the risks inherent in identifying oneself as a rebel, the leaders of this faction in particular were by definition unusually bold and committed to their course of action. They

> had their own independent views of things and . . . enormous capacity to get things done. . . . [E]veryone who joined was self-motivated in some way; no one who was afraid of the consequences would dare to join. They there-fore had more core members and fewer nominal ones, and their effectiveness could not be measured in numbers.
>
> (Liu Guokai 1987: 44, 79)

It sounds feeble to assert that rebel leaders became such because that was the sort of people they were, but although difficult to pin down, the influence of such nebulous factors as personality is inescapable when looking at this question of who became a rebel and why. Perry and Li's effort to explore the 'psychocul-tural approach' to worker mobilization through detailed biographies of rebel leaders in Shanghai is to be commended in this respect (Perry and Li 1997: 44–64).

It should always be borne in mind that factional allegiance was not necessarily unchanging or clear-cut. Liu Guokai records how during the summer of 1967 when the rebels had the upper hand in the cities, it was possible for workers in Guangzhou to conform by belonging to conservative organizations in their large factories in the suburbs, while 'at home in the cities they were "rebel" supporters' (Liu Guokai 1987: 96). As the fortunes of the two factions shifted through the intense fighting of 1967 and into 1968, many of the less-committed followers of both factions changed sides as their original groups fell out of favour with Mao and the party centre (Walder 1996: 179; Perry and Li 1997: 95), and the numbers of committed participants in the movement also declined absolutely as the risks of participation came to many to outweigh the benefits. Wang Shaoguang's study of Wuhan brings out this round of diminishing returns for movement participants very clearly, particularly with regard to remnant factionalism in the 1970s which involved a far smaller proportion of the population than the great pitched battles of the summer of 1967 (Wang Shaoguang 1995: 251–9).

Finally, it should be noted that although conservative workers' organizations had obvious links with enterprise and other local authorities, they were not only the creations and instruments of these forces. Large numbers of well-established, unionized, skilled and secure workers in big enterprises did have genuine reasons of their own for the actions they took, including joining the conservative faction; they were not only obeying orders. For example, in Shanghai Scarlet Guards went on strike to protest against concessions made by the city government to rebel contract and temporary workers, and dockers in the same city put forward their own 'economistic' demands to maintain wage differentials when contract workers received pay rises (Walder 1978: 48–9; Wylie 1981: 102). These outbreaks of conservative 'economism' were later blamed on local party manipulation and instigation, but the evidence is that the main impetus for the demands came from workers themselves (Walder 1978: 48).

The mass movement takes off

We have seen that even into the autumn of 1966 it was relatively easy for enterprise authorities to argue that the imperatives of stable production justified suppression of workers' protests. Rebel workers at the Guangzhou warehouse visited by Dai Xiao'ai's group were reportedly 'severely suppressed by the management' (Bennett and Montaperto 1971: 62) after the students left, with the need to safeguard production cited to legitimize the authorities' action. Enterprise leaders were understandably reluctant to allow students to intervene in the movement in enterprises, fearing that 'the undesirables in their factories, agitated by the students, might also become unruly' (Bennett and Montaperto 1971: 62). This was precisely what was likely to happen where the build-up of grievances among a section of the workers needed very little encouragement to break out into open rebellion. But the strong emphasis through September and October on maintaining production and preventing student rebels from offering any support to restive workers meant that in Guangzhou, workers' protests 'faltered and nearly died out altogether' (Bennett and Montaperto 1971: 62) during this period.

In contrast to the suppression of early rebels in the workforce, conservative-faction workers were more in evidence on the streets during the autumn, often mobilized by provincial authorities to demonstrate against the student Red Guards fanning out from Beijing to promote the movement around the country. Although clearly the actions of these workers were being controlled by authorities in their enterprises and in the local party committee, their own enthusiasm for the task was probably not negligible. Most Red Guards at this point were still the offspring of the 'five red' groups (party cadres, PLA personnel, revolutionary martyrs, workers and poor peasants), with those from cadre backgrounds particularly prominent, and despite the theoretical leading status of the working class in Chinese society, the attitude of these students towards workers (and towards the offspring of workers and peasants as opposed to the other three 'red' categories) was often very condescending:

> [T]hose who suffered most before 1949 (the workers and peasants) owed a debt of gratitude to the revolutionaries who liberated them. As the passive recipients who gained most from the efforts of revolutionary cadres, workers and peasants were not in a strong position to provide class education to the children of their liberators.
>
> (Rosen 1982: 78)

Resentment of the student Red Guards' patronizing attitude towards workers and inflated sense of their own importance may have encouraged conservative workers in their positive response to official mobilization at this stage.

Constant exhortations to students to stay out of factories and let workers 'liberate themselves' were not only motivated by fears of disruption; clashes between workers and students were also a cause for concern (*Red Guard News* 9 September 1966; *People's Daily* 12 September 1966). Aside from the organized confrontations between unionized workers from the larger state enterprises and student Red Guards, especially those from Beijing, student rebels were not always welcomed in enterprises even by the protesting workers they wished to support: 'Many rebel workers were extremely hostile to all forms of intervention from outside the plant' (Andors 1977a: 165). This is hardly surprising when what made workers at the bottom of the heap protest was that they were constantly told by others what to do; the last thing they wanted during the Cultural Revolution was to be told how to rebel.

Rebel workers often shared conservatives' resentment of students' condescending attitudes towards them, and cooperation proved difficult. Once workers were allowed to organize themselves freely, from mid-November, even those students who welcomed this development had some misgivings, being 'aware that [they] would soon have to share leadership responsibility with workers' (Bennett and Montaperto 1971: 144). The Cultural Revolution would no longer be 'their' movement. Early in 1967, workers' groups were still being used as window-dressing in student-dominated power seizures (Bennett and Montaperto 1971: 157), and student Red Guards were laying claim to the same sort of infallibility as had state representatives in factories back in the mid-1950s:

> The '16 Articles' pointed out: 'It will be necessary to trust the masses, rely on them, and respect their pioneering spirit.' Some leaders of the Guangdong Provincial Revolutionary Alliance, however, do nothing of the sort. As soon as they have taken over a certain unit, they rise high above the revolutionary masses of that unit, issue orders and tell the masses what to do. . . . They even say arrogantly: 'We take orders from Chairman Mao, and you shall take orders from us.'
>
> (*Guangzhou Red Guard* 10 February 1967)

This sort of behaviour is of course precisely what rebel workers had revolted against.

Students at a Red Guard conference in Guangzhou in September 1966 similarly had to be reminded to 'respect the revolutionary proposals and opinions of the masses' (*Red Guard News* 9 September 1966), and not simply take over the movement in the factories and direct it themselves, and this was not untypical of their attitudes as a group. Students in China have often seen themselves as the natural and rightful leaders of any protest movement, harking back, as they did during the spring of 1989, to the intellectuals of the May Fourth era and their role in China's social and political development. Although they are often keen to have the support of other sections of (particularly urban) society, including workers, there is a noticeable tendency to guard their leading role and guidance over any movement quite jealously, and to regard workers as unsuited to playing anything more than a supporting role, a more useful source of logistical back-up and occasional street-fighting muscle than of ideas or leadership. Given their exclusion from any sort of political role since the founding of the PRC, it is perhaps not surprising that workers appropriated with such enthusiasm the slogan of 'the masses liberating themselves'[7] and resisted even the intervention of outside activists inclined to support their demands, determined to make the best use of this unprecedented opportunity to organize themselves.

Workers' mass organizations received official sanction with the CCRG decision on 17 November 1966 that workers should be allowed to participate in the movement much as students did, exchanging revolutionary experiences outside working hours and setting up their own representative organizations (Lee Lai To 1986: 108–9). The decision was couched as a call to workers to take part, but in fact it was simply a recognition of what was already happening in the movement in many cities (L T White 1989: 233; Walder 1978: 28). From early October, the campaign to criticize the 'bourgeois reactionary line' (the conduct of the Cultural Revolution under the work-teams sent out by Liu Shaoqi) had begun to encourage more, and more genuine, mass involvement in the movement, since it unmistakably allowed mass criticism of party leaders themselves for the first time and weakened the position of the 'five-red' elite who had monopolized leadership of the Cultural Revolution since the early summer.

Many people were at first inclined to regard this change in the campaign's direction as 'too good to be true' (Liu Guokai 1987: 36), especially those on whom 'black material' had been collected, and who were now told that all this material had to be destroyed. But as it became clear that this instruction was actually being carried out in some units, where it was an important part of the campaign against the 'bourgeois reactionary line', confidence grew: 'Due to the widespread nature of this campaign . . . the broad ranks of people began to dare to rise up. This happened around November and December of 1966' (Liu Guokai 1987: 37). The ranks of both student and worker 'revolutionary rebels' swelled during these months and rebel groups soon came to eclipse their conservative rivals. With this numerical strength and political momentum behind them, during December 1966 and the first half of January 1967 workers used the freedom allowed them by the campaign to criticize the bourgeois reactionary line to 'give their superiors a piece of their mind without fear of being beaten down as anti-party, anti-socialist elements' (Liu Guokai 1987: 45). They turned on cadres in their enterprises demanding action on all the grievances which had been building up over previous years, in some cases dating right back to 1956–7, in a movement that was soon to be branded 'counterrevolutionary economism'. What emerged for a short time was a genuine, bottom-up mass movement, and the momentum of it carried some workers into all-out rebellion against the entire authority structure in their enterprises and beyond in the 1967 'January Storm'.

Economism and the attacks on the contract labour system

The application of the term 'economism' to workers' demands for material improvements clearly showed the party centre's disapproval of what it saw as an attempt to sully the pure political struggle of the Cultural Revolution with economic demands: economism had been 'Lenin's scornful term for the benighted mentality of workers bereft of Communist party leadership' (Perry and Li 1997: 98). Since much of the backlash against economism seemed to be directed at rebel groups, some commentators have tended to conflate the economistic campaign and the rebel movement of December 1966–January 1967, but in fact members of both factions (and of neither) took part enthusiastically, encouraged by the victories of other groups to take advantage of the manifest weakness of the authorities and see what they could get (Walder 1996: 181). The only distinction between the factions was that conservatives, tending to come from the more privileged sections of the workforce, were often behaving in an economistic way to try to protect their differentials against challenges from the less well-off, while the rebels involved were disproportionately drawn from particularly deprived segments of the workforce such as younger workers, apprentices, and, of course, temporary and contract workers.

Perry and Li have found that rebel-group *leaders* mostly stood aloof from the rush to gain back-pay and travel funds and to take over empty state housing, 'careful to distinguish [their] basically political objectives from the materialistic upsurge' (Perry and Li 1997: 117). Not only were political concerns much more important to these individuals than were economic benefits, they also were probably more politically aware and keen to be seen to be keeping to Mao's line in the Cultural Revolution in the furtherance of their objectives. The priorities of the rebel rank and file were also not as mercenary as they are sometimes painted: most rebels were 'politically motivated rather than inspired merely by short-term economic gains' (Wang Shaoguang 1995: 305, n. 3), as the January 1967 wave of enterprise power seizures showed.

The mass movement unleashed, apparently unintentionally, throughout urban China in December 1966 was universally condemned a few weeks later even by those members of the CCRG, particularly Jiang Qing, who initially seemed inclined to back the demands of contract workers when these were first presented to them. Rebel students, too, were often in the forefront of the campaign to get workers to renounce the concessions made to them and return the back-wages which many had received (Liu Guokai 1987: 48), urging them not to be fooled by the plot of 'capitalist roaders' in enterprises and local government, who were claimed to have tried to sabotage the Cultural Revolution by diverting workers' activity into economic demands with 'bribes' of back-wages and other payments. It was insisted that economism could be traced back to these local party and government leaders, who had first incited workers to make demands and then met them, thus disrupting production and causing losses to the state, in an attempt to force the leadership in Beijing to modify the Cultural Revolution which was now beginning to threaten local power holders' own positions.

As Andrew Walder has pointed out, many Western accounts of the Cultural Revolution accept this explanation of economism in part or in whole (Walder 1978: 39), but this is to ignore the fact that workers' resentment and protests on a variety of issues had actually been brewing for months if not years, and the suppression of the earlier attempts of some to use the Cultural Revolution to voice some of their demands can only have added to the pressure. There is really no need to look for evidence of behind-the-scenes manipulation of workers, as it is entirely plausible that, under the unique conditions of the early Cultural Revolution when the usual controls on organizations independent of the party had been lifted and leaders made legitimate targets of attack, workers seized a rare opportunity to press their demands, give vent to their anger and seek redress for some of the wrongs they felt had been done to them over the years.

> It was a cry out of the bottom of the masses' hearts, a cry coming out spontaneously from thousands and thousands of people without prior consultation. . . . There was no need to agitate them or to help them fall into ranks.
>
> (Liu Guokai 1987: 46)

Cadres did not need the motive of plotting to wreck the Cultural Revolution for their decision to give in to many of workers' demands at this time. In many cases they conceded quite simply because it would have been almost impossible to justify a refusal. Where workers had not received overtime pay or subsidised medical treatment to which they were legally entitled (Liu Guokai 1987: 46), cadres did not have firm grounds on which to refuse them, since these could hardly be classed as excessive or 'unreasonable' demands. The Cultural Revolution enabled some groups of workers to obtain documents proving that not all of the money allocated for their wages was actually being used to pay them: the case of Ke Qingshi's reign in Shanghai, where wages were held down to please the party centre in Beijing, has already been noted (Perry and Li 1997: 99), and there was a similar case in Harbin, where rebel transport workers discovered that the local government was paying them less than it was authorized to do. It would have been extremely difficult for any cadre to refuse a demand for back-pay in this situation, and indeed workers

> reportedly demanded and received payment of the difference between the authorized and actual levels of wages, retroactive for three years. Transport workers in Harbin reportedly received about 1,000 *yuan* each in back-wages, whereupon workers in other trades demanded and received similar payments.
>
> (Solomon 1968: 13)

Probably the worst accusation which can be levelled at the cadres who made concessions is that they caved in to some genuinely unreasonable demands instead of adopting the prescribed course of explaining the state's difficulties to workers and persuading them to withdraw excessive claims. However, given the force of the movement it seems doubtful that such a course of action was a real-istic possibility. After all, the same policy had been advocated by high-level union officials and the party alike in 1957, when the ideal of the union cadre who would be able to reason with workers and explain to them why they should drop their demands was equally far from reality. In one 1957 case, two union cadres of the Shanghai Fertilizer Factory were marched to the banks of the Huangpu river by protesting workers and almost drowned in an attempt to force them to agree to workers' demands (Perry 1994: 24–5). Like many aspects of the official unions' mandate, this policy for dealing with unreasonable or excessive demands sounded fine in theory but does not seem to have worked at all in practice, espe-cially when cadres were confronted with '[l]arge groups of workers, fresh from a violent and . . . bloody defeat, possibly still armed with clubs and stones, [and] probably in no mood to negotiate' (Walder 1978: 48).

The attack on economism in the last weeks of January concentrated on the supposed plot by capitalist roaders to disrupt production and corrupt workers' revolutionary will by giving them back-pay, bonuses, and travelling expenses for *chuanlian*,[8] but in fact at least part of what was later condemned as the 'evil wind of economism' stemmed from a 26 December editorial in the *People's Daily*. While encouraging a new upsurge in the Cultural Revolution in enterprises in which the working class would be the 'leading force and the most active factor', this article also revealed what had happened to the workers who had tried to speak out in the preceding few months, and barred enterprise cadres from taking similar retaliatory measures in future:

> The Party Central Committee has ruled that . . . no leaders of industrial and mining enterprises should strike at and retaliate upon the workers who have put forth criticism and disclosed facts, nor are they to reduce the wages of these workers, to discharge these workers from their posts, and, for the same reason, to discharge contract workers or temporary workers . . . all those wrongly accused of being 'counter-revolutionaries' must be vindi-cated. Transfer of any post in production is disallowed. Threatening and persecution of dependents of workers is also disallowed. Revolutionary workers who have been struck off and forced to leave their factories must be allowed to return to their factories to participate in production and in the cultural revolution. These revolutionary workers should be given any wages which were held up when they were forced to leave the factory.
>
> (*People's Daily* 26 December 1966)

These provisions for payment of back-wages to at least some of the workers, perma-nent and temporary, who had been laid off or sacked because of their protest activities paved the way for an even greater upsurge in 'economistic' demands.

This was particularly true of contract and temporary workers, one of the most discontented and rebellious groups in the whole of the Chinese workforce, representatives of whom were widely reported in wall-posters to have met with Jiang Qing on the evening of 26 December and to have received her full support for their claims. Posters in Guangzhou dated 4 January 1967 reported that Jiang 'had denounced officials of the Ministry of Labor and of the All-China Federation of Trade Unions for permitting the worker-peasant system to exist' (Solomon 1968: 9). Liu Guokai gives a similar account of workers' representatives' reception by members of the CCRG:

> On December 25, the Ministry of Labor in Beijing was closed down by petitioners. The next day Jiang Qing received the petitioners, and right in front of them she reprimanded Xi Zhanyuan, vice-minister of labor. She said: 'The Ministry of Labor is simply a Ministry of the Lords. Even though the country has been liberated for so many years, the workers are still suffering so much; it is unbelievable. Does your Ministry of Labor know about this or not? Do you mean to say that contract workers are the offspring of a stepmother? You, too, should work as a contract worker!' Saying this, Jiang even burst into tears.
>
> (Liu Guokai 1987: 47)

News of this support for the contract workers' cause spread throughout the country via telephone calls and posters 'at lightning speed. . . . People were overjoyed, people were excited, and they were ready to whip up an even more powerful wave' (Liu Guokai 1987: 47). Condemnations of the worker-peasant system continued to appear in the press and in wall-posters, although signs soon appeared of a backlash against 'economism', particularly with regard to contract and temporary workers: in a later meeting with Zhou Enlai, contract workers' representatives were told that despite its faults, the worker-peasant system would have to be maintained for the time being for the sake of the national economy (Solomon 1968: 10).

Some posters alleged that Liu Shaoqi and the Labour Ministry were planning to halt all hiring of permanent workers from 1967, and that all demobilized soldiers would henceforth be hired on a contract basis (Solomon 1968: 10). The second of these allegations was very significant, since demobilized soldiers formed some particularly militant Cultural Revolution mass organizations which caused the authorities great concern, given the military skills which they could bring to the increasingly violent movement. In Guangzhou, for example, one of the largest and most militant rebel groups was the August 1 Combat Corps, formed in mid-January 1967, the majority of whose members were demobilized soldiers now working in factories or neighbourhood labour service stations (Hai Feng 1971: 61–2; G White 1980: 207–8). Many of these ex-servicemen had joined the labour force during the GLF and in the years immediately after, and so were disadvantaged in comparison with those demobilized earlier (G White 1980: 202) and formed part of the group of 'new workers' who in the late 1950s and early 1960s lost out to their more established colleagues in terms of pay and conditions and especially job security:

> Most soldiers demobilized around 1955 and 1956 found promising new jobs in recently collectivized enterprises and farms, but those demobilized in the

late 1950s and early 1960s had difficulty finding comparable opportunities. Many veterans complained that local officials failed to give them good work or adequate welfare for their dependents.

(Vogel 1969: 342)

The rumour that demobilized soldiers would now only be employed on a contract basis removed any prospect of permanent, secure employment for an already disadvantaged group, fuelling the militancy of those who already felt they had little to lose in becoming actively involved in the Cultural Revolution, in sharp contrast to the most privileged and secure members of the industrial workforce. There had been reports back in the summer of 1966 in Guangdong that the worker-peasant system would be extended to all enterprises too, so many workers would have found the latest rumours of a universal contract-labour system quite easy to believe. The news would not only make the chances of a transfer to permanent status for any of those already employed on a contract or temporary basis extremely remote, but would also threaten workers who might be included in such a system in the future. Add to this the fact that large numbers of contract and temporary workers had recently been laid off because of the disruption caused by the Cultural Revolution itself (Hong Yung Lee 1978: 131), and it is not surprising that this section of the workforce was so militant in pressing its demands, forming a national organization, the National Red Workers' Rebel Headquarters, to do so as early as the beginning of December 1966 (Hong Yung Lee 1978: 137).

The political content and significance of workers' 'economistic' demands is perhaps most obvious in the case of the revolt of contract and temporary workers. While this system of employment had clear benefits in terms of cost savings for the state, it was not easy to find any ideological justification for giving enterprises such total power over a group of workers. To the ordinary worker, socialism meant fairness, and to be doing the same work as the next person on the line for less pay and with no rights seemed to them manifestly unfair, and therefore not socialist:

> From the contract workers' point of view, the system was obviously 'anti-socialistic'. . . . [They] were not eligible for fringe benefits, such as medicare, accident insurance, job security, retirement pensions, sick leave, and so forth. In contrast even to the capitalist market system, in which the law of supply and demand generally sets up the wage and the labor unions protect the interests of the workers vis-à-vis the owners, in a socialist economy in which the management is strongly motivated toward profit there is no such mechanism to protect the interests of contract workers. The absolute power regarding contractual conditions for hiring rested in the hands of the enterprise. . . . In some places, the management asked for monthly renewals of the contract in order to strengthen their position vis-à-vis the contract workers.

(Hong Yung Lee 1978: 131)

Given this complete lack of rights and leverage in the workplace, we can see why a Soviet observer called the worker-peasant system 'a form of forced labour' (Rozman 1985: 120). Contract workers were discriminated against politically as well as economically, as besides being excluded from the union, they also had no right to participate in institutions such as the workers' congress (Walder 1978: 45). It was thus quite easy for the workers affected to attack the system as one which ' "divides workers into two strata, creating differences, disintegrating the ranks of the workers, eliminating revolutionary enthusiasm, and obstructing the development of the social productive forces" ' (Hong Yung Lee 1978: 131).

Since the contract labour system, as it was constituted in the mid-1960s, had obvious benefits for enterprise management, both financially and in terms of control and leverage over workers, it was particularly hard to counter workers' accusations that the system was a manifestation of Liu Shaoqi's 'bourgeois reactionary line' and the Seventy Articles' emphasis on 'profit and money in command' and strict control in enterprises. At a rally of more than 100,000 temporary and contract workers in Shanghai on 6 January 1967,[9] workers were reported to have called on the party to 'thoroughly abolish the irrational system of contract labour and outside contract labour and establish a brand new labour system in conformity with Mao Zedong's thought'. A *Wen-hui Daily* report described these systems as 'remnants of the capitalist system of labour employment' (Solomon 1968: 11). Articles in Red Guard newspapers during January praised worker-peasants elsewhere who had

'destroyed the reactionary bourgeois line of Liu and Deng and their system of contract and temporary work which harmed the workers'. The system was described as an attempt to 'raise the greatest amount of cheap labour and to extract the maximum profits'.

(Solomon 1968: 11)

Contract workers in Shaanxi couched the issue in similar terms:

'[O]ver 95 per cent of the workers in our construction brigade in the Xi'an Metallurgical and Electrical Industry are temporary and contract workers and we have suffered just as bitterly as our comrades under the old society.' Workers in Xi'an had demanded abolition of the temporary and contract work system at the commencement of the Cultural Revolution, the article stated. Provincial Party leaders reportedly responded that the system was laid down by the CCP Central Committee, 'but we exposed this by saying that it was laid down by the revisionist Liu Shaoqi'.

(Solomon 1968: 11)

It is not clear whether workers emphasized the system's links with Liu Shaoqi because they were aware of the danger of a direct attack on the party centre as a whole, or because they genuinely held the 'bourgeois reactionary line' responsible for the system. Liu had in fact presided over the expansion of the system, and Red Guard publications, especially those produced by Labour Ministry rebels, gave workers plenty of evidence to support this, so it is possible that workers 'believed that the hardships they had suffered in the past were the result of a bourgeois reactionary line executed by leaders at different levels, while the party centre under Mao still cared about them' (Liu Guokai 1987: 46). Whatever the answer, it clearly suited both workers and that section of the top leadership opposed to Liu Shaoqi to make him the main scapegoat for the system. In his discussion of ex-soldiers' organizations in the Cultural Revolution, Gordon White notes that veterans 'tended to cloak sectional demands in the ideological language of "class struggle"', disguising the 'bread-and-butter issues' that actually motivated them (G White 1980: 210), and workers generally were intelligent enough, and experienced enough in the CCP's mass campaign methods, to play the same game. Having said that, it is clear that in the upsurge of the workers' mass movement through December 1966 and into January 1967, important political concerns were also raised which were quite genuine, and not intended as camouflage for politically incorrect material demands.

The political agenda

Despite later official attempts to portray workers' actions in December and January as solely concerned with economic demands, and therefore a dangerous diversion from the real business of a political mass movement, it is clear both that political demands were also raised, and that even purely economic demands had some political content and significance. Perry and Li have described the economism outbreak as a 'cry for worker justice' which, '[i]n pointing the finger of blame at the flagrant injustices inherent in the operations of China's socialist system . . . represented in some respects a more fundamental criticism than did the rebel movement' (Perry and Li 1997: 116–17). The example of temporary and contract workers who argued that their conditions of employment were inherently anti-socialist shows that there could be a genuine political dimension to the pursuit of economic grievances, and many workers had of course been aware back in the mid-1950s that it was their political superiors who determined the workplace conditions and pay against which they were protesting (Perry 1994: 29–30), giving a political edge to disputes which would otherwise be regarded as economic. In the early stages of the Cultural Revolution, 'revisionists' and those who had implemented Liu Shaoqi's line in industry were made legitimate targets of attack, giving new impetus and a distinctly anti-authority and political character to this outbreak of workers' rebellion.

Raymond Wylie has noted that criticism of the employment system and differentiation between types of worker on the Shanghai docks inevitably called into question the authority of the party committee there:

> Since the Party authorities were closely identified with this economic system, the workers' economic discontents were often voiced as criticisms of the Party Committee's political authority. Similarly, those dockers seeking to challenge

the political authority of the Party often appealed to the economic grievances of the rank and file in order to gain support.

(Wylie 1981: 93)

Workers' relationship with their leaders, the mainstay of previous outbreaks of protest, came straight back on to the agenda in the Cultural Revolution. Common accusations made against party and management authorities were that they were 'adopting superior airs and a bureaucratic workstyle, refusing to carry out the mass line', implementing individual prize and bonus systems which 'set worker against worker', and that cadres were 'reluctant to leave their offices, avoiding physical labour . . . enjoying high salaries and personal privileges, and favouring certain workers over others in assignments and promotions' (Wylie 1981: 97). While it is important to remember that economic grievances were real,[10] workers' protests frequently centred on their position and rights in the enterprise and the 'highly political issue of authority' (Wylie 1981: 104); in sum, on whether or not they were the 'masters of the enterprise' in any meaningful sense. This should come as no surprise since it was precisely this issue which brought workers into conflict with party and state authorities immediately after liberation and again in 1956–7.

For many worker rebels in enterprises, '[d]istribution questions were only part of the problem, but the issues of authority and morality were more important ultimately' (Andors 1977a: 167). Objections to the typical Seventy Articles policies of rigid division of labour and tight control over workers in the enterprise surfaced again in the rebel workers' movement, as '[a]rbitrary controls over workshop communications and regimentation of the pace of production, based on quotas made by functionaries in factory offices, antagonized enough people to fuel the rebels' spark' (Andors 1977a: 167). The sense of alienation felt by workers who didn't even have control over the pace of the machinery they operated, so apparent during the Hundred Flowers campaign, is again palpable in the early Cultural Revolution, and rebel workers moved quickly to 'direct criticisms of top factory officials' (Walder 1996: 177).

Morality entered into workers' considerations where they focused not just on questions of their own individual material benefits, but rather on 'the relative distribution between workers and managers. They attacked privileges both on and off the job' (Andors 1977a: 168), as well as the issue of cadre corruption and the misuse of their power to suppress workers' protests in earlier stages of the Cultural Revolution. We have already seen that attempts to reinforce the theoretical political equality and 'comradely relations' between workers and cadres, mainly by compelling the latter to give up the attitude of 'bureaucrats riding over the heads of the people' and participate in labour, had made little progress in the nine years since they began, and the question of whether cadres were 'leaders' or 'rulers' became even more contentious in the highly politicized atmosphere of the Cultural Revolution. What concerned workers was not only who had authority in the workplace, but also how that authority was exercised, 'a decision-making method and a work-style. Officiousness and snobbery were more than marginal concerns of many rebels' (Andors 1977a: 167). They had never enjoyed being treated with contempt by enterprise cadres, but there had been nothing they could do about it until the Cultural Revolution shattered the myth 'that the local authorities represented the Party leadership and Mao, and so were untouchable' (Wang Shaoguang 1995: 80).

In the context of workers' rebellions in Poland, J M Montias has observed that workers often refrained from overtly political protests and demands as they were well aware of the likely consequences of such actions, namely swift suppression and retribution. However, there were clear signs that political and moral issues were very important in workers' protests:

> [I]t is evident both from [workers'] formal complaints and from the points formally raised at meetings with officials, that justice and human dignity – including the right to have a say in working conditions and other pertinent matters – are issues that are virtually as basic to the interests of Polish workers as prices, wages and working hours.
>
> (Montias 1981: 182)

Chinese workers seemed to share this attitude, strongly objecting to their exclusion from the making of decisions affecting their working lives, and showing deep resentment of cadres' high-handed and arrogant disposal of questions of direct concern to them.

Given this concern both with the power exercised by cadres in the enterprise and the way in which they exercised it, and with particular attention to questions of privilege and lack of accountability, there are obvious connections between the issues which were of greatest importance to workers in the Cultural Revolution and the developing rebel paradigm of Chinese society, which saw the main social division as between the masses below and a privileged and exploitative 'red capitalist' minority with power above (A Chan 1992: 70). Thus workers' involvement in the Cultural Revolution cannot be construed as marginal and concerned only with narrow economic issues, despite the fact that only a minority were active rebels. Nor, however, should the possible political significance of industrial action in support of economic demands itself be neglected: Montias finds that of ten major disturbances in the communist countries of Eastern Europe and the former Soviet Union between 1953 and 1977, eight 'had their origin in economically motivated work stoppages' (Montias 1981: 175).

The Cultural Revolution in 1967

January 1967: power seizures and the anti-economism backlash

As happened periodically throughout the Cultural Revolution, the party centre 'discovered' at a crucial moment a document produced by a mass organization condemning economism as sabotage of the movement. This was the 'Urgent

Notice' published by a number of rebel organizations in Shanghai which was broadcast nationally on 9 January 1967 and published in the *People's Daily* on 12 January. The national and local press and mass organizations' own publications were soon dominated by the campaign, and the notice itself revealed the extent of the crisis in the draconian measures it recommended to end economism:

> all those who have opposed Chairman Mao, Vice-Chairman Lin, and the CCRG, and all those who have sabotaged the Cultural Revolution and production will immediately be arrested by the Public Security Bureau [PSB] in accordance with the law ... all those who violate the above [anti-economism] provisions will immediately be punished as saboteurs of the Cultural Revolution.
>
> (*People's Daily* 12 January 1967)

As well as calling a halt to *chuanlian* and demanding that all expense money received for travelling to other units and cities be repaid, in instalments if necessary (it actually proved very difficult to recover money paid out to workers, as many had simply spent it, or refused to admit that the payments made to them constituted economism (Perry and Li 1997: 115–16)), the document laid stress on workers' and cadres' duty to stay at their posts and work their normal eight-hour day, and called on all personnel to return to their original units to 'grasp revolution and promote production'. In addition, enterprise funds were frozen to prevent any further unauthorized payments to workers making 'economistic' demands, and the issues of 'wage adjustments, back-pay and welfare' were shelved until the final stages of the Cultural Revolution 'to avoid shifting the overall direction of the struggle' (*People's Daily* 12 January 1967).

However, it is evident that despite this outpouring of official and unofficial criticism, there was some recognition of the strength of feeling behind workers' demands and protests, and even of their legitimacy in some cases. Not all the problems raised were dismissed out of hand, although almost all had their solution postponed to a later stage of the movement (*Guangming Daily* 16 January 1967). Some adjustments were later made to the terms of apprenticeships in Shanghai, and non-unionized workers were given the same welfare entitlements as union members (Perry and Li 1997: 116). Temporary and contract workers often lost their jobs and might be sent to the countryside, and were banned from setting up their own organizations in February 1967, but power holders were forbidden from taking 'class reprisal' against them and they were accorded the same political (but not economic) rights as other workers, showing that their protests had been justified in part (Solomon 1968: 16).

Students' enthusiasm for the anti-economism campaign might explain why, in mid-January, radio reports said that attacks by workers on rebel students were still a serious problem in some Guangzhou enterprises. In Shanghai, some rebel leaders on the docks also responded to the assault on economism, attempting to persuade workers to concentrate on the overthrow of the local party first and then turn to economic problems, but many workers argued that political and economic reforms were not incompatible and could be pursued simultaneously. This case features the same sort of split between a minority which, like the students, followed the ideological line laid down by the centre, and the rank-and-file who were reluctant to abandon what seemed to them eminently reasonable demands (Wylie 1981: 115–16; Perry and Li 1997: 111–12).

But economism had not been the only manifestation of a genuinely popular mass movement among workers early in 1967. Of equal concern to the party centre was the trend towards 'extreme democratization' or 'ultra-democracy' (*People's Daily* 12 January 1967; *Guangming Daily* 16 January 1967), by which was meant the tendency of some workers 'to oppose, negate, exclude and overthrow all the cadres' (*Guangzhou Radio* 31 March 1967). Through March and April the preferred term changed from 'extreme democracy' to anarchism (*Xinhua News Agency* 18 March 1967), and just for once the term was used fairly accurately rather than as a random term of political abuse. The attacks on 'extreme democratization' marked a swift change of attitude only days after a call for 'extensive democracy' had been made, with the involvement of workers and peasants in the movement hailed as a new stage of the Cultural Revolution. The reason for this change of heart was the phenomenon of power seizures in enterprises. Rebel workers in particular had moved from criticism to simply forcing aside the entire cadre establishment in their factories and taking control through new bodies which they formed themselves.

Power seizures at the provincial and municipal level were encouraged by the CCRG throughout January 1967. They occurred both on the Paris Commune model and on the Heilongjiang 'triple combination' model, which was soon adopted as official policy and promoted as an example to follow nationwide (*Red Flag* 1 March 1967: 12–14), the main problem with the Commune form being that, as a radical form of direct democracy, it left no room for the leading role of the party (P N Lee 1987: 111–12; Walder 1978: 60–3). The triple combination form guaranteed the place of some existing power holders and military representatives in the new power structures, the third element being representatives of mass organizations. The use of the term 'Commune' was actually banned by the party centre during February 1967 (a temporary exception was made for Zhang Chunqiao in Shanghai) in an effort to remove from consideration this subversive idea of direct democracy making all existing power holders redundant, and a similar retreat from radicalism can be observed in official reactions to enterprise-level power seizures.

Recalling the 1967 'January Revolution' in the famous 'Whither China?' article, Yang Xiguang celebrated the success of industrial power seizures:

> It was quite different from the threats of the bureaucrats who, before the revolution, had said: 'Without us, production would collapse, and the society would fall into a state of hopeless confusion.' . . . As a matter of fact, without the bureaucrats and bureaucratic organs, productivity was greatly liberated. . . . The management of industrial plants by the workers them-

selves after January was really impressive. For the first time the workers had the feeling that 'it is not the state which managed them, but us who manage the state'. For the first time, they felt that they were producing for themselves. Their enthusiasm had never been so high and their sense of responsibility as masters of the house had never been so strong.

(Benton and Hunter 1995: 125)

This is obviously a highly idealized picture of production going on uninterrupted and reaching new heights during the January Storm: we know that most workers were able to seize power only for a fairly short length of time, and faced continuous opposition and attacks from conservative workers and the military (who re-imposed control in most cases by the end of February 1967), and all this in a situation where production had been quite severely disrupted before the power seizures even occurred, with the result that production in Wuhan factories, for example, fell in some cases to only 20 per cent of targets during January (Wang Shaoguang 1995: 118). But despite these practical objections, the account does capture something of the spirit of this brief period of radicalism. Before the party, backed by the PLA, had made it clear that only triple-combination power seizures were acceptable, workers were often praised in the press for setting up new 'revolutionary production committees' in their enterprises using the election methods of the Paris Commune whereby delegates could be recalled by workers at any time and had no special titles or privileges (*People's Daily* 14 and 24 January 1967; *Xinhua News Agency* (Shanghai) 15 January 1967).

In one case reported in the official press it was stated with approval that *all* former staff in an enterprise had been relieved of their posts, despite their expertise, in an effort to wipe out bureaucratism in the plant:

Some suggested that, since the members of the former staff were very 'shrewd' in management, they could be kept to take care of technical matters. But the majority disagreed, arguing that revolution meant complete severance with the old and blazing a new trail entirely. Any idea of reconciliation and compromise must be rejected. So the former functionaries were relieved of their posts and went to work in the workshops.

(*Xinhua News Agency* 23 January 1967)

This case occurred in Shanghai before the Commune form was abandoned in favour of the triple combination, and before concern about the number of cadres leaving or being forced out of their posts became widespread (*People's Daily* 11 February 1967). This trend of removing all cadres from their posts never gained official approval in most places and was soon corrected even in Shanghai, and as the weeks passed it was emphasized more and more often that the majority of cadres (95 per cent was the figure often given) were 'good or relatively good' and should be judged on their whole record, not just on a few recent mistakes. The very frequency of these restatements of the 'correct' cadre policy, however, indicates the force of the trend for workers' power seizures in which all cadres stood aside or were overthrown.

Reports on power seizures by rebel workers in a number of enterprises in Guangzhou during the January Revolution did their best to down-play the numbers involved and the amount of support rebels were able to attract from the workforce, with frequent references to a 'handful' of trouble-makers (*Guangzhou Daily* 2 April 1967). But it becomes clear from the details of these accounts (dating from after the imposition of military rule in the city) that the 'tiny handful' were able not only to overthrow the existing enterprise leadership, but also to 'hoodwink' enough workers into backing them to enable them to hold off the counter-attacks of conservative workers, activists and cadres, reinforced by the PLA, with several assaults having to be made before the latter were successful in reimposing control (*Guangzhou Daily* 2 April 1967; *Guangzhou Radio* 15 March 1967). The power seizure phase of the Cultural Revolution, like economism, revealed divisions between students and workers ostensibly on the same side. Where rebel workers disrupted normal working in this period, students might step in, effectively serving as strike-breakers; this happened on the railways in Guangdong, where students worked as ticket-collectors (*Guangzhou Radio* 6 April 1967), and on the Shanghai docks (Wylie 1981: 117) as well.

The 'February Adverse Current' and 'March Black Wind': military suppression of rebels

Once they had found out that the party centre under Mao really would not defend the 'capitalist roaders' they were attacking in local government and enter-prises, the rebels took their challenge the logical next step. As civilian authorities came close to collapse, they passed the crucial personal dossiers, such a threat to the rebels who were always vulnerable to accusations of harbouring bad-class 'ghosts and monsters', to the military. Rebels in many places then turned on 'the last pillar of the old establishment' (Wang Shaoguang 1995: 118) with raids on military installations where files (and arrested comrades) were being held (Vogel 1969: 332). The army had in almost all cases backed the conservative faction once it was instructed to support the genuine proletarian leftists in late January 1967, and rebel raids and defiance provided all the justification necessary for a crackdown on the most radical and troublesome groups, and for the imposition of something close to martial law in many cities.

To see where the danger lay from the authorities' point of view, it is instruc-tive to look at which groups were banned first and treated most harshly through February and March 1967. The usual pattern of more severe treatment for workers than for students is evident: the first targets of mass arrests in Guangzhou were 'organizations of non-student elements' (Zi Chuan 1977a: 8), and according to Dai Xiao'ai, when the military authorities turned on the rebel federation which had taken control of the Guangdong provincial government, 'worker and professional groups . . . were consistently treated more severely than their student affiliates' (Bennett and Montaperto 1971: 166). Just as workers were among the first to be arrested, there is evidence that they were also the last to be released after Mao's April 1967 reprieve of the rebels. In Changsha, non-student rebels served much longer terms than did students (Unger 1991a: 20), and in Guangzhou, rebel workers' organizations did not revive as quickly as those of students once the suppression began to be lifted (Liu Guokai 1987: 69), and were described in an unofficial newspaper as late as August 1967 as having been only recently restored and expanded (*Red Insurrection* 22 August 1967).

The threat posed by some of the groups banned and declared counter-revolutionary was not only ideological, it was also organizational: workers' organizations which extended across different trades, industries, and districts were banned (as were organizations of demobilized soldiers and all those branded 'economist' (*Red Flag* 1 March 1967)). It appears that the threat posed by contract and temporary workers was not just that they were extremely militant, having very little to lose, but also that they sought at a very early stage to form national organizations. It has often been observed that protest is much easier for the CCP to deal with when it can be confined to a single work-unit, or to a limited geographical area; when it cuts across the party's lines of vertical control, it is much harder to nip in the bud. The threat of cross-boundary organizations was not a new discovery of the CCP: its predecessor, the Guomindang, had concentrated in its suppression of organized labour on preventing the emergence of union *federations* above all else (Epstein 1949: vi). The provisions for the disbanding of organizations which cut across the boundaries of different trades and those which united workers in a particular district hit rebel workers' organizations particularly hard, as they relied on these connections for their strength, often being a minority in individual enterprises: 'Few were able to seize power in their own units; most joined citywide, provincewide, or nationwide activities' (Liu Guokai 1987: 79).

After Mao had decided that the factional struggle had not yet achieved its aims and revived the rebels from early April 1967, accounts emerged of how those involved in the banned groups were treated under the 'March Black Wind'. In Guangzhou all members of banned organizations had been closely supervised, having to register with the municipal PSB, and it was later claimed that many more people were arrested in March than was admitted by the authorities (Zi Chuan 1977a: 8), often without proper warrants. When Cultural Revolution violence is invoked it is usually that of the mass organizations, particularly during the summer of 1967, which springs to mind, but the application of force by the state was an equally salient feature of many phases of the movement; memoirs of rebels who lived through these times, particularly in Guangzhou, stress its brutality (Zi Chuan 1977a: 7–8). It was not just the leaders of banned groups who came in for reprisals in the spring of 1967: rank-and-file members and their families were subject to various penalties, as described in this report on the suppression of the August 1 Combat Corps, a rebel workers' group composed mainly of ex-soldiers:

After the dissolution of August 1 Combat Corps, all members were forcibly ordered to surrender and register and to write self-examinations. . . . The homes of many were raided, and many were struggled against and severely beaten up. They and their wives and children were generally discriminated against and denounced. Some were fired, some were transferred to other posts, some had their wages reduced, and for some the welfare benefits to which they were entitled were abolished. This caused some people to lose their jobs and their homes.

(*Steel August 1* 15 October 1967)

These were exactly the sort of reprisals which had initially deterred many workers from participation in the Cultural Revolution. Firing, transferring, docking pay and struggling against workers were familiar methods to those of them who had witnessed earlier campaigns in the 1950s, and the same tactics had been used against workers in the early stages of the Cultural Revolution itself. But it seems that despite the lessons of past experience, the momentum of the 'economism' movement and the January Revolution power seizures had carried workers along into actions and organizations which they knew to carry serious risks.

'We are now the real masters of our plant'

When workers had seized power in their enterprises in the first days of 1967 it was often claimed that they were finally acting as 'the masters' and fulfilling socialist principles by taking management into their own hands. This radical power seizure phase, though, was short-lived, and the rebels' 'expressly political [agenda] of overthrowing workplace . . . authorities' (Perry and Li 1997: 29) temporarily disappeared, replaced by the triple-combination form of new political authority, the revolutionary committee, with its built-in cadre and military dominance. Reinstatement of the cadres overthrown during the January Storm was near-complete in many enterprises (Wang Shaoguang 1995: 127), and communications to workers from the party centre stressed discipline, the maintenance of production, efficiency, economy, keeping to the eight-hour day, attention to quality, cooperation with the PLA, and proper application of Mao's cadre policy (i.e. working with the 95 per cent of 'good' or redeemable cadres) (*Red Flag* 10 March 1967: 3–4). Particularly as the triple combination amounted to military dominance in many places (Wang Shaoguang 1995: 127), it is hard to see how the revolution in enterprise management could have continued.

However, accounts from factories around China during and after the 'March Black Wind' continue to make far-reaching claims about workers' new-found authority in the workplace, implying that the banning of prominent workers' organizations and the arrest of many activists had not stopped the momentum of a real revolution in enterprise management and democracy. The larger questions of authority and the relationship between workers and their managers had now been ruled out of bounds, as 'ultra-democracy' and the overthrow of all authority was condemned, but possibly progress could still be made on reversing some of the more unpopular trends in management systems from the Seventy

Articles era, such as issues of the rigid division of labour, unnecessarily complex and strict rules and regulations, and the exclusion of workers from decision-making.

In the course of triple-combination power seizures in enterprises throughout the country, it was reported, 'the rebels and revolutionary cadres joined forces, took all power into their own hands, and promptly started to institute a new order of things in their factories' (*Xinhua News Agency* 21 February 1967) by tackling the bureaucratism which had long hampered workers:

> The handful of persons taking the capitalist road . . . enforced an out-and-out bureaucratic system which stifled the initiative and ingenuity of the workers . . . some leading cadres sat in their offices like high-and-mighty bureaucrats. All they did was to issue orders, dream up plans and indulge in the formulation of rules and regulations. Division of labour was so rigidly applied that it became a barrier between cadres and workers, between the managing and producing section, and between one workshop and another.
>
> (*Xinhua News Agency* 21 February 1967)

These bureaucrats had been replaced by a new sort of administrator, described as 'pathbreakers in the Cultural Revolution and model workers in production', people with 'high political qualifications' who were elected by workers themselves to be their 'true servants':

> They work among the workers. Planners go to the workers to discuss their ideas and the resulting plan fully tallies with actual conditions. And the managing departments are now beginning to serve, and not just to 'control', the workshops. . . . A worker expressed exactly the sentiments of his comrades when he said: 'We are now the real masters of our plant. Chairman Mao has given us the right to run it and we must do it well.'
>
> (*Xinhua News Agency* 21 February 1967)

We saw in the 1950s that the existence of a system of elections does not guarantee that workers have anything like a free choice in selecting cadres, but at that time elections for administrative, as opposed to union, cadres were only experimented with briefly, so this reform of management would represent a step forward whatever the extent of the choice being offered to workers.

Another example recommended for emulation was that of the Guiyang Cotton Mill, where the plant's twenty-two administrative departments were abolished and replaced with four offices which led revolution and production, bringing about a reduction in the proportion of non-productive personnel and closer relations between workers and especially technical cadres, who now 'have . . . gone to the shops to live, study and struggle together with the rank and file'. This was said to be 'a good beginning . . . for eradicating the evil influence of the former capitalist, revisionist system of management'. But there were also signs that little might actually have changed in some enterprises despite all the rhetoric about putting politics in command and implementing the mass line, for the simple reason that although a 'handful' had been removed from their positions, it was stated that 'many revolutionary cadres have taken part in leadership work and a sound command system has been set up' (*Beijing Review* 7 April 1967: 27–9); in other words, much the same people were in charge in many cases and discipline was still being enforced.

It will be seen in the next chapter that even if these accounts of reforms in particular plants were accurate, this does not necessarily mean that many, or even any, other enterprises not selected as models were experiencing the same changes. Even in the first half of 1967, accounts of sweeping changes in the running of enterprises are noticeably formulaic, sticking closely to the terms and principles laid down in the *People's Daily*; the touches of local linguistic colour which lend authenticity to workers' reported speech in the newspapers of the Hundred Flowers era are absent in much of the Cultural Revolution. Perry and Li offer one explanation for this: that many statements about the Cultural Revolution in factories, both for publication and for internal use, were written not by workers themselves, but by ex-students assigned to this role in enterprises or by intellectuals: 'By late 1968, virtually everything published in the press in the name of workers was really written either by former [student] Red Guards or by radical academics and journalists' (Perry and Li 1997: 26). In all, the new provisional power structures seemed to include large numbers of cadres, including members of the former leadership, and those workers' representatives who were chosen to serve on the new bodies tended to be veteran workers, Mao-study activists and models, representatives of the old establishment, in other words. Moreover, they were selected by 'repeated examination and discussion' among workers and staff, not by any form of election, still less the Paris Commune type of election so strongly promoted a few months before (*People's Daily* 8 May 1967). Thus it does not appear that much real progress can have been made towards workers' gaining meaningful authority in the enterprise.

Nineteen sixty-eight: the fall of the rebels and the rise of 'workers' dictatorship'

Questions of enterprise management and authority were pushed aside during the summer of 1967 by the pitched battles, amounting to a virtual civil war in places, which took place between the factions and between rebels and the armed forces. The extent of the violence finally forced the party centre to acknowledge the most striking feature of the mass organizations through which the Cultural Revolution had so far been conducted, the fact that they comprised two different and opposing factions, with the division running through every section of urban society including the working class. While in public statements this division was blandly wished away as unnecessary and the result of capitalist roaders tricking the masses to turn on each other (*People's Daily* 14 September 1967), action was taken to force all mass organizations into 'great alliances', representatives from which could then be chosen to sit on the revolutionary committees which had temporarily replaced party committees at all levels.

But progress in forging 'great alliances' among workers was slow, dragging on well into the spring of 1968, and such undesirable phenomena as economism and protests by temporary and contract workers (Solomon 1968: 23; Wang Shaoguang 1995: 168–9) also reappeared, even in parts of industry which were under direct military control (*Guangzhou Railway General Headquarters* February 1968; *Spring Thunder Warriors* 25 November 1967). The obvious difficulties experienced in trying to persuade, coax, and threaten workers into forming alliances were rooted in the unresolved issues of this and previous confrontations with workers. Rebel workers were still adamantly opposed to the 'liberation' and return to work of large numbers of deposed cadres, and to the powerful role of the PLA representatives in the revolutionary committees. Concern about continued attacks on cadres prompted the usual measures to remove antagonism on the factory floor, with leading cadres being urged to go down to the masses, spend at least a third of their time there, and display a democratic workstyle, treating others as their equals (*Guangzhou Radio* 19–21 October and 21–2 November 1967 *passim*).

These exhortations, if heeded, might have won a favourable response from workers back in the mid-1950s, but now, after eighteen months of the Cultural Revolution, things had gone much too far for gestures like these to have any real effect. Workers were not now asking cadres to mend their ways and show them more respect; they had already overthrown many of the cadres once, completely rejecting their authority, and had tried, for a brief period, to establish themselves as the true 'masters of the enterprise'. The insistence of the central authorities on the reinstatement of most cadres was bitterly resented by rebels after this. It had also become apparent to many rebels by now that

> all their actions had to fall into some sort of orbit known only to those at the top, or else. Those who were not reconciled to playing this role became angry. They started to shout the slogan: 'We want a genuine mass movement, not a manipulation of the mass movement!'
>
> (Liu Guokai 1987: 115)

This was a dangerous development from the point of view of the top leadership, and was one more motive for turning to the only institution party leaders could still rely on, the PLA, for the suppression, by force wherever necessary, of those forces which were unwilling to submit to the 'restoration of the old' in enterprises and elsewhere.

Resisting restoration and the 'ultra-left trend'

The problems of persistent factionalism and attacks on restored cadres were blamed in part on the re-emergence of the 'ultra-left trend' (Huang Yongsheng 1967) among workers, and there is some truth in this accusation. Left ideas grew in popularity among some of the rebels during the last months of 1967 and the first half of 1968, and the influence of the extreme left 'trend' on Guangzhou's workers led to calls on provincial radio in June 1968 for the smashing of 'illegal solidarities between groups of workers and the Trend' (*Guangdong Radio* 7 June 1968). Between January and March 1968 the radical rebel manifesto, *Whither China?*, produced by Hunan's Provincial Revolutionary Alliance, was circulating nationally with its attack on the exploiting 'red capitalist' cadre class and its call not to 'go down the bourgeois reformist road of the Revolutionary Committees' (Zi Chuan 1977b: 46). Local ultra-leftist 'trends' appeared in response, such as the so-called '5 August thought trend' which posed the question 'Whither Guangdong?' (Zi Chuan 1977b: 46) Echoing the analysis of the Hunan Provincial Revolutionary Alliance's Yang Xiguang, a member of the '5 August' faction stated at a meeting that 'the present contradiction is between the basic level of the labouring people, the rusticated youth, and contract and temporary workers who have suffered the most deeply [on the one hand], and those who have climbed up onto the workers' throne' (Hai Feng 1971: 330). This formulation clearly relates the idea of the existence of a new bureaucratic class exploiting workers and peasants to the conflict we saw in 1966 and early 1967 which pitted the more disadvantaged workers against enterprise and party authorities, showing the close connection between workers' protests and one of the most important ideas to emerge from the Cultural Revolution.

That the danger of this idea that cadres constituted a new exploiting class in enterprises was taken seriously at the centre is shown by an April 1968 *People's Daily* article on revolutionary committees in enterprises, in which it was specifically denied that cadres' political power was that of an exploiting class. Cadres, however, were warned that the proletarian nature of their political power depended on maintaining close ties with the workers, becoming 'common people serving as officials', and guarding against bureaucratism, arrogance and oppressive behaviour (*People's Daily* 3 April 1968). Later in the year, as rebel attacks on the revolutionary committees' 'rightist reversal of verdicts' (i.e. the inclusion of cadres overthrown by rebels) gathered momentum, further attempts were made to emphasize that the revolutionary committee was uniquely well-suited to the mass line and anti-bureaucratism, and that representatives were ordinary labourers with no special privileges; it was even claimed that criticism of the revolutionary committees by some rebels was proof of the democratic atmosphere (*Xinhua News Agency* 30 June 1968).

The stress on the revolutionary committees' status as a 'red political power' won by workers' own efforts during the Cultural Revolution made criticism of the institution problematic, but rebel workers' groups in Guangzhou were very clear in their condemnation of the way in which the old power holders had taken over the new institutions in enterprises, and the fact that both they and the conservatives had effectively shut rebel workers (and cadres) out of the new organs of power, including not just the revolutionary committee, but also the workers' disciplinary teams which were organized in the spring and summer of 1968 to carry out the 'cleansing of class ranks' (*Guangzhou Workers* 28 May 1968):

When revolutionary committees were established in various factories, the rebels . . . suffered from discrimination of all sorts. For instance, in the Canton Iron and Steel Works and other plants, some rebel group leaders . . . were accused of having 'strong factionalist character' or of being 'extreme leftists' and were prevented from joining the 'three-way combination' organs. When a revolutionary committee was set up in the Canton Oil Refinery, all representatives of the rebel group were excluded from it.

(*Guangzhou Workers* 28 May 1968: 9)

It was a similar story with the workers' disciplinary corps, where rebel workers were excluded almost entirely from the organizations, and particularly from their leadership; those who did join were reportedly harassed by conservative faction members who made up the bulk of the force. Rebels also complained that

> Apart from being subject to political attack and discrimination, many rebel fighters also suffered from economic persecution. In the Canton Paper Mill and Canton Shipbuilding Yard cases continued to appear where the wages of workers of rebel groups were unreasonably reduced and hardship subsidies unreasonably abolished, and so on.
>
> (*Guangzhou Workers* 28 May 1968: 9)

Rebels were at a particular disadvantage in Guangzhou because of the strong influence of the military there under Huang Yongsheng, a close associate of Lin Biao, and so the conservative faction had come out on top while the rebels suffered brutal suppression during 1968. But the picture elsewhere was similar: in Wuhan, where rebels had eclipsed the conservatives after the July 1967 Wuhan Incident, as the new organs of power were consolidated, rebel gains swiftly evaporated. Since participation in the groups carrying out the 1968 'cleansing class ranks' campaign depended on good class background, former conservatives dominated the movement and rebels yet again found themselves cast as suspects. At all levels in Wuhan's revolutionary committees reorganization, re-shuffles and consolidation took place during 1968 and into early 1969, and all the changes had the same effect: 'the rebels were replaced by former conservatives, and the cadres who had supported the rebels by the cadres who had not' (Wang Shaoguang 1995: 208).

What most concerned rebel workers everywhere was the 'return to the old'. It seemed to many of them that all the effort and upheaval of the past two years had changed very little in many units. *Whither China?* had insisted that the Cultural Revolution was not about the dismissal of individual power holders, but the overthrow of the entire structure of authority in enterprises and in society, but now it seemed that not only had this sort of revolution not succeeded, but the rebels had even failed permanently to dislodge individuals in the old system. Guangzhou workers were driven to conclude that

> the same group of men are still in actual power, while mass representatives are merely the appendages . . . in Canton at present, both in those units

where revolutionary committees have been set up and in those units where [they] have not, not only do the same group of men remain in power, but the same working systems remain intact also.

(*Guangzhou Workers* 28 May 1968: 15)

The examples given were that the old party committees and the political and militia departments still seemed to be operating within the framework of the 'new red political power', and it was said that 'some people in these departments are even now collecting black material against the masses', and in some cases had made preparations for the arrest of rebel leaders in their enterprises (*Guangzhou Workers* 28 May 1968: 13). It seemed to the 'have-nots' in enterprises that they were more or less back where they had started.

The end of the Cultural Revolution (April 1969)

At the end of 1966 and the beginning of 1967, workers had taken advantage of the unprecedented opportunity presented to them by the lifting of party controls on organizations and the legitimizing of attacks on party and administrative cadres, to press for a solution to all the grievances which had been building up among them over the years, the most fundamental of which – the question of power or authority and who really was the master of the enterprise – can be traced back to both of the previous confrontations between workers and the party-state. In the circumstances of the Cultural Revolution, workers took their growing conviction that cadres were not simply allotted a different sort of work under the rational division of labour, but were actually a privileged and exploitative stratum or new class, to its logical conclusion and, briefly, attempted to take over enterprises themselves. Both this and the more 'economistic' aspects of the mass movement proved equally unacceptable to the central authorities, and the movement was soon brought back onto its proper course. The subsequent struggles of the rebels never looked likely to achieve any radical changes in how enterprises were run or who held power in them, and by mid-1968 they were battling just to avoid total obliteration.

It seems paradoxical that at precisely the moment when rebel workers' groups, and particularly their leaders, were falling victim to a familiar type of campaign to root out trouble-makers, workers seemed finally to have come to the forefront of the Cultural Revolution with the despatch of workers' propaganda teams into schools and universities and all units in the 'superstructure' to exercise 'all-round working class leadership'. But it must be remembered that

only workers with 'high political qualifications' were recruited into the propaganda teams. In places like Guangzhou, where typical 'conservatives' had crushed typical 'rebels', large numbers of workers were not only deprived of the honour of exercising 'overall leadership', but were victims of the 'clean out' movement.

(Liu Guokai 1987: 126–7)

It was not only the movement to 'cleanse class ranks' which targeted former rebels among the workforce: the 'one hit, three anti' campaign and the witch-hunts against the ultra-left, including the fictional 'May 16 conspiracy', also tended to trap the same people in their nets (Walder 1996: 190–1). In the name of the proletariat there developed in 1968 'a period of repression and terror that was as severe as anything seen since 1949' (Walder 1996: 190), conducted not by the working class, as the terminology implied, but much more straightforwardly by the army and the civilian police. 'The Cultural Revolution came to an abrupt, shocking end' (Liu Guokai 1987: 118) as the new revolutionary order was enforced. Again, the situation perhaps can be seen at its starkest in Guangzhou. The report by rebel workers in Guangzhou quoted above was intended to be the first part of a longer document, but there turned out to be no time for them to prepare it. The final suppression of the rebels began in the summer of 1968, and on 15 July the headquarters of the rebel workers' federation which prepared the report was the target of the military's 'mopping-up' operations; four people were killed by stray bullets as troops fought their way up through the building from floor to floor (Zi Chuan 1977b: 48).

It can have been little consolation to rebel workers that their analysis of what was wrong with the way enterprises were run was partially accepted by the new, left-dominated party centre. During 1968 it was acknowledged that cadres had in some cases become an exploiting, privileged stratum usurping the product of workers' labour, and that the relations between workers and cadres had thus degenerated from those between leaders and led to those between exploiters and exploited (*People's Daily* 9 July 1968). But the cause of this was identified as the bourgeois revisionism of Liu Shaoqi and his agents who had imposed 'profit in command' and material incentives, and had caused enterprise administration to become top-heavy, resulting in a split between the party and the people, the proletarian state and the masses (*People's Daily* 13 July 1968). The solution to this was the mass line, closer ties with workers and rejection of privileges, 'crack troops and simpler administration', i.e. retrenchment of administrative staff, and the revolutionary committee (*People's Daily* 13 July 1968). This formulation clearly represents a victory of the Maoist line in industry over that associated with Liu and Deng, but of course this did not necessarily represent a victory for any group of workers, and certainly not for the most outspoken among the rebels.

These sorts of policies in industry, the Maoist line of politics in command and reliance on the masses to get rid of irrational regulations and systems, so-called mass management, persisted not just through what was left of the Cultural Revolution proper but, on paper at least, on into the 1970s; they were the subject of a particularly fierce debate between the Gang of Four and Deng Xiaoping and their respective followers in 1975–6. In fact, when the lasting influence of the Cultural Revolution in industry is discussed, it is usually this policy line which is meant, rather than workers' earlier experiences in self-organization, 'economism', and seizing power. It is important to distinguish here between the three years of the Cultural Revolution proper and the years of Gang of Four dominance from late 1969 to 1976. The former period is one which many workers retrospectively saw as a high point of democratization and freedom of expression and organization in enterprises and in wider society, but in the latter seven or eight years, ubiquitous praise for the superiority of the working class and its leading role in society and politics was not matched by the reality of workers' position and influence, and workers seem to have been subject to the same sort of autocratic rule as the rest of Chinese society; indeed, workers were often prominent among those protesting against this type of rule. The next chapter will consider this period, looking at how far the much-trumpeted 'revolution in mass management' actually occurred, and tracing the causes of the renewed wave of strikes in 1974–5 and the leading role played by young workers in the protests which threatened to bring down the Gang of Four in the spring of 1976.

5 'Long live the people'

Unrest and dissent, 1969–76

'Restoration of the old' in enterprises, 1969–73

At the First Plenum of the Ninth Party Congress in April 1969, Mao said:

> It seemed there was no alternative but to make the great Cultural Revolution, because this foundation of ours was not sound enough. According to my observations, still in a considerable number of enterprises, if not all or a majority of them, leadership was not in the hands of genuine Marxists and the masses of workers.
>
> (P N Lee 1987: 111)

The claim that power in most enterprises now was in the hands of 'genuine Marxists and the masses of workers' was often repeated in the years after 1969, but the return to their posts of many former factory cadres, together with the absence of any effective new mechanism allowing workers to participate in enterprise decision-making, casts doubt on the extent of any real change. The rebels had been in the forefront of demands for substantive changes in the power structure, but increasingly, as was seen in the last chapter, they found themselves on the wrong end of campaigns carried out by the elite beneficiaries of the pre-1966 status quo in industry.

To judge from the propaganda writings of the time, the Cultural Revolution had indeed brought about a revolution in industrial management, one which had put workers in their proper place in the socialist enterprise as the political equals of managers and technicians, able to formulate rules and systems for themselves and playing a full part in technical innovation (Andors 1997b). There was a strong emphasis on reliance on the workers in managing socialist enterprises, and the Anshan Constitution was once again promoted as the guiding set of principles for all management work (*Guangming Daily* 21 March 1970; Andors 1977b). The implication was of a huge quantitative and qualitative increase in workers' participation in management, and some researchers found this to be the case, describing institutions such as the workers' management team as 'attempts to develop organizational structures affording the greatest possibilities for the masses to participate in running the factories and to make their weight felt'

(Bettelheim 1974: 43). Charles Bettelheim, basing his findings on field-work at six model enterprises in Beijing, went furthest in accepting the new line as the reality in Chinese factories, suggesting that China was seeing a transition to 'management by the majority, or mass management' (Bettelheim 1974: 70).

But most of those who have examined the practice of participation in management and all the issues surrounding workers' achievement of their proper position in the socialist enterprise have concluded that both 'the degree of change and its permanence was greatly overstated' (Lockett 1985: 5) by Bettelheim:

> The more radical and egalitarian demands for fundamental changes in the prevailing system of industrial organization, issuing from sections of the working class movement and voiced by some of the more radical leaders in Beijing, were denounced as 'ultra-leftist' well before the Cultural Revolution had run its tragic course.
>
> (Meisner 1989: 104)

In the case of the revolutionary committee, a familiar problem prevented workers from gaining significant leverage over those in charge of the enterprise as 'the appearance of control from below through election was not institutionalized through re-election procedures, and there is no evidence to suggest that there was any form of re-election' (Lockett 1985: 15). As we saw with the workers' congress and unions in 1956–7, this lack of provision for regular re-election of representatives was often fatal in undermining participatory institutions. As for workers' management teams, 'from 1973 they were put under the control of the reformed trade union and by 1975 certainly such bodies neither existed on the scale suggested by Bettelheim nor did they have the autonomy from management and Party structures' (Lockett 1985: 18).

Measures for workers' participation in management and in technical innovation do not seem to have lived up to claims that they represented a revolution in industrial organization and management, being 'at best reformist in character. . . . Most were gradually abandoned in the early 1970s in favor of pre-Cultural Revolution forms of managerial authority, factory work rules, and labour discipline' (Meisner 1989: 104). The results of the other 'participation', that of cadres and technicians in labour, were similarly disappointing. This sort of participation had been going on in one form or another for nearly twenty years, but there still was little sign that it was having the effect desired by the workers who had initially called for it. Cadres' participation in manual labour 'perhaps had a certain symbolic significance, but [its] effects on the consciousness of those involved were problematic in the short term and negligible over the long term' (Meisner 1989: 104).

The 'liberation' and reinstatement of former cadres after the 'cleansing of class ranks' which ended the Cultural Revolution seemed to have the sort of effect rebel workers had feared when they opposed the policy back in 1967–8, as it 'gradually eroded much of the impact of the Cultural Revolution' (Blecher and White 1985: 111). In one enterprise, this was what happened:

As former cadres were 'liberated', they were placed on the revolutionary committee where their numbers, skill and experience came to outweigh the mass representatives. As the unit resumed its normal activities, and political matters increasingly gave way to administrative and professional tasks, moreover, the revolutionary committee as a whole lost power to its standing committee, and the mass representatives on the standing committee became less influential. Their opinions were increasingly ignored, and they spoke less and less often.

(Blecher and White 1985: 111)

This is an almost exact repetition of the fate of workers' representatives on the very first participatory organ set up after liberation, the WRC, as noted in the first chapter of this study. It is particularly ironic in view of all the praise of the Anshan Constitution and corresponding vilification of the Seventy Articles during the early 1970s that 'the basic orientation, and, in some cases, the specific provisions of the "Seventy Articles" had outlived their opponents' (P N Lee 1987: 93).

But if 'the structure of the industrial establishment, together with its vested interests, suffered little discontinuity and disturbance from the early 1960s to the period right after the Cultural Revolution' (P N Lee 1977: 87), we cannot say that the Cultural Revolution had no lasting impact in industry or on workers' lives and ideas. The Cultural Revolution did see a 'marked influx of workers and new cadres into organs of local government' (Andors 1977a: 213), not just in Shanghai but more generally (Perry and Li 1997: 187), even though it proved more difficult for workers or cadres of the rebel faction to gain or keep positions of power within the workplace (Wang Shaoguang 1995: 229–30). And even within the work-unit, the Cultural Revolution also gave workers 'a limited say in some areas from which they had been excluded ... led to the airing of many critical ideas', and also played a part in 'reducing managerial control in areas such as labour discipline' (Lockett 1983: 229–30). Complaints about lax discipline and anarchism in enterprises in the late 1970s invariably cited the Cultural Revolution as its major cause, and not without reason, although this deleterious effect should properly be traced back to the rebellions of 1966–9 rather than being attributed to the Gang of Four's influence over workers during the 1970s. The experiences of the Cultural Revolution led to a crisis of managerial legitimacy (Lockett 1983: 230), and to a certain extent of the legitimacy of all authority, especially among younger workers. Those workers who had overthrown or forced aside the leaders of their enterprises in the January Revolution still resented the way in which these cadres had in most cases been reinstated with military backing, and presented the restored authorities with persistent problems through the 1970s.

Even while the Ninth Party Congress was actually in session unrest continued in some areas, with 'increasingly widespread wildcat strikes' in Wuhan (Wang Shaoguang 1995: 212) during April 1969. Elsewhere the presence of soldiers in enterprises was unable to guarantee anything like normal order and production.

We saw earlier how eagerly workers adopted the slogan of 'everyone liberating themselves' to justify their self-organization in the early stages of the Cultural Revolution, but this phrase also cropped up later in 1968 and 1969 with a slightly different slant on it, being used by workers to resist the reimposition of discipline by enterprise authorities and the military. Cadres reproaching young workers for persistent lateness or absenteeism might be told to mind their own business as the workers were merely exercising their right to 'liberate themselves' from the revisionist rules and regulations enforced by Liu Shaoqi, which had amounted to slavery for workers (*China News Analysis* 711, 7 June 1968, and 769, 15 August 1969).

It seems that the radical rhetoric of the Cultural Revolution and the early 1970s which celebrated the ideological superiority of the worker had some lasting, if unintended, effects, since it could be used by workers themselves in this way. The leadership gave hostages to fortune in the shape of slogans which, however far removed they were from the reality of workers' subordination to party-state authorities, were difficult to counter when thrown back at the authorities by discontented workers in cynical and entirely negative ways, e.g. to justify absenteeism or slow working. Reports of continued indiscipline and defiance of authority, particularly by young workers, abound from the late 1960s onwards (and rise to new heights from 1974), despite the harshly punitive nature of the army-backed campaigns to restore order:

> The tools of terror were turned to the restoration of labour discipline. Workers were threatened with accusation as counterrevolutionaries if they did not report to work; requests for unpaid overtime were phrased as 'loyalty to Mao work' – a clear threat in the reigning political atmosphere.
>
> (Walder 1996: 194)

It is remarkable how ineffective such extreme measures seem to have been. Even after party committees replaced revolutionary committees at all levels and networks of loyal activist-clients were rebuilt in enterprises, the level of discipline and control attainable before 1966 was never recovered (Perry and Li 1997: 191–2).

Leftist criticism of regulations and systems designed for 'control, check and suppression' of workers were particularly vulnerable to subversion by workers, since it gave them ample ideological justification for objecting to almost any control over their working lives as 'an insult to their revolutionary spontaneity' and an encroachment on their right to 'liberate themselves'. Party theoreticians tried to insist that there was such a thing as proletarian, revolutionary discipline which bore no resemblance at all to Liu Shaoqi's alleged insistence on servile obedience by workers, but simply putting the epithet 'revolutionary' in front of everything (as with the 1966 replacement of clock-cards with 'revolutionary cards') did not fool workers. They could play the same game, insisting that their patchy attendance or slow pace of work was an expression of their revolutionary resistance to 'control, check and suppression' by remnant revisionists who wished to return to the days of slavery. Each side knew very well what the other was really saying, but the linguistic constraints of high Maoism resulted in stalemate.

The eulogizing of workers' role as masters in the enterprise does seem to have given them a weapon with which they could resist an overt return to pre-1966 management methods, although this resistance was on the whole unsuccessful; of course, its other main effect would be to breed resentment against the Gang of Four when they proved either unwilling or unable to realize their much-vaunted revolution in industrial management and organization. Just as the pro-working class rhetoric of the Cultural Revolution and early 1970s was of use to workers in asserting themselves politically, in the 1989 protests, while well aware of the dishonesty of claims that workers were the 'leading class' in China, workers still attempted to use their widely proclaimed status as the 'most advanced class' to take what they felt to be their rightful place in the movement when this was resisted by student activists, and were certainly not defensive in their use of classic pro-working-class terminology. This was despite the fact that the reforms of the 1980s had seemed to disadvantage them in that terms such as 'the masses' or 'the working class is the most progressive class' were largely lost to them and to their advocates (Chan 1993: 50). Overall, workers' experience of the Cultural Revolution 'seems to have bequeathed a newfound pride in their proletarian status as well as a powerful language of class with which to challenge unwelcome policies' (Perry and Li 1997: 193).

Renewed factionalism and industrial unrest, 1974–5

Many people were discontented with the position in which they were left when the Cultural Revolution seemed to have come to an end in the spring of 1969. As well as leaders of mass organizations who might have had a brief taste of power before being edged out again by the rivals they had overthrown, workers still had a backlog of unresolved grievances, economic and political, which only became more urgent as time went on and which they would increasingly seek any opportunity to express. The first chance to press for changes in the outcome of the Cultural Revolution came as early as the end of 1971, after Lin Biao's sudden demise and denunciation as a traitor led to a swift reduction in the army's political role and its withdrawal from factories (Walder 1996: 194). Former leaders and activists in mass organizations, particularly rebels, still had to be careful as long as the campaigns against 'class enemies' and the 'ultra-left' were still going on; rumours from around the country that rebels were being released in the aftermath of Lin's death and disgrace turned out to refer only to isolated incidents (Wang Shaoguang 1995: 227). But with their great experience of how to use the centre's vague rhetoric and campaign instructions as cover for pursuing their own beliefs and interests, former activists were quick to take advantage of the next major movement to come along, the campaign to criticize Lin Biao and Confucius (*pi-Lin-pi-Kong*) which ran through 1974.

This campaign has been described as 'one of the most perplexing' remaining mysteries of the Cultural Revolution (Perry and Li 1997: 177). In most accounts,

Zhou Enlai is cast in the role of Confucius and the campaign interpreted as an attack on the Zhou-Deng wing of the party by the leftists, notably Mao and the Gang of Four. Most ordinary people, including those previously active in mass organizations, seem to have made little response to this rather arcane criticism campaign when it first started in mid-1973, but it took off from January 1974 once further explanation was offered that it was actually a campaign against

> anyone who was hostile to the Cultural Revolution. [The masses] were urged to do away with all outmoded rules and regulations and to throw themselves into the campaign. Furthermore, officials at all levels were warned against trying to dampen the masses' enthusiasm about partici-pating in the campaign.
>
> (Wang Shaoguang 1995: 233)

To many this seemed the best opportunity yet to restart the Cultural Revolution and press for the achievement of their aims. As well as renewed contact, and *chuanlian*, between former members of mass organizations in different work-units (Heilmann 1993: 9), a wave of industrial unrest and disrupted production accompanied the campaign. In part this was simply the result of some workers walking off the job to rejoin the factional conflict, but the unrest also included deliberate pressure for the meeting of workers' demands, as renewed factional competition 'provided the opportunity for labor protest that, like the wave of "economism" during the Cultural Revolution, often found radical rhetoric mixed with the suppression of labor demands (the same ones that had been ignored and suppressed since 1966)' (Walder 1996: 196), if not since 1956.

By April 1974 the disorder in many areas, and particularly the activity of a resurgent rebel faction, prompted the party centre to act to rein in the move-ment; in Wuhan there had even been fresh attacks on the army (Wang Shaoguang 1995: 240), although the numbers involved were much less than at the height of 1967's violent summer. Production figures from a number of provinces showed a sharp year-on-year reduction in the first five months of 1974 (Wang Shaoguang 1995: 245), and industrial unrest was reported among workers in many industries (Heilmann 1993: 3), with that among railway workers a particular cause for concern given their previous history of activism and their potential to affect the rest of the economy. The party's response showed an awareness of both the political and the economic dimensions of the threat: Document No. 12, issued in April 1974, banned 'spontaneous mass organiza-tions' and inter-unit or inter-regional *chuanlian*, and also ordered workers to return any payments they had received in response to their demands (Wang Shaoguang 1995: 242), an act reminiscent of 1967's anti-economism campaign. It is hardly surprising that many workers made pay-related demands: many had been subject to a pay freeze since 1963, apart, of course, from the increases they demanded and temporarily received during the 'wind of economism' of the winter of 1966–7. Welfare services to workers are also reported to have deterio-rated greatly in Shanghai by the mid-1970s; the official trade unions had only recently begun to function again, and the political climate made it difficult to raise any kind of economic grievance. The hostility of the left to anything which smacked of welfare trade unionism is illustrated by the example of Wang Hongwen's new 'Shanghai Federation of Trade Unions', which proved if anything even more reluctant to focus on bread-and-butter welfare issues than its pre-1966 predecessor had been (Perry and Li 1997: 188).

As in the 1950s and the Cultural Revolution to 1969, workers' grievances in this latest outbreak of unrest were not purely economic, but also encompassed disappointment over the lack of real improvement in their status and influence at work during and after the Cultural Revolution. Workers on the Shanghai docks in 1974 expressed the widely-felt exasperation that the 90 or 95 per cent of rehabilitated cadres who were back in post by then and were often behaving in much the same way as before, nevertheless constantly parroted the official line that it was the workers who were really in charge:

> The leadership of our district always talks about relying on the masses, but the masses are forgotten when work is carried out. Herein lies the cause of not much change in our district over the past few years. The leadership has looked upon the workers not as the masters of the wharf but as the slaves of tonnage.
>
> (Wylie 1981: 123)

To some extent enterprise authorities could have been caught in a trap of rising worker expectations: the concessions that workers did gain as a result of the Cultural Revolution reforms in industrial management might have satisfied them twenty or even ten years earlier, but in the aftermath of the wave of autonomous collective action and power seizures that marked the Cultural Revolution in 1966–7, they were seen as inadequate.

Also evident was a new unwillingness on the part of workers to endure an unsatisfactory situation, with the resort to self-organization and independent action coming much more quickly in the wake of the Cultural Revolution than it ever did before; ties with former comrades in the same enterprise and in other units and districts could quickly be revived, and workers did not face the same difficulty in renewing these connections as did students who had been sent down to the countryside in large numbers from 1968–9. Even 'administered participation' (Strand 1985), such as the organization of workers into study groups to prepare big-character posters for official campaigns, could now backfire on the party as participants might well decide to use the opportunity to express their own views; this occurred in the 1974 *pi-Lin-pi-Kong* campaign and in the April Fifth Movement of spring 1976 (Heilmann 1993: 15).

One further sign of the political content of unrest at this time is the stress on the issue of cadre privilege and 'going through the back door'. An official campaign against the phenomenon was actually launched in January 1974, and it reportedly gained an enthusiastic popular response. In fact the campaign proved rather too popular for the liking of many of the rehabilitated victims of the anti-cadre, anti-authority phase of the Cultural Revolution, and it was brought to a halt after only a month on the grounds that it was interfering with the simultaneous *pi-Lin-pi-Kong* campaign (Heilmann 1990: 32–3). The *pi-Lin-pi-Kong* campaign was itself curtailed from April 1974, as we have already seen, being put back under the firm control of party committees at all levels on the grounds of protecting production (Wang Shaoguang 1995: 245). But the question of cadre privilege and related issues would not go away. Guangzhou in the summer and autumn of 1974 was described as 'seething with urban protest' (A Chan *et al.* 1988: 8), much of it strongly reminiscent of rebel protests during the Cultural Revolution. The Baiyun Mountain Incident was the culmination of a series of protests:

> A crowd of more than a hundred thousand, mainly factory workers and youth who had been sent to settle in the countryside, climbed Baiyun mountain ostensibly to honour their ancestors according to the traditions of the Mid-autumn festival. But many of them used the occasion to protest against cadre privileges and other inequities.
>
> (A Chan *et al.* 1988: 8–9)

Other accounts of these events also mention the presence of demobilized soldiers with pay-related grievances (Zi Chuan 1977f: 23).

The autumn of 1974 in Guangzhou also saw the posting of the celebrated Li Yizhe big-character poster 'On socialist democracy and legal system', a document which was enormously influential in both the April Fifth and Democracy Wall Movements. This tract returned to some of the main themes of Cultural Revolution protests, namely the existence of a new bureaucratic ruling class or 'new nobility', and the inability of ordinary people to exercise their theoretical democratic rights and to participate in politics. It specifically raised concerns about special privilege and inequalities between cadres and ordinary people (Chan *et al.* 1988: 77–8), and also raised the question of the prolonged pay freeze and the lack of material incentives for workers (Chan *et al.* 1988: 82–3). This intertwining of political and economic concerns had by now become characteristic of workers' protests, and remained so through the April Fifth, Democracy Wall and 1989 Democracy Movements.

It is clear from all these events that the concerns and ideas of young workers in particular were not that different in the early to mid-1970s from what we saw in 1967–8, which suggests that the major underlying problems as far as less privileged workers were concerned had not been solved, and could still be the cause of large-scale protest. Frustration at the lack of political progress since the beginning of the Cultural Revolution combined with discontent at stagnant living standards to produce a general dissatisfaction among workers which found expression most notably in the 1975 summer of unrest in Hangzhou. This undeclared strike involving two dozen enterprises was only brought to an end with large-scale military deployment into factories involving as many as 30,000 troops at its height (Forster 1990: 218). Economic issues were obviously important in generating the Hangzhou unrest: wage disputes have been stressed as a cause in some accounts, and more generally there were problems with working conditions (especially in the exceptionally hot weather of this summer), poor welfare provisions, and cadres' resistance to participation in physical labour, all of which caused workers 'to perceive *unjust* inequality in their daily lives', not to mention exploitation (Andors 1977a: 234–5).

Keith Forster, however, points out that these grievances were common to industrial workers all over China by mid-1975, and finds another explanation for the extent and severity of the Hangzhou unrest in the details of the renewed factional struggle in the city, particularly the involvement of Wang Hongwen in a plot to sabotage production in order to discredit his opponents in the local leadership (Forster 1990: 226–8). He does allow, though, that the use of the army was intended as a general suppression of 'dissidents and malcontents' (Forster 1990: 219) such as could have been found in almost any enterprise in China since 1967, and expresses the view that subsequent propaganda claims of marked improvement in labour discipline among Hangzhou's young workers were greatly exaggerated, as many continued to come and go from work as they pleased (Forster 1990: 224), still 'liberating themselves' from the shackles of the eight-hour day. It was also reported that workers in Hangzhou had gone as far as organizing independent unions during 1975 and in subsequent years (Chiang 1990: 93).

Generally speaking, by the end of 1975 most workers had come to reject the policies of austerity and political incentives associated with the Gang of Four, and instead supported the return of Deng Xiaoping to the top leadership and his pragmatic line on material incentives and other economic issues, as well as the hope for stability and an end to large-scale political conflict which he represented (Perry and Li 1997: 188; Wang Shaoguang 1995: 254–5). In most places only a small minority of diehard rebel-faction leaders still stuck to their leftist allegiance, and only in Shanghai could the Gang be said to have anything amounting to a social base (Perry and Li 1997: 192). To judge from the output of the Gang's propaganda and media empire, workers had never been as powerful or as politically significant as they had become by the end of the Cultural Revolution decade, but like much of the Gang's policy 'line', this situation in fact hardly existed outside the columns of the *Liberation Daily*. In deciding between the Gang of Four's line in industry and that of Deng Xiaoping and the ailing Zhou Enlai, workers were really faced with the choice of no power and no money, or no power and some money, and it is hardly surprising that after more than a decade of struggle and enforced austerity, most opted for the latter. When the Gang launched a fresh campaign against Deng's 'right deviationism' in November 1975, most people reacted with a mixture of trepidation and depression at the prospect of a return to disorder and factional street-fighting (Wang Shaoguang 1995: 254–5), but few dared to oppose the new campaign outright. That changed abruptly, however, with the death of Zhou Enlai on 8 January 1976, the popular response to which proved to be a vital turning-point in the Gang's fall from power.

Workers in the 'April Fifth Movement' of 1976[1]

The April Fifth Movement was unusual in several respects, not least for its spontaneous, bottom-up nature. In its immediate aftermath Deng Xiaoping was blamed for having masterminded it as a challenge to the Gang of Four, but no convincing evidence for this has ever been produced. Instead, both participants and many observers stress that 'the meaning and significance of the movement lay in the very fact that it came from the grass roots, at a time when this seemed almost unthinkable' (Heilmann 1993: 17). It also stood out in the line of popular protests starting with the Hundred Flowers as a movement which was dominated in most places by young workers rather than students, and it gave an unusual degree of emphasis to questions of high-level politics rather than issues closer to home. By 1976 the question of top-level party leadership had in fact become crucial to workers since so much that they objected to in their daily lives flowed from the leadership's leftist dogma against material incentives and welfarism. The movement's final singularity was that it worked, insofar as it helped to depose the Gang of Four and prevent a left succession to Mao on his death in September 1976, instead contributing to Deng Xiaoping's rise to supreme power. This was the minimum goal of everyone involved; some had a further, more radical agenda, as will be seen below, extending beyond the removal of the four hated leftists to a systemic critique of how party power had evolved since 1949.

The 1976 protests began in the provinces and culminated in the capital with the Tiananmen Incident of 5 April. Following the death of Premier Zhou, best-loved and most respected of the remaining top party leaders, activists in a number of Chinese cities (often aware of what was happening elsewhere in the country) began planning unofficial gatherings in his memory which were to take place on 5 April (Williams 1991: 2), the festival of Qing Ming, the traditional day for remembering the dead in China. In fact, many of the wreaths in Tiananmen Square were laid on or before 4 April, which was a Sunday and therefore most people's day off. The numbers visiting the square to read the tributes and offer their own peaked during the weekend of 3–4 April at around half a million (Heilmann 1993: 6), and it was the overnight removal of the tributes from the square which prompted the violent unrest of the following day.

The political overtones of tributes to Zhou were very clear, not least to the Gang of Four; praise for Zhou was an implicit attack on them and their policies. The Gang's control over the media, especially in Shanghai, enabled them to mount coded and eventually overt attacks of their own on Zhou's memory in the months after his death, and it was in part these attacks which inflamed public opinion in some cities to the point where open criticism of the Gang flourished in the form of big-character posters and speeches on the streets. Nanjing was the scene of one of the most outspoken protests against the Gang, beginning in mid-March 1976 (Williams 1991: 2). Heilmann notes that recent Chinese accounts of the April Fifth Movement concur that the movement began in Nanjing and was then taken up in Beijing (Heilmann 1990: 69); one of the earliest slogans to appear in Tiananmen Square read: 'We are determined to support the Nanjing people in their revolutionary struggle' (Williams 1991: 2).

News of events in Nanjing mostly came not through the official media (although the directive circulated to party committees condemning the Nanjing protests had the effect of publicizing the Nanjing events among this group (Heilmann 1990: 72–3)), but from informal contacts between activists and also via the Cultural Revolution method of painting slogans or sticking posters on trains, especially those going to Beijing. These 'mobile billboards' from the movement in Nanjing first began arriving in Beijing on 31 March, and according to Heilmann, in the first few days of April so many arrived that station workers were unable to keep up with the cleaning of them (Heilmann 1990: 70–2). Students and railway workers cooperated in the endeavour, and used tar to paint slogans so that they could not be washed off (Garside 1981: 113; Heilmann 1993: 10). Trains similarly painted with slogans arrived in Shanghai, the Gang's stronghold, from Hangzhou, scene of a great deal of activity in 1976 (Forster 1986: 22) and of course the location of the serious industrial unrest the previous year which was put down by the PLA.

Other cities in which major 'April Fifth Incidents' took place included Taiyuan, Zhengzhou, Wuhan, Xi'an, Luoyang, Anyang, and Kaifeng (Heilmann 1990: 74, 88; 1993: 5; Forster 1986: 17; Williams 1991: 2), and in most of these cases, as in the Tiananmen Incident itself, the backbone of the movement consisted of young workers. The movement in Nanjing was slightly different in this respect, as it originated with students but had a great deal of worker support. Nanjing had an unusual tradition of cooperation between workers and students both before and after 1949, and this had continued even during the Cultural Revolution, when many young workers had developed the habit of going to the Nanjing University campus after work to read the posters there and catch up on the news from elsewhere. This began to happen again in the last week or so of March 1976 (Heilmann 1990: 60–1).

In Beijing students were much less in evidence in March and April 1976, and were in some cases physically prevented from joining memorial or protest marches as campus authorities locked the gates and patrolled the grounds during the 'Tiananmen Incident' (Heilmann 1990: 88, n. 3). This was reminiscent of the tactics used to prevent students from joining workers' protests in Gdansk and Gdynia in December 1970 (Laba 1991: 30), although the key measure there was not just shutting students into their classrooms, but the brainwave of offering them an early start to their Christmas holidays in order to get them out of the cities. In both the Beijing and Polish cases there was probably a certain amount of student apathy at work, and perhaps also an awareness of the risks of political activism. There was also remnant support for the Gang of Four among those students who had had to prove their leftist credentials to get into university and, not yet having to earn a living under prevailing austerity policies, retained their faith in radical Maoism: some of the students who did go to Tiananmen Square were reported to have spoken out *against* Zhou Enlai and been beaten up for their trouble (Garside 1981: 130; Heilmann 1993: 6). The young workers and students who did take part in the movement had in common above all their recent political experiences in the Cultural Revolution; many were also familiar with the widely-circulated Li Yizhe tract 'On socialist democracy and the legal system' (Williams 1991: 3; Zi Chuan 1977e: 41).[2] Former Red Guards were well-represented, including many former rebels (Heilmann 1990: 88) as well as conservatives (Heilmann 1993: 3–7), and many participants went on to be active in the Democracy Wall Movement from 1978 as well.

Not surprisingly, then, the April Fifth Movement showed a high degree of continuity with Cultural Revolution ideas and forms of action. But after the 1978 reversal of verdicts, the Tiananmen Incident in particular was presented by the Deng regime as a spontaneous mass act in support of the late Zhou and his protégé Deng, and against the Gang of Four (and implicitly against Mao as well); it was portrayed above all as a popular *rejection* of the Cultural Revolution. Young workers were indeed rejecting the experience of the years 1969–76, and in the case of those involved in mass organizations during 1966–9, they were also rejecting their own blind faith in Mao, as expressed by Wei Jingsheng in his comments on April 1976:

> We have come a long way since the Cultural Revolution started. In the beginning, people rose up in their anger to defend the man who was the author of their suffering. They opposed the slave system but worshipped its creator. They demanded democratic rights but despised democratic systems. They even tried to use a dictator's thought to win democratic rights. Eventually people recognized their mistakes. During the ten years of the Cultural Revolution great changes took place in their understanding. Many of those who in 1966 had stood in Tiananmen like idiots, with tears in their eyes, before that man who stripped them of their freedom, returned coura-geously in 1976 to oppose him in the same place.
>
> (Garside 1981: 277)

But, as is implied in Wei's words, they certainly were not rejecting the spirit of rebellion and questioning authority of the early Cultural Revolution, nor the opportunity they had then for the first time to exercise their right to political expression (albeit still within the limits of what the personality cult would allow). Many of them saw this taste of political autonomy in expression and organiza-tion as a positive legacy of the Cultural Revolution, despite all the cruelty, suffering and destruction which the movement had brought with it (Liu Guokai 1987: 140).

The posters of the April Fifth Movement showed absolutely unambiguously the deep popular hostility towards the Gang of Four which had developed by 1976: it was still a remarkable act of boldness to put up a poster at that time crit-icizing a serving Politburo member by name, but Zhang Chunqiao was named on several posters in Nanjing (Heilmann 1990: 63); many more poster-writers veiled their attacks in allusion and homophonic puns on the Gang's names. But it is quite a leap to go from this to casting April Fifth as a rejection of the mass movement phase of the Cultural Revolution between 1966 and 1969. The people's respect and support for the former 'capitalist roaders' in April 1976 was as clear as their rejection of the leftists, but as was noted in the last chapter, it is as well to beware of 'two-line struggle' explanations of popular support for one leader or another. While those involved in these high-level power struggles have a vested interest in claiming the maximum possible mass support for themselves, the social forces which helped to generate mass participation in the Cultural Revolution and the April Fifth Movement were more complicated than the 'two-line struggle' model will allow.

As has already been noted, participants in the April Fifth movement, whether young workers or students, had in common a background of Cultural Revolution activism and had been influenced by the 1974 Li Yizhe poster. So we can trace a course of development from Red Guard activity in which Zhou and Deng were the capitalist roaders and therefore the enemy, via the Li Yizhe tract with its denunciation of the new bureaucratic rulers of China and 'CCP ultra-leftism and autocratic lawlessness' (Williams 1991: 3), which was aimed at the Gang of Four in particular, to 1976, when demonstrators attacked the Gang of Four, the victors in the Cultural Revolution so far as the high-level power struggle was concerned, and praised Zhou and Deng. An explanation for this apparent 180-degree turn on the part of the young activists is offered by Xiao Ping:

> At the beginning of the Cultural Revolution the rebels chose Mao's temporary advocacy of rebellion and opposition to the bureaucracy rather than Chou's royalism and the status quo. In April 1976, comparing the Gang of Four's extreme leftism and autocracy with Chou's, people supported and longed for the latter. Pro- or anti-Chou, behind their outward emotions, these people were all fighting against the autocracy of the privileged bureaucratic class.
>
> (Xiao Ping 1986: 162)

Wang Xizhe (one of the four members of the Li Yizhe group) made a similar point when he described the Tiananmen Incident as

> a spontaneous opinion poll . . . an authentic people's election. . . . This was the brave attempt of the people to recapture the Party and the state that had been increasingly alienated from them . . . it was not an accident resulting from the usurpation of power by the Gang of Four. It was only an exposure and verification for society . . . of our Party's alienation from the people.
>
> (Wang Xizhe 1979a: 148)

In other words, the people had acted not only against the Gang of Four but also against the broader problem of their lack of control over the party which ruled in their name, the lack of control which had left them unable to 'recall' the Gang themselves. In doing so, the participants in the April Fifth movement had issued a warning to those in the party who did not support the Gang, making them fully aware of the need for radical change in the party's relationship with the people before it was too late. It was a reproach to those in the leadership who had allowed the Gang's influence (backed, of course, by Mao's tacit support or at least tolerance) to continue for so long in the face of popular desire for change.

Once Deng Xiaoping was back in power the party leadership cast former Cultural Revolution rebels as supporters of the Gang of Four, but in fact by 1974–6 they were among the Gang's boldest challengers (Williams 1991: 4; Chan 1992: 72–3). The April Fifth movement was the moment when they showed what they had learned in the Cultural Revolution, putting the party moderates on notice that where they could not or would not act, the people were now ready and willing to take matters into their own hands. Wang Xizhe drew attention to the significance of the bottom-up, spontaneous nature of the protest:

> The movement's vanguard and main force were mostly young workers. Isn't that like a huge signpost indicating that an entire generation of industrial workers has grown up with socialist consciousness and culture? When the proletarian enterprise was at its most dangerous moment, when the opportunistic politicians were frightened, trembling and scared to talk, was it not they who ventured forth, defended the people's welfare, and expressed their great ability to manage society?
>
> (Wang Xizhe 1979a: 154)

There were many statements of contempt and hatred for the Gang of Four during the April Fifth movement, and also many sincere expressions of respect and support for Deng Xiaoping as the heir to Zhou Enlai's reform programme, but the most striking slogan of all, recurring in different places throughout the movement, referred to neither side in the power struggle. It was 'Long live the people' (Garside 1981: 130; Forster 1986: 21), the phrase Mao had used at the first Red Guard rally in Tiananmen Square in 1966 (Forster 1986: 31), now turned against not just Mao and the Gang of Four, but against any in the party leadership who thought they could ignore the people's wishes.

From the suppression of April Fifth to the fall of the Gang of Four

The April Fifth movement was suppressed before it could develop in the direction of unofficial publishing or autonomous organization, as its successors in 1978–81 and 1989 did. But there were some proposals for autonomous organizations, such as a 'National Committee for the protection of Premier Zhou' proposed by a Beijing worker (Garside 1981: 135; Heilmann 1993: 16), even after the forcible clearing of Tiananmen Square on 5 April. During 4 April small *ad hoc* groups had been formed on the square, and on the following day, with retaliation clearly imminent, 'young workers and middle school students temporarily joined together and acted as bodyguards for authors of poems, speakers, and other prominent activists, trying to protect them from the secret police' (Heilmann 1993: 16). Given the shared experience of so many in the movement of the mass organizations of the Cultural Revolution, it is hard to believe that April Fifth would not have developed its own autonomous organizations had it continued even for a few days longer.

Figures on the numbers killed, injured, arrested, imprisoned, and executed in the April Fifth movement are sketchy, but the available statistics from most cities indicate that it was the workers (particularly young workers) who had dominated the movement who were arrested in the greatest numbers (Forster 1986: 29; Heilmann 1993: 11–12). Participants from all social groups are estimated to have totalled more than 1 million in Beijing, several hundred thousand in Nanjing, and tens of thousands in other cities including Hangzhou, Xi'an, Luoyang, and Taiyuan (Heilmann 1993: 7), and a majority of these were workers. Among the much smaller numbers who can be identified as the most outspoken activists in the movement, workers were also in the majority (Heilmann 1993: 11).

Workers' reasons for turning publicly against the Gang of Four in such large numbers included disillusionment with having dogmatic Maoism forced on them at endless political-study sessions while the economy and their standards of living stagnated and industrial morale fell to an all-time low (Garside 1981: 85). The significance of the younger generation's involvement is not only that they, after their experiences in the late 1960s, were most prepared to challenge authority and pursue their own beliefs and interests, but also that they had no personal memory of the bad old days before 1949, and were consequently much less impressed with the achievements of Chinese socialism (Garside 1981: 86), which seemed to them at best to have marked time during their lives. But despite the importance of the state of the economy in generating discontent with the leftist leadership, economic demands as such were not at all prominent in the movement. In one case in Nanjing where wages were mentioned, the issue was really a political one centring on allegations of favouritism, hypocrisy and inequality. Workers in Nanjing had heard rumours from further down the Yangzi that their counterparts in the Gang's stronghold of Shanghai were receiving unpublicized pay-rises at a time when the Gang was still preaching the virtues of egalitarianism and frugality to the rest of the country (Heilmann 1990: 44, 62–3), and this helped to fuel their protests.

Most people's April Fifth activities had been organized around their work-unit, often with the involvement, or at least the non-interference, of enterprise cadres from the trade unions, management, and even the party. The work-unit had certain obvious advantages for rapid mobilization of a large proportion of the workforce; it was not unusual for more than 50 per cent of those in a unit to participate in the movement (Heilmann 1993: 9). But this form of 'cellular protest' also showed a tendency to compartmentalize the movement and inhibit its broader development (Heilmann 1993: 9–10); it was cross-unit and cross-regional initiatives which had caused the authorities most concern all through the Cultural Revolution, but protest within a unit was much easier to deal with. There were a few examples of cross-unit cooperation in 1976, however, and it is very noticeable that in some cities former rebels were able to work with former conservatives, temporarily at least, despite the resurgence of factionalist struggles locally since 1974 (Heilmann 1993: 6–7, 16–17, 19).

It is also striking that, in contrast to the very successful campaigns of the early 1970s in which large numbers of people were forced to confess and to implicate others in largely fictional political conspiracies, there was no great rush to turn in to the authorities either participants in the April Fifth movement or materials produced during it, such as the poems and eulogies to Zhou which many had copied down in the course of the movement. Some factional score-settling did occur (Heilmann 1993: 7), not surprisingly, but many people showed a new willingness to defy the authorities, concealing documents by burying them in courtyards or out in the countryside, and in some cases secretly compiling collections of documents which began circulating as a form of Chinese *samizdat* publication (Garside 1981: 136), offering a foretaste of the so-called 'people's publications' (*minkan*) of the Democracy Wall movement. Wall-posters appeared to commemorate both the anniversary of Zhou Enlai's death on 8 January and the anniversary of the Tiananmen Incident in 1977 and 1978, and the Democracy Wall movement beginning in November 1978 was seen by many of its participants as a direct continuation of April Fifth (Seymour 1980: 7, 77, 85, 155, 267). Those involved were proud of their movement, and they would not let it be condemned or forgotten.

This defiance, born of the early Cultural Revolution and the permanent diminution of cadre authority which it had brought about, was also reflected in continued unrest through the summer of 1976, with strikes reported in Wuhan, Nanchang, Baoding, Sichuan and Xi'an (Garside 1981: 138; Walder 1996: 468–71). Although much of this unrest was factionalist in appearance, in many cases workers were again using the cover of factional campaigns to press workplace grievances and vent general anti-cadre hostility (Walder 1996: 468–71). Given the scale of popular opposition to the Gang, backed even by many cadres at the lower levels who themselves wished to see Deng Xiaoping, rather than anyone connected with the Gang, succeed the Great Helmsman, their position remained precarious, and within a month of Mao's death on 9 September 1976, the Four and many of their associates were under arrest. This sparked off probably the biggest spontaneous party the world has ever seen, described by Chinese as the 'three empties', meaning that liquor shops, firework shops and even hospital beds were all emptied for the celebrations. Spontaneous celebrations and anti-Gang demonstrations occurred even in their Shanghai base (Perry and Li 1997: 187), where only a single individual had dared to commemorate Zhou Enlai's passing six months before.

Most of the workers involved in what had been, at least in Beijing and Nanjing, a true mass movement (Heilmann 1993: 6) were prepared to allow the new Deng Xiaoping administration a chance to improve things before they would think of renewing their protests, but Deng did not have a blank cheque, despite widespread early enthusiasm for the 'Four Modernizations' programme. Former rebels in particular were on guard against any return to business as usual in Chinese politics, and were ready to speak out, organize and act collectively and autonomously again if dissatisfied with the new regime. This was the attitude which put many of them on a collision course with Deng within two years of his return to power, as we will see in the next chapter, and he found it necessary in 1982 to remove the right to strike from the Chinese constitution for the first time in the PRC's history. The end of austerity policies and successive catch-up pay increases from 1977 to 1979 proved extremely popular, but other aspects of Deng's reforms, with their emphasis on ending the 'iron rice-bowl' and management's right to manage, soon came to threaten workers' security, and the policy of sharper wage differentials, too, was resisted and subverted by workers who proved very set in their old, egalitarian ways despite their rejection of the low-pay austerity policy of the first half of the 1970s. Nineteen seventy-six, then, was not quite such an unalloyed triumph for Deng Xiaoping as it might have appeared, while the Maoist line in industry, based on the Anshan Constitution, was rejected because it had failed to materialize in important respects rather than because its concerns with workers' participation in management and political equality with cadres were not important to the rank and file.

The upheaval of the Cultural Revolution decade returned to the basic themes of all the confrontations between workers and the party-state in China thus far: the question of who held power in the enterprise and how it was exercised, and of whether or not the workers were truly 'masters in their own enterprise'. An important part of this was the issue of how workers were to be represented in the workplace and beyond, and how far they would be allowed to represent and defend their own interests and priorities. It is here that the major impact of the Cultural Revolution can be found, for it saw the first post-liberation instance of large-scale autonomous organization and political action by workers, and this experience had a profound effect on workers' later conduct and protests.

The Cultural Revolution also highlighted the idea of the existence of a new exploiting class in China in the shape of the industrial and party bureaucracy, and this idea came to be accepted by many workers during the course of the movement, even if it was not fully articulated at the point in 1966–7 when the momentum of the mass movement carried rebel workers into a wholesale attack on cadres. It is an idea which we will certainly find to be important when we look at the Democracy Wall movement and the problems of re-establishing both discipline and legitimacy in enterprises, and it also played a major role, though 'devoid of radical rhetoric' (Unger 1991a: 3) in many cases, in the pro-democracy protests of 1989. The spark for the next crisis in workers' relations with party-state authorities was in many cases a familiar one – disputes over methods of participation, the role of the official unions, cadre attitudes and workstyle – but workers' response, autonomous industrial and other protest action, clearly bore the marks of the Cultural Revolution, and debates over these longstanding bones of contention would never be quite the same again because of it.

6 'Others are your masters'

Dissent, democracy and reform, 1976–84

The sources of conflict and discontent in workplaces in the late 1970s and early 1980s were very similar to those of the mid-1950s, as were the main solutions advanced by party and enterprise authorities, including the revitalization of the official unions and the workers' congress. The posters and unofficial journals of the Democracy Wall movement of 1978–81[1] represented an opportunity for workers' grievances to be aired in public, an opportunity which in the 1950s was provided by an unusually outspoken official press during the Hundred Flowers campaign; and the final point of similarity between the two periods was the influence of events in Eastern Europe. The strike at the Lenin Shipyard and the rise of Solidarity were reported by both official and unofficial sources in China, and concerns about the possibility of a Chinese Solidarity seem to have loomed large in the thinking of CCP leaders from the second half of 1980 (Liao Gailong 1980). These concerns are evident throughout the 1980s, and probably contributed to the early targeting of workers' organizations for suppression during the 1989 Democracy Movement.

But the very fact that unofficial journals and sources of information existed shows the difference between the mid-1950s and the post-Mao era, and this difference can be traced in large part to the impact of the Cultural Revolution. Young workers and students who had gained experience of political activity and challenging authority during the Cultural Revolution were the mainstay of the Democracy Wall movement. Former Red Guards dominated the editorial boards of many unofficial journals (Chen Ruoxi 1982: 14–15; Xiao Ping 1986: 155), and the concerns of the Cultural Revolution, such as the rise of a new bureaucratic ruling class in China, questions of ownership and control in industry, and the desirability of a Paris Commune form of organization, were evident in the movement's writings (Lu Min 1979a).

As was mentioned in the last chapter, Liu Guokai and others identified the Cultural Revolution (1966–9) as a time when, albeit briefly, people actually were able to exercise the democratic rights laid down for them in the constitution, speaking out against cadres, and organizing themselves. After the subsequent period of dominance by the Gang of Four, former Cultural Revolution activists were more determined than ever to achieve clear legal guarantees of these rights, so that they would no longer be something which the party could grant or withhold according to its own interests. Harking back to the Li Yizhe group's poster in Guangzhou in 1974, the unofficial journals were full of discussions on socialist democracy and the legal system (Chen Ruoxi 1982: 74), and demanded legal guarantees of citizens' rights, especially the rights of freedom of speech, publication and organization. Given the links between the Cultural Revolution and Democracy Wall in terms of both participants and issues, it is not surprising that the authorities condemned some of the Democracy Wall activists for wanting to launch a 'second Cultural Revolution' against the party bureaucracy (*Red Flag* 1 March 1981: 17).

Democracy Wall

The Democracy Wall movement began in mid-November 1978 in Beijing with the posting of large numbers of big-character posters on the roadside wall in Xidan, to the west of Tiananmen Square, which gave the movement its name. As well as posters, unofficial journals soon began circulating in Beijing and in other cities all over China, including Guangzhou, Changsha, Wuhan, Taiyuan, Tianjin, Qingdao, Harbin, Shanghai, Nanjing, Guiyang and Kunming (Chen Ruoxi 1982: 107–15). The first wave of posters was sparked off by the 16 November *People's Daily* announcement of the decision to reverse the verdict on the Tiananmen Incident of 1976, declaring it a revolutionary act by the masses against the Gang of Four; this followed hard upon reversals of verdicts on high-profile April Fifth protests in other cities, including Nanjing, Hangzhou and Zhengzhou (Garside 1981: 200–1). The protests of March and April 1976 had been declared counter-revolutionary at the time and this verdict had been maintained by Mao's immediate successor, Hua Guofeng, but Deng Xiaoping's re-emergence into the top leadership during 1977 held out hope of a reversal. The November decision came a month before the Third Plenum of the Eleventh Central Committee at which Deng's economic reform programme was launched, marking the ascendancy of his wing of the party in the post-Mao competition for power.

But although Democracy Wall followed on closely from the April Fifth movement, being regarded by many participants as a direct continuation of it (Seymour 1980: 7), it was initially a different sort of movement. It could not really be described as a mass movement in the way that April Fifth in Beijing and Nanjing had been, despite the ready audience which the many unofficial publications and wall-posters found in urban areas: 'for the time being, the broader social forces of April had withdrawn from active political roles and were ready to entrust the affairs of state to the new Deng government' (Benton 1982: 103). The remaining activist minority, however, often had experience not only of April Fifth but of the Cultural Revolution, and their analysis of what had gone wrong in China did not encourage them to sit back now that a 'good' bureaucrat had been installed at the head of the same system over which Mao had presided. As Wang Xizhe, the only member of the Li Yizhe group to play an active role in Democracy Wall, put it:

While the people happily celebrated the October [1976] victory, demands of two types simultaneously arose. A segment of the masses became dissatisfied because they had had none of the spiritual and material means to enable them to recall the Gang of Four directly; they went a step further in their demands for democracy. Another segment of the masses seemed to feel the necessity of discovering anew the 'saviour of the world'. They spread the hope: 'Let's hope that Uncle Deng will live for a few more years'; there are even people who burn incense and pray for him . . . these actions . . . reveal that the people still feel extremely uncertain as far as controlling their own fate is concerned.

(Wang Xizhe 1979a: 149)

The April Fifth movement had been directed not just at the Gang of Four and Mao, but more broadly at a party elite which was a law unto itself, and which enjoyed not only a monopoly of political power but also considerable material privileges. Democracy Wall activists saw themselves as carrying on the process begun by April Fifth, which they saw as 'a revolutionary movement against autocracy and dictatorship' (Seymour 1980: 267). The new Deng regime had made statements on the importance of democratization to its overall reform programme, but vague expressions of good intent would not be sufficient to satisfy the Red Guard generation if they did not result in any concrete improvements in the political system. If economic improvements also failed to materialize, more people might also begin to lose patience with Deng's administration. It was clear that despite the wave of popular support and goodwill so evident in 1976, Deng's honeymoon period with the urban Chinese citizenry could prove to be rather short if he failed to meet their expectations of reform. Wei Jingsheng argued that Deng's regime had to continue to support the just demands of the people and to protect their legitimate interests if it was to keep their trust: 'Do the people support Deng Xiaoping as a person? No, they do not. Without his fight for the people's interests, he himself has nothing worthy of the people's support' (Wei Jingsheng 1979: 198). An enormous backlog of workers' grievances, economic and political, had built up since the mid-1960s or even earlier, and these could now find public expression in Democracy Wall's 'people's publications', many of which were written and edited by groups of workers.

Workers' concerns in Democracy Wall: living standards, pay, and cadre privilege

Although the main issue which brought hundreds of thousands onto the streets in 1976 had been the prevention of a leftist succession to Mao, the state of the economy, stagnating production, and the prolonged wage freeze had formed the economic backdrop to the protests. The Four Modernizations programme developed by Zhou and Deng had already been announced in 1975 and had drawn widespread popular support. Thus the question of the future economic direction of the country and the prospect for an improvement in standards of living had been integral to the movement's concerns, and economic problems, both macro and micro, were also an important concern of Democracy Wall, with many contributing to the debate on how reform should proceed. These economic questions were, of course, closely bound up with the political issues of democracy, representation and accountability, as is shown by the way in which the question of economic reform was tackled in the unofficial journals of the Democracy Wall movement. This link was also acknowledged initially in Deng's programme of economic reforms, although whereas Democracy Wall activists asserted that economic development was dependent on democratization and effective public supervision of government, the party centre under Deng had it the other way around (Rosen 1988: 9–10; Brodsgaard 1981: 773).

The urban housing shortage, the cause of much discontent back in the mid-1950s, came back on to the agenda in the late 1970s. A new feature of the complaints this time, however, was that it was not just inequality, but China's overall state of underdevelopment which was now being called into question by young people who looked at what had been achieved by thirty years of 'building socialism' and were distinctly unimpressed (Chen Ruoxi 1982: 75). Unfavourable comparisons of China with the capitalist West were common during Democracy Wall and later in the 1980s, although this did not mean that activists were uncritical of the West either. Doubts clearly existed about the 'superiority of socialism' and specifically about workers' position in society, since they were supposed to be 'the masters', yet in most cases had a very low standard of living. Questions along these lines required the authorities to demonstrate the advantages workers enjoyed under socialism, especially the right to participate in management and to elect democratically some of the enterprise leadership. These comparisons and criticisms of China therefore helped to increase pressure for real democratization of management, as well as for more obvious remedies such as price stabilization and improved housing and welfare.

The inadequate living space of many workers' households in Beijing was highlighted in many issues of the Beijing unofficial journal *Beijing Spring* (*Beijing Spring* 8 January, 17 June, and 10 August 1979), while in Qingdao *Theoretical Banner* claimed that since the fall of the Gang of Four, it had become common practice for the 'red bigwigs' to build luxurious properties for themselves and their families, even in a China where the economy was 'on the verge of collapse' and ordinary people were suffering from a shortage of housing (*Theoretical Banner* February 1981: 35). Ye Wenfu's poem, 'General, you cannot do this!', was inspired by a particular case of abuse of privilege to obtain luxury housing, that of a high-ranking PLA officer alleged to have ordered a kindergarten to be demolished to make way for his new mansion (Siu and Stern 1983: 157–71). Clearly the resentment of cadre privilege which had briefly emerged during the 1974 anti-privilege campaign was still a force to be reckoned with, as the extremely cramped living conditions of many households were repeatedly contrasted with the building by cadres of luxurious dwellings for themselves and their relatives. As in the mid-1950s, it was perceived inequality and inequity rather than poor housing per se that was the politically significant issue.

In Guangzhou, the seriousness of the problem of official abuse of power in the building or allocation of housing was confirmed by official newspaper reports on various cases which began to appear from 1980 (*Southern Daily* 9 February 1980, 6 May and 5 October 1981; *Guangzhou Daily* 21 and 29 January 1984). Corruption cases involving housing were identified as a key cause of worker dissatisfaction with management and the higher levels of bureaucracy, with (corrupt) mishandling of housing allocation sometimes mentioned as the issue which sparked off a strike in this period of relatively frequent industrial unrest (*Xinhua News Agency* 28 April 1984; *China Daily* 8 October 1981). The extent of concern about cadre abuse of power in the enterprise can be judged from a 1982 *Southern Daily* article praising an enterprise where the workers' congress had been put in charge of the sensitive tasks of housing allocation and the recruitment of employees' offspring to vacancies in the plant. The clear implication of this account is that this had the effect of preventing abuses of power which were otherwise extremely common; it was specifically noted that of fifty young people who had so far been given jobs, most were the offspring of shopfloor workers, and none were scions of 'leadership' families (*Southern Daily* 15 April 1982).

The phenomenon of different pay for the same work, a major cause of dissatisfaction in the 1950s, when it led to the widespread adoption of the 'work according to pay' attitude among disgruntled workers, also gave rise to discontent in the late 1970s and early 1980s. The economic reforms, by giving some enterprises more autonomy to retain and dispose of some of their profits and set wages and bonuses as they saw fit, seem to have exacerbated the problem. In some cases the objection was to disparities in pay between workers at different plants, where employees of one enterprise might see their pay rapidly falling behind that of workers at another plant with a higher value-added output (*Southern Daily* 25 April 1980). In other cases, bonuses within an enterprise would depend on the achievement of norms set for particular work-processes, and it soon became apparent that some workers were unjustly receiving lower bonuses than their colleagues simply because of the specific work-process in which they were engaged, not because they were working less hard or contributing less to the success of the enterprise (*Southern Daily* 28 April 1980). Complaints about the unfair distribution of pay and bonuses appeared in a regular 'Workers' Forum' column in the Guangzhou unofficial journal *People's Voice*,[2] as did many general items on local living standards, housing problems, prices and workers' standard of living (Chen Ruoxi 1982: 57, 76).

In many respects early reform measures and the debate about future changes seemed to pose a threat to workers' job security and to the welfare benefits they had hitherto enjoyed. Articles in the official press suggested that far too much was expected of enterprises, particularly smaller ones, in the form of welfare services, and that the provision of these services was an 'irrational burden' detracting from the enterprise's principle economic purpose and its efficiency (*Southern Daily* 10 January 1979). Condemnations of 'eating from one big pot' were soon joined, too, by speculation that the 'iron rice-bowl' of job security might become untenable in the new economic circumstances. Moves in this direction were, naturally, extremely unpopular among workers, especially when the system of lifetime tenure for cadres (the 'iron armchair') was still in place (*People's Voice* December 1979). Many Democracy Wall activists saw the latter as a far more serious problem, an obstacle to democratic accountability in the workplace as well as in government.

So to the mid-1950s concerns about housing and welfare had been added a threat to job security, and also worries that rising incomes might be overtaken by inflation. *Beijing Spring* published a list of prices of basic foodstuffs showing prices before and after 'adjustment' and percentage increases (*Beijing Spring* 2 April 1979: 26), and in Guangzhou, *People's Voice* kept an eye on wage levels and prices of everyday necessities in its 'Window on the world' section (Chen Ruoxi 1982: 57). By the early 1980s, the view that many workers' standards of living had actually dropped since the beginning of Deng's reform programme had become so widespread that articles appeared in the official press attempting to refute the claim. In a 'campaign to draw up detailed accounts', the authorities insisted that real wage increases had more than kept pace with rising prices (rising food prices were in part a knock-on effect of the agricultural reforms), and also pointed to some success in finding temporary work for the offspring of worker households, thus reducing the burden on the household budget (*Southern Daily* 3 May 1982). Whatever the truth of the matter, it is clear that many workers *perceived* their standard of living to have dropped, contrary to the promises made by the reformers in the leadership; the 'feel-good factor' was most definitely lacking. Party leaders in China would have been aware of the fact that increases in food prices had sparked off the strikes in Poland both in December 1970 and in August 1980 (*Xinhua News Agency* 18 December 1980).

In sum, it was not just obviously disadvantaged groups (such as the unemployed, rusticated youth illegally returned to the cities, or peasants come to the capital to seek redress for injustices and reduced to begging on the streets) who were concerned about their livelihood and had economic grievances for which the unofficial press of Democracy Wall provided an outlet. Ordinary workers' households were greatly concerned about present difficulties and possible future threats to their livelihood posed by the economic reforms, and the many unofficial journals edited by workers not surprisingly gave a great deal of space to their views.

Workers' concerns in Democracy Wall: participation and control

More obviously political issues, such as how workers could exercise control over their working lives and how their views and interests should be represented in the enterprise and in society, were also reflected in the 'people's publications'. Behind a large number of the criticisms raised in the unofficial publications and posters of Democracy Wall was one overriding question, namely whether, or to what extent, workers' theoretical status as masters of the enterprise and the leading class in society had actually been realized. It is this debate which is behind all arguments about the role of management, the enterprise party committee and the union, the powers and scope of the workers' congress, the possibility of self-management, democratic election of cadres, and the problems of public ownership.

This question of workers' status in the enterprise and in society had been at the heart of previous confrontations between workers and the party, but it was now addressed more explicitly and more bluntly than ever before by Democracy Wall activists and by protesting workers. There were a number of reasons for this. One was the Cultural Revolution rebel background of many in the movement: ideas of a new, exploiting ruling class emerging from China's post-revolution elite were not new to them. Thanks to discussion of the ideas of the Li Yizhe group and others, neither were systemic critiques of 'actually existing socialism' in China a completely new departure. With these earlier movements and ideas providing the foundations of the new movement, the way was open for criticism and protest to be taken further. There was a feeling after Mao's death and the fall of the Gang of Four that now nothing was sacred, and that there was an urgent need to say the previously unsayable and to expose the shortcomings in the way in which Chinese society and the economy were organized. Calls for a complete reassessment of the whole history of CCP rule were now commonplace. With the 'Open Door' trade policy initiated by Deng Xiaoping there was also more knowledge of the outside world, and this probably also contributed to a more critical attitude towards the achievements of the People's Republic thirty years on from liberation.

Common themes in Democracy Wall writings were the lack of democratic rights enjoyed by workers in Chinese enterprises, which many writers saw as a cause of China's relatively poor economic performance in recent years, and the fact that, although 'the people' nominally owned all state-run industrial enterprises, in fact they had no control over their operations whatsoever. Instead, this control was in the hands of party and management cadres appointed for life. One wall-poster put up in Beijing in December 1978, in the early weeks of the movement, put this quite bluntly:

> According to the concepts of Marxism-Leninism, the people should control the means of production. But ask yourselves, Chinese workers and peasants: Apart from the small wage which you receive each month, what do you control? What belongs to you? The answer is shameful: Others are your masters. In a socialist society, the product of labor should belong to the worker. But what do you get? Just enough so that you can continue to work! Higher salaries have not sufficed to compensate for soaring prices, and our standard of living has not improved.
>
> (Anon. 1978)

Another article related the problem of actual control over the means of production to the dominance of the party at all levels and to the system of lifetime tenure for cadres:

In our country, the means of production are not directly controlled by the people but are entrusted to people's representatives – administrative cadres at all levels. For this reason, the people cannot control the means of production unless they have control over the cadres. Since the 'system of posting according to grades' has rendered the people unable to supervise and control the cadres, the socialist economic base will be threatened if this old system is not gradually abolished. And, sooner or later, people's ownership will be turned into ownership by bureaucrats and emperors, and people will be enslaved again.

(Lu Min 1979a: 76–7)

The April Fifth Forum, like most Democracy Wall groups, was generally in favour of the reforms then beginning to be implemented and supported the 'Four Modernizations', but held the success of reforms in industry to be conditional on democratization in enterprises. One of its early statements observed that in China, 'the power of the people is the most uneconomically utilized of all', and went on to describe the situation in Chinese industry thus:

If a small number of non-producers in our country control the production workers with regard to their personal files, wages and transfers, it will be impossible to expect the workers to surpass the productivity of labor attained under the capitalist system. It is precisely those who dislike others airing independent political views that are suppressing production workers from expressing their views on production, distribution and exchange. If this is so, laborers under socialism will only be expected to mind their own business as handicraft workers traditionally did in the past.

(*April Fifth Forum* 1979: 159–60)

Wei Jingsheng, in 'The fifth modernization', argued that the poor position of ordinary workers in Chinese society was not simply due to the backwardness of the productive forces; even if that were no longer the case, 'the questions of authority, of domination of distribution, and of exploitation' (Wei Jingsheng 1978: 51) would still arise. The question as to whether exploitation and oppression could exist under socialist public ownership was specifically addressed in some of the unofficial journals. *Sea Spray* of Qingdao, noting that the question had hitherto been ruled out of bounds in what it sharply termed the 'nominally socialist world', expressed the view that exploitation and oppression could actually become worse under a system of bureaucratic, one-party rule as existed in China, where privilege could act as a form of capital (*Sea Spray* 1980: 34).[3]

This theme within the Democracy Wall movement provides evidence of a post-Cultural Revolution and post-Gang of Four diminution in party legitimacy, and a corresponding increase in political and organizational self-confidence, most notably among the movement's activists, but also among workers and the public at large. It was specifically argued by some that workers (or the people in general) had now shown that they were ready to take over much more of the direct running of their enterprises and of wider economic and political systems as well. This they saw as the beginning of the process of the withering away of the party and the state as predicted in Marxist theory. The negative example of what might happen if the party did not yield to popular demands in this area was the Soviet Union, while the positive example worthy of emulation was Yugoslavia, with its system of workers' self-management. Wang Xizhe, as observed in the previous chapter, saw the Tiananmen Incident itself as evidence that a new generation of workers was ready to replace the party's direct administrative leadership with its own. He went on to propose a change in the old Anshan Constitution formula for workers' participation in management in the economic sphere and workers' participation in dictatorship in the political sphere, advocating instead:

> 'direct democratic management by the workers'. The class dictatorship of the proletariat can have its firm material foundation only under conditions in which workers manage the means of production themselves directly and democratically. This was the aim of the Paris Commune, the aim of the October Revolution.
>
> (Wang Xizhe 1979a: 156)

The level of the industrial enterprise was seen by many as a suitable starting point for workers to take over direct, democratic management while the party organization took a back seat:

> [I]t is necessary to give the workers genuine democratic rights and do away with the administrative leadership power of the basic-level party organization in industrial enterprises. . . . Since class struggle is withering now, the party should also gradually wither away. This should first take place in the basic-level units of industrial enterprises.
>
> (Lu Min 1979b: 163)

Another article by a Beijing worker argued similarly that 'if we want to have a system of democracy in politics, we must insist on a system of people's democracy in economic management' (Han Zhixiong 1979: 162).

Many writers were not only making direct connections between the low morale and poor performance of industrial workers and undemocratic organization in enterprises and in the country as a whole, stating, for example, that the long-term deterioration in both economic performance and the people's livelihood was entirely 'due to a lack of democracy' (Han Zhixiong 1979: 162). They were also critical of some of the early reform measures taken to remedy the acknowledged lack of democracy in enterprises. One article noted that there was little point in workers being allowed to elect the heads of workshops, sections, shifts and groups when the real power on the shopfloor belonged to the enterprise party organization: 'therefore, this sort of partial democratic election cannot fundamentally arouse workers' enthusiasm for production. And the workers have taken a cool attitude towards this minor reform' (Lu Min 1979b: 163). This dismissal of the right to elect management cadres at certain levels as unimportant shows the gulf between what some Democracy Wall activists were demanding and what was being offered even by the reformists in the top party leadership. These cadre elections had been billed as 'an important right' of workers when promoted during 1979, and it was reported at the same time that the restoration of the workers' congress was meeting with considerable cadre resistance at the lower levels (*Southern Daily* 8 November 1979), even though the powers of that body were quite limited at the time. So what was derided as not enough by some activists and workers was clearly already too much for the management personnel it affected.

Workers' designated representatives did not escape criticism either. As in the Hundred Flowers era, the official unions were in crisis at the end of the 1970s, with workers' faith in them at a very low ebb and again some suggestions that there was no point in their continuing to exist: in his address to the Ninth ACFTU Congress in October 1978, Deng Xiaoping found it necessary to state that the official unions were 'no longer an unnecessary organization as some believed' (Deng Xiaoping 1978: 7). Workers described their official representatives as 'sign-board unions' (*Xinhua News Agency* 10 October 1979), i.e. unions in name only, who did nothing for them, did not represent their views (or even know what their views were), did not stand up to the party committee or management on their behalf, and did not even hold regular meetings in some cases (*Workers' Daily* 18 November 1980).

Some of the unions' earlier problems were more openly acknowledged in the post-Mao period than they had been before, and the unions did gain a greater degree of independence of action from the party for a time, at least in theory. As part of the general process of reassessing the PRC's history and politics right back to 1949, it was admitted that 'left' errors had been made with regard to trade unions as early as the 1950s. Li Lisan and Lai Ruoyu were both posthumously rehabilitated in 1980 and 1979 respectively, and it was stated the accusations against them of syndicalism and economism had been 'erroneous and groundless' (Ni Zhifu 1981; *Workers' Daily* 13 October 1981). However, in the early stages of the post-Mao period, the unions' role was not defined in a way which was strikingly different from that of the 1950s. Mobilizing workers for production and for the realization of the four modernizations was still regularly cited as the unions' core task (*Southern Daily* 3 March and 8 November 1979; *People's Daily* 19 October 1983), with tasks such as labour protection, education, improving skill levels, and safeguarding workers' democratic rights coming further down the list. When in Guangzhou in the spring of 1979 there was a certain amount of unrest connected with Democracy Wall around the anniversary of the April Fifth movement, the unions were called upon by the city authorities to guide workers in the 'correct' exercise of their democratic rights, oppose extreme democratization and individualism, and lead the workers to combat the 'small minority' of criminals who were 'destroying social order and production order' (*Southern Daily* 9 April 1979). So it would seem that the unions were still being cast in the role of controllers, mobilizers and educators of workers, rather than representatives of their special interests.

These criticisms of how Chinese industry was run, more obviously a challenge to the party than the still politically-charged issues of housing and living standards, were expressed with considerable forcefulness and articulacy by many worker-activists who wrote for or edited unofficial journals. But as time went on there was evidence that such views were not limited to this politically-conscious and active minority. Demands for independent unions made during a number of disputes and strikes in 1980–1 indicate the political content of industrial unrest. In one of the best-documented strikes of the period, at the Taiyuan steel works, striking workers 'labelling themselves "the poorest workers in the world", called for "breaking down the rusted door of socialism", the right to decide their own fate, the end to dictatorship, and the overthrow of the system of political bureaucracy' (Wilson 1990b: 263). Given that we know of the occurrence of many other strikes in this period,[4] although in most cases detailed reports are not available, it is possible that this was not the only case of industrial unrest where workers acting collectively put forward demands which went every bit as far as the criticisms of China's political system being articulated in the unofficial journals. He Qiu, of Guangzhou's *People's Voice*, hinted that the journals were only keeping pace with workers' views, describing them as 'the organs as well as the avant-garde of the democratic movement' (Chen Ruoxi 1982: 36).

Democracy Wall under pressure, January 1979–August 1980

The suppression of Democracy Wall was a gradual process which began as early as January 1979 and lasted, with greater or lesser severity, for more than two years. January 1979 saw the arrest of China Human Rights League activist Fu Yuehua, whose main crime had been to lead petitioning peasants up from the provinces in a demonstration in the centre of Beijing. By March the Chinese press was carrying articles denying that the 'foreign' type of human rights protection had anything to offer to a socialist country like China, and attacking a minority who were campaigning for 'extreme democratization' and 'bourgeois democracy' (*Workers' Daily* 22 March 1979). Wei Jingsheng's arrest on 29 March followed his publication of the essay 'Do we want democracy or a new dictatorship?', in which the measures employed by Deng's regime in dealing with popular protest and political activity were likened to 'the customary methods of fascist dictators old and new' (Wei Jingsheng 1979: 32).

Deng Xiaoping had initially tolerated the posters and publications, not least because they were primarily hostile to his own opponents on the left of the party. Democracy Wall had also provided a useful opportunity for him to demonstrate to the outside world how much China had changed and how tolerant of dissent he was in comparison with Mao and the Gang of Four, an attitude which went well with the ten-gallon hat he sported on his end-of-January visit to the United States, with which China had just resumed full diplomatic relations. But clearly Democracy Wall's systemic critiques of China's political and industrial systems were much less to his liking, and as the foremost surviving 'capitalist roader' victimized in the Cultural Revolution, like many of his generation he reacted immediately to any signs of mass politics taking to the streets again. In a speech on 30 March he set out the limits of free debate in the shape of the four cardinal principles, 'Party leadership, the socialist path, the dictatorship of the proletariat (now termed "the people's democratic dictatorship"), and Marxism-Leninism-Mao Zedong Thought' (Munro 1984a: 75). New regulations restricting the places where posters could be posted were announced on 1 April, although the original 'Democracy Wall' at Xidan in Beijing was not closed down until December 1979.

Over the next eighteen months publishers of and contributors to unofficial journals were subject to more or less constant pressure from the authorities to cease their activities. The 'four big freedoms' (the freedom to speak out freely, air views fully, hold great debates and write big-character posters) were removed from the Constitution in September 1980 (Chen Ruoxi 1982: 27). In response to efforts to close down unregistered unofficial journals, many groups and individuals switched to publishing in correspondence form, with journals being circulated to subscribers only rather than being on public sale, in an attempt to evade closure. Nineteen-eighty also saw the beginnings of a national organization linking the surviving journals and activists. In December 1980, in the wake of Solidarity and its impact on China, Democracy Wall activists were officially branded counter-revolutionaries who were stirring up social unrest and trying to wreck the economic reforms. A mass campaign against the 'two illegals' (illegal publications and organizations) was launched in all work-units with the promulgation of CCP Document No. 9 in February 1981, and this heralded the final round of arrests and closures of unofficial journals, with the final issue of *Duty*, published in June 1981, being the last such publication to find its way out to Hong Kong (Chen Ruoxi 1982: 36–8).

In Guangzhou the pressure on the movement was initially somewhat more subtle than was the case in most other cities, which is why the south became the centre of the movement from about the middle of 1980. In its early stages, the city was even described by some as a 'liberated area' for the democracy movement, and Wang Xizhe confirmed that this was an accurate description as of autumn 1979 (Wang Xizhe 1979b: 11). There are a number of explanations for this relative tolerance, one of which could be the city's proximity to Hong Kong, which meant that news of a harshly repressive reaction would quickly find its way to the outside world, harming the country's image at a time when the 'Open Door' policy of attracting foreign technology and investment was just getting off the ground. In addition, the movement could be useful to the authorities as a testing-ground for new ideas; activists often protested at being labelled anti-party when so many of the ideas first aired in the unofficial journals were actually taken up by the CCP later on (Rosen 1988: 2–3). The movement seems to have been comparatively weak initially and to have developed more slowly in Guangzhou than in other cities (Wang Xizhe 1979b: 11–12), and thus it probably seemed a less serious threat.

Stanley Rosen has pointed out that student journal editors were more suscep-
tible to official pressure to stop publishing, since their activities were a heavy
drain on both their finances and their study time, and since they were aware that
obstinacy in the face of official disapproval might affect their employment
assignments after graduation. The student-edited journal *Future* was the first to
cease publication voluntarily in Guangzhou, after provincial First Secretary Xi
Zhongxun suggested that it was unhelpful of the journal to dwell on the admit-
tedly important issue of the masses' low standard of living at a time when the
CCP was already working hard to solve the problem, undoing the damage of
previous errors committed by the likes of the Gang of Four (Rosen 1988: 16).
Workers such as He Qiu and Liu Guokai were less likely to respond in the
desired way to being leaned on like this, although, as Rosen notes, for this very
reason they were sometimes singled out for different treatment (Rosen 1988: 18).

In 1980, as in 1989, activists came up against the problem of registering a
publication or an organization with the authorities in order to keep their activities legal. The Guangzhou journal *People's Voice* suspended publication in the
spring of 1980 after being told by the Propaganda Department of the provincial
Party Committee that the journal had to comply with the 1952 'Temporary [sic]
Law on the Registration of Publications', which was still in force. Both *People's
Voice* and its offshoot *People's Road* protested that they had tried much earlier to
register with the authorities, but to no avail, and that it was unreasonable to
expect them to comply with such an out-of-date law. The particular measure to
which they objected was that the publications had to obtain the legal guarantee
of two privately-owned shops before they could be registered. This might not
have been an onerous requirement in 1952, but in 1980, as the editorial board of
People's Road pointed out, 'since the [socialist] transformation of commerce was
completed as early as 1956, after which private shops ceased to exist, it is now a
complete impossibility for us to go out and obtain the guarantee of two shop-
owners' (*October Review* 1980: 12). Similarly, in May 1989 the Beijing Workers'
Autonomous Federation (*gongzilian*) was refused registration by the Public
Security Bureau when it tried to achieve legal status, and then condemned as an
illegal organization (Walder and Gong 1993: 7).

But despite all this pressure, some 'people's publications' continued to appear
in various cities around China into 1980, and the groups of workers producing
them, as noted above, were less easy to intimidate than students. They shared in
the strong sense of working-class pride that seemed to emerge from the Cultural
Revolution, and presented this class identity as their defence when resisting the
closure of their journals, describing themselves as 'permanently employed
workers' (*People's Road* 1980: 12), or 'ideologically aware young factory workers'
(*Free Talk* 1981: 21) to emphasize their status in Chinese society and their right, as
workers, to participate in decision-making on the future of that society. Many of
them were of the generation denied the chance of higher education by the
upheavals of the Cultural Revolution, and factory jobs had been the best they
could hope for, but in putting them into the industrial workforce, far from
ridding itself of potentially troublesome campus radicals, the CCP had ended up

creating the type of person which, according to Liu Guokai, it feared the most, 'people who can think independently coming from the ranks of the working class' (A Chan 1992: 79). The 'Thinking Generation' who had 'graduated' from mass organizations and the April Fifth movement to play the leading role in Democracy Wall made it much more of a working-class movement than most of its predecessors since 1949 (Brodsgaard 1981: 774).

Workers' response to reform, to August 1980

Those worker activists who were able to keep publishing their unofficial journals through 1979 and into 1980 still did not lack material, as widespread labour discontent and unrest continued to be a feature of the early reform period. The new regime attempted to sell itself to workers as a provider of greater material benefits *and* greater democracy in enterprises, drawing an explicit contrast between its policies and practice under the Gang of Four (*Southern Daily* 7 January and 7 February 1979), but there were many aspects of the reforms in enterprises to which workers objected. We have already seen that apparent threats to the work-unit welfare system and employment security caused concern among workers, and wage issues were also controversial. Individual bonuses, a key feature of the reforms, were a particular bone of contention. These payments were intended to break the egalitarian, 'eating from one big pot' mentality among the industrial workforce by rewarding workers individually for their performance under the principle of 'more pay for more work'. In fact, in the short term at least, the use of individual performance-related bonuses proved singularly unsuccessful in ending wage egalitarianism. Susan Shirk has noted that the awarding of bonuses by workers themselves in small-group 'evaluation and comparison' sessions resulted in a strongly egalitarian distribution of the extra money. Measures to combat this seem to have been easily circumvented by such means as informal rotation systems, with workers taking turns to receive the highest bonuses, or simply by exerting pressure on those receiving high bonuses to share their good fortune with their workmates in the form of gifts or meals (Shirk 1981: 585).

Despite repeated assertions in the press that 'eating from the same big pot' was damaging to the interests of the state, the enterprise and the individual alike, and that egalitarianism, contrary to many workers' views, was not equivalent to socialism (*Southern Daily* 9 October 1979, 21 June and 21 August 1981; *Guangzhou Daily* 14 May 1984), these attitudes seem to have persisted. It is interesting that although the low-wage policy in force from the 1950s up until 1978 was itself a source of discontent, with the Cultural Revolution-era wage freezes a particular cause of complaint, there seems to have been little enthusiasm for widening income differentials in industry, with many workers instead favouring a relatively egalitarian distribution of a bigger 'cake'.

The 'them and us' hostility towards cadres characteristic of the Cultural Revolution seems to have lingered on here, with some workers emphasizing that all of them 'made a contribution to socialism' and 'created wealth' for society (and thus should be rewarded equally), while the cadres who were criticized for building themselves luxurious villas created nothing (*Theoretical Banner* 1981: 35; *Sailing Ship* n.d.: 11). This does not seem to have been a cynical or subversive use of the regime's own rhetoric such as we saw in the late 1960s. Rather it seems, like the spirited self-defence statements of the journal editors quoted earlier, to reflect a genuine sense of the rightful place of the working class in society. Even after more than ten years of reform, workers active in Beijing's Workers' Autonomous Federation in 1989 were still claiming their status as 'the rightful masters of this nation' (Walder and Gong 1993: 12), showing the persistence of these values despite the vast changes that had taken place in China's economy and society by the end of the 1980s. This was all sharply at odds with the general direction of the reforms, which tended to take power away from the party committee in the enterprise only to give it to management, not the workers. Managers' right to manage and to hire and fire dominated early discussions of how reform should proceed, and 'scientific management' was discussed with no hint now of any ideological objection to Lenin's 'blood and sweat system' of capitalism.

Reform in enterprises and the impact of Solidarity

With the examples of the Cultural Revolution and April Fifth before it, however, the party leadership knew it could not safely ignore rising discontent among the urban workforce, and was aware of the need to re-establish and revitalize institutions for workers' representation and participation in management, and to make a better job than the Gang of Four had of realizing workers' status as 'the masters'. Democracy Wall's working-class nature and input only made this a more urgent requirement, and at least in the early stages, a considerable degree of overlap can be detected between the demands of the Democracy Wall mainstream and the proposals of the 'reformists' in the party and government. In the same speech in which he had insisted that the official unions still had a role to play, Deng also called for democratic management as an essential part of the successful implementation of reform. Democratization of management was to be achieved by means of the revitalized workers' congress (usually with the union committee as its working body), which in addition to its usual remit of supervision, discussion and criticism would also organize the election of workshop, section and group leaders within the enterprise. Addressing some of the main concerns of Democracy Wall activists, Deng argued that an extension of the role of the workers' congress was needed in order to tackle the 'overconcentration of power within the Party and the state and the undesirable consequences stemming from this (such as bureaucratism, organizational rigidity, paternalism, extensive privileges, and the life-tenure [cadre] employment system' (P N Lee 1987: 138).

Similarly, the Democracy Wall debate on the realities of public ownership in China had its counterpart in official circles. We have already seen claims in some unofficial journals that 'ownership by the whole people' had over time turned

into control, if not actual ownership, of the means of production by a minority
of cadres, who thus came to be living exploitatively on the fruits of others'
labour. But it is more surprising to come across this type of argument in the
pages of the party-controlled *Beijing Review*:

> In some places and units where democratic life is lacking and a patriarchal
> system is in effect, the rights to manage an enterprise and to distribute its
> products are in fact in the hands of the Party secretary and the factory
> director. . . . [Workers' congresses] are nothing but rubber-stamp organiza-
> tions without real power . . . socialist public ownership is, to say the least, far
> from complete or even devoid of content.
>
> (*Beijing Review* 29 December 1980: 16)

The date of this article, December 1980, is significant, as this places it at the
height of the official panic about Solidarity and Chinese unrest.

It is debatable whether management democratization was an end in itself in
the post-Mao period or merely instrumental in the overall reform programme.
Many see promotion of the workers' congress as simply a means to an end,
necessary for the support of one of the main policies of that programme:
increased enterprise autonomy. If decentralization of some powers to the enterprise was to be successful, it was essential to have technically competent
management who enjoyed a certain amount of support and legitimacy in the
workplace. Put at its simplest, it was thought that giving enterprises, for example,
more scope for retaining profits to be distributed in the form of bonuses for
productivity and fulfilment of quotas would give workers an incentive to elect
the most competent personnel to run the enterprise, since inefficient management would have a direct adverse effect on workers' pockets. This view sees the
workers' congress as a by-product of the reform process mainly used 'to buttress
enterprise autonomy' (Hong and Lansbury 1987: 152).

In a slightly broader sense, there was a concern that the extent of worker
alienation from both management and the official unions could not but have an
effect on efficiency and productivity, making enterprise democratization a vital
part of the reform effort. Furthermore, taking into account the impact of
Democracy Wall, the possibility emerges that democratization was important in
itself as a means of diverting popular demands for democratic participation back
into officially-sanctioned channels, as well as being a prop of the reforms. What
gave impetus to enterprise democratization, in this view, were 'reasons of
management effectiveness and others relating to pressures for democracy . . .
including the unofficial "democracy movement"' (Lockett 1983: 232). Besides
accepting the enterprise autonomy argument, Peter Nan-shong Lee goes further
in crediting Deng with the promotion of industrial democracy in a different
(institutional rather than mobilizational) form from that practised by Mao, but
stemming from the same 'deep intellectual roots in Marxism' (P N Lee 1987:
140).[5] However, if industrial democracy was in fact desirable in itself to the top
leadership, it was certainly a subordinate goal to that of improving economic

performance and maintaining 'unity and stability'. Otherwise, it is difficult to see why a new era of democratic management in Chinese enterprises did not in fact emerge during the reforms of the early 1980s.

The workers' congress is an interesting case in point, as an examination of the debate on its powers between 1979 and 1981 shows the influence on the Chinese reforms of the changing nature of the Democracy Wall movement and of events in Eastern Europe. In the process of developing a workers' congress for the post-Mao era, a process which began with experimentation with radical reforms but ended in a return to the formalism and disillusionment of the mid-1950s, the demands of Democracy Wall activists and some workers gradually diverged from what enterprise and party leaders were prepared to concede, until the gulf between them became unbridgeable. This ultimately led workers to look for other ways of asserting their right to a greater degree of control over their working lives, in the shape of autonomous organizations with a political as well as an industrial remit.

After falling into disuse during the Cultural Revolution, the workers' congress began to be promoted again from 1978, but the Provisional Regulations governing its operations were not published until July 1981, and were not made permanent until 1984. This left a relatively long period of time when practice varied widely in different enterprises and in different parts of the country. There was a great deal of experimentation, and much discussion in the national, local and specialist trade union press of how the pitfalls of the workers' congress system of the 1950s might be avoided this time around. At times proposals were made which, if implemented, would have made the workers' congress a genuinely powerful body in the enterprise, not just within its traditional remit of welfare and bonuses but in the making of all major decisions. Such proposals 'gave rise to some speculation that China was about to embark on a more active form of worker participation than had occurred in the past' (Henley and Nyaw 1987: 144). But this speculation was limited to outside observers, while workers and also many union cadres were initially quite suspicious of the proposals and doubted that they could be made to work in their own enterprises, suspicions that were far from groundless in view of the ineffectiveness of past attempts to promote participation and democratization.

Official interest in applying the Yugoslavian example of decentralized workers' self-management was taken by some outside observers as a sign that the Chinese authorities' commitment to the democratization of management might be genuine this time. Many Democracy Wall activists such as Wang Xizhe spoke approvingly of the Yugoslav system (Wang Xizhe 1979b: 4–6; Han Zhixiong 1979: 162), apparently unaware of its actual limitations, and some official sources disseminated a similarly rosy view of the self-management system. But Nina Halpern has identified Chinese praise for this and other aspects of East European practice as being prompted primarily not by any perceived appropriateness of Yugoslavia (or Romania) as a model for China, but by foreign policy concerns (Halpern 1985: 98–101). Thus articles on the Yugoslav economy seem mainly to have been intended to provide evidence (from a partial, overly positive picture) of the likely success of policies the Chinese leadership had already put into practice, or had decided to adopt. It seems likely, then, that favourable references to Yugoslav-style 'workers' self-management' were merely being used to bolster official promotion of the workers' congress in China, and did not necessarily imply any radical departure from past Chinese practice.

Looking at articles on enterprise reform and democratization, and particularly at those on the workers' congress, from the period 1979 to 1981, it is hard to avoid the conclusion that the demands of Democracy Wall and the emergence of Solidarity had a major impact on policy in the second half of 1980. The change in the tone and content of the discussion from about September 1980 is striking, and the most likely explanation for this change is that it was part of the official reaction both to the rise of Solidarity and to the welcome it received from Democracy Wall activists and restive workers in China.

This is not to say that there was no impulse for reform and democratization from the top leadership prior to the appearance of Solidarity in Poland. There was; as was noted above, as early as 1978 in his speech to the Ninth ACFTU Congress, Deng had called for all enterprises to be democratically managed (though still under unified party leadership). The need to extend the powers of the workers' congress was discussed in a *People's Daily* article in March 1980; the article also suggested that elections for factory directors were a necessary reform (*People's Daily* 6 March 1980). Further evidence is provided by Liao Gailong's 1980 report on the 'Gengsheng reforms', which discusses democratization and trade union reform at length (Liao Gailong 1980: U1–2). The editorial note accompanying the version of the report printed in *The Seventies* reveals that much of the content of the report had already been discussed by the party centre in July, and had been set out in a speech by Deng Xiaoping at a Politburo meeting on 18 August 1980, four days after the sit-in at the Lenin Shipyard began and on the day when the strike was first reported in the Chinese press. However, the final October version of Liao's report makes specific reference to the 'Polish crisis', suggesting that the Chinese working class, too, was likely to 'rise in rebellion' unless workers were 'allowed to enjoy freedom and democracy in electing their own trade union leaders' who would provide genuine representation of workers' interests Liao Gailong 1980: U11).

This explicit later reference to events in Poland supports the view that pressure for real concessions on enterprise democratization and worker representation in China greatly intensified as the nature and dimensions of the Polish uprising became clear. As the culmination of the decision-making process, the establishment of workers' congresses in all enterprises and the promotion of democratic management was endorsed at the Third Plenum of the Fifth National People's Congress in September 1980, and several articles on the workers' congress in subsequent months made reference to this decision (*Workers' Daily* 21 October 1980; *Southern Daily* 22 October 1980). But even a high-level decision such as this does not fully account for the appearance in the official press of articles linking enterprise democracy through the workers' congress with wider socialist democracy (*Southern Daily* 22 October and 29 November 1980), and calling for workers to exercise real power in the enterprise as a prerequisite to taking over the management of state political, social and economic affairs (*Workers' Daily* 21 October 1980).

This was what the reforms of the late 1970s and early 1980s set out to do, and the language in which the reforms were discussed, as well as the actual measures proposed, shows quite clearly that a dialogue was going on between Democracy Wall and those officials who favoured reform. Some of the early proposals for reforming industrial organization, especially those concerned with the role of the workers' congress, were genuinely radical, and this would not have been the case without the very strong influence both of Democracy Wall and of protesting workers who had shown themselves to be prepared, in the face of management intransigence, to go outside authorized channels in order to press demands they considered to be legitimate.

The promotion of greater democratic rights for workers, for a short time, went far beyond anything which had been proposed even at the height of the Hundred Flowers period; it was unprecedented in the history of the People's Republic. This quite sudden departure from previous language and practice occurred at a time when the party was greatly concerned about the activities of Democracy Wall activists, especially those who had stood in local people's congress elections, and was within months of the final suppression of that movement, the trial of the Gang of Four, and the final party verdict on Mao's historical legacy; the party was voicing concerns about 'extreme democratization' and the threat this posed to hard-won unity and stability. In other words, this was not a time when radical new policy initiatives in the direction of greater democracy in enterprises would normally have been on the agenda. So the explanation for this sudden display of commitment to workers' role as masters of the enterprise and the state must lie in external pressures on the authorities, namely Democracy Wall and Solidarity.

The shift in attitudes regarding democratic management and workers' proper role can be discerned in the *Southern Daily*'s coverage of the enterprise reform debate. Up until September 1980 articles on economic reform had all focused on enterprise autonomy and ways of loosening the bureaucratic controls on factory directors. Guangdong was in the vanguard of the early economic reforms, and the many articles centred on efficiency, decentralization, contracting out, management's right to manage, etc. were in keeping with the region's reputation for placing enthusiasm for rapid economic reform above political dogma about the nature of the socialist enterprise. Typical of the tone of pre-Solidarity reports on enterprise reform are a number of pieces from the spring and early summer of 1980 which were mainly concerned with such subjects as increasing enterprise profit through greater autonomy, competition between enterprises, and the use of individual economic incentives to motivate workers (*Southern Daily* 21 March, 25 April, 21 May and 28 June 1980).

But the tone and content of articles on enterprise reform changes abruptly after the month of August, and it is hard to believe that the radicalism and forthright language of some of the proposals that were made in the autumn and winter of 1980 represented a spontaneous restatement of commitment to workers' role as masters of the enterprise, rather than being prompted by fear of Democracy Wall linking up with large numbers of disgruntled workers to create a 'Polish crisis' in China. Articles now appeared, stressing that all power devolved to the lower level had to be in the hands of the workers, who should run factories, and in time the state itself, themselves. A different attitude towards workers was apparent, too: references to indiscipline and the lingering influence of the Gang of Four disappeared (temporarily), and workers were portrayed instead as reasonable and responsible people who could be trusted with power. By the end of November the *Southern Daily* was posing the question: 'To whom does power in the enterprise belong?', and answering itself: 'In a socialist society, it should undoubtedly belong to the broad mass of workers and staff'. The same article went on to describe the workers' congress as a mere 'democratic ornament' in the past, ignored or treated as a rubber stamp by the party committee and management, and noted that the proper relationship between 'humble servants' (cadres) and 'masters' (workers) had for a long time been transposed (*Southern Daily* 29 November 1980). Much of this line of argument could have been lifted straight out of one of Guangzhou's unofficial publications.

It is very noticeable that in this period, official sources to a large extent admitted the shortcomings of the workers' congress as it had previously been constituted, noting that only recent experiments had given democratic management 'genuine content' (*Southern Daily* 5 October and 23 November 1980). The influence of Democracy Wall, i.e. the extent to which official sources accepted its arguments and its agenda, is apparent in praise for experimental enterprises where workers, through the workers' congress, now had 'a genuine right to speak . . . the right to be consulted and to decide on important matters . . . [and] the right to distribute a part of the fruits of their own labour'. The same article reported that these enterprises had turned over some of the work of recruitment and allocation of jobs within the enterprise to the workers' congress, to make it more difficult for cadres to make 'back-door' appointments and practise favouritism (*Southern Daily* 5 October 1980). This is another example of the reforms addressing specific grievances aired in the unofficial Democracy Wall journals.

Various measures were proposed, and in some cases tried out, for preventing the new 1980s system of democratic management based on the workers' congress from degenerating into formalism as it had in the past. The *Workers' Daily*, not surprisingly, was the most outspoken about past problems, calling for China's enterprises to be made socialist in fact as well as in name, and arguing that public ownership was only a necessary condition for workers' becoming the masters of the enterprise, not a sufficient one. Exactly the same argument was of course used by the Qingdao unofficial journal *Sea Spray* in August 1980 (*Sea Spray* 1980: 34), showing again the way in which quite radical ideas first expressed in Democracy Wall writings, and condemned by the authorities, could later on crop up as acceptable components of reform policy.

But in spite of the radicalism of some of the discussion of the workers' congress, in the early 1980s, 'the approach adopted was to a large degree a return to the policies of the mid-1950s' (Lockett 1983: 233). One article in 1980 actually used the same form of words as Lai Ruoyu had in 1956, asserting that 'democratic management is one of the signs that distinguishes socialist enterprises from capitalist enterprises' (*People's Daily* 6 March 1980). There was an awareness, though, that the 1950s system of workers' congresses had failed to establish institutional safeguards of workers' right to participate in management which could not easily be circumvented by cadres, and a number of proposals were made, many by the official unions, which were intended to make the workers' congress a body with real authority in the enterprise. But these ultimately failed to establish any more effective form of participation or representation for workers than had existed in the 1950s.

In an attempt to ensure that workers' congresses were not once again dominated by cadres and more skilled workers, it was stipulated that 60 per cent of congress representatives should be shopfloor workers (*Beijing Review* 1 September 1980: 22) rather than cadres, technicians or union representatives. In one experimental enterprise, the Guangzhou No. 1 Cotton Mill, rank-and-file workers were also reported to constitute 60 per cent of the congress's standing body, the presidium. Since it was this body which was responsible for overseeing the implementation of congress decisions, and for taking decisions when the congress was not in session, ensuring a shopfloor majority on the presidium could be said to be even more important than making sure that a majority of congress representatives were workers. In the past, it was reported, workers had constituted only 10 per cent of the presidium, and so could easily have been overruled by the body's cadre members. The report on this enterprise took a similar line to many others at the time in criticizing the efficacy of the workers' congress in the past. Before the reforms, the workers' congress was said to have met only twice a year, and to have been nothing more than a forum where the factory director made a report, the party secretary gave instructions, and the workers pledged their support (*Southern Daily* 23 November 1980), a familiar description of the body's traditional role.

When the Temporary Regulations for workers' congresses were published in mid-1981 it was stipulated that ordinary workers should form a majority of the congress and of its standing body. However, this was a much less significant concession than it might seem, because in the Temporary Regulations, almost all of the new powers experimentally granted to the workers' congress were downgraded from the power to take decisions itself to the right to be consulted over decisions and to ratify some of them (*People's Daily* 20 July 1981). The Guangzhou No. 1 Cotton Mill was an experimental enterprise, and most enterprises would not have introduced the 60 per cent rule in any case. In addition, even in this plant which was being allowed to go further than others in experiments with management democratization, no cadre elections had been held, even though the right to elect and recall cadres was supposed to be one of the most important innovations of the 1980s.

There were also proposals to make the congress the policy-making body of the enterprise while the party committee concentrated on wider issues of ideology and political education (Lockett 1983: 246). The party committee of the Foshan No. 5 Plastics Plant was criticized in the autumn of 1980 for going beyond its proper role of ideological and political leadership and for trying to limit the workers' congress to discussion and implementation of decisions after they had been taken by the enterprise leadership. The leadership was rebuked for having refused workers permission even to convene the workers' congress to discuss a possible merger with another enterprise, and was reminded that the party was not an administrative organ, and that the authoritative structure within the scope of enterprise autonomy was the workers' congress (*Southern Daily* 29 November 1980). It was also reported from another Guangdong enterprise that the party committee there was passing important matters over to the workers' congress for discussion and decision, including production and financial plans, the use of retained profits to construct workers' housing, the recruitment of new employees by public examinations, and the establishment, amendment and removal of regulations and systems. It was emphasized that workers' congress must be involved in implementing the increased powers available under enterprise autonomy, and that there was no contradiction between this and the party's leading political role (*Southern Daily* 8 November 1980).

In some experimental enterprises new standing organizations were set up with the remit of ensuring the timely implementation by cadres of decisions of the workers' congress. These bodies were given the powers to enforce cadre compliance with congress decisions, and it was further stated that no regulation or system set up by decision of the workers' congress could be overturned except by another congress resolution, in contrast to past practice (*Southern Daily* 8 and 29 November 1980). In addition to various groups set up expressly to oversee implementation of congress decisions, the enterprise union still played a part, and the workers' congress was also convened more often than in the past, twice a quarter in the case of one experimental enterprise. However, as was the case with the built-in workers' majority on the congress presidium, these innovations became much less significant once the Temporary Regulations reduced the congress's powers to the right to be consulted about important decisions in the enterprise. Ultimately the workers' congress was left with the power of decision only within its traditional remit of safety, welfare and some decisions on pay and bonuses. This meant that its power to exert influence within the enterprise was not significantly greater than it had been in the 1950s. It seems that in spite of some early over-optimistic assessments of its significance, the best that can be said of the 1980s version of the workers' congress is that could provide

a consultative forum that imposes limited obligations on top management. Like most representative bodies in capitalist economies, congresses tend to be dominated by more skilled workers and supervisors . . . since the Party secretary is the final arbiter in disputes with management, his influence tends to be pervasive.

(Henley and Nyaw 1987: 144)

While some observers nevertheless considered that workers' congresses could still offer 'some scope for meaningful participation beyond the mere "formalism" of the past' (Henley and Nyaw 1987: 144), in many enterprises this was not the case, and possibilities for genuine participation still depended on the attitudes of management rather than on the institutionalization of workers' rights. As in the 1950s, the one management reform measure on which all others ultimately depended for their efficacy was the holding of direct elections in enterprises, elections not only of workers' congress and union representatives, but also of group, section and workshop heads, and even of factory directors. Unless workers could affect the career prospects of their managers in some way they would be unable to exert any real authority in the workplace. Cadres with life tenure and no threat of losing their position in an election would be able to go on disregarding the proceedings of bodies like the workers' congress, so that the organization's reputation among the workers would become tarnished and they too would cease to expect anything of it. This was the chain of events in the 1950s; the next section will look at the theory and practice of workplace elections in the 1980s, identifying the reasons why a similar programme of democratization fared little better in this later period.

Enterprise elections

The importance of making cadres accountable to the people through some form of election was stressed in the writings and public statements of a number of Guangzhou Democracy Wall activists. For example, at an official forum sponsored by the provincial Communist Youth League, Li Min noted that cadres' attitudes towards the rank and file had changed for the better when they were facing re-election, but that now that elections were no longer on the agenda, attitudes had changed back (*The Seventies* 1980: 56). This insistence on the need for democratic elections was part and parcel of the campaign to replace arbitrary personal rule by individuals with democracy and a transparent and impartial legal system; it was integral to the concerns of Democracy Wall.

Democratic elections were another point on which there was some agreement between the movement's activists and party reformers. Enterprise elections for cadres below the level of the factory director had been promoted since the beginning of the reforms in 1978, with mixed results. But in the second half of 1980 the importance of democratic elections as a check on cadre bureaucratism and misuse of power began to be stressed very heavily (*Southern Daily* 9 October and 8 November 1980). It was also acknowledged in the national press that 'the very urgent demand of the working masses for the power to elect and recall leading cadres including factory directors and managers has basically not been realized' (*People's Daily* 5 October 1980). As is often the case with the post-Mao reforms, there is a mixture of motives governing policy choices here. Cadre elections were not made a plank of the enterprise reform programme solely because the party was ideologically committed to the democratization of management: as was mentioned above, there were also reasons of economic efficiency to be considered. The linking of workers' bonuses to enterprise performance was supposed to ensure that workers would be strongly motivated to elect competent managers; in this way, cadre elections could serve as a way of bringing in younger, better-educated and more competent managers to replace the 'dead wood' of ex-army or ex-rural cadres of an older generation who owed their positions more to their political standing than to any expertise in industrial management (Lockett 1983: 234–5). Reform of the system of lifetime cadre employment (the 'iron armchair') thus could be underpinned by democratic elections.

But in addition to these efficiency considerations, the combined impact of Democracy Wall, Solidarity, and industrial unrest in China helped to create pressure for democratic elections. As had happened on other issues, what had been written in unofficial journals up to a year before in the second half of 1980 found its way into the state-controlled press in only slightly milder language. Wang Xizhe, defending his right to talk about the problem of China's bureaucratic (and, in his view, un-Marxist) system of government, had noted that no matter how bad the relations between cadres and the masses, cadres were still sure of a job for life and could only ever go up the career ladder, not down (Wang Xizhe 1979b: 16–17). In November 1980 the *Southern Daily* concurred that bureaucratism was generated by the cadre system in which officials were only responsible to those above them, and not to their 'masters' below, and that democratic elections would allow the masses finally to make some progress in ending bureaucratism and autocracy. Unlike Wang, the paper didn't invoke the Paris Commune as its ideal, but it did state that China's democratic systems at all levels were fundamentally unsound, with a resolution of the National People's Congress having less influence than a few words from a top cadre, making China in some respects even less democratic than capitalist nations (*Southern Daily* 8 November 1980). The authors of the Li Yizhe tract had of course been detained for saying as much in 1974, an irony which was not lost on Wang.

Solidarity's demands, the first of which was the right to elect independent trade unions, had been published in full in a number of unofficial journals (*October Review* 1982: 45–9), and were also reported in the official press in August 1980. Striking Chinese workers in the winter of 1980–1 made demands ranging from special representation on the workers' congress to the right to form independent unions, clearly influenced by Solidarity, and it seems likely that reports of Polish workers' demands also intensified pressure from below for Chinese workers to be allowed a much greater degree of influence over their managers. Liao Gailong's report, which stressed the importance of democratic elections for union representatives in China if a 'Polish crisis' was to be avoided, also emphasized the need to allow workers to recommend the removal of incompetent managers, and in time to elect enterprise personnel (Liao Gailong 1980: U13).

But although the election of cadres, including factory directors, had been acknowledged as an 'urgent demand' of workers, and despite the party's apparent acceptance of the case for democratic accountability of management through workplace elections, little progress was ultimately made in setting up a system of regular enterprise elections. It will be remembered that proposals put forward by Lai Ruoyu back in the mid-1950s had included provisions for the election of cadres up to and including factory directors, but that this had been one of the first management democratization measures to be ruled out of bounds, the argument being that factory directors had to be appointed by the state rather than being elected by the workers' congress since they represented the interests of the whole people, and not just those of the workforce of the particular enterprise. Similarly, although the election of factory directors had received a certain amount of official support during the years of experimentation, there was no mention of this when the Temporary Regulations on the Congress of Workers and Staff Members in State Enterprises were promulgated in July 1981. The regulations only provided for the election by the workers' congress of 'leading administrative personnel', while the congress was also charged with 'upholding the authority of the factory director', who had only to accept that body's 'inspection and supervision' (*People's Daily* 20 July 1981).

So even before the regulations governing the new system of democratic management were finalized, this measure, which would have taken workers' power in the enterprise an important step further than it had ever been before, had apparently been dropped. The election of factory directors was still discussed as a desirable future development (*Southern Daily* 26 October 1981), and elections were actually held in some enterprises, reportedly with good results (*Southern Daily* 15 April 1982), but it does not seem to have become common practice. Trials of factory director elections in Shenzhen were reported in 1984 (*Guangzhou Daily* 11 April and 27 June 1984), but it was also proposed in that year that factory directors, appointed by the state, should have the right to make their own cadre appointments within the enterprise and could transfer cadres who had been elected to their posts (*Guangzhou Daily* 8 and 27 June, 29 December 1984), so it seems that although experimentation was continuing, not all of it was in the direction of more widespread election of top management. On the whole it seems that in this phase of the reforms, workers' congresses and similar bodies were only empowered to make proposals and recommendations to the higher levels regarding the appointment or dismissal of top managers.

At other levels of management, however, cadres were to face election either by the whole workforce or by the workers' congress. We saw earlier that elections for heads of groups, sections, and workshops initially aroused little enthusiasm among workers who were aware that the real power in the enterprise lay with the party committee and the director. There was widespread scepticism, too, about how free and democratic elections would be, and given the experiences with elections for enterprise cadres and union representatives in the 1950s, not without justification. There was sometimes a degree of self-censorship in the nomination process in these elections whereby workers would refrain from nominating anyone who, for reasons of family background or previous political problems, might not be approved by the higher levels (all appointments were subject to such approval), and if nominated, such people might seek to withdraw from the ballot (*China Reconstructs* 1979: 7–8). Not all enterprises were deemed to have the appropriate conditions for holding elections, and in some cases 'the government advocated the use of opinion polls at regular intervals to provide workers with a means of examining and evaluating the work of the leading cadres in the enterprise', where elections were 'not feasible' (Tung 1982: 165). In recent years the contracting-out of enterprise management has further complicated matters, and annual democratic *evaluation* of leading cadres in these enterprises has been recommended, while elections can still take place in collective enterprises (*Union Bulletin* 1 April 1991: 9).

Election procedure was not standardized in the early years of the reforms, varying between cities and between different types of enterprise. In the early 1980s, some enterprises voted by a show of hands while others held secret ballots, and some held 'primaries' as part of the nomination process. In most cases the list of candidates arrived at by a process of open nomination, group discussion and gradual elimination contained the same number of people as there were posts to be filled; only in exceptional circumstance, such as when two or more candidates had almost equal support, would the final slate have more candidates than posts (*China Reconstructs* 1979: 7–8).

There was no reason why cadres should not be re-elected to their posts in these elections, and they very often were, especially in the case of technical staff who were generally better qualified for their position than anyone else in the enterprise who might challenge them. But it is easy to see why cadres 'accustomed to issuing administrative orders' might 'worry about their prestige if they are subject to the supervision of the masses' (*Beijing Review* 1 September 1980: 23), and might see elections as a threat and do their best to obstruct them. Overt attempts to manipulate elections, for example by numbering ballot papers so that workers voting against a cadre could be identified, or by threatening reprisals against opponents, were 'by no means unknown' (Lockett 1983: 237), but the influence of leading management and party cadres often did not even need to be exercised in such an obvious way. It is possible that workers' doubts about the fairness of elections may have made them less than enthusiastic about active participation, leaving cadres to dominate the process, so that workers' views were not in fact reflected in the results. Cadres could also find legitimate reasons for opposition to elections: 'Objections to control from below' could be couched in terms of 'the supposed need for secrecy in management work and the possibility that the workforce will not make the "right" choice', and 'the legacy of the Cultural Revolution in the area of work discipline' (Lockett 1983: 238) could also be used as an excuse for opposing elections in case 'production order' was disturbed as a result. Again, these arguments are familiar to us from the 1950s.

The main obstacle to increasing the powers of the workers' congress and to the institution of regular cadre elections in enterprises seems to have been resistance from cadres. Interference in election procedures was not unusual, and cadres elected by the workforce could be transferred without notice or consultation by the factory director or the higher levels. Accounts of cadre resistance hampering management democratization and the work of the workers' congress accompanied the reforms throughout (*Southern Daily* 8 November 1979, 22 October and 29 November 1980; *People's Daily* 6 March 1980, 27 October 1983), but were especially frequent during 1981 (*Workers' Daily* 18 February and 7 November

1981; *Southern Daily* 26 October 1981; *People's Daily* 10 June 1981). This raises the possibility that the quite radical proposals of the previous few months, during which time it had been stated categorically that enterprise autonomy meant giving more powers to workers, not cadres, had generated a backlash among management and party officials.

It is also noticeable that the most outspoken support for a powerful workers' congress and for cadre elections came from the labour movement press, namely the *Workers' Daily*. It was the *Workers' Daily* which, in a seminal article on the workers' congress system in October 1980, had adopted the language of Democracy Wall in describing how in the past, the role of the workers' congress had been limited to consultation and discussion, and how workers had had no systemic or legal guarantees of their right to participate. The paper insisted that in future, the exact powers of the workers' congress must be clearly defined and protected in law, so that the congress's decisions no longer depended on 'the quality of a few top cadres', and that laws and regulations must be established governing the election and recall of congress representatives and presidium members to avoid the congress's powers ending up in the hands of a minority (*Workers' Daily* 21 October 1980). In late 1981 the paper was still insisting on the 'innumerable advantages' of the workers' congress, which it saw as the way to establish 'democracy and a legal system' within enterprises (*Workers' Daily* 7 November 1981), but it is likely that support for management democratization was less strong in other quarters.

Reports on progress in setting up and running workers' congresses during 1981 revealed that although a majority of enterprises had set up a workers' congress (90 per cent of large and medium enterprises in major cities had them by June 1981), only about 25 per cent of them were running well. Sixty per cent were said to be operating more or less satisfactorily, while 15 per cent were performing poorly and had already degenerated into formalism (*People's Daily* 10 June 1981). Vice-Premier Wan Li urged all cadres, as communists, not to be afraid of the masses and to be willing to hand over powers to the workers' congress, and it was re-stated that the workers' congress did not represent a negation of centralism and was not tantamount to anarchism. Cadres were assured that the powers of the workers' congress were limited to consultation on matters not affecting workers' direct personal interests, and that cadre elections would only be introduced gradually (*People's Daily* 10 June 1981). But despite these assurances, cadre support for democratization and the workers' congress system does not seem to have been forthcoming. The *Southern Daily* identified the main misgivings in enterprises about the workers' congress as the 'four afraids': the party secretary was afraid that the workers' congress would go on for far too long; the factory director was afraid of losing authority to a body which would 'refuse to leave the stage'; the union chair was afraid that it would deadlock relations between management and workers; and the workers and staff themselves were afraid of being made to 'wear small shoes' (i.e. of management reprisals) if they exercised their democratic rights through the workers' congress (*Southern Daily* 10 June 1981).

The situation in Guangdong was acknowledged to be even worse than else-where. It was reported towards the end of 1981 that many large and medium-sized enterprises had still not set up a workers' congress, and that even in those enterprises experimenting with increased autonomy, where the reforms had gone furthest, few workers' congresses were running well after their establishment (*Southern Daily* 26 October 1981). An evaluation of the reforms in Guangdong published a decade later painted a similar picture, observing that democratic management and the role of the workers' congress had been neglected in the province, weakening workers' sense of being masters and leading to a pervasive 'wage-labourer' mentality among workers who felt that they were 'working for the factory director' (Wang and Wen 1992: 265–6).

The reasons for Guangdong's poor performance in this respect seem to lie in the province's otherwise rapid reforms, which resulted in greatly increased powers, under enterprise autonomy, for the factory director. In theory the 'factory director responsibility system' was integrated with democratic management and participation in management by workers and staff, but in practice, the result was often similar to the one-man management of the past. Many references to this problem can be found in the trade union and general press of the late 1980s and early 1990s in China. The 'hired hand' and 'work according to pay' mentality among workers is frequently noted as a problem in these years, and the difficulty of preserving workers' democratic rights under the factory director responsibility system is also discussed, as is the reappearance of 'one-man management' by factory directors who regularly by-pass or fail to convene the workers' congress (*Union Bulletin* 1 February 1991: 18–19).

The potential contradiction between increased autonomy for factory directors and management democratization was recognized at an early stage; in fact, the factory director responsibility system was seen by some as making the role of the workers' congress more important than ever if the danger of a return to one-man management was to be averted. Zhao Ziyang reminded state enterprises of the importance of guaranteeing workers' right to participate in management once all powers to direct production and to manage the enterprise had been entrusted by the state to the factory director (*Guangzhou Daily* 16 May, 26 August and 19 October 1984). But despite this awareness of the potential problem, it does not seem to have been possible to protect workers' existing, quite limited rights to participate in management alongside the other planks of the management reforms. This again casts doubt on the claim that management democratization and the promotion of the workers' congress was anything other than instrumental in the reform programme. By the early 1990s, workers generally seem to have felt that the economic reforms had weakened their role as masters and democratic management, even though these were now enshrined in the Enterprise Law. A reflection of the way in which power shifted within the enterprise during the 1980s but still remained out of the hands of rank-and-file workers was the comment that 'in the past, trade union cadres took orders from the party secretaries and now they take orders from the factory managers' (Chiang 1990: 86).

The trade unions

It is a measure of the extent of the unions' crisis that they have not loomed as large in this discussion of the early reform period as they did in the mid-1950s. Many discussions of democratic management, even in the *Workers' Daily*, make no mention whatsoever of a role for the unions. There were proposals that the unions should again serve as the standing body of the workers' congress, but in many enterprises bodies to oversee the implementation of congress resolutions were set up quite separately from the official unions.

From 1979, and particularly after the advent of Solidarity, more emphasis was given to unions' duty to protect the legitimate interests and democratic rights of workers first and foremost, while still also bearing in mind the interests of the enterprise and of the state. Unions were said to have swapped 'fear' for 'daring' in representing workers' views to the enterprise party committee (*Workers' Daily* 23 March 1979). A concerted effort was underway to recover the confidence of workers in grass-roots union organizations, and some within the unions admitted that their difficulty in asserting operational independence from the party in the past had in part been their own fault: 'Unions not representing the interests of the workers are bound to be weak' (*Workers' Daily* 18 November 1980). Union officials and activists seem to have been aware that if the unions lacked the confidence of their members, there was indeed 'no meaning to their existence'. An article in the *Workers' Daily* summed up what had happened to the official unions since the Hundred Flowers: 'Since 1957, many union organizations have gradually lost their original prestige and role, falling back on a role of education, the organization of labour emulation campaigns, and some redundant work of the Party and the government'. According to another piece in the same issue, the trade unions had shown 'very little interest in the immediate interests of the workers', and consequently workers 'have never taken seriously the things the unions did' (*Workers' Daily* 18 November 1980).

In response to workers' criticisms of unrepresentative 'signboard' unions, basic-level union cadres were criticized for tending to pit their duty to the party against their duty to workers, and were reminded that the unions were to be the workers' own trusted organization, and one which had every right to speak out on its members' behalf when orders from above conflicted with workers' wishes or interests (*Workers' Daily* 9 October 1979). But although at least some in the union hierarchy seem to have been sincere in this effort, overall only changes in emphasis were being made with regard to the unions' role; they were not being given free rein to stand on the side of the workers and represent their interests first and foremost. The reforms are perhaps best characterized as 'attempts to make the unions appear more independent of the Party' (Saich 1984: 164).

The influence of Solidarity and Democracy Wall can be seen as we trace the development of the unions' 'new line' from 1978 through to the early 1980s. The labour movement press exhibited much greater concern about the extent to which workers had become alienated from their unions in the autumn of 1980 than it had done previously, and in articles permeated with the language of

Democracy Wall. In November 1980 the *Workers' Daily* ran a number of articles on this subject, one of which insisted that the unions' 'fundamental objective . . . is to protect the legal rights and interests of all workers, for which the union cadres should be responsible first'. The two points to note here are, first, that cadres' duty to workers is explicitly put before their duty to other authorities in the enterprise and beyond; and second, the reference to legal rights. In terms strongly reminiscent of Li Yizhe's and Democracy Wall's demand for a socialist legal system institutionalizing protection for citizens' rights, the unions now called for 'the necessary protection of law and support from the government', and demanded that the relationships between the unions and the workers' congress, administrative and party organizations 'should be clearly defined in the law or by the institutions' (*Workers' Daily* 18 November 1980).

Liao Gailong's report, also dating from the autumn of 1980, was very clear about the likelihood of a 'Polish crisis' in China if the official unions were not revitalized, made more democratic, and freed from arbitrary party interference, citing Lenin on the necessity of trade union representation even under socialism (Liao Gailong 1980: U10). The problem of the unions' own internal lack of democracy was brought up by others as well, and the importance of workers being able to elect their own union representatives was stressed. Mention was also made of cases where democratically elected union representatives were arbitrarily moved from their posts by party officials without consultation (*Xinhua News Agency* 4 December 1980). All this discussion was of course taking place against the background of Democracy Wall's praise for Solidarity coupled with industrial unrest and sporadic self-organization among Chinese workers; by the middle of 1981, once this stimulus to reform had receded in importance, the more outspoken statements in support of a greater degree of union independence were no longer heard. At the Tenth ACFTU Congress in October 1983, Ni Zhifu's address included among the unions' core tasks speaking and acting for the workers and protecting their lawful interests, and called for closer relations between unions and masses, but paid more attention to the unions' role in improving economic results, and in educating workers in patriotism, collectivism, socialism, and communist ideals, morality and culture, a very conventional pre-1978 view of what the unions should regard as their main tasks (Ni Zhifu 1983).

Solidarity's impact on Democracy Wall activists and workers

If the rise of Solidarity in Poland frightened the CCP, this was nothing to its inspirational effect on Democracy Wall activists and on workers. Discontent among workers had been rising steadily. Two years of economic reforms, while successful in some respects, had given rise to some serious problems. Shortages of energy and raw materials were also quite severe at this time (Halpern 1985: 79, 101), and in these conditions, many industrial enterprises had no option but to run at reduced capacity, or even, temporarily, to suspend production altogether. This inevitably led to hardship for the workforce, who received only their basic pay with no performance-related bonuses on top. In the 1950s it was claimed that some workers' basic pay, without bonuses for over-fulfilment of norms, was not enough to live on, giving rise to great anger among workers when managerial incompetence led to the non-arrival of supplies and the suspension of production, thus threatening their livelihood. There were similar fears again in 1980, by which time bonuses had become a significant proportion of many workers' pay-packets and were widely seen as part of workers' basic income, not an optional extra (Shirk 1981: 586).

Price rises early in the reform period placed extra strain on workers' household budgets, and were also seen as a threat to workers' security. Later on, in 1989, the fear of inflation outstripping wage increases was a major factor influencing workers to support the Democracy Movement. There was every reason to suppose that discontent among workers would intensify and possibly crystallize into collective protest under conditions like these in the early 1980s. From the point of view of the authorities, Solidarity could hardly have happened at a worse time, and the way in which it was publicized by a Democracy Wall movement now beginning actively to seek mass support among workers made it all the more alarming.

Workers' grievances had always been able to find expression in Democracy Wall's publications, and there were signs of workers' support for its aims (Chen Ruoxi 1982: 35–6). But initially the movement had not really sought to develop a mass base. It was not until 1979 that some activists began to look to sent-down youth or petitioning peasants (Benton 1982: 6), and not until 1980 did attempts to build up support among workers become significant in the movement. During the earliest weeks and months of Democracy Wall some groups and individuals were addressing their ideas as much to the reformists in the leadership as to the public at large. It was only later, when the movement's continuation was gravely threatened by arrests and changes to the Constitution restricting freedom of expression, that it began trying 'to break out of its isolation and to find new allies outside the fickle elite' (Benton 1982: 11). With the example of Solidarity before them, activists like He Qiu now called for Democracy Wall to forge links both with Chinese labour *en masse* and with the international labour movement (*Observer* 1980: 14; *October Review* 1982: 3). Some of the movement's activists 'tried hard to widen its social base by organizing, publicizing and defending struggles for higher wages and better conditions in the factories' (Benton 1982: 120).

Solidarity's impact was two-fold. First, it showed restive Chinese workers that they were not the only ones contending with a system which praised them to the skies as leaders of the nation while actually offering them political powerlessness and a low standard of living. Workers involved in autonomous organizing in the 1989 protests had sometimes tracked Solidarity's progress all the way through the 1980s, seeing it as a test-case for workers' political will and power in a socialist country (Lu Ping 1990: 90). Second, Solidarity showed Democracy Wall's activists that a movement against a regime which had degenerated into a military-bureaucratic dictatorship could gain mass support, despite the general post-Cultural Revolution disenchantment with political activism in urban China. The authorities had drawn links between Democracy Wall and the rising tide of industrial unrest even before Solidarity emerged, with official newspapers condemning the 'methods of a minority' who were resorting to strikes, demonstrations, petitions and speech-making in pursuit of rapid democratization or 'extreme democratization' (*Southern Daily* 31 May 1979; *People's Daily* 8 February 1980), and predictions of a 'Polish crisis' in China reinforced its determination to shut down Democracy Wall before things went too far (Wilson 1990b; Liao Gailong 1980: U10).

Despite the lack of an organizational framework encompassing mass industrial unrest and the unofficial journals that were the mainstay of Democracy Wall, we must conclude that the authorities were right to fear the power of the two combined. Democracy Wall activists in Beijing, Qingdao, Shanghai, Guangzhou, and Taiyuan reported the activities of Poland's Solidarity (*Theoretical Banner* 1981: 94–5; *Sea Spray* 1980a: 34; *October Review* 71 (1982: 45–9); Benton 1982: 86–7), in some cases printing all of Solidarity's '21 Demands' and 'Charter of Rights of the Polish workers', and drew explicit parallels between the economic and political crisis which had given rise to the independent union and conditions in China. Many looked forward to a Chinese Solidarity, recording Chinese working-class examples of resistance to the rule of the 'bureaucratic privileged class' in support of their predictions, and in one case in Wuhan Democracy Wall activists were even reported to have led a strike (Benton 1982: 11).

Given the extremely high level of dissatisfaction with the unions' performance, it is not surprising that there were a number of attempts by striking and protesting workers in China to form independent unions, especially once they had the example of Poland's Solidarity before them. Several outbreaks of industrial unrest in China in the early 1980s were reported to have culminated in a demand for free trade unions to be established (Wilson 1990a: 54; Benton 1982: 85; *FBIS-CHI* 29 January, 2 February, 3 March and 9 October 1981; *SWB/FE/*6175/B11/4–6), including the dispute at the Taiyuan Iron and Steel works in 1981 (Benton 1982: 120–1). This started as a protest by single workers living in at the plant (i.e. workers who, although married, lived away from their families in factory dormitories) over their living and working conditions. These could be construed as narrowly economic demands, but, as with the undeclared strike on the Guangzhou docks in 1957, the dispute inevitably became a confrontation between the workers and the party organization, with whom real power in the enterprise still lay.

One of Taiyuan's unofficial journals, *Sailing Ship*, made clear the view within the movement that such spontaneous collective actions by workers signalled a challenge to the party itself, since it showed that workers were aware of the need to organize themselves when their official representatives failed them:

> They understand that if they want to change their wretched conditions, they cannot rely on any messiah, but must begin to organize themselves, to rely on their own strength, and to elect their own representatives to speak for them, and if at any time their elected representatives do not represent them properly, they will be recalled and another election held. This sort of

demand on the part of the broad popular masses is the social basis for China's democratic reforms.

(October Review 1981a: 11)

The journal's account also made it clear that the dispute was about the defence of workers' legal rights; this is a phrase which crops up continually in Democracy Wall writings, and it too gives political content to what might otherwise be classed as economic demands.

One of the demands of the workers concerned was to have their own special representatives on the workers' congress (Chen Ruoxi 1982: 35–6). This shows that as things stood, despite two years or so of reform and the official promotion of the workers' congress, these workers still felt that it could not represent or defend their interests. It is not that big a step from wanting separate representation on an officially-sanctioned body to deciding that it was necessary for workers to have their own, self-organized and autonomous unions if they were not to succumb to further exploitation and oppression. *Sailing Ship* explicitly linked contemporary workers' protests with a long line of struggles against exploitation going right back to the nineteenth century, and gave as the motive for the most recent outbreaks of unrest the following description of workers' situation:

> Under the bureaucratic system, their glorious title of master bears no resemblance to their actual position of powerlessness; their standard of living bears no resemblance to that of the privileged bureaucrats; the improvement in their livelihood bears no relation to the development of the social productive forces.
>
> *(October Review* 1981a: 11)

This account of the Taiyuan unrest makes no mention of any involvement of the official unions. Only 'leadership cadres' and party committee members are mentioned, which probably indicates that workers didn't expect the unions to help them in pressing what they saw as reasonable claims for improved conditions, instead going straight to those in authority who did have some power in the enterprise. As in the 1950s, the official formula for dealing with workers' grievances was that if their demands were reasonable, they should be met; if they were justified but could not be met straight away, then the reasons should be explained to the workers concerned; and if they were not reasonable, then the workers should be told why they were not reasonable. But in this case, the reaction of enterprise leaders was immediate condemnation: the workers were accused of holding 'black meetings' when they met together to discuss demands, and were accused of carrying out *chuanlian* when they visited each other, in an apparent attempt to paint them as Red Guard-type hooligans and supporters of the Gang of Four. Given that the approved channels for presenting demands and resolving disputes appeared not to be working at all, it is not surprising that self-organization began to occur. The backlog of economic grievances and widespread resentment at official privilege fuelled it, and Cultural Revolution experiences of organized action outside party control provided a relevant precedent. But the influence of Solidarity, among ordinary workers as well as Democracy Wall activists (Chen Ruoxi 1982: 35), was undoubtedly also extremely important in pushing Chinese workers to form their own independent trade unions.

No matter how concerned the party leadership was about the 'Polish disease' spreading to China's workers, it was not sufficiently worried to go so far as actually meeting their demands for democratization and independent representation. Once the initial panic of autumn 1980 had died down, older patterns of limited reform stymied by lower-level cadres' resistance reasserted themselves, so that the gap grew ever wider between workers' demands and what the authorities were prepared to concede. This would eventually necessitate drastic action, such as Deng Xiaoping's 1982 removal of the right to strike from the Constitution for the first time since 1949; it would also leave a legacy of party distrust and fear of independent organized labour which would be expressed in particularly harsh treatment of autonomous unions in 1989. But before the final suppression of Democracy Wall and the accompanying industrial unrest took place, one final manifestation of workers' support for Democracy Wall occurred which should not be overlooked in any account of this period.

Workers and other activists in 1980 local elections

In 1979 a new election law had been passed which provided for direct election of representatives to county- and township-level people's congresses, and which allowed for more candidates to stand than positions available, and 'a more open nominating process' (Strand 1989: 41) in which candidates no longer had to have the approval of their local party committee (Benton 1982: 11); any elector could stand if nominated by three others (Munro 1984b: 12). Many Democracy Wall activists took advantage of this (temporary, as it proved) relaxation of the rules and stood as candidates in local elections in their work-units in a number of Chinese cities. This was far easier to do on university campuses where party control was more lax and debate was seen as less of a serious threat (Strand 1989: 42); workers who stood in their units tended to come under rather greater pressure from enterprise authorities, but despite these adverse conditions, a number did stand and won a significant amount of support from their fellow workers.

Two Democracy Wall activists and unofficial journal editors from the Guangzhou region stood as candidates in the 1980 elections. One of these, Fang Zhiyuan, actually stood in Beijing in the elections at Beida where he had been a student since 1978 (Munro 1984a: 79). While there he acted as the Beijing liaison representative of the Guangzhou journal *People's Voice* with which he had been associated at home. During the campaign Fang made the point that public ownership of the means of production did not equal socialism, but that democracy was also necessary, as both a means and an end. He also expressed the view that the Cultural Revolution had been a failed anti-bureaucratic revolution which the reactionary Gang of Four and Lin Biao had tried to use for their own ends. Both these points show the influence of the Li Yizhe poster of 1974, with which Fang, like virtually all Democracy Wall activists from Guangzhou and elsewhere, was familiar (Benton 1982: 91–3).

By all accounts debate during the Beida election campaign was lively and often controversial, with frank discussion of 'such sensitive topics as whether or not China was really a socialist society, whether it sustained a bureaucratic stratum that may already have become a new ruling class, and whether or not China had essentially the same political nature as the Soviet Union' (Munro 1984a: 79). Again, the nature of this debate shows quite clearly the Cultural Revolution and early 1970s heritage of Democracy Wall. Another Guangdong candidate in the local elections was Zhong Yueqiu of Shaoguan, a worker in a smelting plant in Shaoguan who was the editor of two local unofficial journals, *Voice of the Common People* and *North River*. Unfortunately, given the metropolitan bias of much reporting on the movement and the fact that independent election candidates stood a much better chance of being able to publicize their views and mount a real campaign on a university campus rather than in a factory, very little is known about Zhong's election activities (Chen Ruoxi 1982: 30).

One of the best-known cases of worker-activists standing in local elections during 1980 was the candidacy of Fu Shenqi in Shanghai.[6] Fu was already well known in the movement in Shanghai as the editor of *Voice of Democracy*; later on, he was active in the National Federation of People's Publications, and edited the Federation's journal *Duty* for a time (Munro 1984a: 77–78; Chen Ruoxi 1982: 27, 32, 54–6). Fu's candidacy was strongly opposed by the enterprise party committee at the engine factory where he worked. Although he went through the required legal procedures in registering himself as a candidate, he eventually had to stand as an unofficial candidate after the leadership refused to recognize his nomination. His complaint to his local election committee about this and other instances of interference in his campaign resulted in the committee branding him a counter-revolutionary and anti-socialist element (Chen Ruoxi 1982: 27; Munro 1984a: 77–8).

Nevertheless, he was still able to publish a number of statements during his campaign (Chen Ruoxi 1982: 27), and the day before the election he addressed 500 of his fellow workers, pointing out that China's problems did not just stem from the acts of a few villains like Lin Biao and the Gang of Four, but were systemic, having their roots in China's development of over-centralized government and organization modelled on that of the Soviet Union. 'The solution lay in a thoroughgoing political reform which would transfer the fate of the country from the hands of a privileged minority into the hands of the "legalized popular will" ' (*Observer* 20 October 1980: 15; Munro 1984a: 77). Fu's campaign gained a great deal of support from workers in the plant, despite some rather heavy-handed tactics on the part of the enterprise party committee, which shortly before the election even threatened workers with loss of bonuses and losing promotion if they voted for Fu. He came second in the first round of voting, but was denied the chance to clinch the second of two seats in a run-off election when, contrary to the newly passed Election Law, the authorities simply appointed a candidate to the second post (Chen Ruoxi 1982: 27).

There were also cases of workers standing for election in Beijing, and as else-where, they and their supporters in the workforce were subjected to considerable pressure and harassment on the part of enterprise authorities. The election campaigns of two Beijing workers, He Defu and Gong Ping, were reported in *Duty*, and showed the sort of problems which commonly arose when workers defied enterprise authorities, even when they had the law on their side. He, a worker at the Organic Chemical Factory, and Gong, an oxygen factory worker, prepared a joint manifesto which was fairly typical of the concerns and argu-ments of Democracy Wall:

> The Chinese people suffered for ten long years from the ravages of the Cultural Revolution. This was clear proof that because the people did not rule the country or control their own destinies, power fell into the hands of a small minority whose mistakes have cost us dear. . . . At present the position of master and servant are reversed in China. But the people strongly want those that they elect truly to represent them. The role of the people's repre-sentatives is to defend and fight for the people's basic interests, and to supervise the policies and measures of the ruling party. . . . We view this election as a test of the ruling party. Does it believe in the people and stand together with the people? Or does it stand against the people?
>
> (Zheng Xing 1981: 101–2)[7]

Their election platform also called for improved standards of living to be made a national priority, and for this commitment to be enshrined in the Constitution and included in a wide-ranging programme of socialist modernization (Zheng Xing 1981: 102). He Defu came third in the elections, while Gong Ping came fourth in his factory. In his case, however, there was overt interference in the campaign from leading cadres, who 'held "individual discussions" and "greeting sessions" with each voter, so there were many abstentions' (Zheng Xing 1981: 102). This indicates that the favoured 1950s method for dealing with trouble-makers, 'one-to-one threats', was still being practised where workers' demands for democracy clashed with cadres' desire to maintain their position and quell shopfloor opposition.

In their manifesto, He and Gong noted the general belief in the factory that 'elections are a mere formality and that the representatives will have been secretly chosen in advance', adding that 'we believe that this was true of previous elections. But now we must resolve that from now on things will be different' (Zheng Xing 1981: 102). The previous year, shortly before the passing of the new Election Law, an article produced as part of the official reform campaign for limited democratization had made very similar observations, acknowledging that worker scepticism about democratic elections was under-standable given that

> [I]n previous elections – for positions like people's congress deputies and various kinds of workers' representatives – a list of candidates had been

announced by the factory Communist Party committee. . . . This was often done without the democratic consultation that was supposed to take place first, and voting was a mere formality.

(Zhi Exiang 1979: 6)

Other instances of experimental elections were reported where workers were similarly suspicious of procedures, holding back from participation and saying, 'We'd rather wait and see if the election is going to be carried out in a democratic way or not!' (*Beijing Review* 1 September 1980: 24). Given these well-founded doubts about the integrity of both internal enterprise elections and external elections to local people's congresses, as well as the sometimes explicit threat of reprisals, it is all the more significant that various worker-activists came so close to winning elections during 1980 (Munro 1984b: 12). Financial as well as electoral support was also forthcoming from workers in some cases, as in Changsha, where a large amount of money collected by workers funded the campaign of a student candidate who was struggling to keep going in the face of official harassment and opposition (Benton 1982: 11). Changsha workers were also reported to have posted big-character posters outside the premises of the local party committee in support of student activities (Chen Ruoxi 1982: 35).

But this opportunity for Democracy Wall activists to go out and seek mass support for their views was short-lived. As seen in several of the cases discussed above, local authorities were in a position to disrupt the elections and to prevent the election of candidates considered a threat, and the legal provisions which should have protected the right of such candidates to campaign freely proved to be inadequate. The next round of local people's congress elections, in 1984, were held 'in a far more controlled atmosphere' (Strand 1989: 42), although in 1986 local elections again became a medium for expressing dissent, as will be seen in the next chapter.

The final suppression of Democracy Wall

Ultimately the fate of Democracy Wall was probably sealed by the national consolidation which finally began to occur in the movement from September 1980, together with the rise of industrial unrest and calls for independent unions which the party saw as linked with it (Chen Ruoxi 1982: 36). The formation of the National Federation of People's Publications (Rosen 1988: 13, 26–30) moved the protests up a level from the largely local, comparable to work-unit, cellular protest in 1976, making it inherently more of a threat to party control, just as the large rebel federations in the Cultural Revolution had been. Meanwhile, restive workers were not only organizing themselves to pursue enterprise-specific disputes, but were demanding and sometimes forming fully independent unions, and even advocating an explicitly political role for them: one unofficial publication, *Sea Spray* of Qingdao, insisted that Solidarity was a workers' political party in all but name, and that it was only necessary caution which prevented the organization itself from admitting this. It also described the general strike and the organizing of autonomous unions as obviously political acts in their own right (*Sea Spray* 1980: 20). There was also the case of three Taiyuan printing workers jailed in March 1981 for organizing a 'China Democracy Party' (*October Review* 1982: 47).

Democracy Wall had been too slow to realize the potential which existed for a mass movement for democratization and autonomy from the party. Initially there were many good reasons for most people to shy away from active involvement in the movement, not least disenchantment with politics, and fear of being associated with those the party branded anarchists, disruptive elements, criminals, counter-revolutionaries and 'Gang of Four' types (*Southern Daily* 9 and 18 April, 31 May 1979; *People's Daily* 8 and 21 February 1980; Rosen 1988: 20; Chen Ruoxi 1982: 25–6); the *Southern Daily* went so far as to bracket Democracy Wall 'trouble-makers' who had clashed with the police with rapists and murderers, all of whom had to be dealt with using the 'iron fist' of dictatorship (*Southern Daily* 9 February 1980). David Strand has argued that the early focus on individual rehabilitation hindered the transition to a movement with mass participation, and that 'in its more obviously collective manifestations . . . the movement's turbulence made association with it dangerous' (Strand 1989: 29). There is something in this, although Democracy Wall was sparked off not by any individual rehabilitation, but by the reversal of verdict on April Fifth, an entire movement involving hundreds of thousands of people (Heilmann 1990: 80).

The party was ahead of Democracy Wall activists themselves in perceiving the danger of a connection between the dissident publishing movement and widespread industrial unrest and self-organization by workers. In blaming Democracy Wall for the unrest, it was partly demonstrating its conviction that whenever ordinary, uneducated workers started causing trouble, someone cleverer must be behind the scenes pulling the strings (Leijonhufvud 1990: 136), but the threat of a joint assault on the CCP, the new ruling class which had usurped the name of the working class the better to exploit it, was a real one. Spring 1981 saw a campaign in the official press to refute the main arguments of Democracy Wall, and to prepare the way for the CCP's definitive verdict on the Cultural Revolution and on Mao's leadership. A series of articles denied that any bureaucratic class or privileged stratum existed in China, and accused those who claimed to be attacking this new class of Cultural Revolution-style anarchism and of attempting to overthrow the party and the socialist system. It was denied that the party or the state appropriated the fruits of others' labour in an exploitative way, and, in the CCP's defence, its consistent opposition to bureaucratism and its many campaigns to eradicate the problem were highlighted, without, however, any reference to the very limited progress which such major campaigns as the Three-Anti had actually made (*Liberation Army Daily* 9 February 1981; *Red Flag* 1 March 1981: 12–18; *Southern Daily* 2 April 1981).

The document containing the official appraisal of Mao and the Cultural Revolution, the 'Decision on certain questions in Party history' adopted by the Sixth Plenum of the Eleventh Central Committee on 29 June 1981, had been under discussion for a year before it was finalized and had gone through numerous revisions, mainly, it seems, to make it less critical of Mao (MacFarquhar 1990: 329–30). Its formal adoption, and the show trial of the Gang of Four which ended early in 1981, marked a turning point in the high-level power struggle following Mao's death which was significant for the Democracy Wall Movement (Benton 1982: 12–13). The movement ceased to serve any useful purpose for Deng and his supporters in the top leadership once these questions had been decided in their favour, and so the final round of arrests could begin.

Given this context, the trial of the Gang and the verdict that the Cultural Revolution launched by Mao had been an unqualified disaster for China, it should not surprise us to find Democracy Wall activists being linked with Lin Biao and the Gang of Four, and activists' attacks on bureaucratism and privilege being denounced as calls for a 'second Cultural Revolution' (*Liberation Army Daily* 9 February 1981; *Red Flag* 1 March 1981: 12–18). Once again, former rebels were 'turned . . . from victims of Lin Biao, Mao and the Gang of Four into the Gang's so-called running dogs', ignoring the fact that 'the rank and file members of the Rebel Faction had no connection with the Gang of Four or its clique. In fact, former Rebels like the Li Yizhe group took dangerous risks by criticizing the Gang's radical policies' (A Chan 1993: 72–3). What is perhaps more surprising is to find the same line being taken eight years later against worker-activists in the 1989 Democracy Movement, when members of the Beijing Workers' Autonomous Federation and other workers' groups were compared in the press to the Gang of Four and labelled ' "sinister remnants of the Gang of Four" ' by their own state-appointed representatives, the ACFTU (Lu Ping 1990: 16; *Workers' Daily* 28 June 1989).

Although none of the proposals to give real power in the enterprise to workers bore fruit early in the 1980s, foundering as usual on cadre resistance and the lack of commitment to democratization among the party's top leadership, rising living standards as the reforms progressed from 1982 prevented the industrial unrest which had been building up from posing a serious threat once Democracy Wall had been suppressed. But this set a dangerous precedent for the party in that it was now relying solely on its ability to keep incomes rising and living standards improving in order to keep urban workers' allegiance. This meant that if the economy should falter, or if inflation ate too far into the income of workers' households, a group which now had considerable experience of autonomous political and industrial action might again prove willing and able to challenge its leaders. The next chapter looks at how this came about in 1989 as part of the Democracy Movement sparked by the death of Hu Yaobang.

7   'Let the whole nation know the workers are organized', 1984–94

To a large extent it was faltering confidence in the party's ability to manage the reforms, together with worries over very high urban inflation and outrage at increasingly obvious official corruption, which brought so many urban workers to support the student-initiated Democracy Movement of the spring of 1989. Having first become involved in a supportive role, worker-activists in the movement went on to forge forms of organization and a political programme which in many respects went beyond anything proposed by the students in terms of its radicalism and the potential threat which it posed to continuing party rule in China. Workers' involvement in the 1989 protests was described by many observers at the time as unprecedented; this study has already shown that this was not the case, but it is true that 1989 saw the most widespread, overt formation of autonomous workers' organizations in the history of the PRC.

During the course of the industrial reforms of the 1980s workers began to lose many of the benefits, such as security of employment, which had hitherto offered some recompense for their powerlessness and lack of a voice in the workplace, while at the same time pressure increased on them to work harder and produce more and better goods, leading to a more widespread sense of alienation and exploitation than ever before. We turn first, then, to an examination of how the reforms were perceived by workers and how they affected workers' interests during the 1980s, as the party's apparent abandonment of its socialist principles in industry revealed the extent of workers' own genuine commitment to some of those principles, leading to the political confrontation of 1989.

Impact of the industrial reforms, 1984–9

Following the final suppression of Democracy Wall in 1981, the economic reforms proceeded unhindered by any great concern about the problems which still remained in workers' relationships with enterprise management, the party, and the official unions. It was unlikely that workers' democratic rights would be able to make much headway in the early and mid-1980s in the context of a continued campaign against Cultural Revolution-era 'extensive democracy', excessive individualism and anarchism (*Guangzhou Daily* 25 September 1984).

Any attempt to assert the rights of those at the bottom of the hierarchy could be cast as a Red Guard-style attack on legitimate authority and ruled out of bounds. More recent confrontations with restive workers also seemed to play on the minds of workers' official representatives, as unions were warned at an ACFTU meeting in late 1984 to discourage by all means any ' "national, transregional, and transindustrial activities" ' among workers (Wilson 1986: 237); the right to strike had, of course, already been removed from the constitution. Having weathered the first such storm, the leadership was determined to prevent any further outbreaks of the 'Polish disease' among China's workers (Perry 1995: 314).

The official unions' role was once again formulated in a very orthodox way after the end of Democracy Wall, with the brief period of emphasizing workers' right to run the enterprise and the unions' duty to their members quickly forgotten once the beginnings of a Chinese Solidarity-style movement had been nipped in the bud. Although it was admitted that cadre–worker relations in the enterprise were not perfect, little stress was put on solving this problem, and instead the emphasis was all on unions' role in mobilizing workers to achieve the Four Modernizations and in carrying out ideological education among them (*People's Daily* 19 October 1983). A sure sign of a period of orthodoxy and unresponsiveness to workers' grievances is the insistence in the press of the identity of workers' interests and those of the state; no suggestion that workers still had legitimate grievances could be put forward as long as this was the case.

The recession in much of the capitalist world in the early 1980s gave the Chinese authorities an opportunity to remind workers at home that they had never had it so good, pointing to high unemployment in the West as proof of the superiority of socialism (*People's Daily* 27 October 1983). It was safe to do this by the end of 1983 once China's own late-1970s peak of youth unemployment, often associated with protests and violence during Democracy Wall (G White 1987: 369–70), had passed, and at a point where some workers were already feeling the benefits of increased pay and bonuses under the reforms and all expected to benefit in the near future. The success of the agricultural reforms in increasing peasant incomes was well known in urban areas, and some suggested that the benefits of reform would be even greater among workers, since they were an organized and disciplined group with a higher cultural level than their rural counterparts (*People's Daily* 22 July 1981), and thus better equipped to understand reform and to push it forward. Workers' expectations of the reforms were high, not just in terms of material benefits, but also of greater efficiency and better organization and management in the workplace; they had often felt their own hard work to have been wasted in the past by the managerial incompetence and supply bottlenecks which had been a feature of the planned economy. But expectations were high not least because official pronouncements on the reforms deliberately raised them (M M Yang 1989: 55), something which was regretted later on as discontent was generated by the failure of reality to measure up to the hopes which had been created in the minds of workers and their families.

Breaking the iron rice-bowl

The party was faced with difficulties of presentation with many aspects of the reform programme in industry, as it was anxious not to appear to workers to be abandoning socialism in any respect. Yet there was no getting round the fact that measures such as contract employment and the diversification of forms of enterprise ownership (both of which began during the 1980s, although the latter has become a much more significant component of the reforms in the 1990s) could be construed as introducing elements of capitalism into the Chinese economy. The authorities went to great lengths to establish that the system which they were criticizing and planning to dismantle, the so-called 'iron rice-bowl' of lifetime job security and work-unit welfare, was not an essential feature of socialism in China but rather a distortion of the system, and moreover one which was largely responsible for China's low level of labour productivity and quality problems in industry. But it was always a struggle to convince workers that the reforms did not represent an assault on their most cherished achievements under CCP rule.

The campaign against the 'iron rice-bowl' and 'eating from one big pot' is a case in point. Press accounts of the flaws of the old system stressed the negative effects on productivity of workers' knowledge that they would be paid, and paid about the same, regardless of their work performance (*Guangzhou Daily* 8 July 1984), and also strove to link the old system with the era of Cultural Revolution leftism, so that it became difficult to defend egalitarianism or social security without appearing to be defending late Maoism and the extremism of the Gang of Four (*Guangzhou Daily* 28 May 1984). Presumably because workers' attitudes seemed to be the easiest part of the equation to change, reformists stressed 'the mentality of the "iron rice-bowl" employee' as the sole cause of China's low labour productivity, ignoring, as Pat Howard has pointed out, debates on appropriate technology and the goal of full employment as factors in that low level of productivity (P Howard 1991: 94). Workers were in effect being told that their laziness was to blame for the poor performance of their enterprises, and that they were envious of others' hard-earned success if they objected to greatly increased bonuses being paid to a minority. The unanimity of the media on this issue left no room for a stand to be made on 'claims for equity or social justice' under the reforms, with all such claims cast as stemming from the 'discredited, remnant Maoist-era mentality of "eating from the same big pot", undue "egalitarianism", and infection by the "red-eye disease"' of jealousy (A Chan 1993: 41).

But despite the constant public denigration of egalitarianism and excessive job security, workers were not at all convinced that their attachment to these features of the old system was the product of old-style leftist dogmatism and the politics of envy. On the contrary, many older workers in particular felt deep resentment as the security which they had always seen as the one unequivocal benefit of socialism slipped away from them during the 1980s, complaining that they had not 'risk[ed] their lives in the struggle for the new society only to return to the nightmare of fear and anxiety over job and wage security' (P Howard

1991: 114). This belief that ' "many of our revolutionary comrades struggled all their lives so that the people of the whole country could have an iron rice-bowl" ' (G White 1987: 379) persisted most strongly among workers. The party insisted that the iron rice-bowl and egalitarianism did not equal socialism (*Guangzhou Daily* 29 December 1984), but few in the factories seemed convinced. It appeared that thirty years of indoctrination with socialist ideology had been rather more successful than the party had anticipated, particularly on the question of employment security and workers' status in China as more than just hired labour (G White 1987: 384).

There was very little acceptance among workers of Deng Xiaoping's idea that it was all right if 'a few people get rich first'; they saw this simply as unfair distribution (Leung Wing-yue 1988: 207–8; Wang Shaoguang 1993: 184), since how could these few really be worth ten or twenty times the value of an ordinary worker? Workers often reacted to sharply differentiated individual bonuses by subverting bonus allocation, pressuring managers to ensure a relatively egalitarian distribution of the available funds (Walder 1987: 26), and even devising ways of pooling bonuses among themselves to ensure that roughly equal benefits came to everyone (Shirk 1981: 585). Many workers were deeply offended even by wage differentials which would not be considered very great by Western standards where these were nevertheless perceived as unfair (A Chan 1993: 40; Walder 1991: 479). Particularly sharp resentment was generated by the widening gap between the bonuses paid to workers and those received by top management in the enterprise, which on occasion might be twenty or thirty times greater than the equivalent payment to workers, and which were not always subject to prior approval by the workers' congress, further reducing their legitimacy in workers' eyes (*Beijing Worker* May 1989). Even where the workers' congress did approve such payments, this had the effect of making the growing disparity between rewards to workers and those to cadres obvious to all, 'invit[ing] enhanced collective antagonism towards cadres' (Walder 1991: 480).

Inevitably, workers who found their own security threatened raised the question of whether the 'gold rice-bowls' enjoyed by bosses did not present a stronger case for abolition than their own humble iron ones. But the adverse effects of the reforms on worker–cadre relations went beyond disputes over increased inequality of income, serious though these were. At a time when ever greater efficiency was being demanded of workers, the deficiencies of management became a more significant bone of contention than ever before. It had often been a cause of complaint back in the 1950s that workers lost pay through failing to meet production quotas because managerial incompetence had led to a shortage of materials, and as bonuses became an important component of workers' normal wage under the reforms, being forced to slow or halt production and miss targets because of errors by management generated great discontent among the workers affected, sometimes resulting in unofficial actions such as absenteeism or go-slows by groups of workers (M M Yang 1989: 52–4). Managerial incompetence was cited as just as important a cause of low productivity as workers' attachment to the 'iron rice-bowl' (G White 1987: 379), and although at the very beginning of the reforms it had been suggested that workers could improve the quality of management by being permitted to elect managers below the factory-director level, this system had never been widely implemented, leaving workers adversely affected by poor management unable to do much about it, except withdraw their labour in whole or in part. Managers still seemed only to feel responsible to those above them, not to the workers below (M M Yang 1989: 49).

'Scientific management' and the authority of the factory director under the reforms

If the party was defensive about its apparent retreat from socialist principles in the state sector, in the Special Economic Zones (SEZs) established for foreign investment as part of Deng's 'Open Door' policy there was no need to disguise the fact that essentially capitalist forms of management and labour relations were in force, since these areas were quarantined off from the rest of Chinese industry and regarded as experimental zones. Workers were aware, however, that what happened in Shenzhen today could happen in their own enterprise a year or two later, and watched the introduction of measures such as short-term employment contracts with trepidation. The way in which foreign-invested enterprises in the SEZs were run does seem to have had a noticeable influence in the surrounding area, with features such as 'much greater managerial control and supervision, the more rapid pace of assembly lines . . . [and] the amount of overtime' striking observers as a contrast with the situation in long-established state enterprises away from the SEZs where such reforms had as yet hardly been implemented (P Howard 1991: 106–7). While Taylorism or scientific management was only fully and openly implemented in the areas most influenced by the SEZs, such as Guangdong, a general shift towards greater managerial authority, regimentation and discipline was more widely discernible in Chinese industry. This was true not only in small and medium-sized collective and township enterprises, but also anywhere where the reform-driven shift in power from the party secretary to the factory director had left the latter, now responsible for the enterprise's profit and loss, looking at 'tightening labour discipline, imposing heavy penalties, raising production norms, and restructuring the award system' (A Chan 1993: 42) to try to ensure higher productivity from a docile workforce.

Guangdong was a pioneer of many of the industrial reforms, not only within the SEZs at Shenzhen and Zhuhai, but more generally throughout the province. The *Guangzhou Daily* in mid-1984, only months after the official beginning of the urban reform programme, ran an admiring article on the Haizhu District Watch Assembly Plant, which it praised for its boldness in drawing on overseas and Hong Kong experience to introduce 'rigorous scientific management systems'. What the factory was implementing was classic Taylorism: quotas revised upwards and the time taken to complete a given task measured in seconds; workers trained to 'eliminate superfluous movements' so as to reach the maximum physically possible level of productivity; work-stations arranged with all employees facing away from the door so that they did not waste valuable seconds looking up when people came in, and absolutely no talking, smoking, eating or drinking permitted during working hours; piece-rate wages; and such strict discipline that a single late start would lose a worker the whole month's bonus (*Guangzhou Daily* 10 July 1984). But unlike in the 1960s and 1970s, no-one now was straining logic to prove that this sort of system was anything other than a Tayloristic, capitalist style of 'scientific management'; the plant, an early experiment in enterprise autonomy, boasted of its rare freedom to hire and fire without the interference of the 'mothers-in-law' of the industrial bureaucracy, and proudly announced that more than thirty workers who had not come up to scratch had already been sacked. This sort of 'management method designed to squeeze as much surplus labour as possible out of these human machines' (A Chan 1995: 48) has become increasingly common in the 1990s, particularly in foreign-invested manufacturing operations in southeast China, but it is striking to find it being boasted of as early as 1984.

Those who advocated this sort of management 'rigour' took pains to portray such reforms as opposed by the conservative-leftist old guard, and therefore themselves progressive, liberalizing and democratic, but in fact many of the technocrats who advocated scientific management also had very specific definitions of democracy, favouring elite neo-authoritarianism rather than mass democracy (A Chan 1993: 46), which might explain why an undemocratic, extractive version of the labour process had such appeal for them. While state enterprises did not experience Taylorist rationalization of the labour process to anything like the same extent, they did during the 1980s undergo a parallel process of power in the enterprise being concentrated more and more in the hands of the factory director, to the exclusion of workers, the workers' congress, the official unions, and even the party branch. Such was the extent of the factory director's authority that this trend has been described by some as tantamount to a return to one-man management (Wilson 1986: 233; Leung Wing-yue 1988: 99).

It was clear from the outset of the reforms that there was a contradiction between plans for decentralization and greater enterprise autonomy, giving authority to the factory director, and the goal of democratic management and participation by workers. This was particularly so once the 'Factory Director Responsibility System' (FDRS) was introduced in 1984. The FDRS provided for the enterprise party committee to retire to a role of political and ideological education while the director took over sole authority for the enterprise's day-to-day management, forward planning and meeting of production quotas, subject only in some areas to consultation with the union or the workers' congress, whose objections could in any case be vetoed (Child 1994: 66). The director also had the right to appoint, transfer and dismiss middle managers, even in those enterprises where these people had been democratically elected to their posts by the workforce (*Guangzhou Daily* 8 June 1984), showing clearly the contradiction between the institutions intended to give workers a voice in enterprise decision-making and the new direction of enterprise reform.

When the FDRS was introduced in 1984 it was accompanied by warnings in the press, including one from no less a figure than Zhao Ziyang, that democratic institutions such as the workers' congress and the unions would have to be strengthened if an unacceptable shift in power was not to occur away from the majority of workers and into the hands of a single top leader (*Guangzhou Daily* 16 May, 26 August, and 19 October 1984). But judging by the results after three to five years of the system, these warnings were not heeded. The *Workers' Daily*, which had pressed into use the old Maoist slogan of the 'unity of opposites' to describe how these fundamentally incompatible systems might be successfully combined (*Workers' Daily* 5 May 1987), was among those reporting that, as workers and union cadres had originally feared (Leung Wing-yue 1988: 99), the all-powerful role of the factory director had in practice been over-emphasized, while democratic management had been allowed to wither (*Workers' Daily* 27 June 1989), resulting in the FDRS becoming as dictatorial as the Soviet-inspired one-man management of the 1950s. While experiments in enterprise autonomy and decentralizing power down to the factory director had begun as early as 1979, it was not until 1995 that workers' rights in the new environment gained protection under the Labour Law, showing how far concrete measures to defend workers' interests lagged behind the increase in the power of top management. A sharp deterioration in worker–management relations was the main result of the spread of Tayloristic practices in Chinese industry (Wang Shaoguang 1993: 185; Chan 1993: 40).

Workers' voice in the autonomous enterprise: unions and workers' congress

Many of the criticisms of the factory director's increased authority in the enterprise concerned reports of interference in union appointments or failure to support and implement the resolutions of the workers' congress. We saw in the last chapter that the reform of these institutions for the representation and protection of workers' interests in the enterprise had not, in the early 1980s, resulted in any changes which would guarantee their effectiveness: 'China's enterprises ended the 1980s with the same powerless trade unions and workers' congresses with which they began them' (Walder 1991: 479). The effectiveness of the workers' congress still depended on the attitude of the party committee and, increasingly, the factory director (Leung Wing-yue 1988: 110), while the official unions had not been able to win back the allegiance and trust of workers who had on occasion resorted to self-organization in disputes during Democracy Wall, seeing the official unions as part of the problem rather than a useful ally in their struggles. From this unpromising start in the reform era, things had if anything got worse by the end of the 1980s as the increased authority of the factory director reduced even further the influence of both unions and workers' congress. By the end of the 1980s the unions' own prediction of increased conflict in the enterprise if democratic management was not developed further as a counter-weight to the all-powerful position of the factory director was borne out by an increase in strikes, a significant proportion of which were attributed to the failure of the unions and the workers' congress to defend workers' rights in the autonomous enterprise (Leung Wing-yue 1988: 117; *FBIS-CHI-89–042* 6 March 1989: 32; Perry 1995: 315).

Reports throughout the 1980s give the impression that little had changed since the Mao era with regard to the main problems of the official unions. In mid-1984 the Guangzhou Municipal Federation of Trade Unions, responding to an ACFTU call to basic-level union organizations to make themselves the 'family and friend' of the workers, reported that a large proportion of enterprise union branches in the city were failing to live up to this ideal, and needed to rectify their organization and forge close ties with workers as quickly as possible, speaking out on workers' behalf, acting to solve their problems, and thus gaining their trust (*Guangzhou Daily* 28 May 1984). Even more damning was the verdict of a survey undertaken by the ACFTU itself in spring 1988. Less than 10 per cent of respondents in the survey considered that trade unions could 'speak for workers and solve their problems', while 25 per cent said unions had 'only collected dues and conducted recreational activities'. When asked whether their enterprise trade union could be called the 'family' or 'friend' of the workers, less than 20 per cent replied in the affirmative while nearly 55 per cent answered 'no' or 'not really'. Thirty per cent thought workers' congresses were effective or very effective, but 70 per cent said they were only occasionally effective or did their duties in form only. The only difference noted by workers in the way in which the unions operated towards the end of the 1980s was that union cadres were now ordered about by factory directors, rather than by enterprise party secretaries as before. Workers said that in general they did not turn to the union for help with their problems (Chiang 1990: 85–6).

A comparable ACFTU survey of workers' views two years earlier had also revealed a negative assessment of the unions' performance among a majority of workers, with younger and better-educated workers the most critical of all (Wu Shouhui and Guo Jinhua 1987: 55–6). The same response pattern was repeated when workers were questioned about the workers' congress and democratic management, and here even the respondents aged over 45 were more negative than positive in their assessment of its role (Li Hua 1987: 69–70). The ACFTU researchers who analysed the survey data claimed to find little evidence of strong demand among workers for democratic management, with most workers instead far more concerned at the incompetence of the unions in welfare work and in assisting them in improving their skills and standard of living (Li Hua 1987: 72, 79). But by 1988 the lack of democratic rights in enterprises was regularly being cited by ACFTU officials as a cause of strikes and workplace disputes (*Workers' Daily* 13 April and 8 July 1988; Leung Wing-yue 1988: 117).

It is possible that over the two-year gap workers' perception grew that their weak political position and lack of rights in the enterprise was the cause of their economic difficulties and increasing insecurity at work, particularly as the issues of inflation and corruption came to politicize workplace disputes (Walder 1989b: 34). Equally it is entirely possible that workers' responses to an official questionnaire were guarded; other researchers found workers willing to voice demands for democratic management in some situations, but not when top management were present (M M Yang 1989: 48). The apparent lack of demand could also be a sign of very low expectations for democratic management, of the 'unavailability' of this option (Pateman 1970: 81–3) to many rank-and-file production workers, whereas it was a minimum expectation that the union would provide welfare benefits and social services, and thus discontent was readily expressed when the organization failed in this basic role.

To illustrate the depths to which the unions' reputation among workers had sunk, in 1987 a case emerged in Qingdao where an enterprise union branch had proved incapable even of protecting its own, siding with management against a representative democratically elected by workers themselves. A worker in a pressure-gauge factory was forced out of his workers' congress post after making criticisms of the enterprise leadership for falsifying production figures and applying rules on compensation for medical expenses too rigidly and simplistically. A dispute over the medical bills of a worker who had subsequently died raised the emotional temperature of the confrontation. The removal of this worker representative from his production post was ordered by the head of the enterprise union in violation of proper procedures, and the worker was left 'awaiting re-assignment' on living expenses of one *yuan* per day (*Workers' Daily* 15 June 1987).

Workers at the plant were predictably unimpressed that someone elected to serve on the workers' congress could nevertheless be treated in this way, with the enterprise union backing up management's retaliation, commenting: '"Talk about democracy all day long, but we can't even speak the truth at our workers' congress"' (Leung Wing-yue 1988: 110–11). The ACFTU commented that when a union failed to uphold workers' democratic rights and the democratic management role of the workers' congress, it not only lost workers' confidence, but came to be opposed to the workers, and that such a union was worthless (*Workers' Daily* 15 June 1987). Many union officials had become seriously concerned by the end of the 1980s that incidents such as this, which further reduced workers' confidence in the approved channels of participation and representation set up for them in the workplace, could only lead to workers abandoning the official unions, much as they had in 1956–7, and organizing themselves in the event of disputes (*Workers' Daily* 11 August 1987; *FBIS-CHI-89–042* 6 March 1989: 32).

Where unions did try to defend workers' rights, they often ran up against the power of the factory director, finding themselves subject to management harassment and intimidation, or transfer, demotion, or even dismissal, as a punishment for their legitimate union activities (Leung Wing-yue 1988: 116; *Workers' Daily* 9 and 11 August 1987). Urgent calls for union reform and democratization, to make the unions truly representative of shopfloor workers and independent from management and the party, were still being made (*Workers' World* February 1989) weeks before the 1989 demonstrations broke out and proved the concerns about workers' resort to autonomous organization to be well-founded. While at the top level the ACFTU was able to push for more independence for the official unions, despite the generally conservative political line prevailing within the party at this time (Wilson 1990b: 271), at the grassroots of union organization, dominance by the factory director or the party committee was still the rule (Wilson 1990a: 56). Efforts to shore up unions' independence from the party and management and to bring them under the democratic control of their members manifestly failed to divert workers from responding to the worsening economic situation in the cities with strikes and stoppages in 1987 and 1988, and from taking part in the Democracy Movement of 1989.

This familiar state of affairs – a rubber-stamp workers' congress giving mean-ingless affirmation to management decisions, and a union under the thumb of those with real power in the enterprise and held in contempt by most of its members – meant that there were still no properly functioning official channels through which workers' grievances could be expressed and resolved before they turned into major confrontations. As workers' grievances mounted from 1986 up to the eve of the Democracy Movement, this set the scene for growing unrest, strikes, slow-downs and other protests by workers who could not see any other way of solving their problems or registering their dissent from the general trend of increasing insecurity and their relegation from the status of 'masters of the enterprise' back to that of 'hired hand'. However local, small-scale and short-lived many of these strikes were, they nevertheless showed that 'some workers had come to realize the importance of organization', with the formation of inde-pendent unions during the 1989 movement not 'the product of a sudden impulse [but] an indicator of an important trend' (Wang Shaoguang 1993: 186–7).

The urban reforms falter: insecurity, corruption and inflation, 1986–9

As had been the case in all previous confrontations, specific economic circum-stances and the background of workers' everyday lives played an important part in generating support for the protest movement of 1989. A possible explanation for the very rapid emergence of autonomous workers' organizations in the spring of 1989 was the extent of discontent with what many perceived as a marked worsening of workers' situation under the reforms during the second half of the 1980s. It was noted in the last chapter that restive workers were to a certain extent successfully 'bought off' by rising incomes in the early stages of the reforms, although even then concerns about rising prices and decreased job security were also very evident, and it seemed clear that the party was only being allowed a limited chance to make good on its promises. If improvements failed to materialize, then the unrest and self-organization beginning to occur in 1980 and 1981 might very quickly return in China.

What happened in the second half of the decade, and particularly from 1987 onwards, was that rising expectations of improved living standards came into conflict with a perceived worsening of most working-class households' economic circumstances. Whether or not this perception was borne out by the facts is not really the point; it was the perception, almost universal, of promises broken and hopes betrayed which was important in generating support among urban workers for the Democracy Movement (Walder 1991: 470–3). In a survey of the reform period, the Hong Kong periodical *Mingbao Monthly* located a crucial change in the public mood on reform taking place from early in 1987, and passing through several distinct stages until by the spring of 1989, widespread distrust of the government and pessimism about living standards, together with disgust at official corruption, formed the basis of near-universal urban support for the Democracy Movement (*Mingbao Monthly* October 1991: 24–8). A first point to note with regard to popular views of the reforms is that before 1987, urban incomes had on the whole been rising, and, in an ironic echo of the high expectations generated in the cities by the successes of land reform in the late 1940s, hopes were high that the success of contract responsibility in the country-side could be repeated in urban areas, resulting in a similarly striking year-on-year improvement in living standards (*Mingbao Monthly* October 1991: 24). By 1987 many urban citizens had actually come to regard rising incomes as synonymous with reform, and this posed problems for the regime when the increases faltered and in some cases went into reverse. When further price reforms were carried out in 1988 without the cushion of rising urban wages, panic-buying and runs on the banks resulted (*Mingbao Monthly* October 1991: 27).

The *Mingbao Monthly* article noted that in two 1987 surveys of public opinion, security was rated more important than increased individual income by most respondents (*Mingbao Monthly* October 1991: 26), and although the threat posed by the reforms to this cherished security had been apparent since 1979, it was only at the end of the 1980s that the government really began to dismantle the system of socialist welfare provision set up in the 1950s, with reforms being implemented in the areas of housing, medical care, and employment (specifically the promotion of insecure contract employment, which implied an acceptance, for the first time since 1949, of the existence of urban unemployment as a permanent feature of the economy). Workers who in the late 1970s and early 1980s had already reacted with alarm and hostility to reformist slogans about 'smashing the iron rice-bowl' now finally faced the reality of it. As cases of laid-off workers falling ill and being unable to obtain help with medical bills began to occur (Wang Shaoguang 1993: 186), workers in general became increasingly concerned about the lack of social support now available to them; for many it was the first time in their lives that they had had to worry about things like being unable to pay for medical treatment (Wang Xiaodong 1993: 156).

At the same time, the development of a tight money policy through 1988 meant that by early 1989, as many as two-thirds of urban factories were running at less than full capacity, and that as a consequence, workers on short-time working, often a two- or three-day week, were not receiving their full salary, still less their usual bonuses for meeting production quotas. Many were only on 70 per cent of their usual pay (*South China Morning Post* 9 March 1990), and in the context of further price reform and the highest inflation rates of the reform period so far, this was a major cause for complaint among workers. It is generally agreed that, mainly as a result of very high urban inflation, but also influenced by the prevalence of short-time working and suspension of bonuses, real urban industrial incomes actually fell slightly between the end of 1986 and the end of 1988 (Walder 1989b: 31; 1991: 471; *Mingbao Monthly* October 1991: 26). The ACFTU itself estimated that in 1988 a majority of urban households experienced a drop in real income, with 25 to 30 per cent of workers reduced to subsistence level (Wilson 1990b: 270).

Despite the fact that it only affected a minority of the workforce, and a small minority at that in the state sector, the introduction of fixed-term contract employment in 1986 was one of the most significant reform milestones in terms of the build-up of workers' discontent prior to the demonstrations of 1989. To workers the end of permanent employment was 'both insulting and threatening' (G White 1987: 377), and it had the effect of evaporating once and for all the illusion of their 'masters' status:

> Workers may still be persuaded to feel that they are in control even when wages are being redistributed or reduced; but it would take a great deal of imagination for those workers facing retrenchment to believe that they are the masters of their enterprises.
>
> (Leung Wing-yue 1988: 97–8)

It was difficult for the authorities to develop any convincing ideological justification for a measure which quite plainly was intended to make it easier for management to sack superfluous or otherwise undesirable workers; nor was it easy to distinguish the 'new' contract employment from the system of the 1960s associated with Liu Shaoqi, which had played such a significant role in generating worker militancy in the early Cultural Revolution (G White 1987: 377; Warner 1995: 61). The implicit division of workers into first- and second-class employees in effect replicated the dual employment system characteristic not only of the Soviet Union, not regarded as a suitable model for China since the end of the 1950s, but also, and more damagingly, of capitalism in general (P Howard 1991: 105–6).

Initially only new employees were supposed to be subject to contract employment, and it was emphasized in the earliest experiments with the system in Guangdong that these new-style contract workers would not be an inferior and exploited group in enterprises, but would be recompensed for their lack of long-term security by being paid slightly higher wages than regular workers while enjoying the same rights in the enterprise (*Guangzhou Daily* 5 June 1984), the lack of political rights for contract and temporary workers in the 1960s having been perceived as a blatant injustice. But it is clear from reports of how the system actually worked that contract workers in the late 1980s were often regarded and treated in enterprises much as their 1960s counterparts had been, and did not enjoy equal rights with the permanent workforce (*Guangzhou Daily* 9 November 1984):

> There were complaints of discriminatory pay despite being allocated the most difficult, dirty and dangerous jobs. There were accounts of breaches of

contract and of workers being denied promotions after serving apprenticeships with minimal remuneration. There were reports of workers being
excluded from membership in the trade union and the workers' congress in
'many' units. There were reports of workers being fired when they became
ill [or] injured.

(P Howard 1991: 100)

Implementation of contract employment had been projected to take in a
majority of the workforce by the year 2000 (P Howard 1991: 98), but it actually
proceeded (and at the time of writing is still proceeding) rather slowly (Walder
1987: 41; Wilson 1990a: 50), particularly in the state sector, where it was estimated that by 1992–3 less than 20 per cent of the state industrial workforce were
on fixed-term contracts (M Warner 1995: 61). A major reason for this slow
progress was 'passivity, disagreement and resistance', not just on the predictable
grounds of vested interests being attacked, but also 'in terms of general ideological principle' (G White 1987: 378–9). Objections to the system were raised not
just by those workers immediately affected, but by all the others who worried
that it was only a matter of time before it was applied to them; as on the eve of
the Cultural Revolution, rumours circulated that universal application of the
system was the ultimate aim, and some state enterprises did apply contract
employment to all their workers, not just new employees (P Howard 1991: 98–9),
adding credence to this fear. Thus even among workers still permanently
employed, a 'job security panic' (Walder 1991: 478) had been engendered by the
end of the 1980s.

Contract employment added further to the power of the factory director,
since the non-renewal of employment contracts, unlike dismissals of permanent
workers, did not have to be ratified by the workers' congress (P Howard 1991:
102), but was within the power of top management. But even without actually
sacking workers, managers had other measures at their disposal with which they
could bring pressure to bear on workers, including the compulsory transfer of
unwanted workers, on a significantly reduced salary, to a labour service company
to await reassignment to another post, thus using the labour service companies
set up to provide the beginnings of a labour market in China 'to punish recalcitrant or rebellious workers' (Walder 1991: 478). The lack of constraints on the
behaviour of factory directors in this new era of enterprise autonomy also
enabled some to act in an obviously corrupt or self-serving way (A Chan 1993:
42), something which could only add to the anger and discontent of workers
who were coming to see themselves as the main casualties of the urban reforms.

A sense of relative deprivation among previously privileged workers in the
larger state enterprises (Chan 1993: 43), and the gap between expectations of
reform and the reality, despite generally rising urban incomes (Unger 1991b: 3;
Wilson 1990a: 58), have both been offered as explanations for the scale and
intensity of workers' backing for the 1989 Democracy Movement. There is
considerable truth in both of these explanations, but they do not fully capture
the many ways in which workers' political as well as material position had

sharply worsened by the end of the 1980s (Wang Shaoguang 1993: 187). Measures such as the leasing of enterprises to managers for fixed periods greatly eroded what sense workers had previously had of being 'the masters' in any real sense (Leung Wing-yue 1988: 207–8), and the situation was worsened in cases where no formal announcement about contracting-out was even made to the workforce who, on learning about the decision from the evening news, could not be blamed for concluding that they were being treated simply as part of the unit's fixed assets, owned by managers who could keep them on or dispose of them as they saw fit (Leung Wing-yue 1988: 100). Added to contract employment's promotion of the 'hired hand' mentality (G White 1987: 380), this measure helped to break down any remaining notion that the relationship between workers and management was not one of rulers and ruled, or exploiters and exploited.

Once the opposing sides were so clearly drawn up, it became harder to explain why workers did not need their own independent organizations to defend their interests against the extensive new powers of management, not only where diversification of ownership meant that they were now in a quasi-capitalist employment relationship (*Workers' World* February 1989), but even in state enterprises. Measured against the 1950s, when many workers also displayed a strong sense of alienation from management and the regime and compared themselves unfavourably with workers under capitalism before 1949 even as the transition to socialism in industry was completed, by 1989 workers had an even stronger case for feeling the necessity of autonomous collective resistance to the impositions of the authorities; the level of alienation observable in enterprises made its emergence inevitable (Wilson 1990a: 59; P Howard 1991: 113–14).

Workers' low sense of their group's status and social worth on the eve of the Democracy Movement is striking, as they compared the rewards to be had for honest work unfavourably with those gained through corruption by the well-connected (*China News* 4 January 1989: 6; Walder and Gong 1993: 20). In the labour movement press it was openly argued that workers were right not to feel that they were the masters since, although they were much better off than before 1949 and had benefitted from reform in some respects, they were nevertheless without democratic rights or power in the workplace (*Beijing Worker* April 1989). Even basic safety and working conditions suffered under the trend of 'marketization' in industry (Wilson 1990a: 52). As before, workers had no means of enforcing their rights to be consulted and to give approval for management decisions, since in the absence of democratic elections, the only possibility was for factory directors to be persuaded to share their power with workers (Chan 1993: 58), and this proved extremely difficult in the absence of sanctions for behaving like an old-style 'boss'. A punitive style of management prevailed, with some enterprises having literally hundreds of regulations setting out punishments to which workers were subject (*China News* 4 January 1989: 6), and with the unions and workers' congress often themselves dominated by the factory director's or the party secretary's personal appointments (*Workers' World* February 1989), there was little possibility of workers' being able to use the designated channels to express their objections to the style or content of reform-era management.

One revealing detail of several commentaries on workers' relations with management at the end of the 1980s was the trend among top managers to hire bodyguards for themselves, apparently not out of a general fear of increasing violent crime in cities, but rather specifically to protect themselves from the wrath and violent retribution of 'down-sized' or otherwise disgruntled workers (*Beijing Worker* April 1989; *FBIS-CHI-89–022* 3 February 1989). These attacks appeared to be particularly common in the northeastern heavy-industrial 'rust-belt', with 276 incidents of violence against managers in the first half of 1988 in Liaoning province, and at least three managers murdered in Shenyang during the year, while workers generally took the view that the victims deserved their fate (Wang Shaoguang 1993: 186). It was noted that capitalists in the old society had also had bodyguards to protect them from workers, but that this had been a reflection of the sharpness of class struggle at that time; the implication for managers in the 1980s did not need to be spelled out (*Beijing Worker* April 1989).

Overall workers' mood by 1989 was characterized by very low morale, as they increasingly felt themselves to be nothing more than hired labour or even part of the machinery; by a sharp increase in antagonism towards enterprise management (Walder 1991: 433–4), often expressed through strikes or other industrial action; by profound worries about insecurity, all the more so as not all of those who were laid off could find new jobs (*FBIS-CHI-89–042* 6 March 1989: 32); and growing disgust at open official corruption while their own standards of living stagnated or declined. Workers had never been convinced that the implicit deal offered by the reformists – more pay as compensation for less security – was one which they ought to accept, but at the end of the 1980s the state had even failed to keep its side of this suspect bargain (Saich 1990: 11). As on previous occasions when workers met their side of a bargain with their employers but found that the promised reward, whether this consisted of democratic rights and authority in the workplace or higher pay, was not forthcoming, they turned away from the ineffective and discredited official channels for grievance expression and resolution and, inspired by the student protests following the death of Hu Yaobang in April 1989, took matters into their own hands.

Workers in the 1989 protests

The student demonstrations which began in April 1989 had a forerunner in the protests of December 1986 and January 1987 in a number of Chinese cities. On that occasion most commentators suggested that workers had remained aloof from the protests as 'largely passive observers' (Wilson 1990b: 270). Other accounts, however, indicate that workers were involved, or at least were protesting at the same time as students in Hefei, Shanghai, Beijing and elsewhere were demonstrating over political reform and their own economic grievances. Workers as well as other urban residents registered a protest of sorts in the 1986 local people's congress elections, invalidating their ballot papers by writing in fictional names of candidates (from Water Margin heroes to the more contemporary

Mickey Mouse), to such an extent that in some districts in Shanghai the first round of the poll itself was rendered void by the number of spoiled papers. In one factory in Shanghai workers were threatened with having a fine deducted from their wages to force them to vote at all (Wang Ruowang 1987). Discontent over party interference in these elections and the lack of progress on political reform helped generate the winter demonstrations, and at the same time as students were taking to the streets, strikes were reported and a circular was sent to enterprises warning workers against participation in the movement and supportive striking. It has even been suggested that top party leaders only became seriously concerned about the movement once the threat of workers' involvement became apparent (Leung 1988: 119).

It was later explained by worker-activists in the 1989 protests that in the earlier movement, the authorities had successfully practised divide-and-rule tactics by portraying students as a selfish and pampered elite who frittered away the public funds accumulated through the toil of workers and peasants, and who had no real cause for complaint (Mok and Harrison 1990: 111), thus making workers disinclined to act in sympathy with such a privileged group. Virtually every account of workers' activities in 1989 mentions their greater concern with bread-and-butter economic issues, as compared with students' and intellectuals' more abstract political concerns, but in fact students and intellectuals in both 1986–7 and 1989 were very much concerned with how they as a group had lost out in material terms under the reforms (Erbaugh and Kraus 1991: 159; A Chan 1991b: 142). One could not spend more than five minutes with a mainland Chinese academic in the late 1980s without hearing about how much more money was being earned by hairdressers, restaurateurs and taxi-drivers than by learned professors, and during the 1989 protests a workers' handbill appeared warning the students not to alienate ordinary people by over-emphasizing 'the treatment of intellectuals and the budget for higher education' (Mok and Harrison 1990: 110). Right from the beginning of the reform period, some intel-lectuals had seen workers as the main beneficiaries of urban reform (Benton 1982: 92), and this idea seems to have persisted through the 1980s, with more notice taken in intellectual circles of reports of the high bonuses earned by a minority of workers in certain industries or firms, while the effects of increased job insecurity, inflation, and punitive management practices on workers received much less attention.

Students had not sought workers' active support in 1986–7, and neither did they go out of their way in 1989 to seek more than sympathy and logistical support (which was readily forthcoming) from the urban citizenry as a whole; they did not see workers as a group likely to be able to contribute to the move-ment's agenda. In part their preference for keeping workers out of the movement was based on an accurate calculation that a workers' movement would face immediate suppression, whereas the right of students and intellectuals to 'remonstrate' with the government would be accepted and their protest allowed to continue. But contempt for the intellectual and political capabilities of workers was also important in making students disinclined actively to extend the movement to encompass other social groups (Walder and Gong 1993: 24; Unger 1991b: 4). When this did happen, it was 'more in spite of than due to student efforts to broaden the societal base of participation' (Wilson 1990b: 273), an ironic state of affairs given that the overriding concern of the authorities in Beijing and nationally seems to have been preventing workers from linking up with the student movement (Chan and Unger 1990: 278; Wang Shaoguang 1993: 178), something which they saw as an obvious and natural development.

Beginnings of the workers' movement: participants and agendas

The best-known of the many autonomous workers' organizations in 1989, the Beijing Workers' Autonomous Federation (BWAF; *gongzilian*), emerged very early in the movement out of a nucleus of young worker-activists who made contact after work in Tiananmen Square through informal evening discussions of the shortcomings of the party leadership, inflation, corruption, and workers' treatment in the enterprise. Handbills denouncing the security forces' violence towards peacefully protesting students appeared under the name of the BWAF as early as 20 April (Walder and Gong 1993: 1–2; Lu Ping 1990: 2), although the organization was not formally established until 18 May. Independent workers' organizations of varying size and composition, many using the WAF title, were also formed in Changsha, Fuzhou, Guangzhou, Guiyang, Hangzhou, Hohhot, Jinan, Kunming, Lanzhou, Nanjing, Shanghai, Suzhou, Wuhan, Xi'an, and Xining (Wang Shaoguang 1993: 179; Lu Ping 1990: 17); in some of the larger cities several different autonomous groups existed. In addition, the BWAF also included workers from elsewhere in northeast and north-central China, including Tianjin (Lu Ping 1990: 13). Although the core activists of the BWAF numbered only about 150 at the peak of the group's activities just before the military suppression of 3–4 June, it claimed nearly 20,000 registered members by that stage (Walder and Gong 1993: 9), and also had links with other workers' organizations in the capital.

The movement consisted mainly of young workers from a variety of enterprises (Lu Ping 1990: 13), who generally had little or no previous history of political activism or rebellion and also had had relatively little in the way of formal education (Walder and Gong 1993: 15). While older workers and lower-level management and union cadres tended not to be prepared to risk direct involvement by joining the movement, quite a few of them shared in the general opposition to the CCP government's corruption and mismanagement, and they were prepared to mingle with the crowds around the BWAF stand on the north-western edge of Tiananmen Square and to offer moral support and advice to activists (Walder and Gong 1993: 12). Elsewhere in China, the Guangdong WAF was reported to have significant numbers of lower-level management, white-collar workers and 'worker-intellectuals' in its ranks, as well as ordinary shopfloor workers (Chan and Unger 1990: 275, n. 19; *China Spring* April 1990: 60).

Workers from the largest state enterprises had always been considered by the party as the least restive and most reliable section of the working class, but although they had on the whole been a privileged group in the past, they were at least as badly affected by the changes in industry under the reforms as any other group of workers, and they were well represented in the 1989 movement in Beijing and elsewhere. Great controversy has surrounded this involvement, however, as the government went to enormous lengths after the movement had been crushed to establish that no regular, permanently-employed workers from such high-profile firms as Shougang (Capital Iron and Steel) or Yanshan Petrochemicals had in fact taken part. The intensity of this effort suggests the political importance which the regime still attached to being able to make a credible claim to have the backing of the core of the urban working class. But despite the official denials and hair-splitting, there is ample evidence of the high-profile involvement in 1989 of workers from well-known large state corporations such as the two named above (Wang Shaoguang 1993: 179; Lu Ping 1990: 16–17); Shougang even had its own WAF, affiliated to the BWAF (Walder and Gong 1993: 11–12).

Some in the BWAF expressed disappointment, however, that more workers from Shougang (which employs 120,000 at its site in western Beijing (Hassard and Sheehan 1997: 74)) did not come out in full support of the movement. Similarly, in Changchun students made contact with workers of the Changchun No. 1 Auto Plant, but no strike resulted in the end despite much debate among workers over whether they should come out in support of the movement, although a go-slow was reported to have occurred within the plant (R Howard 1991: 61–2). In neighbouring Liaoning, another area where large, heavy-industrial state owned enterprises (SOEs) are concentrated, it was not until six days after martial law had been imposed that workers and other citizens began to join the demonstrations (Gunn 1991: 73). Anita Chan has suggested that the official channels for dealing with grievances, the union and the workers' congress, operated more satisfactorily in this sort of large and relatively prosperous state enterprise where they were better resourced, reducing the appeal to workers of the independent option; she nevertheless stresses the significance of the presence in autonomous organizations of any workers from the largest and most prestigious SOEs (Chan 1993: 55–6).

Marginal workers, including those already laid off from state enterprises, temporary workers and the unemployed, also featured prominently in the movement (Chan and Unger 1990: 274), not surprisingly as they were the most directly affected by the new insecurity and lack of status of workers. It has also been observed that the extent and nature of workers' involvement in the movement varied by geographical area in accordance with the benefits or dis-benefits which had accrued to that area under the reforms. This meant that in the booming coastal areas of Fujian and Guangdong the movement as a whole was relatively mild (at least until after 4 June, when reaction to news of the massacre brought workers and citizens out to the barricades in Guangzhou). In Fujian little worker involvement in the movement was reported (Erbaugh and Kraus 1991: 150); when students did try to make contacts in factories, management complaints to campus authorities about this disruption soon put a stop to it, although there were signs of workers' support for protesting students, such as a 10,000 *yuan* donation to the cause collected by one factory's workers (Erbaugh and Kraus 1991: 160). In contrast, the only places which experienced major violent incidents involving workers prior to 4 June were Xi'an and Changsha, both located in interior provinces which had yet to see any great benefit from the economic reforms (Unger 1991b: 3).

On the whole, then, workers from a wider variety of backgrounds than ever before soon came to form a very significant force in the 1989 movement, not least because in their main concerns they genuinely spoke for the vast majority of the urban population. Although they shared in the sincere respect and mourning for Hu Yaobang (Walder and Gong 1993: 21), they quickly moved on from commemorative activities to issues such as official privilege, the mismanagement of economic policy and its effects on workers' livelihoods, and the uselessness of the official unions (Walder and Gong 1993: 5). Their particular concern with inflation should not be seen as evidence of a purely material agenda, since their analysis of the issue was 'deeply political' (Walder and Gong 1993: 17), and in general workers' critique of the government's economic management was inherently political rather than being based on a defence of economic vested interests (although Alan Liu has pointed out that at a time of rapid change, the defence of tradition can be politically radical or even revolutionary rather than conservative, seeing workers in 1989 as a good example of this (A P L Liu 1996: 130)). None of the various demands put forward by workers in the movement was important in itself compared with the key demand that workers must have workplace and political representation and democratic rights to enable them to defend their interests (Walder and Gong 1993: 17). As this study has shown, this lack of effective political remedies when workers' interests were infringed upon had been a feature of workers' previous confrontations with the regime, but in 1989 it was given even greater emphasis.

Whether discussing their own treatment within the enterprise or the management of the national economy, workers returned repeatedly to the lack of accountability of those in power, their dishonesty to the people, and their ability, by virtue of their administrative power, to line their own pockets at a time when many urban households were struggling to make ends meet. The verdict of the BWAF on the government of Deng Xiaoping and Li Peng referred to the Chinese regime as a typical fascist dictatorship, 'this twentieth-century Bastille, this last stronghold of Stalinism' (Walder and Gong 1993: 12–13), a type of language that had hardly been heard since Wei Jingsheng was imprisoned ten years earlier for making similar accusations against Deng.[1] Workers emphasized their sense of powerlessness and their resentment at being lied to and kept in the dark by leaders who did not suffer from the consequences of their own actions as ordinary citizens did (Walder 1989b: 34–5; Mok and Harrison 1990: 108–9):

> You people have made a mess of China, a country rich in human and natural resources. It is too easy to say that China lacks experience in building

socialism, and that you are leading the people across a river, locating each stepping stone as you go. In what direction are you taking us? And what about those who find no stepping stone, and drown? Is the life of the people so worthless that it can be handled like a gambling chip by the bureaucrats?

(Mok and Harrison 1990: 117)

Paralleling their calls for democracy and a proper impartial legal framework for the nation, workers also denounced one-man dictatorship in the workplace, calling for collective formulation and impartial enforcement of enterprise rules (Walder and Gong 1993: 18) rather than the absolute authority of the factory director. As well as being fully aware of the need to form their own independent organizations in the workplace if their interests were to be successfully defended, organizations like the BWAF also insisted on their right to a national political role supervising the CCP (Mok and Harrison 1990: 116). When workers declared that they were not 'prison labourers who happen to live in society, but legal citizens of the republic' (Mok and Harrison 1990: 118), they brought together their concerns about their status in the workplace and beyond it, and in both cases the attacks on their position under the reforms had helped to generate 'a growing desire . . . to be treated as full citizens' (Walder and Gong 1993: 28–9).

A strong sense of working-class identity and workers' proper political status as the leading class in society comes through as strongly in 1989 as it did in the mid-1970s, but despite the display by marching workers of portraits of Mao and other former leaders (Esherick 1990: 224; A Chan 1991b: 141), workers were not seeking to turn back the clock in China. Although they looked back on the Mao era as a time when they had at least rhetorically enjoyed high status (A Chan 1991b: 141), and moreover as a time of relatively incorrupt government still in touch with the original ideas of the revolution, the 'unabashed working-class trade-union mentality' (Walder and Gong 1993: 4) expressed in 1989 was of a piece with the changes in industrial life wrought by the reforms. If workers were to be treated as hired labourers, forced to obey autocratic management by the threat of punishment, then they would assert their rights as a group quite separate and independent from their supposed class vanguard, organizing themselves. Cultural Revolution rebels had talked of the fundamental division in society being that between rulers and ruled, but now it was not just the 'have-nots' of the working class who saw things this way, but the vast majority (Walder and Gong 1993: 8).

The nature of workers' organizations and relations with students

Workers' political radicalism contrasted more sharply with the concerns and direction of the student movement the longer it went on, particularly as the efforts of intellectual think-tank staffers close to Zhao Ziyang to swing the students behind their man began to take effect in the second half of May (Han Minzhu 1990: 246–51). Although some in the student movement had started out with an awareness of the fate of previous movements which leadership factions had used for their own ends and then abandoned, they were increasingly drawn towards the internal power games of the political elite (Walder and Gong 1993: 23). The workers, though, seemed to have learned the lesson of Democracy Wall, as seen in this proclamation of 17 May 1989 from the Beijing Workers' Union:

> We must now be on our guard against political careerists within the Chinese Communist Party who will use the current Democracy Movement to usurp power for their own purposes. Deng Xiaoping used the people's movement of April 5, 1976, to obtain power. Afterward, his evil intentions were exposed.
>
> (Han Minzhu 1990: 234)

Given the focus of the movement on the issue of corruption, especially that of top leaders' children, it is all the more remarkable that the student movement became so well-disposed towards Zhao Ziyang after his tearful encounter with them in the Square in the early hours of 19 May, since at the outbreak of the movement Zhao and his two sons had been the most notorious example of such corruption in most people's minds (Wang Shaoguang 1993: 185). Workers' profound opposition to and distrust of the whole top party leadership inclined them to put Zhao into the same category as the hated Li Peng and Yang Shangkun, the ' "harm-the-people faction" ' (Walder and Gong 1993: 21–2).

As they had done with apparent success in 1986–7, the authorities once again attempted to fan antagonism between workers and students to prevent the two parts of the movement from linking up (Chan and Unger 1990: 278), but the students themselves ensured that cooperation would prove extremely difficult; this failure to cooperate has been identified as a crucial weakness of the student movement (Saich 1990: 32). The Beijing students' attitude towards the workers' movement was made clear by their prolonged refusal to allow the BWAF or any other workers' group to set up a headquarters on Tiananmen Square itself; they only relented on this point at the very end of May, well into the period of martial law and at a time when student numbers in the square were dwindling and they were feeling increasingly vulnerable to forcible suppression. At least two previous attempts by workers to get onto the square had been rebuffed (Walder and Gong 1993: 24). Apart from the symbolic insult of this quarantining of workers away on the far side of Chang'an Avenue, it also put worker-activists at greater risk of being picked off by plain-clothes police, as began to happen by the end of May (Lu Ping 1990: 16).

Student leaders played a key role in preventing the organizing of a general strike for 20 May, and again for 28 May, which workers proposed after the imposition of martial law, insisting on workers' obedience to the priorities of 'their' movement (Walder and Gong 1993: 25). The BWAF and other groups had had great difficulty in organizing within workplaces and had decided to focus their efforts elsewhere, since they could organize huge demonstrations of a scale which made a great impression on the party without the need for this sort of workplace presence (Walder 1989b: 37). Their reliance on purely informal ties with work-units might thus in any case have meant a very limited response to the call for a general strike (Walder and Gong 1993: 3), although it has been strongly rumoured that the ACFTU (which showed its sympathy for the student cause with a 100,000 *yuan* donation, a unique gesture for a government-controlled organization) would have supported the proposed 20 May general strike (Wang Shaoguang 1993: 179). When, as the PLA began to move into Beijing on 3 June, students called in panic for a general strike, it was too late, as workers would not then jump to obey student orders having been thwarted by them so often in the previous few weeks (Walder and Gong 1993: 25).

Workers in the movement increasingly came to recognize some of the elements of elite behaviour which most outraged them being replicated by the student proto-elite. The student leadership's tendency towards power struggles and factionalism, individual glory-seeking, hierarchy, secrecy, privilege, and even corruption, have been widely documented since the end of the movement (A Chan 1991b: 146; Walder and Gong 1993: 25; Forster 1991: 178; Wasserstrom and Liu 1995), and as workers became more aware of what was going on within the student leadership, they increasingly came to define their own organization and movement in opposition to that of the students (Walder and Gong 1993: 26), whom they termed 'capitalists' out of contempt for student squabbling over money and misappropriation of funds. Workers' groups were far more careful about dealing with funds and donations from the public, realizing, as the leading activists of the Guangdong WAF did, that student misuse of money donated by the public was a propaganda gift to the authorities (*China Spring* April 1990: 62).

If it was in many ways the antithesis of the student movement, the workers' movement also defined itself in opposition to the structure of the centralized socialist state, and in this Chinese workers' organizations were strikingly similar to Solidarity in Poland, which also developed as a consciously non-hierarchical institution in opposition to the Leninist state (Laba 1991). Solidarity was a direct inspiration for many workers, with some activists having followed the progress of the Polish organization ever since 1980, according to a member of the Guangdong WAF:

> [T]he Solidarnosc union in Poland inspired us a lot. Although Poland had a socialist system, the workers there set up Solidarnosc in the eighties. After many years of hard work and struggle, they managed to gain legitimacy. We wondered whether we could borrow the experience of Solidarnosc in Poland to form an independent political force outside the Communist Party.
> (Lu Ping 1990: 79–80)

After a resurgence of industrial unrest the previous summer, Solidarity had re-emerged as a major political force in Poland, and, having entered into negotiations with the government in February, had its legal status restored on 17 April 1989 (Lewis 1994: 237–8). Many workers were as aware of developments regarding Solidarity and reform elsewhere in Eastern Europe as were the party's top leaders, who of course saw it as less of an inspiration and more of a warning, and a number of speakers in Tiananmen Square referred approvingly to Solidarity's legalization in the early days of the movement in China (Wilson 1990b: 271–2). At least one of the independent unions formed during the 1989 movement, in Nanchang, actually called itself 'Solidarity' (Chiang 1990: 97).

The BWAF insisted on collective leadership of the workers' movement by activists who were allocated certain responsibilities, but who did not have any official title or any authority whatsoever to order others to do anything; this was as important a principle to them as any aspect of the cause for which they were fighting (Walder and Gong 1993: 25–6). It is not hard to see why feeling was so strong on this point. In the 1960s workers had joked grimly about being at the bottom of the workplace hierarchy and only able to order the machines about; and in the Cultural Revolution, worker rebels had rejected student-rebel leadership, since they were told to do things all their working lives, and would not accept being told how to rebel against that. At the end of the 1980s workers had had ample opportunity in their enterprises to see all-powerful factory directors throwing their weight about in an arbitrary and unaccountable way, and they had not the slightest desire to emulate this leadership style which had been such a major factor in their rebellion in the first place. They reacted very strongly to student attempts to tell them what to do, since to them the importance of not reproducing the existing hierarchical, undemocratic and arbitrary system was obvious: ' "nobody had to be any more powerful than anyone else. Although we workers didn't have any education, we were very clear about that!" ' (Walder and Gong 1993: 26).

The more workers came to see the student wing of the movement as a privileged elite primarily interested in power, the less convinced they were that the students were actually on the same side as them, but this did not prevent them from rushing to block the path of the army as it began to advance toward the Square during 3 June, 'while most of the remaining students huddled more tightly around the monument to await their expected martyrdom' (Walder and Gong 1993: 15). In fact, most if not all of the remaining students were able to leave the Square alive as troops advanced onto it in the early morning of 4 June, whereas members of the BWAF and other workers' organizations bore the brunt of the slaughter at the intersections away from the Square on the PLA's path into the centre of the capital (Lu Ping 1990: 12). Workers had by this stage come to dominate the movement in Beijing, which perhaps gives a certain grim appropriateness to their much higher casualty rates in the final suppression of the movement.

The workers' movement before and after 4 June and the party's response

The party leadership had in previous confrontations demonstrated more concern over organized resistance and opposition from workers than from any other social group, and especially once the example of Poland was before them (Wang Shaoguang 1993: 180), the top leaders became mildly obsessed with the possibility of a similar workers' uprising in China. Early on in the 1989 movement they made it a priority to prevent workers from linking up with students, and in some cities youth league and union activists were mobilized in enterprises to try to prevent young workers in particular from joining the movement (Forster 1991: 177–8). As we have just seen, the authorities in fact need hardly have concerned themselves with the effects of student agitation among workers, as although factory visits were attempted or successfully carried out by students in a number of Chinese cities, student activists themselves were often no keener on a major working-class contribution to the direction of the movement than were the old guard in Zhongnanhai.

But workers did not need any outside agitation to mobilize them in 1989, given the powerful groundswell of politicized discontent which had built up as a result of the urban reforms. By the time of the demonstrations commemorating the May Fourth movement of 1919 and its iconoclastic call for democracy and science, workers had come to outnumber students in the protests (Walder 1989b: 38), and in contrast to the decline in student numbers and commitment once martial law was declared, the workers' movement actually grew, with outrage over martial law acting as a powerful recruiting agent for the WAFs (Walder and Gong 1993: 9). It has been noted elsewhere in the former socialist camp that workers, initially well aware of the harsh repression they are likely to attract if they rebel, gain in confidence in the course of their confrontations with the regime (Pravda 1981), and this was borne out in China in 1989 as the BWAF began to take more of a leading role in the movement as a whole, making a particular stand over the refusal of the authorities to allow them to register as a legal organization (Walder and Gong 1993: 14).

It must always been borne in mind that workers knew what a serious risk they were taking with their very lives in becoming involved in a movement against the top party leadership (they stressed that they did not oppose the party as a whole or socialism). Given their knowledge of their likely fate at the end of the movement, it is all the more remarkable that so many did in fact join the movement, and that activists like Han Dongfang publicly identified themselves by name in it. Aware that they would suffer a much harsher fate than students guilty of exactly the same political offence, they nevertheless decided that to organize, raise their profile and set a precedent for other groups of workers in the future was still worth doing:

'You know, with students it's nothing – they arrest you for a couple of days and let you go. But when we workers get arrested they shoot us. . . . The government is ruthless towards us. And they say the workers are the ruling class. What a load of horseshit! The workers who were arrested [after 4 June] were all beaten half to death. . . . About halfway through, a lot of us thought that we would be defeated anyway, and that the government would suppress us. But we couldn't break up. If we broke up, we would be suppressed, and if we didn't we'd be suppressed. So we felt we might as well do it right, and let others know that there was a group of people like us, an organization like ours'.

(Walder and Gong 1993: 24–5)

One feature of the end of the 1989 movement which has not always received much attention was workers' and citizens' reaction in cities around China to the news, no less shocking for not coming as a total surprise, that the army had opened fire on and killed unarmed citizens in Beijing. Popular outrage as the news spread in the early hours of 4 June overwhelmed many people's reservations about the dangers of active involvement in the movement, giving renewed impetus to the workers' movement in a number of cities. A new branch of the WAF was set up in Hangzhou on 5 June, and the official founding of the Guangdong WAF was announced on 4 June:

Now that the soldiers have opened fire in Beijing, and the people lie bleeding, the nation has reached a critical juncture. A historic burden falls on the shoulders of every worker. We have no other choice than to oppose the violence, support the students, and promote both democracy and knowledge.

The nation is confused and disrupted, flooded with bureaucracy, with a corrupt political and economic system. The future of the nation has become the personal concern of each individual worker. The Guangdong workers cannot stand by, and the Guangdong Workers' Autonomous Union urgently appeals to people from every walk of life to support and participate in the nationwide, patriotic, Democratic Movement.

(Mok and Harrison 1990: 120)

Rumours swept the country in the days after 4 June, and it is difficult to know how much credence to give to the numbers claimed to be on strike, such as the 600,000 rumoured to have come out on strike in Shenyang on 6 June (Gunn 1991: 76). But there are so many reports of strikes and mass absenteeism, of enterprises and whole industrial districts at a standstill, and of a sharp drop in industrial production from May and on into July 1989, that the impression of widespread protest and industrial action by workers cannot have been purely the wishful thinking of those who hoped the movement might still survive in some form even after its symbolic centre in Tiananmen Square had been destroyed. Monitoring service reports from the days after 4 June reveal roads, bridges and railway lines blocked in cities all over China, and although the official press accounts attempted to down-play the involvement of workers, portraying those on the barricades as hooligans and criminal elements, unemployed or migrant workers, there is no concealing the key role played in the post-massacre popular backlash by non-students (*FBIS-CHI-89–107–22* June 1989 *passim*).

In Xi'an strikes were reported at many enterprises, including some of the high-profile large state-owned enterprises, and a foreign observer had the impression that there were many more young workers than students at the barricades around the city (Esherick 1990: 230). The official press in Xi'an blamed a small minority for surrounding enterprises and denying the loyal, law-abiding majority the opportunity to go back to work, but there is no way of knowing from these accounts how much support there really was for the stoppage; as usual, the official version fails to explain how such a 'small minority', if resolutely opposed by 300,000 loyal workers, could bring a major city to a virtual standstill for six days and cause a loss in industrial output of 40 million *yuan* (*FBIS-CHI-89–111* 12 June 1989: 90–1). Strikes, as well as road and rail blockades, were also reported in Hangzhou, with workers there much more willing to become active in the movement after 4 June than they had been before, despite the 'carrot' of payments of up to 300 *yuan* for those who stayed on the job and the 'stick' of commensurately steep financial penalties for those found taking part in street protests (Forster 1991: 183). Given the magnitude of the rewards and penalties applied to keep workers at work after 4 June, it is possible that there was some truth in the heroic tales in the official press of workers walking miles to clock on or spending their own money on taxis when the buses failed to run.

In the northeast there were rumours that the workers of Harbin were on strike, while workers at the Shenyang Aircraft Factory also came out; the story was that one of the workers there had lost a child in the massacre in Beijing (Gunn 1991: 77). In previous bouts of unrest a large SOE with military links, such as the Aircraft Factory, would have been the last place one expected to find rebellion or industrial action, showing how far the discontent and hostility towards the authorities had spread by 1989. The Tiexi industrial area of Shenyang also appeared to be at a standstill, and, in contrast with other areas where older workers seemed more inclined to accept the party-line that turmoil and disruption of public order and production had to be stopped (Chan and Unger 1990: 277), in Liaoning even retired workers remained convinced that the students had been right to continue their protest (Gunn 1991: 77).

Shanghai, though, stands out in the immediate aftermath of 4 June for the lack of militant action by workers there. Workers' groups in the city did put their names to posters calling for a national strike, and Shanghai, like most of urban China, was at a standstill through 5–6 June, with a quiet but very tense gathering composed mostly of workers outside the offices of the municipal government (S Warner 1991: 220–2). But on the whole workers seem to have decided to let go of a lost cause and to make every effort, despite the severe transport disruptions, to get to work if possible and avoid deductions from their pay; many were reported to be angry at being prevented from travelling to work, not only because of the money they stood to lose, but also because of the increasing shortages of essential goods in the city (S Warner 1991: 225, 230–1). This lack of militancy in Shanghai, a stronghold of the workers' movement in China since the 1920s and still the country's premier industrial city, came as a great disappointment to workers elsewhere in the movement, such as Xiao Yaqun of the Guangdong WAF:

[W]hat makes one lose hope is that the workers of Tianjin, Shanghai and Nanjing, with their glorious democratic traditions, didn't mobilize. Shanghai workers on the contrary opposed the student movement, and for the sake of one day's bonus they preferred to rush back to the factories and sign in when they clocked on and off, creating a shameful episode in the history of the Chinese workers' movement.

(*China Spring* April 1990: 62)

As mentioned before, the authorities had started to target workers in the movement even before 4 June, but from that date on they intensified their repression. Theirs was a dual strategy of punishing workers much more harshly than students or intellectuals for their role in the movement, while at the same time denying that any 'real' workers had been involved at all, despite all the evidence to the contrary. All accounts of the crackdown agree that workers were much more likely than students to be arrested at the end of the movement, to receive long prison sentences or to be executed, and to be maltreated while in custody (Lu Ping 1990: 18–19; Wilson 1990b: 274–6; Walder and Gong 1993: 24). Workers were reported to make up the majority of those arrested in Shanghai (S Warner 1991: 229), Shenyang (Gunn 1991: 78) and Chongqing, with detained workers in the latter city displayed on television 'battered and humiliated' as a warning to others (Chan and Unger 1990: 276). Leading BWAF activist Han Dongfang preferred to give himself up to the police rather than wait for the same treatment to be meted out to him as the manhunt progressed.

As workers' organizations around the country were banned one after another in the two weeks following 4 June, the official union federations often took a leading role in denouncing these 'fake' organizations of criminal elements and agitators who had 'usurped the name of the workers' (*Guangzhou Daily* 11 June 1989) to cover up counter-revolutionary or criminal activities. The unions needed to prove their own loyalty in the face of the expected purge of those leaders who had backed the student movement, or even the workers' movement, prior to 4 June, and hence many provincial and municipal union federations called on the government to shut down the illegal and disruptive WAFs (which, of course, were only illegal because the authorities had refused to allow them to register as legal; the official unions had not supported independent groups' attempts to gain legal status (Walder and Gong 1993: 7)).

Those enterprises known to have supplied recruits to workers' organizations and whose banners had been seen prominently displayed on demonstrations (Walder and Gong 1993: 7) also had to take the lead in the condemnation to avoid the risk of guilt by association, and in seven articles condemning the WAFs in the *Workers' Daily* on 28 June, institutions such as the Shougang Corporation, the Beijing Rail and Public Transport Unions, and the People's Engine Manufacturing Company Union, as well as the municipal FTU itself, went to great lengths to distance themselves from the movement (Lu Ping 1990: 16), claiming that those workers who had carried 'their' banners in the movement were not permanently employed, a common excuse being that they were either young trainees or workers who had already been laid off before April 1989. Some enterprises took steps to ban any employees from carrying the work-unit banner in public without prior approval of the workers' congress (*Guangzhou Daily* 23 June 1989), which seems to indicate that at least some of those who had previously marched under work-unit banners were in fact regular employees who were perfectly entitled to do so.

Arrested workers' alleged previous criminal records were emphasized (Warner 1991: 229; Gunn 1991: 78), as were stories of violence and extortion of money from the public, with the widespread prejudice against migrant workers from the countryside fanned in an attempt to tar all non-students in the movement with the same brush as 'lawless elements'. An exiled member of the Guangdong WAF noted that when the local wanted list was compiled after 4 June, many of the white-collar worker-activists and others who had had responsibility for handling money at work were listed not as counter-revolutionaries but as wanted for fraud or embezzlement, something calculated to reduce their chances of being granted political asylum if they managed to escape abroad (*China Spring* 1990: 62). The party-controlled press also carried stories of how workers' pickets had helped to restore order in the cities after 4 June, giving the impression of solid proletarian loyalty to the party when in fact many of those in the so-called workers' pickets were enterprise party and management cadres selected for their political reliability (S Warner 1991: 228). The overall effect, though, was to create the impression that real workers had remained aloof from the protests or had actively opposed them, defending the party and the national interest, while a minority of hooligans and criminals had run riot under the name of the workers in so-called 'independent unions'.

Thus the party's version of the 1989 workers' movement was sharply at odds with the reality, giving no hint that workers' challenge to the party had often been couched in explicitly socialist and class terms reminiscent of earlier confrontations, as in the anonymous comment of a Beijing worker that 'the words "owned by the people" actually mean "owned by a small group of the bourgeoisie"' (Mok and Harrison 1990: 109). It is very noticeable that although some of the ideological heat had gone out of the language of the 1989 protests (no references to 'red capitalists', for example), nevertheless, workers at least were still identifying their leaders as an exploitative minority which lived off others' labour; and the document quoted above did use the term 'bourgeoisie' to refer to privileged officials. This analysis of the power relations between workers and the party can be traced back through Democracy Wall, April Fifth, the Li Yizhe poster, and the Cultural Revolution, all the way back to the Hundred Flowers period when it was first suggested that officials might constitute 'a privileged class standing above the people' (Fu Rong 1957: 20). Workers in 1989 asserted their right, even their duty, as the most advanced class in society, to participate in politics. Recalling the words of the Communist Manifesto, the BWAF gave this statement of its purpose:

The working class is the most advanced class and we, in the Democratic Movement, should be prepared to demonstrate its great power. The People's Republic of China is supposedly led by the working class, and we have every right to drive out the dictators. . . . To bring down dictatorship and totalitarianism and promote democracy in China is our undeniable responsibility. In the Democracy Movement, 'we have nothing to lose but our chains, and a world to win'.

(Mok and Harrison 1990: 115)

This was hardly the call to arms of a group of criminals bent on disruption and petty personal gain.

Workers under continuing reform since 1989

It has been noted that immediately after the 1989 Democracy Movement, the party 'tried to win the workers' loyalty by apparently re-establishing their position as the "premier" class in China' (Lam 1995: 273). A change in slogans was certainly noticeable, with managerialist rhetoric temporarily replaced by talk of the importance of democratic management and social justice under the reforms (A Chan 1993: 57). The official unions also, despite their unavoidable role in the condemnation of the independent unions of 1989, continued to press workers' grievances about unfair distribution, one-man management under the FDRS, and why workers' theoretical status as masters was so far from being realized (Chan 1993: 56), showing that they believed workers' protests to have been justified in part. While in public the official unions were brought firmly back under party control (*People's Daily* 1 February 1990), during 1990 they complained in internal communications that they were being treated as a work department of the party committee in enterprises, and that they were thus unable to do much more than make sympathetic noises when workers brought them their problems. Consequently, they reported, the workers whose interests they were unable to protect tended to reject the party's slogan of 'relying on the working class' as mere words (*Union Bulletin* 15 September 1990: 8–9).

So it seems that in spite of efforts to win them over, workers remained distinctly unimpressed with rhetoric about their leading position as long as they had no effective union representation and no say in management. Workers' complaints about enterprise organization and management conduct in the 1990s often bore a striking resemblance to those voiced back in the 1950s. After 1989 there were still reports of workers being excluded from participation in management because managers thought they were incapable of effective participation. Where this happened, the official unions responded in terms which could have been lifted straight out of a summer 1950 report, restating the argument that workers would only learn to participate effectively in management if they were actually allowed to participate, and that although they might not know about all sections of the enterprise and its activities, they did have expertise in specific areas and practical knowledge, and collectively they were extremely important to the successful functioning of the enterprise.

Thus in the reform period the case for democratic management was having to be made all over again, as managers grown accustomed to asserting their right to manage proved even less receptive to it than their 1950s counterparts (*Workers' Daily* 25 July, 8 and 22 August 1989; *Union Bulletin* 15 January, 1 February and 15 April 1991). In the 1950s when Chinese enterprises were moving away from capitalist management forms and towards socialism, the ideological imperative of respect for workers' status was strong, but as enterprises under the reforms moved in the opposite direction, managers no longer even had to pay lip-service to democratic ideals in the enterprise if these were seen as hampering economic efficiency. References abounded not only to one-man management in the 1990s and to the difficulties workers faced in exercising their democratic rights under the FDRS, but also to the prevalence of the 'hired hand' and 'work according to pay' mentality among workers (Wang Zhuo and Wen Wuhan 1992: 265–6), and to widespread worker discontent over unfair distribution, with particular reference to undemocratic or corrupt wage and bonus decisions being taken by managers without consulting the workers' congress, in contravention of the Enterprise Law (*Workers' Daily* 25 July and 8 August 1989; *Union Bulletin* 15 September 1990: 8–9, 15 January 1991: 30, 1 February 1991: 18–19, and 15 April 1991 7–8).

Not only had the complaints of the 1950s, 1960s, 1970s and 1980s not gone away, but workers even felt that the reforms had weakened their position further, despite the fact that their status as masters of the enterprise and provisions for democratic management were now laid down in the Enterprise Law and other legislation. The reality, however, well-established on the shopfloor before the Enterprise Law was passed, was of a further reduction in workers' influence and a great increase in the authority of management. Increased enterprise autonomy meant a weakening of direct state control over enterprise management, with contract management a case in point. As the second round of contracts was being negotiated in 1990, concerns were expressed that workers saw the contract management as the 'owner' of the enterprise (Wang Zhuo and Wen Wuhan 1992: 265), and felt that this reform left no room for democratic management. The official unions pushed for regular democratic evaluation of managers by workers and for the participation of workers' congress representatives in awarding contracts and evaluating management (*Union Bulletin* 1 November 1990: 22–5, 1 April 1991: 9). But the problems posed by the changing nature of state enterprise management tended to reinforce workers' feeling that their supposed democratic rights in the enterprise were a fiction.

Increasingly in the 1990s workers in China have found themselves in a position in which the language of exploitation is much more relevant to them than it was fifteen or twenty years before (A Chan 1993), and this does not only apply to the growing numbers employed in private or foreign-invested enterprises, notorious though some of these operations are for their harsh, almost militarized conditions of work (A Chan 1996b). An emphasis on control and punitive regulation and the extraction of maximum production from the workforce is also observable in many state enterprises, where the work system is characterized by 'quota increases and speed-ups; longer working hours; the adaptation of "socialist labour emulation" to production for profit; new draconian controls over labour attendance; and the use of monetary sanctions and penalties to control labour' (Zhao and Nichols 1996: 1). The idea of linking workers' pay more directly with performance, a keystone of the economic reforms, has become lost in a welter of complicated regulations in some plants which leave workers unable to work out from one month to the next how much they should be paid (Zhao and Nichols 1996: 15). One thinks of Miklos Haraszti wrestling with the hundreds of pages of rules governing piece-work calculations in pre-1989 Eastern Europe (Haraszti 1978), and the same powerful sense of alienation and betrayal among workers comes through in 1990s China.

Unrest among Chinese workers, including strikes and attempts to organize independent unions, has continued since 1989, and among state workers levels of unrest have risen sharply towards the end of the 1990s. The plans outlined at the Fifteenth Party Congress in September 1997 to allow most SOEs to be sold off, merge, or go bankrupt, will only increase unrest, and even those large or strategically significant state corporations which are not to be forced to the market in the foreseeable future are planning large-scale lay-offs of up to 50 per cent of their workers by the year 2000 (Hassard and Sheehan 1997: 92). Workers seem more and more willing to take to the streets in defence of their interests as they are told that they will have to bear the brunt of the short-term pain which must accompany vital restructuring of China's industrial economy, but see no sign of managers or party cadres being thrown out of work. While economic grievances, such as late wages or unilaterally-imposed changes to welfare entitlements or pensions, are often the cause of unrest, a politicized suspicion of corruption not infrequently accompanies protests on these issues (Sheehan 1996: 555), as well as a strong sense that such measures are a violation of social justice.

The political nature of workers' unrest even after 4 June 1989 was openly admitted in internal union documents, which stated that the international political upheavals in the socialist camp were the major cause of strikes, stoppages and petitions among Chinese workers through 1989 and 1990, only in 1991 giving way to economic issues at the enterprise level as the main 'hot-spot' on which unrest was focused. It was admitted that the suppression of the Democracy Movement and the subsequent East European revolutions had had great repercussions among China's workers and had shaken the faith of some of them in the socialist system (*Union Bulletin* 15 April 1991: 28). In 1991 the Ministry of State Security was said to be investigating fourteen underground workers' organizations in Beijing alone, organizations each with a membership of between twenty and 300 workers; two of these organizations modelled themselves explicitly on Solidarity, and 'vowed to form an alternative, workers-based party that championed "real democracy" '. These groups were also putting out unofficial publications (Lam 1995: 273–4). Other reports cite independent union activity in Luoyang and Zhuzhou in 1990 (*South China Morning Post* 9 March 1990). One former BWAF member stated in 1993 that workers involved in the protests had continued to meet secretly after the crackdown, and that underground activities were 'well-organized' (*South China Morning Post* 25 February 1993). Autonomous organization thus seems to be continuing on some scale and is likely to be a common feature of future bouts of workers' unrest in China.

In addition to the above reports of independent organization, in March 1994 a 'League for the Protection of Working People in China' (*Laomeng*) was established. Several of the organizers, one a founder member of the BWAF, were arrested in March 1994 in connection with their efforts to organize a petition to the National People's Congress demanding that the right to strike be restored to the Chinese constitution and that workers and peasants be allowed to form independent unions (Lam 1995: 277; Human Rights Watch – Asia 1994: 1–2). Making the case for including the right to strike in the Chinese constitution, and referring specifically to the state and collective sector as well as to other forms of ownership, the league put forward the following argument:

> Confronted with capitalist owners and their managers, workers and employees can only protect their own interests by invoking the specific rights of citizens bestowed upon them by law. Absolute power corrupts absolutely. Unrestrained wealth will also alienate into a source of social injustice. And the citizens' rights – the right to strike included – constitute a basic factor restraining the unjust use of wealth. Once the working people lose these rights, their fate is dominated by the capitalist owners and their managers. . . . Under these circumstances, violations of the rights and interests of the working people will become unavoidable, and conditions will worsen. Society will be tragically split into violent non-legal conflicts. In order to maintain stable development of society, we therefore put forward the following proposal: Adopt a constitutional amendment to amend Article 35 of the Constitution as follows: 'Citizens of the People's Republic of China enjoy freedom of speech, of the press, of assembly, of association, of procession, of demonstration, and of strike'.
>
> (Human Rights Watch – Asia 1994: 7)

Anita Chan has cast some doubt on the league's credentials as a real organization for workers, pointing out that the conditions for membership imposed by the board (most of whom are not workers but professionals) included the achievement of ' "a certain level of theoretical grounding" ', and concluding that 'Chinese intellectuals still condescendingly resist making common cause with the masses even when they are prepared to go to jail in defence of their rights' (A Chan 1996a: 181). Notwithstanding reservations about the nature of this particular organization, the overall point – that under 'market socialism' workers need independent organizations to defend their interests just as much as labour does in a fully capitalist economy – is one which increasing numbers of Chinese workers are taking up. If the idea of the workers as masters provokes mirth among the new breed of SOE manager in the late 1990s, workers themselves retain few illusions about their actual status, and hence for them a return to the weapons of the strike and the sit-in, as well as go-slows and deliberate under-performance on the job (C K Lee 1998), seems an obvious response.

To date what has developed in China in the 1990s is a dual pattern of labour movement militancy, with migrant workers in the foreign-invested enterprises and sweat-shops of southeastern China yet to join forces with increasingly pressurized and insecure state-sector workers (A Chan 1995). The divisions between different sections of the working class, visible in the late 1980s as one group suspected another of benefitting more and unfairly from the reforms, were temporarily submerged during the 1989 movement in the overriding hostility towards the corrupt and incompetent top leadership, but are evident again now, particularly as laid-off and long-term unemployed former state workers lower their sights and begin to compete directly with migrant labour from the countryside for scarce urban jobs. But both groups' restiveness is likely to cause continuing difficulties for the authorities, with a particularly serious challenge posed by the growing willingness of state workers affected by the latest phase of the transition away from socialism to mount a collective defence of their rights and interests, on the streets if necessary.

8 Conclusion

Despite a number of recent studies offering evidence to the contrary, the prevailing image of Chinese workers remains that of a relatively quiescent and politically passive group. In most accounts it is still Chinese students and intellectuals who receive the most attention in movements such as the Hundred Flowers, the Cultural Revolution, and Democracy Wall. Yet as Elizabeth Perry has noted, 'alongside each of these famed outbursts of protest by intellectuals have occurred little-known, but highly significant, labour movements' (Perry 1994: 4). The aim of this book has been to make these periodic labour protests better known, and to highlight the political nature and content of these outbreaks which, if they are acknowledged at all, are usually portrayed as being opportunistic attempts to win material benefits on the back of more idealistic political agitation by the intelligentsia.

In fact, not only have workers played an important part in all of the significant anti-party movements in China from the 1950s to 1989, but the government's reaction to workers' activities seems to indicate that it has been the labour aspect of these movements which has posed the most significant threat to the regime (Perry and Li 1997: 194). Various explanations have been offered for the consistently harsher treatment meted out to worker activists and participants in successive movements. For example, with reference to the 1989 movement, workers' lack of international contacts is often argued to have placed them at a disadvantage compared to students and intellectuals whose names were known abroad and whose arrest, imprisonment or execution would have brought strong reaction from international human rights groups and foreign governments (Wilson 1990b). But as well as repressing workers more severely because it can, the regime does genuinely seem more concerned about workers' oppositional activities than those of other social groups, and this was reflected in its attitude towards Chinese workers' protests long before Solidarity came on the scene to give a concrete example of how a grassroots workers' movement could undermine a communist ruling party. Solidarity certainly heightened CCP fears of a workers' uprising, but 'the Chinese leadership was hardly being irrational in harbouring such fears' (Perry and Li 1997: 194) even before.

Andrew Walder's model of how the regime in China controls workers, a model of worker dependency based on an enterprise network of patron–client ties ensuring quiescence and an inability to organize collective resistance in most circumstances (Walder 1986), even if it only ever applied to a minority of workers in the larger state enterprises, nevertheless has to be revised in the light of the findings of this and other studies of workers' protests in China. His argument that the Chinese authorities' networks of control precluded the necessity of the use of coercion and terror is undermined by the actual frequency with which the party-state has resorted to such methods, and by the disproportionate application of these methods to restive workers in comparison with other groups involved in protests; Deborah Davis has pointed out that 'the post-1949 urban polity has been characterized by high levels of coercion and terror' (Davis 1988: 496), and much of this has been directed at workers. Walder himself in a recent publication noted that 'with the exception only of Poland, China's working class has mobilized for collective protest more often than any other Communist regime's' (Walder 1996: 168), a statement which goes far beyond the picture he painted in *Communist Neotraditionalism* which admitted the possibility of such action by Chinese workers only in abnormal, rare circumstances.

One such rare circumstance identified by Walder was the 1989 Democracy Movement, when the specific impact of certain reform measures in the late 1980s had created a broad groundswell of urban hostility to the regime, and when 'the division of the leadership and the temporary paralysis of its formidable apparatus of repression' (Walder 1991: 492) meant that the normal means by which such unrest was usually suppressed were unavailable. This analysis admits the importance of police measures in maintaining control over workers, but in my view it still exaggerates the extent to which the 1989 movement was an unprecedented instance of worker mobilization. It has been argued that workers' organizations in the Cultural Revolution, extensive and powerful though they were, do not represent a true precedent for 1989 because workers then were mobilized through the factional activities of local and national power holders rather than spontaneously organizing and acting on their own. But this neglects the extent to which workers became adept at taking advantage of the political space afforded them by factional campaigns to pursue their own independent agendas, as was seen in Chapters 4 and 5 of this study.

One completely new factor affecting the spread and the impact of autonomous workers' groups in 1989 was the fact that the domestic and international press were able to report on events in China more openly and in more detail than ever before, thanks to the 'Open Door' policy of the reform era. Workers elsewhere in China could take inspiration from the BWAF by reading about it and seeing pictures of its banners in their local paper, as well as through personal contacts with activists, whereas back in the 1970s they had had to resort to methods like painting slogans on the sides of trains in tar to tell the next city or province about their protests. The speed with which groups such as the WAFS emerged, their scale in some cities, notably Beijing, and their nationwide spread, are all striking features of the 1989 movement, but given the short lifespan of the movement, the constant threat of suppression and the pressures of martial law, it developed in a very uneven and uncoordinated way nationally and made little inroads in terms of organizing within workplaces. Given more time and space it would undoubtedly have improved its position in these respects, but as things were, it does not to my mind look as if 1989 represented a 'new species of political protest' (Walder and Gong 1993: 3–4) among workers as compared with, say, the early 1980s, when politicized labour unrest and the formation of independent unions also took place in a number of Chinese cities, as discussed in Chapter 6.

In 1989 it was certainly true that the specific impact of the urban reforms, with their undermining of what workers perceived to be the most, or even the only, valuable achievements of Chinese socialism, helped to generate near-universal sympathy and support for the Democracy Movement among workers and citizens, hence the appearance of independent workers' groups in so many parts of urban China within a very short space of time (not forgetting, though, that some of these groups only came into being as part of the popular reaction of outrage to the 4 June massacre itself). However, groups such as the WAFs and worker-activists in general were essentially making many of the same points as their predecessors had in movements going right back to the 1950s. Some observers have recognized the extent to which the 1989 Democracy Movement was concerned with the same issues as not only its immediate predecessor, the Democracy Wall movement, but also the Cultural Revolution; Jack Gray (Gray 1994: 1157) and Jonathan Unger (Unger 1991a: 3) have both made this point. But a concentration on workers' activities helps to bring this connection into sharper focus. The effects of the marketizing reforms had made obvious the fundamental conflict between workers' interests and those of the state, but that conflict had always existed, and in the absence of any effective channels for representation or participation in the workplace or in society, workers had always responded at times of particular pressure with self-organization in order to make their voices heard.

In the 1950s most of these organizing efforts were limited, being confined to a single enterprise, but once the unusual freedom of organization of the early Cultural Revolution had allowed much larger, non-party workers' organizations to emerge, there was a precedent for inter-factory, cross-regional and cross-industrial workers' organizations. After the Cultural Revolution, partly because of this organizational precedent and the political experience and confidence gained during the movement by worker-participants, and also because of the lasting damage which the movement had caused to the party-state's authority and prestige, groups of discontented workers showed far more readiness to organize autonomously in order to press their grievances, and moreover were themselves increasingly aware of the political significance of this trend, with some independent groups in China specifically modelling themselves on Solidarity as a workers' political party as well as a union.

The divisions within the Chinese working class have been highlighted in studies of the Hundred Flowers and the Cultural Revolution, and Elizabeth Perry's work in particular has made a strong case for the importance of these divisions in generating unrest among Chinese workers (Perry 1994; 1995). Wang

Shaoguang has also drawn attention to the internal divisions among both workers and cadres which he considers helped obscure the fundamental political cleavage between the two groups until the reform era (Wang Shaoguang 1993: 181). But, as was observed in Chapter 2, although workers' perceptions of the unfairness of the party-state's differential treatment of segments of the working class fuelled protests and rebellion, their anger was generally directed at the architects and enforcers of this unfairness rather than at its beneficiaries. One striking commonality of all the instances of protest covered in this study is the palpable sense of 'them and us' hostility between workers and cadres which seems to have been the dominant feature of strained workplace and social relations. The key division in Chinese society, according to the workers involved in one protest movement after another, has been that between 'rulers and ruled', and this fundamental division has been far more significant politically than the divisions between workers because of the specific challenge which it poses to the regime when voiced by workers. Workers in every decade from the 1950s returned to this basic dichotomy between those with power and those without, tracing to this their other myriad grievances about status, conditions, pay, representation, and participation, and thus turning virtually every major dispute with the authorities into a political confrontation.

After all its confrontations with workers, the CCP has attempted to replace the reality of workers' involvement in challenges to its political authority and legitimacy with its own version of history, a version in which workers have been the reliable defenders of the party and the national interest against the selfish or misguided attacks of students and intellectuals. With regard to the earlier confrontations, the party has had some success in getting its version of events accepted within China, but the much more open domestic reporting of the 1989 protests might have made this more difficult to achieve with regard to 1989. Certainly many observers outside China have recognized the significance of workers' activities in 1989 and also the essentially political nature of the workers' Democracy Movement, in contrast to the views which still often prevail of workers' activities in the earlier movements as being of minor importance and economically motivated. Perhaps this more accurate perception of 1989 will help to change views on the earlier confrontations as well, with the image of Chinese workers as the ever-reliable defenders of the regime replaced by that of a group whose activist vanguard was as prepared as any student or intellectual to face the regime's bullets in defence of its ideals.

If the previous pattern of workers' confrontations with the CCP has mostly been that these outbreaks accompany or are part of a more general anti-party protest movement, often led by students or intellectuals, does this mean that we will have to wait for the next such movement to see workers becoming active again? In my view, it is unlikely that this pattern will be repeated in the near future, not least because there seems little chance of a student-initiated movement like that of 1989 emerging in the present climate. The party's tactics against known activists during the 1990s have generally been very effective, particularly the use of voluntary exile from China. Many activists have been persuaded to accept exile, given that those who choose to remain in China face the unattractive options of long periods in prison, or constant harassment of themselves and their families and mandatory unemployment outside prison. Exiles from the labour movement in 1989 testify to the effectiveness of this sanction, recognizing their inability to contribute much to the workers' struggles and self-organization which have continued through the 1990s; such help is often rejected by those remaining inside China (*Far Eastern Economic Review* 16 June 1994: 36), whether for reasons of safety (because of the risk of being charged with treasonous activities if foreign countries are involved), or because of a perception that exiles have taken an easy way out and no longer have enough understanding of conditions inside China to be able to offer worthwhile assistance. Many figures well known from 1989 or from Democracy Wall are now exiled from China and restricted to reporting on activity there for the outside world; so many are either abroad or in prison that one of the few who remained at large grimly joked that there were not enough people left to get up a decent petition to protest when Wang Dan was given another long prison sentence in 1995.

But this does not mean that workers will remain inactive until such time as the student/intellectual opposition to the CCP recovers its strength. Many of them cannot afford to wait for such an opportunity; at the end of the 1990s, there are many pressing reasons for workers to look to self-organization outside party auspices to defend their interests in an increasingly hostile economic and social environment. As the numbers laid off from the state sector increase, particularly in areas like the northeastern 'rustbelt' or the old 'Third Front' industrial areas in Sichuan, and the workers affected find little prospect of re-employment or of adequate social welfare to tide them through the most difficult phase of industrial restructuring, politicized protests are being fuelled by the strong perception that many workers' plight is the direct result of government policy, and moreover is not being shared by members of the over-staffed government and industrial bureaucracies. At the time of writing, a large-scale programme had just been announced at the National People's Congress of March 1998 which would streamline the whole party-state bureaucracy and do away with many of the industrial ministries altogether. But it remains to be seen how much effect this will have in the short term, and workers have long been pointing out the unfairness of the continued cast-iron job security available to the very cadres who lecture them on the need for flexibility and the 'no pain–no gain' theory of economic restructuring. This standing incitement to protest thus seems likely to continue to exist for some time to come.

Similarly, obvious and widespread official corruption remains as a constant provocation to disgruntled workers facing economic hardship, and as with rising unemployment, the present policy of selling off, merging, or allowing to go bankrupt small and medium-sized SOEs is likely to worsen the situation. Corruption and the illegitimate role of personal connections can often be seen, and are now nearly universally suspected, in decisions to close enterprises down or to sell them to particular local buyers. Workers again are making the comparison between the rewards available for honest hard work and those to be gained from the right *guanxi*, and feel that their bosses are trying to make fools of them in pretending to consult, at the last minute, over the closure or merger of a plant whose fate has already been settled between those in the know.

In China's post-socialist economy, workers in both the state and private sectors increasingly feel the need for independent organizations through which they can defend their collective interests, and given the party's own abandonment of the socialist economy, which in theory provided better protection for workers' interests than any capitalist-style adversarial union could, it is more and more difficult for the CCP to come up with compelling reasons why this cannot be permitted. But the existence of any autonomous organization in the PRC would open up the first crack in the CCP's monopoly of political power, and is as unacceptable to the leadership now as it was in the spring of 1989. Thus the aspiration for autonomous self-organization shared by groups of workers all over China is still likely to clash with what the CCP is prepared to concede. But such are the pressures on large numbers of workers in China at present, where even those still in work in the state sector can go unpaid for months at a time, that confrontation is likely to become increasingly sharp and frequent, and a common feature of many of these confrontations will undoubtedly be the organization of autonomous workers' groups with both industrial and political agendas, as occurred in 1989.

Notes

1 Chinese labour under 'New Democracy' 1949–55

1 This document is the source of all subsequent information on the structure and functions of the FMC and WRC unless otherwise stated.

2 Contradictions among the people, 1956–7

1 Elizabeth Perry cites one case of conflict between permanent and (sacked) temporary workers at the same enterprise (Perry 1994: 13), but generally concurs that discontented workers directed their protests at those in authority who were ultimately responsible for the situation.

2 More detailed accounts of the Guangzhou dock strike and additional newspaper references can be found in Gipouloux (1986: 196–8), and Sheehan (1995: 190–4).

3 This is the road at the northwestern edge of Tiananmen Square which runs past the Forbidden City and the Zhongnanhai compound where most of the CCP's top leaders live and work. Mao's prediction came true more than thirty years later, as it was at this corner of the square, on the northern side of the road, that the Beijing Workers' Autonomous Federation first had its headquarters during the 1989 protests. The party, just as he said, still had the army on its side, and that was enough to keep it in power.

3 'Hard work and plain living', 1958–65

1 Commonly referred to as the Seventy Articles, the document's official title is 'Regulation of tasks in state-owned industrial enterprises (Draft)', issued by the CCP Central Committee, 15 September 1961.

2 The Constitution of the Anshan Iron and Steel Corporation in Liaoning, northeast China. Mao personally endorsed the Anshan Municipal Party Committee Secretary's 'Report concerning technical reform and the technical revolutionary movement on the industrial front' in March 1960.

3 This is the phrase (*guan, ka, ya*) commonly used by supporters of the Gang of Four in their polemics against Deng Xiaoping's policies for industry, particularly in 1975–6.

4 This hardy perennial among workers' complaints has reappeared among workers in foreign-owned enterprises in Shenzhen: see the translation attached to Anita Chan's 'PRC workers under "capitalism with Chinese characteristics"', *China Information* 5, 4 (Spring 1991). Taylorism, universally reviled in China up to 1976, made a comeback in Shenzhen as early as 1984.

5 Strictly speaking, there is a distinction between urban contract or temporary labour and contract or seasonal labour in industry in rural localities or in agriculture-related industry, as is pointed out in Andors (1977a: 298, n. 68). This study is mainly

concerned with the use of temporary and contract labour in urban industry; this pre-dates the use of the term 'worker-peasant system', but seems to have become a major cause of conflict only from 1964, when the 'worker-peasant system' began to be promoted. There is clearly a connection between the two forms of employment, hence the use of the terms 'worker-peasant' system and contract labour system inter-changeably by many writers. For an account of the development of contract labour in China, particularly the controversial developments from 1964, see the translations from unofficial Cultural Revolution publications in *Survey of China Mainland Magazines* 616: 21–30.

6 The other is the difference between mental and manual labour; the 'two participa-tions' were intended to tackle this.

7 Unless otherwise stated, the details of this account of changes to the contract and temporary labour system are drawn from a series of articles by two mass organiza-tions at the Ministry of Labour, the Red Rebel Team and the Revolutionary Rebel Team of Workers and Staff, published in the Guangzhou Red Guard publication *Red 'Criticizing Liu Shaoqi' Combat Corps of Canton* [Guangzhou], and translated in *Survey of China Mainland Magazines* 616: 21–5.

4 'To rebel is justified': workers in the Cultural Revolution, 1966–9

1 At the time, the Cultural Revolution was generally understood by both those in power and ordinary Chinese people to have come to an end with the Ninth Party Congress of April 1969, and this is the period covered in Chapter 4. It was only after Mao referred to the Cultural Revolution as ongoing in a 1974 document that officials began to refer to the movement again as current. The post-Mao Chinese leadership has adopted the ten-year (1966–76) periodization of the Cultural Revolution, as have most current researchers on China, but despite some important elements of conti-nuity between 1966–9 and 1969–76, the two periods are so different in many ways as to require, in my view, some sort of distinction of terminology. I have sought in this study to distinguish between the Cultural Revolution proper, the mass movement of 1966–9, and the following seven years of political dominance by the Gang of Four and their followers, for reasons which will become apparent. Since there is no gener-ally accepted term for the latter period, I refer to it simply by its dates. Anita Chan has developed a detailed exposition of the problems of Cultural Revolution peri-odization and the competing paradigms of social cleavage during the movement (Chan 1992: 69–70, 73–4).

2 The Cultural Revolution was an exceptionally complex event and it is even more than usually dangerous to generalize across the whole of urban China when making statements about it. So as not to tire the reader with constant digressions, however, I simply record here that there are likely to be exceptions in particular cities to any of the general assertions about workers in the Cultural Revolution made in this chapter; only the most important will be noted in the text. Shanghai is a special case throughout the Cultural Revolution (Perry and Li 1997), since there a coalition of rebel-faction groups, albeit under the overall leadership of the Gang of Four's Zhang Chunqiao, took power and retained it to a significant extent right up until 1976. The special circumstances of Shanghai's January 1967 'power-seizure' (actually a reimpo-sition of order under Zhang) meant that it escaped the worst of the violence (between conservative and rebel factions and between the latter and the army) which wracked most Chinese cities in 1967–8.

3 See for example reports of workers' rallies in Guangzhou from the city's radio station, translated in *News from Provincial Radio Stations* (*NPRS*) 158 (19 May 1966: 20–1 and 26–7), and 159 (26 May 1966: 23–4).

4 I have not found much clear evidence to support this, but it seems that women workers were more likely to lose their permanent status and benefits in enterprises than men, particularly given the fairly generous maternity benefits for which women union members were eligible, an expense which managers would be keen to avoid. Perry and Li (1997: 101) indicate that women may have been over-represented among the disadvantaged in the industrial workforce, and certainly women have been among the first to be laid off by enterprises anxious to save on welfare expenses during the recent economic reforms in China.

5 These details are drawn from Guangzhou city radio reports on 10 September 1966, translated in *NPRS* 174 (15 September 1966: 49); 14 September 1966, translated in *NPRS* 175 (22 September 1966: 28); and 15 November 1966, translated in *NPRS* 184 (24 November 1966: 23).

6 Even in a city such as Changsha where the majority of workers joined the rebel faction, those at the larger enterprises tended to be less militant (Unger 1991a: 20). For the proportion of rebel and conservative workers in some of Guangzhou's main enterprises, see Table 5 in Hong Yung Lee 1978: 135; rebel workers in these enterprises constituted between 21 and 46 per cent of the rank-and-file workforce. In Shanghai an initial conservative majority evaporated by the end of December as the rebels were seen to have Mao's seal of approval (Perry and Li 1997: 85), while in Wuhan the conservatives remained strong until the crisis of July 1967, with their 'Million Heroes' title not that much of an exaggeration of their numbers (Wang Shaoguang 1995: 135).

7 See the account in *China News Analysis* 711 (7 July 1968: 3–4), for the uses to which this slogan was put by workers resisting the PLA's reimposition of discipline in enterprises.

8 'Linking up', i.e. travelling to other units all over the country, to exchange revolutionary experiences.

9 By the time the Cultural Revolution began, there were estimated to be 10 million contract workers in China, and in some enterprises they constituted 95 per cent of the workforce (Hong Yung Lee 1978: 130). Shanghai, like Guangzhou, had large numbers of these workers as it was a regional and national centre for light industry and transportation, sectors where this form of employment was commonly used.

10 Most workers' wages had remained at roughly the same level since the GLF under the CCP's policy of wage stabilization (Wylie 1981: 99); and apprentices were forced to train for three years on very low pay when most could master their jobs comfortably in six months, making them one of the most aggrieved and active groups in Guangzhou and elsewhere (Solomon 1968: 21; Perry 1994: 13).

5 'Long live the people': unrest and dissent, 1969–76

1 The protests of late March and early April 1976, including the well-known Tiananmen Incident in Beijing, are referred to in China as the April Fifth Movement. The term has the merit of not implying any geographical limitation of the movement to the capital alone. On the movement in other cities, see Philip Williams, 'Some provincial precursors of popular dissent movements in Beijing', *China Information* 6, 1 (Summer 1991: 1–9); Keith Forster, 'The 1976 Ch'ing-ming Incident in Hangchow', *Issues and Studies* 22, 4 (April 1986: 13–33); Sebastian Heilmann, *Nanking 1976: Spontane Massenbewegung im Gefolge der Kulturrevolution*, and 'The social context of mobilization in China: Factions, work units, and activists during the April Fifth Movement', *China Information* 8, 3 (Winter 1993–4: 1–19). Williams identifies a distinct causal relationship between certain provincial protest movements and the Tiananmen Incident. On the significance of the Tiananmen Incident itself and the relevance of feeling for or against Zhou Enlai, see Xiao Ping, 'The rise and decline of China's Democracy

Movement', originally published in the underground journal *Yecao* (Weeds) in 1983, and translated in *Issues and Studies* 22, 1 (January 1986: 157–8).

2 Although see also Stanley Rosen's comments on how widely the poster had been read (Rosen 1988: 8). Even if the numbers who had actually read a copy of the poster were small, discussion of the case was undoubtedly widespread, and in Guangdong in particular, Li Yizhe members seem to have been allowed on occasion to use 'struggle sessions' organized to condemn them to propagate their views further, even before their well-publicized official rehabilitation early in 1979 (A Chan *et al.* 1988: 13–14, 109–14).

6 'Others are your masters': dissent, democracy and reform, 1976–84

1 This movement was widely referred to just as the Democracy Movement (e.g. in Munro 1984b) during the 1980s. I will be referring to it as the Democracy Wall movement to distinguish it from the spring 1989 movement. The term is intended to encompass the whole of the 'unofficial publications' movement which lasted until April 1981, and not just the initial wall-poster phase of the movement from November 1978 to the first arrests in February–March 1979, which was sometimes referred to as the 'Beijing Spring'.

2 *People's Voice* was published by a group called the Guangzhou Socialism Society, most of whom were workers. Liu Guokai and He Qiu, a shipyard worker and former Red Guard, were the main editors, and Wang Xizhe was also a frequent contributor (Chen Ruoxi 1982: 57–9).

3 The idea of 'privilege-capital' was developed by Chen Erjin in 'On proletarian-democratic revolution', translated by Robin Munro (Munro 1984b: 18–19). Munro believes Chen Erjin to have been one of the editors of the Qingdao unofficial journal *Theoretical Banner*, and to have written for it under the pen name of Lu Ji. That the article quoted above uses Chen's formulation of 'privilege-capital' is not surprising given that the two journals were produced in the same city, and it was common for Democracy Wall activists to contribute ideas and articles to journals other than their own. But since this particular article is attributed to the editorial board of *Sea Spray*, Chen may well also have been a member of the board at this time.

4 For reports of strikes in this period, see for example An Zhiguo 1981: 3; *China Daily* 8 October 1981: 3, in *FBIS-CHI* 9 October 1981: Q1; *SWB/FE/*6715/BII: 5; Wilson 1990b: 260–3. A series of strikes and other 'economic disturbances' in Guangdong province were reported at the end of January 1981 (Hezhong News Agency, Beijing, cited in *October Review* 1982: 18). Reports of attempts to form independent unions can also be found in Wilson 1990b: 263; and to the list compiled by Wilson of places where strikes and demands for independent unions had occurred (Wuhan, Taiyuan, Anshan, Shanghai and Kunming), *October Review* adds Shandong (1982: 18), and a report of demonstrating workers in Lhasa demanding an independent trade union (1982: 47). Chen-chang Chiang reports demands for free unions made by Shanghai workers from a steel mill, a diesel engine plant and other enterprises early in 1981, citing Taiwanese sources, and also notes the Shanxi case and others in Chongqing, Nanchang and parts of Xinjiang (Chiang 1990: 91–2).

5 For an alternative view on Deng's acquaintance with the intellectual roots of Marxism, see Meisner 1989: 107.

6 Fu Shenqi was arrested during the final crackdown on Democracy Wall in the spring of 1981. After his release, he appears to have continued to be politically active in recent movements, serving a three-year prison sentence for protesting about the arrest of independent labour activists in Shanghai, and for speaking to foreign reporters about various cases, in the early 1990s (*Guardian* 21 February 1994: 14).

7 Reference is also made to He Defu and Gong Ping in *October Review* 1982b: 18–19. This article includes quotations from the two workers' manifesto in the original Chinese. Their campaign is also mentioned in Munro 1984b: 12, where the two are described as both working at the chemical plant and being editors of the unofficial journal *Beijing Youth*. The *Duty* account only lists He as an editor of this journal.

7 'Let the whole nation know the workers are organized', 1984–94

1 As well as being the tenth anniversary of Wei's imprisonment, the fortieth of the founding of the PRC, and the seventieth of the May Fourth movement, 1989 also marked 200 years since the French Revolution. It was probably this which suggested the Bastille reference rather than Wei's own essay of 1978 on China's political prisons, entitled 'A twentieth-century Bastille'.

Bibliography

Chinese newspapers and periodicals

All dates and pages in text; only articles identified by author are listed in the bibliography. Publications where no *pinyin* title is given are published in English.

Beijing Review
Beijing Worker (*Beijing Gongren*)
China Daily
China News (*Zhongguo Xinwen*)
China Reconstructs
Chinese Worker (*Zhongguo Gongren*)
Chinese Youth (*Zhongguo Qingnian*)
Chongqing Daily (*Chongqing Ribao*)
Economic Research (*Jingji Yanjiu*)
Far Eastern Economic Review
Guangming Daily (*Guangming Ribao*)
Guangxi Daily (*Huangxi Ribao*)
Guangzhou Daily (*Guangzhou Ribao*)
Guangzhou Labour Movement (*Guangzhou Gongyun*)
Guangzhou Red Guard (*Guangzhou Hongwei Bao*)
Liberation Army Daily (*Jiefangjun Bao*)
Liberation Daily (*Jiefang Ribao*) (Shanghai)
Mingbao Monthly (*Mingbao Yuekan*) (Hong Kong)
Observer (*Guanchajia*) (Hong Kong)
October Review (*Shiyue Pinglun*) (Hong Kong)
People's Daily (*Renmin Ribao*)
People's Electricity Industry (*Renmin Dianye*)
Red Flag (*Hongqi*)
Red Guard News (*Hong Wei Bao*)
Shanghai Labour News (*Shanghai Laodong Bao*)
South China Morning Post (Hong Kong)
Southern Daily (*Nanfang Ribao*)
Union Bulletin (*Gonghui Xinxi*) (Internal ACFTU publication)
Wenhui Daily (*Wenhui Bao*) (Shanghai)
Wen-hui Daily (*Wenhui Bao*) (Hong Kong)
Workers' Daily (*Gongren Ribao*)

Workers' World (Gongren Tiandi)
Xinhua News Agency (Beijing unless otherwise stated in text)

Monitored radio broadcasts and press monitoring services

FBIS-CHI Foreign Broadcasts Information Service, China section (monitoring service).
Guangdong/Guangzhou Radio 15 March 1967 '*Guangzhou Ribao* on uniting with PLA', translated in *News from Provincial Radio Stations* 199: M4–9.
—— 'Canton workers' praise for Red Guards', translated in *News from Provincial Radio Stations* 202: M8–9.
—— 'Setting up of the Preparatory Committee for the Canton "Workers' Alliance" acclaimed', translated in *News from Provincial Radio Stations* 234: M1.
—— 'Canton Rally to support the centre's resolution on Guangdong problem, in *News from Provincial Radio Stations* 235: M1–7.
News from Provincial Radio Stations (monitoring service)
Survey of China Mainland Magazines (monitoring service)
S*WB/FE Survey of World Broadcasts, Far East Section* (monitoring service)

Works cited in the text

All-China Federation of Labour (1950) 'Annual Report of the All-China Federation of Labour', *Chinese Worker* 15 May, translated in *Current Background* 24: 10 November.
All-China Federation of Trade Unions (ACFTU) (1949) 'Resolution on the present tasks of the Chinese labour movement' (Guanyu Zhongguo zhigong yundong dangqian renwu de jueyi), in *Selected documents of the Chinese labour movement* (Zhongguo zhigong yundong wenxuan), Beijing: Workers' Press.
An Zhiguo (1981) 'On the question of disturbances caused by small numbers of people', *Beijing Review* 24, 15: 3–4.
Andors, S (1977a) *China's industrial revolution: Politics, planning and management, 1949 to the present*, London: Martin Robinson and Co. Ltd.
—— (1977b) *Workers and workplaces in revolutionary China*, White Plains, NY: M E Sharpe.
Anon. (1978) 'Who should be the masters?', wall poster, Beijing, December 1978, translated in J D Seymour (ed.) (1980) *The Fifth Modernization – China's Human Rights Movement, 1978–1979*, Stanfordville, NY: Human Rights Publishing Group.
April Fifth Forum (1979) 'The state of the economy', original title 'The people's democratic movement and the style of "upright officials" the people expect', *Bei-Mei* Daily 9 (29 April 1979), translated in J D Seymour (ed.) *The Fifth Modernization – China's Human Rights Movement, 1978–1979*, Stanfordville, NY: Human Rights Publishing Group.
Becker, J (1996) *Hungry ghosts: China's secret famine*, London: John Murray.
Beijing Spring (Beijing Zhi Chun), dates in text, in C. Widor (ed.) *Documents on the Chinese democratic movement 1978–1980* (see under Widor).
Bennett, G A and R E Montaperto (1971) *Red Guard – The political biography of Dai Hsiao'ai*, London: Allen and Unwin.
Benton, G (ed.) (1982) *Wild lilies, poisonous weeds: Dissident voices from People's China*, London: Pluto Press.
—— and A Hunter (eds) (1995) *Wild lily, prairie fire: China's road to democracy, Yan'an to Tian'anmen 1942–1989*, Princeton, NJ: Princeton University Press.

Bettelheim, C (1974) *The Cultural Revolution and industrial organization in China*, New York: Monthly Review Press.

Blecher, M J and G White (1985) *Micropolitics in contemporary China – A technical unit during and after the Cultural Revolution*, New York: M E Sharpe.

Brodsgaard, K E (1981) 'The Democracy Movement in China, 1978–1979: Opposition movements, wall poster campaigns, and underground journals', *Asian Survey* 21, 7: 747–74.

Brugger, W (1976) *Democracy and organization in the Chinese industrial enterprise, 1949–1953*, Cambridge: Cambridge University Press.

Chan, A (1991a) 'PRC workers under "capitalism with Chinese characteristics"', *China Information* 5, 4: 75–82.

—— (1991b) 'Protest in a Hunan county town: The profile of a Democracy Movement activist in China's backwaters', in J Unger (ed.) *The pro-democracy protests in China: Reports from the provinces*, Armonk, NY: M E Sharpe.

—— (1992) 'Dispelling misconceptions about the Red Guard movement: The necessity to re-examine Cultural Revolution factionalism and periodization', *Journal of Contemporary China* 1, 1: 61–85.

—— (1993) 'Revolution or corporatism? Workers and trade unions in post-Mao China', *Australian Journal of Chinese Affairs* 29: 31–61.

—— (1995) 'The emerging patterns of industrial relations in China and the rise of two new labor movements', *China Information* 9, 4: 36–59.

—— (1996a) 'The changing ruling elite and political opposition in China', in G Rodan (ed.) *Political oppositions in industrialising Asia*, London: Routledge.

—— (1996b) 'Boot camp at the shoe factory', *Washington Post* 3 November.

—— and J Unger (1990) 'Voices from the protest movement, Chongqing, Sichuan', *Australian Journal of Chinese Affairs* 24: 259–79.

——, S Rosen and J Unger (eds) (1988) *On socialist democracy and the Chinese legal system – The Li Yizhe debates*, Armonk, NY: M E Sharpe.

Chen Erjin (1984) *China: Crossroads Socialism*, translated and introduced by R Munro, London: Verso Editions.

Chen Ruoxi (1982) *Democracy Wall and the unofficial journals*, Berkeley, CA: University of California (Center for Chinese Studies).

Chesneaux, J (1968) *The Chinese labor movement*, Stanford, CA: Stanford University Press.

Chiang, Chen-chang (1990) 'The role of trade unions in mainland China', *Issues and Studies* 26, 2: 75–98.

Child, J (1994) *Management in China during the age of reform*, Cambridge: Cambridge University Press.

China News Analysis (1968) 'Army rule', *CNA* 711 (7 June 1968).

—— (1969) 'Workers and discipline', *CNA* 769 (15 July 1969).

China Spring (Zhongguo Zhi Chun) (1990) 'The Guangdong Workers' movement before and after June 4th', *China Spring* April, 60–62.

Chung, Chong-wook (1980) *Maoism and development: The politics of industrial management in China*, Seoul: Seoul National University Press.

Davis, D (1988) 'Patrons and clients in Chinese industry', *Modern China* 14, 4: 487–97.

Deng Xiaoping (1978) 'Greeting the great task', *Beijing Review* 21, 42: 5–8.

Denitch, B (1981) 'Yugoslav exceptionalism', in J F Triska and C Gati (eds) *Blue-collar workers in Eastern Europe*, London: Allen and Unwin.

Dirlik, A (1997) 'Narrativizing revolution: The Guangzhou Uprising (11–13 December 1927) in workers' perspective', *Modern China* 23, 4: 363–97.

Epstein, I (1949) *Labor problems in Nationalist China*, New York: International Secretariat, Institute of Pacific Relations.

Erbaugh, M S and R K Kraus (1991) 'The 1989 Democracy Movement in Fujian and its aftermath', in J Unger (ed.) *The pro-democracy protests in China: Reports from the provinces*, Armonk, NY: M E Sharpe.

Esherick, J W (1990) 'Xi'an Spring', *Australian Journal of Chinese Affairs* 24: 209–35.

Fletcher, M D (1974) *Workers and Commissars*, Bellingham, Washington, DC: Western Washington State College, Program in East Asian Studies Occasional Paper.

Forster, K (1986) 'The 1976 Ch'ingming Incident in Hangchow', *Issues and Studies* 22, 4: 13–33.

—— (1990) *Rebellion and factionalism in a Chinese province: Zhejiang 1966–1976*, Armonk, NY: M E Sharpe.

—— (1991) 'The popular protest in Hangzhou', in J Unger (ed.) *The pro-democracy protests in China: Reports from the provinces*, Armonk, NY: M E Sharpe.

Free Talk (1981) 'Who are the real law breakers?' (Jinjing shei wei fu?), in *October Review* 55, (1981) 20–21.

Friedman, J R (1949) 'Labor in Nationalist China, 1945–48', in I Epstein, *Labor problems in Nationalist China*, New York: International Secretariat, Institute of Pacific Relations.

Fu Rong (1957) 'My understanding of the contradictions among the people under the socialist system', *Study* (Xuexi) 24, translated in *Extracts from China Mainland Magazines* 123: 12–23.

Garside, R (1981) *Coming Alive: China after Mao*, London: André Deutsch.

Gipouloux, F (1986) *Les cent fleurs à l'usine – Agitation ouvrière et crise du modèle Soviètique en Chine, 1956–1957*, Paris: Éditions de l'École des hautes Études en sciences sociales.

Gong Xiaowen (1976) 'Deng Xiaoping and the "Twenty Articles"' (Deng Xiaoping yu 'ershi tiao'), *Study and Criticism* (Xuexi yu Pipan) 4: 14–19.

Gray, J (1994) 'Review of Rafe de Crespigny, "China this century"', *China Quarterly* 140, December: 1157.

Guangzhou Railway General Headquarters (Guangtie Zongsi) (1968) 'Notice from CCP Central Committee, State Council, Central Military Commission and Central Cultural Revolution Group on dealing further blows to counterrevolutionary economism and speculative, profiteering activities', *Guangzhou Railway General Headquarters* 28 (February 1968), translated in *Survey of China Mainland Press* 4129: 1–6.

Guangzhou Workers (1968) 'The present state of the movement in some factories in Guangzhou – An investigation report', *Guangzhou Workers* 34 (28 May 1968), translated in *Survey of China Mainland Press* 4208: 7–16.

Gunn, A (1991) '"Tell the world about us": The student movement in Shenyang, 1989', in J Unger (ed.) *The pro-democracy protests in China: Reports from the provinces*, Armonk, NY: M E Sharpe.

Hai Feng (1971) *An account of the Cultural Revolution in the Guangzhou area* (Guangzhou diqu wenge licheng shilue), Hong Kong: Union Research Institute.

Halpern, N (1985) 'Learning from abroad: Chinese views of the East European economic experience, January 1977–June 1981, *Modern China* 11, 1: 77–109.

Han Minzhu (1990) *Cries for democracy*, Princeton, NJ: Princeton University Press.

Han Zhixiong (1979) 'Democracy in economic management', translated in J D Seymour (ed.) (1980) *The Fifth Modernization – China's human rights movement, 1978–1979*, Stanfordville, NY: Human Rights Publishing Group.

Haraszti, M (1978) *A worker in a workers' state*, translated by Michael Wright, original title *Piece-rates*, New York: Universe Books.

Harper, P (1969) 'The Party and the unions in Communist China', *China Quarterly* 37: 84–119.

—— (1971a) 'Workers' participation in management in Communist China', *Studies in Comparative Communism* 3: 111–40.

—— (1971b) 'Trade union cultivation of workers for leadership', in J W Lewis (ed.) *The city in Communist China*, Stanford, CA: Stanford University Press.

Hassard, J and J Sheehan (1997) 'Enterprise reform and the role of the state: The case of the Capital Iron and Steel Works, Beijing', in A Bugra and B Usdiken (eds) *State, market and organizational form*, Berlin: Walter de Gruyter.

Heilmann, S (1990) *Nanking 1976: Spontane Massenbewegungen im Gefolge der Kulturrevolution*, Bochum: Brockmeyer.

—— (1993) 'The social context of mobilization in China: Factions, work units and activists during the 1976 April Fifth Movement', *China Information* 8, 3: 1–19.

Henley, J S and Mee-Kan Nyaw (1987) 'The development of work incentives in Chinese industrial enterprises – Material versus non-material incentives', in M Warner (ed.) *Management Reforms in China*, London: Frances Pinter.

Hong, Ng Sek and R D Lansbury (1987) 'The workers' congress in Chinese enterprises', in M Warner (ed.) *Management Reforms in China*, London: Frances Pinter.

Hong Yung Lee (1978) *The politics of the Chinese Cultural Revolution*, Berkeley, CA: University of California Press.

Howard, P (1991) 'Rice bowls and job security: The urban contract labour system', *Australian Journal of Chinese Affairs* 25: 93–114.

Howard, R W (1991) 'The student Democracy Movement in Changchun', in J Unger (ed.) *The pro-democracy protests in China: Reports from the provinces*, Armonk, NY: M E Sharpe.

Huang, Mab and J D Seymour (1980) 'Introduction', in J D Seymour (ed.) *The fifth modernization – China's human rights movement, 1978–1979*, Stanfordville, NY: Human Rights Publishing Group.

Huang Yongsheng (1967) 'Report on the situation of the Great Proletarian Cultural Revolution in Guangdong', *Guangzhou City Radio* 14 December, translated in *News from Provincial Radio Stations 238* 21 December: M3–7.

Human Rights Watch – Asia (1994) 'Report on suppression of independent workers' organizations in China', New York: Human Rights Watch – Asia.

Kaple, D (1994) *Dream of a red factory: The legacy of High Stalinism in China*, Oxford: Oxford University Press.

Laba, R (1991) *The roots of Solidarity: A political sociology of Poland's working-class democratization*, Princeton, NJ: Princeton University Press.

Lai Ruoyu (1953) 'Report on the trade union work in China', in *The Seventh All-China Congress of Trade Unions*, Beijing: Foreign Languages Press.

—— (1956a) 'The current tasks of trade unions in joint state–private enterprises', *Xinhua News Agency* (Beijing), 23 November 1956, translated in *Survey of China Mainland Press* 1422: 2–4.

—— (1956b) 'Summing up of national conference of basic-level trade union cadres in joint state–private enterprises', *Xinhua News Agency* (Beijing), 29 November 1956), translated in *Survey of China Mainland Press* 1423: 10–11.

—— (1957a) 'Trade union chief on tests of democratic institutions in industry', *Xinhua News Agency* (Beijing), 7 March 1957, translated in *Survey of China Mainland Press* 1487: 22.

—— (1957b) 'How contradictions within the people are handled by the trade unions', *Workers' Daily* 9 May 1957, translated in *Survey of China Mainland Press* 1535: 8–12.

Lam, W Wo-lap (1995) *China after Deng Xiaoping*, Singapore: John Wiley and Sons.

Lee, C K (1998) 'The labour politics of market socialism', *Modern China* (January) 24(1): 3–33.

Lee Lai To (1984) *The structure of the trade union system in China, 1949–1966*, Hong Kong: Centre for Asian Studies, University of Hong Kong.

—— (1986) *Trade unions in China, 1949 to the Present*, Singapore: Singapore University Press.

Lee, P N (1977) 'The Gang of Four: Radical politics and modernization in China', in S S K Chin (ed.) *The Gang of Four: First essays after the fall*, Hong Kong: Centre for Asian Studies, University of Hong Kong.

—— (1987) *Industrial management and economic reform in China, 1949–1984*, Oxford: Oxford University Press.

Leijonhufvud, G (1990) *Going against the tide: On dissent and big-character posters in China*, London: Curzon Press.

Leung Wing-yue (1988) *Smashing the iron rice-pot: Workers and unions in China's market socialism*, Hong Kong: Asia Monitor Resource Centre.

Lewis, P (1994) *Central Europe since 1945*, London: Longman.

Li Chun (1957) 'Why democracy must be broadened in enterprise management' (Weishenme yao kuoda qiye guanli de minzhu), *Chinese Worker* 6: 3–4.

Li Hua (1987) 'The democratic management of enterprises and workers' awareness of democracy', *Chinese Economic Studies* 22, 4: 69–80.

Li Lisan (1949) 'Some points of explanation on the policy of developing production and benefitting both labour and capital' (Guanyu fazhan shengchan laozi liangli zhengce de ji dian shouming), in *Selected documents of the Chinese labour movement* (Zhongguo zhigong yundong wenxuan), Beijing: Workers' Press.

Liao Gailong (1980) 'The "1980 reform" programme of China', reprinted in *The Seventies* 134 1 March 1981, translated in *FBIS* 16 March 1981.

Lin Lean Lim and G Sziraczki (eds) (1995) *Employment challenges and policy responses: Chinese and international perspectives*, Beijing: International Labour Office, Area Office Beijing.

Liu, A P L (1996) *Mass politics in the People's Republic*, Boulder, CO: Westview Press.

Liu Guokai (1987) *A brief analysis of the Cultural Revolution*, translated and abridged by A Chan, Armonk, NY: M E Sharpe.

Liu Ningyi (1956) 'Overcome the tendency not to care about the livelihood of workers and staff', *Southern Daily* 25 June.

Liu Zijiu (1951) 'On the belated introduction of the lesson of democratic reform in factories and mines', *Workers' Daily* 12 September 1951, translated in *Current Background* 123: 1–9.

Lockett, M (1983) 'Enterprise management – Moves towards democracy?', in S Feuchtwang and A Hussain (eds) *The Chinese economic reforms*, New York: St. Martin's Press.

—— (1985) *Cultural Revolution and industrial organization in a Chinese enterprise: The Beijing General Knitwear Mill, 1966–81*, Oxford: Oxford Centre for Management Studies.

Lu Min (1979a) 'Gradually do away with the bureaucratic system and establish a Paris Commune-style democratic system', *Beijing Spring 1*, translated in J D Seymour (ed.) (1980) *The fifth modernization: China's Human Rights Movement, 1978–1979*, Stanfordville, NY: Human Rights Publishing Group.

—— (1979b) 'How to run a factory' (original title: 'Do away with the power of administrative leadership of basic-level organizations in factories, mines and other enterprises'), *Beijing Spring 2*, translated in J D Seymour (ed.) (1980) *The fifth modernization – China's human rights movement, 1978–1979*, Stanfordville, NY: Human Rights Publishing Group.

Lu Ping (1990) *A moment of truth: Workers' participation in China's 1989 Democracy Movement and the emergence of independent unions*, Hong Kong: Asia Monitor Resource Centre (also published in Chinese as *The workers have risen* (Gongren qilaile)).

MacFarquhar, R (1960) *The Hundred Flowers*, London: Steven and Sons Ltd.

—— (ed.) (1990) *The Politics of China 1949–1989*, Cambridge: Cambridge University Press.

Mao Zedong Sixiang Wansui! (Long live Mao Zedong Thought) (1969), no publisher.

Mehnert, K (1969) *Peking and the New Left: At home and abroad*, Berkeley, CA: Centre for Chinese Studies, University of California Press.

Meisner, M (1983) 'The concept of the dictatorship of the proletariat in Chinese Marxist thought', in V Nee and D Mozingo (eds) *State and society in contemporary China*, Ithaca, NY: Cornell University Press.

—— (1989) 'Marx, Mao and Deng on the division of labour in history', in A Dirlik and M Meisner (eds) *Marxism and the Chinese experience*, Armonk, NY: M E Sharpe.

Mok Chiu Yu and J F Harrison (eds) (1990) *Voices from Tiananmen Square: Beijing Spring and the democracy movement*, Montreal: Black Rose Books.

Montias, J M (1981) 'Observations on strikes, riots and other disturbances', in J F Triska and C Gati (eds) *Blue-collar workers in Eastern Europe*, London: Allen and Unwin.

Munro, R (1984a) 'China's Democracy Movement: A midwinter spring', *Survey* 28, 2: 70–98.

—— (1984b) 'Introduction', in Chen Erjin, *China: Crossroads Socialism*, London: Verso Editions.

Nathan, A J (1989) 'Chinese democracy in 1989: Continuity and change', *Problems of Communism* 38, 5: 16–29.

Ni Zhifu (1981) 'Implement the guidelines of the 6th Plenum, give full play to the initiative of the workers as masters of the land and strive to push the economy forward', *Workers' Daily* 13 October 1981, translated in *Survey of World Broadcasts* 6870/BII (3 March 1981), 1–10.

—— (1983) 'Report at the opening of the 10th ACFTU Congress', *People's Daily* 19 October 1983.

North China People's Government (1949) 'Decision on the establishment of factory management committees and factory workers' representative congresses in state- and collective-run industrial enterprises' (Guanyu zai guoying, gongying gongchang qiye zhong jianli gongchang guanli weiyuanhui yu gongchang zhigong daibiao huiyi de jueding), in *Selected documents of the Chinese labour movement* (Zhongguo zhigong yundong wenxuan), Beijing: Workers' Press.

Ong, Shao-erh (1953) *Labor problems in Communist China (to February 1953)*, Lackland, TX: Air Force Personnel and Training Research Center, Lackland Air Force Base.

Pateman, C (1970) *Participation and democratic theory*, Cambridge: Cambridge University Press.

Peng Qingzhao (1951) *Gongren Zhengzhi Keben* (Workers' political textbook), Beijing: Gongren Chubanshe.

People's Road (Renmin Zhi Lu) (1980) 'On events around the Qin's arrest and our attitude' (Guanyu He Qiu lei pu qianhou yu women de tai du) in *October Review* 48 (1980) 12–13.

Perry, E J (1993) *Shanghai on strike: The politics of Chinese labor*, Stanford, CA: Stanford University Press.

—— (1994) 'Shanghai's strike wave of 1957', *China Quarterly* 137: 1–27.

—— (1995) 'Labour's battle for political space: the role of worker associations in contemporary China', in D S Davis, R Kraus, B Naughton and E J Perry (eds) *Urban spaces in contemporary China*, Cambridge: Cambridge University Press.

—— and Li Xun (1997) *Proletarian power: Shanghai in the Cultural Revolution*, Boulder, CO: Westview Press.

Pravda, A (1981) 'Political attitudes and activity', in J F Triska and C Gati (eds) *Blue-collar workers in Eastern Europe*, London: Allen and Unwin.

—— and B A Ruble (eds) *Trade unions in Communist states*, Boston: Allen and Unwin.

Questions on the labour movement (1950), 3rd collection, Beijing: Workers' Press.

Red Insurrection (Hongse Baodong) (1967) 'The current situation in Canton and our policy', *Red Insurrection* (22 August 1967), translated in *Survey of China Mainland Press* 4026: 7–12.

Richman, B (1969) *Industrial society in Communist China*, New York: Random House.

Rosen, S (1982) *Red Guard factionalism and the Cultural Revolution in Guangzhou (Canton)*, Boulder, CO: Westview Press.

—— (1988) 'Guangzhou's Democracy Movement in Cultural Revolution perspective', *China Quarterly* 101: 1–31.

Rozman, G (1985) *A mirror for socialism*, London: I B Tauris.

Ruble, B (1981) *Soviet trade unions: Their development in the 1970s*, Cambridge: Cambridge University Press.

Saich, T (1984) 'Workers in the workers' state: Urban workers in the PRC', in D S G Goodman (ed.) *Groups and politics in the PRC*, Armonk, NY: M E Sharpe.

—— (1990) 'The rise and fall of the Beijing People's Movement', in J Unger (ed.) *The pro-democracy protests in China: Reports from the provinces*, Armonk, NY: M E Sharpe.

Sailing Ship (no date) 'The new awakening of the Chinese working class' (Zhongguo gongrenjieji de xin juexing), reprinted in *October Review* 51 (1981): 11.

Schoenhals, M (1997a) 'The Central Case Examination Group, 1966–1979', *China Quarterly* 145: 87–111.

—— (ed.) (1997b) *China's Cultural Revolution, 1966–1969: Not a dinner party*, Armonk, NY: M E Sharpe.

Sea Spray (Hai Lung hua) (1980a) 'A new era in the history of the Communist movement' (Gongcha yundong shi shang de xin jiyuan), reprinted in *October Review* 60 (1981) 34.

Sea Spray (1980b) 'Seeing the inevitability of a multi-party system from the Polish independent trade union' (Cong Polan duli gonghui kan duodangzhi de bu ke kangjuxing), reprinted in *October Review* 61 (1982): 20.

Seventies, The (Qishi Niandai) (1980) 'China's new era is an era of deep thought' (Zhongguo de xin yidai shi sisuo de yidai), *The Seventies* June 1980: 54–6.

Seymour, J D (ed.) (1980) *The fifth modernization: China's Human Rights Movement, 1978–1979*, Stanfordville, NY: Human Rights Publishing Group.

Sheehan, J (1995) 'Conflict between workers and the party-state in China and the formation of autonomous workers' organizations, 1949–1984', unpublished doctoral dissertation, University of London.

—— (1996) 'Is there another Tiananmen uprising in the offing?', *Jane's Intelligence Review* 8, 12: 554–6.

Shengwulian ([Hunan] Provincial Proletarian Revolutionary Rebels Allied Committee) (1968) 'Whither China?', translated in *Survey of China Mainland Press* 4190: 1–18.

Shirk, S L (1981) 'Recent Chinese labour policies and the transformation of industrial organization in China', *China Quarterly* 88: 575–93.

Siu, H F and Z Stern (1983) *Mao's harvest: Voices from China's new generation*, Oxford: Oxford University Press.

Solomon, R (1968) 'Sources of labour discontent in China: The worker-peasant system', *Current Scene* 6, 5: 1–26.

Spring Thunder Warriors (Chunlei Zhanshi) (1967) 'Warmly hail the imposition of military control on Canton Railway Sub-bureau', *Spring Thunder Warriors* 19 (25 November 1967), translated in *Survey of China Mainland Press* 4120: 5–6.

Steel August 1 (Gang Ba-yi) (1967) 'Report on an investigation into the facts of the persecution of the August 1 Combat Corps', *Steel August 1* 15 October 1967, translated in *Survey of China Mainland Press* 4019: 1–7.

Strand, D (1985) *Political participation and political reform in post-Mao China (1985)*, Copenhagen: Centre for East and Southeast Asian Studies, University of Copenhagen.

Sturmthal, A (1964) *Workers' Councils – A study of workplace organization on both sides of the Iron Curtain*, Cambridge, MA: Harvard University Press.

Su Ke (1957) 'The problem of democratic management of state-private enterprises viewed in the light of workers' experience in industrial management', *Workers' Daily* 5 May.

Theoretical Banner (Lilunqi) (1981) 'Death knell of the rule of the bureaucratic privileged class is tolling' (Guanliao tequanjieji tongzhi de shangzhong), reprinted in *October Review* 53–4: 94–5.

Triska, J F (1981) 'Workers' assertiveness and Soviet policy choices', in J F Triska and C Gati (eds) *Blue-collar workers in Eastern Europe*, London: Allen and Unwin.

—— and C Gati (1981) 'Introduction', in J F Triska and C Gati (eds) *Blue-collar workers in Eastern Europe*, London: Allen and Unwin.

Tung, R L (1982) *Chinese industrial society after Mao*, Lexington, MA: D C Heath and Co.

Tyson, L D (1981) 'Aggregate economic difficulties and workers' welfare', in J F Triska and C Gati (eds) *Blue-collar workers in Eastern Europe*, London: Allen and Unwin.

Unger, J (1991a) 'Whither China? Yang Xiguang, red capitalists and the social turmoil of the Cultural Revolution', *Modern China* 17, 1: 3–37.

—— (1991b) 'Introduction', in J Unger (ed.) *The pro-democracy protests in China: Reports from the provinces*, Armonk, NY: M E Sharpe.

Vogel, E (1969) *Canton under Communism: Programs and politics in a provincial capital, 1949–1968*, Cambridge, MA: Harvard University Press.

Walder, A (1978) 'Zhang Chunqiao and Shanghai's January Revolution', *Michigan Papers in Chinese Studies* 32.

—— (1982) 'Some ironies of the Maoist legacy in industry', in M Selden and V Lippit (eds) *The transition to socialism in China*, Armonk, NY: M E Sharpe.

—— (1986) *Communist Neotraditionalism*, Berkeley, CA: University of California Press.

—— (1987) 'Wage reform and the web of factory interests', *China Quarterly* 109: 22–41.

—— (1989a) 'Factory and manager in an era of reform', *China Quarterly* 118: 242–64.

—— (1989b) 'The political sociology of the Beijing upheaval of 1989', *Problems of Communism* 38, 5: 30–40.

—— (1991) 'Workers, managers and the state: The reform era and the political crisis of 1989', *China Quarterly* 127: 467–92.

—— (1996) 'The Chinese Cultural Revolution in the factories: Party-state structures and patterns of conflict', in E J Perry (ed.) *Putting Class in its Place: Worker Identities in East Asia*, Berkeley, CA: University of East Asian Studies, University of California.

—— and Gong Xiaoxia (1993) 'Workers in the Tiananmen protests: The politics of the Beijing Workers' Autonomous Federation', *Australian Journal of Chinese Affairs* 29: 1–29.

Wales, N (1945) *The Chinese labor movement*, New York: John Day.

Wang Haofeng (1958) 'Important reform of management of industrial enterprises', *People's Daily* 26 April 1958, translated in *Survey of China Mainland Press* 1774: 4–13.

—— (1960) 'Consolidate and develop the "Two participations, one reform and triple combination system", raise the standard of enterprise management in all respects', *Red Flag* August: 6–15.

Wang Ruowang (1987) 'Some interesting things that took place at the recent election of deputies to the People's Congresses', *Pa Shing Semimonthly 148* 16 July, reprinted in *Democracy Wall* 3: no date, Hong Kong.

Wang Shaoguang (1993) 'From a pillar of continuity to a force for change: Chinese workers in the movement', in R V Des Forges, Luo Ning and Wu Yen-bo (eds) *Chinese democracy and the crisis of 1989*, Albany, NY: State University of New York Press.

—— (1995) *Failure of charisma: The Cultural Revolution in Wuhan*, Oxford: Oxford University Press.

Wang Xiaodong (1993) 'A review of China's economic problems: The industrial sector', in R V Des Forges, Luo Ning and Wu Yen-bo (eds) *Chinese democracy and the crisis of 1989*, Albany, NY: State University of New York Press.

Wang Xizhe (1979a) 'Strive for the class dictatorship of the proletariat', translated in A Chan *et al.* (eds) (1988) *On socialist democracy and the Chinese legal system – The Li Yizhe debates*, 132–56.

—— (1979b) 'Mao Zedong and the Cultural Revolution', translated in A Chan *et al.* (eds) (1988) *On socialist democracy and the Chinese legal system – The Li Yizhe debates*, 177–260.

Wang Zhuo and Wen Wuhan (eds) (1992) *An evaluation of Guangdong's opening and reform* (Guangdong gaige kaifang pingshuo), Guangzhou: Guangdong People's Press.

Warner, M (1995) *The management of human resources in Chinese industry*, London: Macmillan.

Warner, S (1991) 'Shanghai's response to the deluge', in J Unger (ed.) *The pro-democracy protests in China: Reports from the provinces*, Armonk, NY: M E Sharpe.

Wasserstrom, J N and Liu Xinyong (1995) 'Student associations and mass movements', in D S Davis, R Kraus, B Naughton and E J Perry (eds) *Urban spaces in contemporary China*, Cambridge: Cambridge University Press.

Wei Jingsheng (1978) 'The fifth modernization', translated in J D Seymour (ed.) (1980) *The Fifth Modernization – China's Human Rights Movement, 1978–1979*, Stanfordville, NY: Human Rights Publishing Group.

—— (1979) 'Democracy or a new dictatorship?', translated in G Benton (ed.) (1982) *Wild lilies, poisonous weeds: Dissident voices from People's China*, London: Pluto Press, 45–50

Wen Jin (1956) 'Democracy must serve socialist construction' (Minzhu bixu wei shehuizhuyi jianshe fuwu), *Chinese Worker* 16: 5–7.

White, G (1980) 'The politics of demobilized soldiers from liberation to Cultural Revolution', *China Quarterly* 82: 187–213.

—— (1987) 'The politics of economic reform in Chinese industry: The introduction of the Labour Contract System', *China Quarterly* 111: 365–89.

White, L T III (1989) *Policies of chaos: The organizational causes of violence in China's Cultural Revolution*, Princeton, NJ: Princeton University Press.

Widor, Claude (ed.) *Documents on the Chinese democratic movement, 1978–1980: Unofficial magazines and wall-posters* vol. 2, joint publication, Paris: Éditions de l'École des Hautes Études en Sciences Sociales and Hong Kong: The Observer Publishers.

Williams, P C (1991) 'Some provincial precursors of popular dissent movements in Beijing', *China Information* 6, 1: 1–9.

Wilson, J L (1986) 'The People's Republic of China', in A Pravda and B Ruble (eds) *Trade Unions in Communist States*, Boston: Allen and Unwin.

—— (1990a) 'Labor policy in China: Reform and retrogression', *Problems of Communism* 39, 5: 44–65.

—— (1990b) ' "The Polish lesson": China and Poland 1980–1990', *Studies in Comparative Communism* 23, 3–4: 259–79.

Wu Shouhui and Guo Jinhua (1987) 'Workers' evaluation of and hopes for trade unions', *Chinese Economic Studies* 22, 4: 55–68.

Wylie, R F (1981) 'Shanghai dockers in the Cultural Revolution: The interplay of political and economic issues', in C Howe (ed.) *Shanghai: Revolution and development in an Asian metropolis*, Cambridge: Cambridge University Press.

Xiao Ping (1986) 'The rise and decline of China's democracy movement', originally published in *Yecao* (Weeds) (PRC unofficial journal), translated in *Issues and Studies* 22: 155–75.

Xu Zhizhen (1953) 'Report on the amendment to the constitution of the trade unions of the People's Republic of China', *The Seventh All-China Congress of Trade Unions*, Beijing: Foreign Languages Press.

Yang, M M (1989) 'Between state and society: The construction of corporateness in a Chinese socialist factory', *Australian Journal of Chinese Affairs* 22: 31–60.

Yao Wenyuan (1968) 'The working class must lead in everything' (Gongrenjieji bixu lingdao yiqie), *Red Flag* 2: 3–7.

Yi Han (1956) 'How to understand the Hungarian Incident' (Zenyang renshi Xionggali shijian), *Chinese Worker* 22: 8–9.

Zai Heng (1957) 'Develop the supervisory role of the workers' congress' (Fahui zhigong daibiao dahui de jiandu zuoyong), *Chinese Worker* 11: 6–7.

Zhao Minghua and T Nichols (1996) 'Management control of labour in state-owned enterprises: Cases from the textile industry', *The China Journal* 36: 1–21.

Zheng Xing (1981) 'The election movement is in the ascendant', in G Benton (ed.) (1982) *Wild lilies, poisonous weeds: Dissident voices from People's China*, London: Pluto Press.

Zhi Exiang (1979) 'The election for shop-heads', *China Reconstructs* 28, 5: 6–8.

Zhu Xuefan (1948) 'On the labour movement in Guomindang-ruled areas: Report to the 6th All-China Labour Congress', *Xinhua News Agency*, 26 July, reprinted in *All-China Federation of Trade Unions, Selected Documents of the Chinese Labour Movement* (Zhongguo zhidong yundong wenxuan), Beijing: Workers' Press.

Zi Chuan (1977a) 'Li Yizhe and me' (Li Yizhe yu wo), *Big Dipper* (Beidou) 1: 4–13.

—— (1977b) 'Li Yizhe and me' (Li Yizhe yu wo), *Big Dipper* (Beidou) 2: 43–51.

—— (1977c) 'Li Yizhe and me' (Li Yizhe yu wo), *Big Dipper* (Beidou) 3: 33–8.

—— (1977d) 'Li Yizhe and me' (Li Yizhe yu wo), *Big Dipper* (Beidou) 4: 11–16.

—— (1977e) 'Li Yizhe and me' (Li Yizhe yu wo), *Big Dipper* (Beidou) 6: 36–41.

—— (1977f) 'Li Yizhe and me' (Li Yizhe yu wo), *Big Dipper* (Beidou) 7: 25–8, 41.

Zinner, P E (1956) *National Communism and popular revolt in Eastern Europe. A selection of documents on events in Poland and Hungary, February–November, 1956*, New York: Columbia University Press.

Index

All-China Federation of Trade Unions
(ACFTU) 196, 206; *Chinese Worker*
official journal of 64, 66, 89; concern
over safety, welfare expressed by 56;
condemned by Jiang Qing 119; conflict
with CCP over autonomy 34–6, 43, 88,
165, 184, 185, 203–4, 223; and
Democracy Movement 194, 216, 221;
Eighth Congress of (1957) 81; election
regulations reformed by 68; failure to
protect members admitted by 63, 203;
irrelevance of 79–80, 88, 165, 184,
202, 203; Lai Ruoyu as head of 34, 88,
165; Li Lisan as head of 13, 23, 34,
165; Liu Ningyi as head of 88; Ni Zhifu
as head of 185; Ninth Congress of
(1978) 165, 173; Seventh Congress of
(1953) 13, 15, 23, 34, 36, 43, 63; strikes
and unrest reported by 48, 54–5;
surveys of workers' views by 202; Tenth
Congress of 185; Workers'
Autonomous Federations attacked by
194, 221; weak links with basic-level
unions 36; *see also* Chinese Communist
Party; Gao Yuan; Lai Ruoyu; Li Lisan;
Liu Ningyi; Ni Zhifu; unions, official
All-China Federation of Labour (ACFL):
report on workers' leftism (1950) 24;
Sixth Congress of (1948) 15
anarchism 182, 193; in Cultural
Revolution 126, 141, 193
Anshan Constitution: *see* management
anti-rightist campaign (1957–8): and
Cultural Revolution 101, 106, 107; as
end of collective action by workers 69,
79, 85; intimidatory effect of 79, 106;
union officials in 78, 79, 88–9; workers'
criticisms of intellectuals in 6, 49;

workers punished as criminals in 49,
79; *see also* Hundred Flowers Movement
Anyang: April Fifth Movement in 149
apprentices: in Cultural Revolution 110,
116; grievances acknowledged by CCP
80; in Hundred Flowers 38, 48, 79, 99;
terms of apprenticeships 69, 125, 207
April Fifth Movement 145, 146, 170;
against Gang of Four 148, 151–2, 154,
158; against Mao 150, 152, 158; as
anti-party movement 151–2, 158; in
Anyang 149
autonomous organizations in 152–3; in
Beijing 148–9, 153, 154, 157; bottom-
up nature of 148, 150; cadres in 153;
casualties and arrests in 153;
communication and organization of
148–9, 152–3; Cultural Revolution
factions in 150, 152, 154; and
Democracy Wall 150, 154, 157, 158,
193; and Deng Xiaoping 148, 150, 151,
152, 154, 215; economic grievances in
148, 153, 158; former Red Guards
dominant in 150, 153; in Hangzhou
149; left opposition to 149; Li Yizhe's
influence on 150; in Kaifeng 149; in
Luoyang 149; in Nanjing 148, 149,
153, 154, 157; 'new class' paradigm in
151, 222; numbers involved in 148,
153, 154, 157, 158; popular refusal to
inform on participants after 154;
publications of 154; in Shanghai 149;
similarities with Cultural Revolution of
149, 153, 222; students in 148; students
prevented from participating in 149; in
Taiyuan 149; verdict reversed on 157,
193; Wang Xizhe on 151, 152; Wei
Jingsheng on 150; worker-student
cooperation in 149, 152–3;

Daqing oilfield 105
demobilized soldiers: in Cultural
Revolution 119, 129, 146;
disadvantaged in employment after
1957 119–20; economic and political
grievances of 122, 146
Democracy Movement (1989): in Beijing
211, 212, 215, 217, 218, 219, 222;
casualties in 217, 218; in Changchun
212; in Changsha 211; in Chongqing
221; and corruption 208, 209, 213,
214, 215; and Cultural Revolution 214,
230; and death of Hu Yaobang 194,
209, 213; and Democracy Wall 230;
and Deng Xiaoping 213, 215;
economic grievances in 204–7, 209,
210, 213; in Fujian 212; in Fuzhou 211;
general strikes called in 215–6; in
Guangdong 211, 212, 216, 219, 220–1,
222; in Guangzhou 211; in Guiyang
211; Han Dongfang in 218, 221; in
Hangzhou 211, 219, 220; in Harbin
220; in Hohhot 211; impact of on CCP
223; influence of Solidarity on 186,
216–7; in Jinan 211; June 4 massacre in
212, 217, 219, 230; in Kunming 211; in
Lanzhou 211; leaders of criticized 216;
and Li Peng 213, 215; in Liaoning 220;
and Mao Zedong 214; martial law 212,
215, 218, 229; money donated to 213,
216; in Nanchang 217; in Nanjing 211,
220; 'new class' paradigm in 155, 222;
participants exiled after 231–2; political
demands of workers in 195, 202,
213–4, 216–7, 218, 222, 231; protests
after June 4 219–21; repression of
workers after 5, 217; in Shanghai 211,
220–1; in Shenyang 219, 220, 221;
state-enterprise employees in 207,
211–12, 221–2; strikes in 215–6,
219–20; students in 195, 209, 210,
212–3, 214–6, 218, 219, 220–1;
support for 229, 230; suppression of
217, 218, 219–20, 221, 225, 229, 231;
in Suzhou 211; in Tianjin 220; violence
in 213, 217–8; worker-student conflict
in 210, 211, 214–7, 218; workers'
involvement in 1, 195, 204, 205, 207,
209, 212, 213, 218, 219, 220, 221, 230;
workers' organizations in 1, 156, 168,
185, 187, 189, 195, 203, 204, 208,
211–2, 216–7, 218, 220, 222–3, 233; in
Wuhan 211; in Xi'an 211, 219–20; in

Xining 211; and Yang Shangkun 215;
and Zhao Ziyang 214–5; *see also*
Democracy Wall Movement; economic
reforms
Democracy Wall Movement (1978–81)
146, 155, 196; April Fifth Forum in
163; and April Fifth Movement 157,
158, 168, 193; arrests in 166, 167; in
Beijing 157, 159, 164, 166, 167, 187,
189, 191; in Changsha 157, 192; China
compared with West in 159, 162; China
Democracy Party in 193; China
Human Rights League in 166; *chuanlian*
in 188; civil/human rights demanded
in 156–7; and Cultural Revolution 155,
156–7, 188, 190, 194, 230; and
Democracy Movement 230; Deng's
attitude towards 159, 164, 166, 194,
215; economic reform debated in 158,
160, 191; enterprise democratization
debated in 159, 162, 163, 164, 172; ex-
Red Guards in 156, 158, 168–9; in
Guangdong 190; in Guangzhou 157,
160, 166, 167, 168, 175, 178, 187,
189–90; in Guiyang 157; in Hangzhou
157; in Harbin 157; industrial
organization debated in 156, 159, 162,
166, 170–1, 174, 189; influence of on
CCP 167, 170–1, 172, 173, 174, 175,
178, 179, 186; influence of Solidarity
on 167, 173–5; in Kunming 157;
labelled counter-revolutionary 167;
mass support for 157, 186, 187, 190,
192, 193; in Nanjing 157; National
Federation of People's Publications
190, 192; national organization of 167,
190, 192; 'new class' paradigm in 156,
187, 222; Paris Commune as ideal of
156, 164, 179; participants exiled after
232; and people's congress elections
189–92; political system debated in
162, 164, 222; publications of 154, 156,
158, 159, 160, 166, 167, 168, 169, 175,
179, 187, 189, 190; in Qingdao 157,
175, 187, 192; in Shanghai 157, 187,
190; in Shaoguan 190; and Solidarity
173–5, 179, 185, 186, 187; strikes in
166, 187; as student/intellectual
movement 3, 228; students in 156, 168,
189, 190; support for Deng in 163;
suppression of 166–7, 187, 189, 192,
193–4, 195; in Taiyuan 157, 166,
187–8, 193; 'Thinking Generation' in

commitment to 60, 155, 169, 197; *see also* socialism

employment, security of: 'downsizing' of workforce 209, 232; full employment in PRC 197; 'iron arm-chair'/'gold rice-bowl' security of cadres 161, 162–3, 170, 178, 179, 198, 225, 232; 'iron rice-bowl' security of workers 98, 197, 198, 205; lay-offs under reforms 205–6, 209, 212, 225, 227; reduced under economic reforms 160–1, 169, 195, 197, 202, 204, 205, 212, 227; restriction of those eligible for 91, 93, 98–9, 102; temporary/contract workers' lack of 97–8, 205, 207; sacking of workers 98, 109, 118, 130, 200, 206, 207; transfer of workers as punishment 130, 203, 207; union members advantaged in 91, 93, 98; workers' attachment to 160, 197, 198, 205, 207, 209, 225, 230; *see also* contract workers; demobilized soldiers; temporary workers; unemployment

enterprise democratization: as aid to production/efficiency 18, 24, 38, 162, 164, 170, 171, 178–9, 183; aided by Cultural Revolution 141, 155; cadre resistance to 8, 31–3, 75, 76, 90, 93, 94, 164, 176, 177, 181–2, 191, 194; contradicted by management reforms 200–1, 223–4; demanded by workers 4, 13, 18, 33, 37, 39, 70, 83, 159, 161, 162, 164, 173, 178, 179, 187–8, 189, 191, 202–3, 213, 214, 217, 223; decline of after end of Five-Anti 50; and Democracy Wall 152, 162, 163, 171, 173–4, 189; discredited by Cultural Revolution association 195–6; 'extreme democratization' 24–5, 30, 34, 37, 39, 75, 76, 126, 130, 165, 166, 174, 187, 194, 195; failure of institutions for 4, 7, 10, 13–14, 33, 48–50, 53, 73–5, 77, 81, 88, 95–6, 139, 171–2, 176, 178, 194, 208, 230; hindered by post-Liberation moderate policy 33, 37, 39; influence of Eastern Europe on 48, 172–3; official unions' failure to support 27, 32–3, 223; political significance of 8, 19, 27, 32, 70, 71; 159, 170, 175; promoted by CCP 13, 18, 37–8, 41, 43, 46, 48, 71, 72, 95–6, 105, 133, 159, 169, 170–83, 196, 223; reduced after nationalization of enterprises 44, 50, 70, 73; and

Solidarity 173–5; subordinate to production 45, 49, 171, 208, 224; *see also* enterprises, elections in; factory management committee; joint state-private enterprises; labour-capital consultative conference; private enterprises; state enterprises; workers' congress; workers' participation in management; workers' representative conference

enterprises: autonomy of 160, 171, 174, 177, 182, 183, 199, 200, 202, 224; CCP in 164, 165, 170, 171, 176, 177, 180, 182, 183, 188, 190, 192, 200, 202, 204; contracting-out of 174, 181, 208, 224; elections in 73–4, 75, 105, 131, 132, 159, 164–5, 170, 171, 173, 176, 178–83; Enterprise Law 183, 224; foreign-invested 200, 224, 226; mergers of 177, 225, 232, 233; nature of under socialism 160, 174, 175, 176; ownership of diversified 197, 208, 226; small and medium (SMEs) 199; township 199; reform of 174, 179, 225, 226; workers' position in weakened by reforms 181, 183, 195, 200–1, 204, 207, 208, 209, 212, 213, 214, 223, 224, 226; *see also* cadres; economic reforms; enterprise democratization; joint state-private enterprises; management; private enterprises; state enterprises; unions, official; welfare

exploitation: continuation after Liberation acknowledged by CCP 17, 137; in old society 86; of workers by CCP 70, 77, 78, 82, 105, 134, 137, 162, 163, 171, 188, 193, 208, 222, 224

factory director: corruption of 207; dominant role of in enterprise 22, 49, 51, 66, 74, 92, 93, 171, 180, 183, 200–1, 204, 207, 208, 214, 217; election of 73–4, 173, 176, 178, 179–80, 208; factory director responsibility system 45, 183, 200–1, 223, 224; greater power of under reforms 199, 200, 207, 214, 217; official unions disregarded by 200, 201–2, 208; retaliation against worker critics by 51, 207; right of to transfer elected cadres 180, 181, 200; workers' congress by-passed by 183, 200, 201,

136, 143, 155, 159, 161–3, 170, 174–5,
183, 188, 191, 196, 204, 206, 208, 223,
224, 226; as masters of state 8, 159,
162, 163, 170, 174, 175, 186, 188, 191,
214, 223; migrant workers 219, 222,
226, 227; model workers 132; political
inequality of with cadres 72, 81–2,
85–6, 88, 96–7, 105, 123, 132, 136,
139, 147, 153, 155, 159, 186, 188, 191,
209, 222, 231, 232; politically
motivated in protests 207–8, 209, 213,
217, 218, 222–3, 225, 228, 230, 231,
232; position of in enterprise weakened
under reforms 181, 183, 195, 200–1,
204, 207, 208, 209, 212, 213, 214, 223,
224, 225, 232; pride in pre-1949 labour
movement of 14–15, 111; punished for
criticisms 51, 59, 64, 75–6, 78, 81, 82,
104, 106–7, 108–9, 113, 116, 118,
129–30, 163, 203, 207; recruitment of
160, 161, 175; seen as beneficiaries of
liberation 26, 113; seen as beneficiaries
of reform 210; self-management by
162, 164, 172–3; sense of class of 6,
143, 168, 170, 214, 222; standard of
living of 58, 159, 160, 161, 166, 168,
186, 188, 191, 194, 202, 204–7, 209;
and technical innovation 93, 139; use of
CCP campaigns for own agenda by
143–4, 145, 154, 229; veterans used in
CCP campaigns 91, 132; view of
management/party as new ruling class
10–11, 82, 124, 134, 136, 146, 148,
151, 155, 193, 222; violence by 76, 77,
117, 129, 149, 196, 222; violence
towards 106–7, 129–30, 137, 152, 153,
217, 218, 221, 229; wage-labour
mentality of 70, 160, 183; withdrawal
of labour by 69, 82, 199, 204; 'work
according to pay' attitude of 61, 69,
224; young more prominent in protests
48–9, 78–9, 99, 116, 141–2, 150, 153,
196, 211, 218, 219; *see also* April Fifth
Movement; Cultural Revolution;
Democracy Movement; Democracy
Wall Movement; enterprise
democratization; exploitation; Gang of
Four; Great Leap Forward; Hundred
Flowers movement; labour discipline;
management; socialism; strikes; unions;
Workers' Autonomous Federations;
workers' confrontations with CCP;
workers' participation in management

Workers' Autonomous Federations (1989)
1, 10, 12, 84, 230; attacked by ACFTU
194, 221; Beijing Workers'
Autonomous Federation 168, 170, 211,
212, 215–6, 217, 218, 222–3, 225, 226,
229; Guangdong Workers'
Autonomous Federation 211, 216, 219,
220–1, 222; Hangzhou Workers'
Autonomous Federation 219; after
martial law 218, 229; linked with Gang
of Four 194; refused legal status 168,
218, 221; Shougang Workers'
Autonomous Federation 212; *see also*
Democracy Movement; Han
Dongfang; unions, independent
workers' confrontations with CCP: in April
Fifth Movement 2, 138, 148, 150–1;
CCP denial of 78, 80, 103, 212, 221,
222, 231; in Cultural Revolution 2, 85,
102, 110, 122–3, 130, 134, 136, 138,
155, 163, 172; in Democracy
Movement (1989) 84, 143, 195, 204,
212, 213, 217–8, 220, 221, 222, 233; in
Democracy Wall Movement 2, 84, 166,
173, 193; in enterprises 5, 68, 69, 72,
75, 231; escalation of 11, 204, 233; in
Hundred Flowers movement 2, 49, 70,
72, 77–8, 80–1, 83, 84, 85, 110, 123,
136; increased confidence of workers
after 11, 156, 163, 218; in 1949–52 2,
13–14, 34–5, 37, 45–6, 48, 123, 136;
since 1989 225, 233
workers' congress: and economic reforms
171, 172, 198, 200–2; elections to 73,
74, 82, 140, 176, 178; failure of 96,
171, 172, 175, 176, 201–2, 203, 224; in
Great Leap Forward 88, 90, 95; in
Guangzhou 176; members of chosen
by cadres 95, 203, 208; more effective
in large SOEs 212; and official unions
73, 170, 172, 176, 177, 182; powers of
72–3, 74–5, 170, 172–8, 198, 207, 222,
224; production role of 95; Provisional
Regulations on 172, 176, 180; reform
of 95–6, 156, 162, 164, 170, 172–8;
reliant on management goodwill 8, 73,
76, 90, 176, 178, 183, 201; right of to
elect cadres 73, 74, 75, 170; as rubber-
stamp for management 171, 175, 204;
as successor to workers' representative
conference 21; temporary/contract
workers excluded from 121; workers'
rejection of 71–2, 81, 82, 172, 178,